MEDIEVAL PHILOSOPHY OF RELIGION

THE HISTORY OF
WESTERN PHILOSOPHY OF RELIGION

MEDIEVAL PHILOSOPHY OF RELIGION

Edited by Graham Oppy and N. N. Trakakis

VOLUME 2

THE HISTORY OF
WESTERN PHILOSOPHY OF RELIGION

ACUMEN

First published in 2009 by Acumen
First published in paperback by Acumen in 2013

Acumen Publishing Limited

4 Saddler Street
Durham
DH1 3NP

ISD, 70 Enterprise Drive
Bristol, CT 06010, USA

www.acumenpublishing.com

ISBN: 978-1-84465-682-0 (paperback Volume 2)
ISBN: 978-1-84465-679-0 (paperback 5 volume set)
ISBN: 978-1-84465-221-1 (hardcover Volume 2)
ISBN: 978-1-84465-181-8 (hardcover 5 volume set)

British Library Cataloguing-in-Publication Data
A catalogue record for this book is available from the British Library.

Typeset in Minion Pro.
Printed and bound in the UK by CPI Group (UK) Ltd, Croydon, CR0 4YY.

CONTENTS

EDITORIAL INTRODUCTION

Bertrand Russell's *History of Western Philosophy* (1946; hereafter *History*) provides a model for *some* of the significant features of the present work. Like Russell's more general history, our history of Western philosophy of religion consists principally of chapters devoted to the works of individual thinkers, selected because of their "considerable importance". Of course, we do not claim to have provided coverage of all of those who have made important contributions to Western philosophy of religion. However, we think that anyone who has made a significant contribution to Western philosophy of religion has either seriously engaged with the works of philosophers who are featured in this work, or has produced work that has been a focus of serious engagement for philosophers who are featured in this work.

Like Russell, we have aimed for contributions that show how the philosophy of religion developed by a given thinker is related to that thinker's life, and that trace out connections between the views developed by a given philosopher and the views of their predecessors, contemporaries and successors. While our primary aim is to provide an account of the ideas, concepts, claims and arguments developed by each of the philosophers under consideration, we think – with Russell – that this aim is unlikely to be achieved in a work in which "each philosopher appears as in a vacuum".

Again like Russell, we have only selected philosophers or religious writers who belong to, or have exerted a significant impact on, the intellectual tradition of the West (i.e. western Europe and the Anglo-American world). We realize that this selection criterion alone excludes from our work a number of important thinkers and religious groups or traditions, such as: Asian philosophers of religion, particularly those representing such religions as Hinduism, Buddhism, Confucianism and Taoism; African philosophers of religion; and individuals, texts and traditions emanating from indigenous religions, such as those found in the native populations of Australia and the Pacific Islands. Clearly, the non-Western world has produced thinkers who have made important, and often overlooked, contributions to the philosophy of religion. We have decided, however, not to include any entries on these thinkers, and our decision is based primarily on the (admittedly not incontestable) view that the Asian, African and indigenous philosophical and religious traditions have not had a great impact on the main historical narrative of the West. It would therefore have been difficult to integrate the various non-Western thinkers into the five-volume structure of the present work. The best way to redress this omission, in our view, is to produce a separate multi-volume work that would be dedicated to the history of non-Western philosophy of religion, a project that we invite others to take up.

Where we have departed most significantly from Russell is that our work has been written by a multitude of contributors, whereas Russell's work was the product of just one person. In the preface to his *History*, Russell claimed that:

> There is … something lost when many authors co-operate. If there is any unity in the movement of history, if there is any intimate relation between what goes before and what comes later, it is necessary, for setting this forth, that earlier and later periods should be synthesized in a single mind. (1946: 5)

We think that Russell exaggerates the difficulties in, and underestimates the benefits of, having a multitude of expert contributors. On the one hand, someone who is an expert on the work of a given philosopher is bound to have expert knowledge of the relation between the work of that philosopher, what goes before and what comes after. On the other hand, and as Russell himself acknowledged, it is impossible for one person to have the expertise of a specialist across such a wide field. (Indeed, while Russell's *History* is admirable for its conception and scope, there is no doubt that it is far from a model for good historical scholarship.)

Of course, Russell's worry about a multiplicity of authors does recur at the editorial level: the editors of this work have no particular claim to expertise concerning any of the philosophers who are featured in the work. In order to alleviate this problem, we invited all of the contributors to read drafts of neighbouring contributions, acting on the assumption that someone who is an expert on a particular philosopher is likely to have reasonably good knowledge of contemporaries and near contemporaries of that philosopher. Moreover, each of the five volumes comes with an expert introduction, written by someone who is much better placed than we are to survey the time period covered in the given volume.

Obviously enough, it is also the case that the present work does not have the kind of narrative unity that is possessed by Russell's work. Our work juxtaposes contributions from experts who make very different theoretical assumptions, and who belong to diverse philosophical schools and traditions. Again, it seems to us that this represents an advantage: there are many different contemporary approaches to philosophy of religion, and each of these approaches suggests a different view about the preceding history. Even if there is "unity in the movement of history", it is clear that there is considerable disagreement about the precise nature of that unity.

Although our work is divided into five volumes – and despite the fact that we have given labels to each of these volumes – we attach no particular significance to the way in which philosophers are collected together by these volumes. The order of the chapters is determined by the dates of birth of the philosophers who are the principal subjects of those chapters. While it would not be a task for a single evening, we do think that it should be possible to read the five volumes as a single, continuous work.

* * *

Collectively, our primary debt is to the 109 people who agreed to join with us in writing the material that appears in this work. We are indebted also to Tristan Palmer, who oversaw the project on behalf of Acumen. Tristan initially searched for someone prepared to take on the task of editing a single-volume history of Western philosophy of religion, and was actively involved in the shaping of the final project. He also provided invaluable advice on the full range of editorial questions that arise in a project on this scale. Thanks, too, to the copy-editors and others at Acumen, especially Kate Williams, who played a role in the completion of this project, and to the anonymous reviewers who provided many helpful comments. We are grateful to Karen Gillen for proofreading and indexing all five volumes, and to the Helen McPherson Smith Trust, which provided financial support for this project. We also acknowledge our debt to Monash University, and to our colleagues in the School of Philosophy and Bioethics. Special thanks to Dirk Baltzly for his suggestions about potential contributors to the volume on ancient Western philosophy of religion and for his editorial help with the chapter on Pythagoras.

Apart from these collective debts, Graham Oppy acknowledges personal debts to friends and family, especially to Camille, Gilbert, Calvin and Alfie. N. N. Trakakis is also grateful for the support of family and friends while working on this project, which he dedicates to his nephew and niece, Nicholas and Adrianna Trakakis: my prayer is that you will come to share the love of wisdom cultivated by the great figures in these volumes.

Graham Oppy
N. N. Trakakis

CONTRIBUTORS

Richard Cross is John A. O'Brien Professor of Philosophy at the University of Notre Dame. He has published four books and numerous articles on medieval philosophy and theology, including *Duns Scotus* (1999), *The Metaphysics of the Incarnation* (2002) and *Duns Scotus on God* (2005). Until 2007 he was Professor of Medieval Theology at the University of Oxford.

Gerhard Endress is Emeritus Professor of Arabic and Islamic Studies at Ruhr University, Bochum, Germany. His research interests include the intellectual history of medieval Islam, Arabic literature and especially the reception of Greek philosophy and science in the Arabic Islamic milieu. He has authored *Islam* (2nd edn, 2002) and *Der arabische Aristoteles und sein Leser* (2004), and has co-edited *Averroes and the Aristotelian Tradition* (1999).

G. R. Evans is Emeritus Professor of Medieval Theology and Intellectual History at the University of Cambridge. She is the author of many books, including *Anselm and Talking About God* (1978), *Anselm and a New Generation* (1980), *The Mind of St Bernard of Clairvaux* (1983), *Alan of Lille* (1983), *Augustine on Evil* (1983), *The Anselm Concordance* (1984), *The Thought of Gregory the Great* (1986), *Philosophy and Theology in the Middle Ages* (1993), *The Medieval Epistemology of Error* (1998), *Bernard of Clairvaux* (2000), *Law and Theology in the Middle Ages* (2002), *Faith in the Medieval World* (2002) and *Wyclif, a Biography* (2005).

Jeremiah Hackett is Professor and Chair of Philosophy at the University of South Carolina. He is co-author of "A Roger Bacon Bibliography, 1957–1985" (1987) and *Roger Bacon in der Diskussion* (2001). He is also editor or co-editor of *Aquinas on Mind and Intellect* (1996), *Roger Bacon and the Sciences* (1997), *Being and Thought in Aquinas* (1999) and *Philosophy of Religion for a New Century* (2004).

Syed Nomanul Haq is currently on the faculty of the School of Humanities and Social Sciences at Lahore University of Management Sciences, Pakistan. Previously, he served as Assistant Professor at Brown University and the University of Pennsylvania. Author of *Names, Natures and Things* (1994) and numerous articles on Graeco-Arabic intellectual history, he is also co-editor of *God, Life, and the Cosmos* (2002), General Editor of Oxford University Press's *Studies in Islamic Philosophy* and serves on the editorial boards for *Islamic Studies* and the *Journal of Islamic Science*.

Jasper Hopkins is Professor of Philosophy at the University of Minnesota. He is a translator and an interpreter of Nicholas of Cusa's philosophy and theology, and a member of the international scholarly advisory board of the *Cusanus-Gesellschaft*. Among his works of interpretation are *Glaube und Vernunft im Denken des Nikolaus von Kues* (1996) and *A Concise Introduction to the Philosophy of Nicholas of Cusa* (3rd edn, 1986).

Gyula Klima is Professor of Philosophy at Fordham University, New York. He is Director of the International Society for Medieval Logic and Metaphysics and editor of the Society's *Proceedings*. His publications on medieval nominalism include: *Ars Artium* (1988); John Buridan: *Summulae de Dialectica* (2001); *Medieval Philosophy* (2007); *John Buridan* (2008); "The Nominalist Semantics of Ockham and Buridan: A Rational Reconstruction", in *Handbook of the History of Logic* (2008); "Nominalism", in *Elsevier's Encyclopedia of Language and Linguistics* (2006); and "Ockham's Semantics and Ontology of the Categories", in *The Cambridge Companion to Ockham* (1999).

Stephen E. Lahey is Assistant Professor of Classics and Religious Studies at the University of Nebraska. The chief focus of his research is John Wyclif and theological Wycliffism in later medieval Europe. He is the author of *Philosophy and Politics in the Thought of John Wyclif* (2003) and *John Wyclif* (2009), and is engaged in the translation and re-editing of several of Wyclif's Latin works, including treatises of the *Summa de Ente* and *Trialogus*. He is also active as a parish priest in the Episcopal Diocese of Nebraska.

Charles Manekin is Associate Professor of Philosophy at the University of Maryland, where he specializes in medieval Jewish and Islamic philosophy. He is the author of *The Logic of Gersonides* (1991) and *On Maimonides* (2004). He is also an editor of *A Straight Path* (1988), *Freedom and Moral Responsibility* (1997), *The Jewish Philosophy Reader* (2000) and *Philosophers and the Hebrew Bible* (2008), and he is the editor and translator of *Medieval Jewish Philosophy* (2006).

John Marenbon is Senior Research Fellow at Trinity College, Cambridge. He has published *Boethius* (2003) and *Le Temps, l'éternité et la prescience de Boèce*

xii

à Thomas d'Aquin (2005), and has edited *The Cambridge Companion to Boethius* (2009).

Michael Marmura is Professor Emeritus in the Department of Near and Middle Eastern Civilisations at the University of Toronto. His fields of expertise are Arabic literature and Islamic thought. He has published many articles, and editions of texts and translations. The latter include a face-page translation of al-Ghazali's *The Incoherence of the Philosophers* and Avicenna's (Ibn Sina's) *The Metaphysics of "The Healing"*.

James McConica chairs the Editorial Board of the *Collected Works of Erasmus* (Toronto) and is Vice-President of the International Council responsible for supervision of the new, critical edition (from Amsterdam) of Erasmus' *Opera omnia*. He is a Fellow of the Pontifical Institute of Mediaeval Studies, of which he is President Emeritus. His publications on Erasmus focus on theological methodology and on Erasmus' reforming agenda, derived from scriptural and patristic sources, as well as from a humanistic commitment to active participation in the public sphere. His biography of Erasmus, first published in 1991 and often reissued, has been translated into Japanese, Greek, Turkish and Korean.

Jon McGinnis is Associate Professor of Classical and Medieval Philosophy at the University of Missouri, St Louis. He has written numerous articles on various aspects of Avicenna's (Ibn Sina's) philosophy, ranging from topics in Avicenna's philosophy of science (or epistemology), natural philosophy, psychology and metaphysics. He has also edited (with the assistance of David Reisman) *Interpreting Avicenna: Science and Philosophy in Medieval Islam* (2004), translated Avicenna's *The Physics of the Cure* (2009), and recently written *Avicenna* for the Oxford University Press Great Medieval Thinkers Series.

Brian Patrick McGuire is Professor in the Department of History and Social Theory at Roskilde University, Denmark. He has published extensively on Cistercian history and spirituality, including a collection of articles on Bernard of Clairvaux and his legacy: *The Difficult Saint* (1991). He is presently working on a Danish-language biography of Saint Bernard and is editing the Brill Companion to Bernard.

Constant J. Mews is Professor in the School of Historical Studies, Monash University, where he is also Director of the Centre for Studies in Religion and Theology. He specializes in medieval intellectual and religious history, with particular interests in issues of gender, scholasticism and monastic life. He is the author of *The Lost Love Letters of Heloise and Abelard* (1999) and *Abelard and Heloise* (2005), as well as numerous articles and book chapters relating to Abelard and Heloise and their contemporaries in the twelfth century.

Dermot Moran holds the Chair of Philosophy at University College Dublin and is a member of the Royal Irish Academy. He has published widely on medieval philosophy (especially Christian Neoplatonism) and contemporary European philosophy (especially phenomenology). His medieval studies include: *The Philosophy of John Scottus Eriugena* (1989), *Eriugena, Berkeley and the Idealist Tradition* (co-edited with Stephen Gersh, 2006), and "Cusanus and Modern Philosophy" in *The Cambridge Companion to Renaissance Philosophy* (2007). He is the founding editor (since 1993) of the *International Journal of Philosophical Studies*.

Tamar Rudavsky is Professor of Philosophy at Ohio State University. She specializes in medieval Jewish philosophy and is the editor of three books: *Divine Omniscience and Omnipotence in Medieval Philosophy* (1984), *Gender and Judaism* (1995) and (with Steven Nadler) *The Cambridge History of Jewish Philosophy* (2009). Her book *Time Matters* appeared in 2000. In addition, she has written numerous articles on Gersonides' cosmology and philosophical theology.

Thomas Williams is Professor of Philosophy and Religious Studies at the University of South Florida. He is the translator of *Anselm* (2007) and co-author, with Sandra Visser, of *Anselm* (2008). He is editor of *The Cambridge Companion to Duns Scotus* (2003) and *Thomas Aquinas* (2005), and has contributed to other books in the *Cambridge Companions* series on Augustine, Anselm, Abelard and medieval philosophy.

John F. Wippel is Theodore Basselin Professor in the School of Philosophy at the Catholic University of America, Washington, DC. His works include *Metaphysical Themes in Thomas Aquinas* (1984), *The Metaphysical Thought of Thomas Aquinas* (2000); *Metaphysical Themes in Thomas Aquinas II* (2007) and *Thomas Aquinas on the Divine Ideas* (1993). He is a past president of the American Catholic Philosophical Association, the Society for Medieval and Renaissance Philosophy and the Metaphysical Society of America.

1

MEDIEVAL PHILOSOPHY OF RELIGION: AN INTRODUCTION

G. R. Evans

I. PHILOSOPHY AND THE 'GREAT WORLD RELIGIONS' IN THE MIDDLE AGES: AN OVERVIEW

The transition from the ancient world

The period from the collapse of the Roman Empire to the beginning of the sixteenth century saw several significant transitions in the way students of philosophy and religion understood the relationship of the two, and whether they saw them as distinct at all. For the Greeks and Romans they were closely allied, if not one, because philosophy was a way of life as well as a way of thinking about the universe. A philosopher could be a 'practitioner', even an 'adherent', as well as a student. In the ancient world, philosophy had been concerned with moral as well as intellectual explanation of the universe and how to live in it. It is not too much to call it a 'vocation'.

In Christianity, Judaism and Islam, 'rules for living' and a 'framework of belief' were distinctive to each religion, and stood in a particular relationship in each case. Each arrived at its own 'settlement' with ancient philosophy, while preserving its integrity. Christianity and some forms of Judaism found it comparatively easy to identify the 'love of wisdom' in the Wisdom literature of the Old Testament; and once the doctrine of Christ as Logos developed in Christianity, Christ himself was frequently portrayed as a philosopher, teaching his disciples much as philosophy tutors taught young men in the late antique world. But the era of persecutions in late antiquity had made it clear that neither Jews nor Christians could engage in a simple syncretism.

The Christians

From the point of view of direct influence on Western civilization, the adoption of Greek philosophical ideas by the early Christian community was of the first importance, not least because this more perhaps than any other factor drove the Latin speakers among them to enlarge the capacity of their language for the expression of abstract ideas. The heritage of Rome, with its synthesis of Greek and Roman intellectual traditions and its ultimate dependency at many points on the Greek, also lingered in the oriental Orthodox churches which divided from the rest after the Council of Chalcedon in 451, bringing in Syriac speakers to this process. Classical philosophy left the Middle Ages a booklist, which the burgeoning intelligentsia of the Christian community largely shared with Judaism, too, especially Hellenic Judaism, and it found its way into Islam, where indeed it was exploited with particular intellectual skill. We might usefully begin with a general overview of this mixed process of transmission, modification and 'incul-turation' as it affected each category of believers.

Points of view, and ways of understanding the relationship of 'philosophy' and 'religion', were different, and increasingly diverged in the Greek-speaking East and the Latin-speaking West, as they became two increasingly distinct 'language communities' with the end of Empire. It was primarily in the West that the leading authors represented in this volume emerged, for the Western tradition was a good deal more analytical and argumentative than that of the East. But in the lands that lay at the Eastern end of the dying Empire there were also subtle shifts of understanding and emphasis.

Greek-speaking Christians

The Greeks went through the Middle Ages in a spirit that discouraged the kind of debate and writing we see going on so energetically in Western authors. They took it that the Christian faith was a 'given', certainly after the end of the period of the Ecumenical Councils, and its truth a fixed quantity. In Christology the Council of Chalcedon of 451 formed a decisive endpoint, separating the oriental Orthodox or non-Chalcedonian churches from the rest. In Greek eyes, development of doctrine, any form of innovation, even if apparently right in itself, was unacceptable if it made a change in the way something was expressed or thought about. That became plainer still when the West added 'and the Son' (the *filioque* clause) to the Creed in the Carolingian period and the Greeks objected that this was heresy, and that even if it had not been heresy it would be wrong because it was something new.

A second reason for the distinctiveness of the understanding of the relationship of philosophy and religion in the Greek East of medieval Europe was the fact that philosophers were reading and thinking in Greek. Something of the crucial difference between the way Platonism persisted in the West and in the Greek East may be seen in Volume 1, Chapters 19 and 20, "Proclus" and "Pseudo-Dionysius". Late Platonism (Platonism had become inextricably mingled with Stoicism and Aristotelianism from the Neoplatonist stage of its evolution) had also fostered a taste for mysticism. The West had its mysticism, too, but it had, again, a more analytical character. It involved the climbing of a ladder to God in the mind rather than a trusting leap into the unknown. The mysticism of the medieval Greek Christian world was developed in a monastic and eremitical tradition where the individual soul, stripping itself of all worldly connections, often in extremes of suffering from deprivation of food and from physical discomfort, travelled into the far distance of contemplation in the search for union with God.

Latin-speaking Christians

Few Western philosophers were fluent in Greek by the sixth century. Even though Gregory the Great had spent time in Constantinople, it remains uncertain whether he had any command of Greek. Among the authors discussed in this volume, only Eriugena can claim to have been competent to discuss certain of the questions Greeks were thinking about and the way they approached them, and even he could not do so as an insider.

This language divide alone meant that for centuries Western access to Aristotle and Plato remained limited. Boethius (*b. c.*476) had planned to translate the whole corpus, but he was executed *c.*525 in the political turmoil of the times, with only a part of Aristotle's logic completed, not all of which survives. The early medieval West was able to study only the *Categories* and the *De interpretatione* (On interpretation). In the twelfth century new translations of the remainder of Aristotle's logic were made and by the thirteenth century Aristotle's writings on science, ethics and politics (the last about 1270) were arriving in Latin in the West partly by way of Arabic scholarship and some directly from the Greek.

A diffuse 'Platonism' was mediated through Augustine and others, including references to Plato in Aristotle. Platonic themes were also to be found in Cicero's popular *Dream of Scipio* and in the commentary Augustine's contemporary Macrobius wrote on it, this also becoming quite widely studied in the medieval West. A translation of the *Timaeus*, which became fashionable to study for a time in the mid-twelfth century, presented a considerable challenge to Genesis with its different explanation of the way the world was made by its creator. The *Meno* and the *Phaedo* were also available in translations by Henry Aristippus, although they never became central to academic study. Otherwise, Plato remained almost literally a closed book in the West until the revival of the study of Greek from the fifteenth century. Once Plato began to be studied again directly, problems of compatibility with the Christian faith re-emerged. Marsilio Ficino (1433–99) revived Platonic notions of the existence of a 'World Soul', which had been controversial in the early Christian world and again in the twelfth century.

An additional strand in which there was an admixture of Platonism was the 'hermetica', a body of probably second- to third-century writings linked to Egypt, comprising debased late antique philosophical notions that proved attractive to medieval minds. An example is the idea that human beings are creatures poised between beast and god, who become more like beasts if they behave like beasts, and more like gods if they lift up their heads and concentrate on spiritually and intellectually 'higher' things. This material was discussed by Augustine and therefore became familiar in an abbreviated form to his medieval Western readers.

Judaism and Jewish scholars

Jewish scholarship also had its particular medieval concerns. It has been suggested that the account of the creation of the world in Genesis prompted philosophical discussion of the question how the world began in ways that changed the emphasis of ancient philosophical discussions, especially those on the eternity of the world. This was an issue for Jews as much as for Christian scholars. Could a creator who made the world from nothing have made it in any way he chose? This was a very different being from Plato's craftsman-creator, and a very different situation from the one presented by a world that had somehow always been there, as Aristotle argued.

The twelfth-century Maimonides helped to frame a Jewish philosophical tradition in Arabic, which took forward earlier Islamic scholarship (Inglis 2002: 202). Among his concerns was this question of the beginning of things, on which he disagreed with Aristotle. But Maimonides also took a view on the nature of the highest good in which he found it unsatisfactory to believe that the highest good did nothing but think; and he disputed Aristotle's views on the nature and divisions of the virtues.

For Western Christian Europe, Jews could be a source of advice on the meaning of certain Old Testament Hebrew terms. Peter Abelard (1079–1142) seems to have consulted Hebrew speakers for this purpose. But talking with Jews presented challenges, since they, like the Arab scholars, thought in terms of a monotheism in which the complexities of Christian Trinitarian theology and the Christian theology of redemption had no place. Abelard was the author of one of the experimental philosophical and religious literary dialogues between Jews and Christians that were briefly fashionable in the late eleventh and early twelfth centuries, although unlike Gilbert Crispin, he left Christological questions out of the debate. In such dialogues, as in the related 'anti-heretical' writings such as the *Contra haereticos* (Against the heretics) of Alan of Lille in the later twelfth century, it is Christology that is typically the sticking-point.

Islam and the Nestorian Christians

Nestorian and Jacobite Christians who spoke Syriac and Arabic, as well as Islamic scholars, translated Greek philosophers from Syriac or Greek into Arabic. This work was done mainly in the eighth and ninth centuries during the period of the Abbasid caliphs. Al-Kindi (*d. c.*870) was one of the leading figures (Inglis 2002: 24). These generations seem to have been struck by points at which the texts chimed with the pre-Christian beliefs of their region. They commented; they

4

wrote monographs. Al-Kindi, for example, realized the importance of clarity in the use of terms and wrote a treatise on definitions to help Arabic speakers in their study of the translated Greek. But he also took a more extended view of the questions that were presenting themselves about the nature of philosophy. In his *On First Philosophy*, he encourages Muslims to welcome perceptions of truth even if they come from outside their own tradition. He extols Aristotle, he tackles the question of the origin of the world, and he creates his own synthesis of Greek and Islamic thinking in the spirit he encourages others to adopt.

The rise of Islam created still more new scholarly communities, for the translations were of a high standard and stimulating to their Muslim readers. After al-Kindi's death, the links with Nestorian Christians continued. Al-Farabi (*d. c.*950) was a member of a circle of students of logic and philosophy that included Nestorians, and he was a pupil of at least one of these. Al-Farabi became a leading logician and philosopher in his own right and an influential commentator on Aristotelian texts.

The encounter with Aristotle was probably more direct than that with Plato, for although Arabic histories record the existence of Plato's *Republic*, the *Laws*, the *Parmenides* and the *Timaeus*, it seems that the translations were probably from summaries such as Galen's synopsis of Plato's dialogues. It was not until the twelfth century that the translations were seized on by a hungry West and rendered into Latin for Western use.

Avicenna (Ibn Sina, *d.* 1037), who impressed Albert the Great (1193/1206–1280), was an even bolder synthesizer of Greek and Islamic thought. Among the Islamic thinkers represented in the present volume is al-Ghazali, whose late-eleventh- and early-twelfth-century career coincided quite closely with that of Anselm of Canterbury. Al-Ghazali was struck by the contradictoriness of the opinions of the ancient philosophers he read. Also discussed in this volume is Averroes (Ibn Rushd, *d.* 1198), who was based in Spain and in a part of the Islamic world in much closer touch with the West, and wrote a rebuttal that sought to retrieve the ancient philosophers' reputations.

We turn now to the developments and emphases that entered what was to become, in terms of its subsequent influence on the history of philosophy, the mainstream of medieval European culture.

II. KEY ASPECTS OF THE MEDIEVAL RELATIONSHIP
OF PHILOSOPHY AND RELIGION

The changing syllabus

The main energy of Western medieval thought went into the study of philosophical and theological method and the underlying questions of the nature of logic and language. Here the Western medieval contribution was considerable.

Epistemology and the theory of language were taken well beyond the point they had reached in ancient philosophy. Aristotle's logic was added to, as medieval Western scholars became interested in questions of logic and language, and the conflict between Aristotle and some points in Priscian's teaching of Latin grammar. The doctrine of transubstantiation arose directly out of this line of study, for it is framed in terms of a reversal of the norms of Aristotle's Categories. Ordinary bread changes in its accidents (i.e. perceptible qualities) when it grows mouldy but remains bread in substance. The doctrine claims that the consecrated bread of the Eucharist remains the same in its accidents for its appearance does not alter, but its substance has changed completely, for it has now become the actual body of Christ.

From the early thirteenth century, physics and metaphysics became established as additions to the old staples of the 'arts' course (the grammar, logic and rhetoric of the *trivium*, and the arithmetic, geometry, music and astronomy of the *quadrivium*), and their inclusion in the syllabus of the emerging universities led to challenging debate about their relationship and the way they might fit into the study of philosophy and theology. Universities were to be one of the major contributions of the Middle Ages to the intellectual life of the Latin West. Within them there was, from the first, highly competitive debate, not least between the 'arts' students and their teachers and the older students and more senior teachers of theology. Faculties of theology came into being in some universities and there could be energetic debate between the 'theologians' and the 'philosophers' of the arts faculty about what was essentially common ground, as occurred at Paris. The notion that assertions about the natural world and its workings might be tested and verified experimentally was not to gain ground until the sixteenth century, however, with the work of Francis Bacon. The underlying philosophy was still that reality lay in abstraction or 'ideas' and that nothing could be learned from the particular exemplifications of those ideas in the world the senses can perceive, which can alter the truth of ideas that belong in a higher realm. Mathematics was another matter, with Thomas Bradwardine (*c.*1290–1349) and others doing original work in that area.

In the West, 'religion' began to be written about from at least the twelfth century within the framework of an increasingly 'systematic' Christian theology (although the term 'theology' was slow to emerge as the natural label for the body of Christian doctrine). 'Philosophy' mutated into a study of those questions that are susceptible to reasoning and do not necessarily require scriptural revelation for their resolution, and was given an uneasy position on the edge of Christian theology. Aquinas saw the problem clearly and makes it the first article of the first question of his *Summa theologiae* on whether there is a need for anything more than what reasoning can discover by philosophy alone.

We must now look more closely at the way these implications for the understanding of the relationship of philosophy and religion were worked out in the centuries covered by this volume.

Questions of vocabulary

Philosophia is a common term and *theologia* a comparatively rare one for much of the medieval period in the West. Isidore (*c*.560–636) says in his *Etymologiae* (Etymologies) that theologians (*theologi*) are so called because they "speak of God in their writings" (*quoniam in scriptis suis de deo dixerunt*; in *Etymologiae* VIII. vi.18 [1909]). It was not until the twelfth century and after that the word *theologia* came to be used regularly to describe the whole spread of themes of Christian theology that were to be included in 'systematic theology'. *Studium sacrae scripturae* or even *sacra doctrina* came more naturally.

Augustine and especially Boethius had used the terminology as writers of the late antique world, for whom *theologia* belonged within *philosophia*. Augustine wrote in *De civitate Dei* (On the city of God) VI.5 of the distinction between a theology (*theologia*) that deals with the natural world, a civil *theologia* that shapes the *pietas* of the citizen and encourages him to respect the emperor as a deity, and the *fabulosa theologia* that is mythology, stories of the pagan gods. Cassiodorus (*c*.485–*c*.585), in his short encyclopedia the *Institutiones* (Institutions) gives a series of definitions (1937: 110). Philosophy is the knowledge of things divine and human at the level of what is probable (as all syllogistic argument was taken to be, for it can have only as much certainty as the propositions from which its conclusions are drawn): "*Philosophia est divinarum humanarumque rerum, … probabilis scientia*". He also sees philosophy as the all-embracing art and science, the *ars artium et disciplina disciplinarum*. And, like the classical writer he essentially is, he understands philosophy to be the study of the deep questions of life, which he sums up in the phrase *meditatio mortis*.

The personified *Philosophia*, from whose advice Cassiodorus' contemporary Boethius drew 'consolation', was of this last sort. She concerned herself with the great philosophical topics of the ancient world, which taught a person how to live as much as how to think and believe. Boethius' *Consolations* concentrates particularly on the question of the purpose of life and how far its ultimate outcome was under the care of a providence which cared and could ensure a good outcome.

Boethius wrote in a different frame of reference and using different terminology in the *De Trinitate*, where he discusses 'theology'. He divides intellectual activities (*speculativa*) into *theologia*, *mathematica* and *physica*. Of these "*tres … speculativae partes*", *naturalis* considers the forms of bodies in matter; *mathematica* considers forms as though they were abstracted from bodies although in reality they cannot be; and *theologia* considers what is truly not material, for "the substance of God lacks both matter and motion" (1973: 9).

On this understanding, *theologia* confines itself to the highest and most abstract ideas: topics that can be dealt with by reasoning. Reason alone can equip a thinker to come to conclusions about the existence of a God and whether there is one God or many. It may even, at a stretch, make it possible to formulate the doctrine of the Trinity and to discuss the creation of the universe. For that which is spread before the eye of the mind in the natural world may also be regarded as a form of divine revelation. What reason cannot do is to arrive unaided at the historical facts of revelation and discuss those aspects of Christian belief that depend on knowing that Jesus was born and taught and died, and what he said to his disciples, although once those are 'given' reason may struggle with the technicalities of the Incarnation, as the Church had been doing during the fourth- and fifth-century Ecumenical Councils.

This distinction was very apparent to Hugh of Saint-Victor (*d.* 1141), a keen pedagogue who went to great trouble to help his pupils learn. For example, he was much concerned to ensure that the canons of the Abbey of Saint-Victor in Paris understood the underlying structure and divisions of their studies, in ways which would chime with the expectations they would encounter in their reading. There was an exchange of ideas between the Victorines, the students and masters of the cathedral school in Paris, and the rival schools that were coming into existence round Sainte-Geneviève, from which the University of Paris was to emerge. So this was a way of understanding the deep structure of Christian theology, which had a wider potential importance and influence. In his *De sacramentis ecclesiae* (On the sacraments of the Church), Hugh divided Christian theology into two broad areas: the *opus creationis*, which deals with the existence and nature of God, the Trinity and the creation; and the *opus restaurationis*, which is concerned with the matters known about only through the pages of Scripture and not accessible to reasoning alone.

He wrote in this way, in a period when the question what authorities could be relied on in constructing arguments was the subject of widespread debate. It was beginning to be realized that not everyone would accept the same proof-texts, or indeed any proof-texts. If Christian theology depended on the Bible for a significant part of its content, there were going to be problems in winning converts. Accordingly, Gilbert Crispin (*c.*1055–1117) takes different approaches to the use of biblical authorities in his *Dialogue with a Gentile* and his *Dialogue with a Jew*. In the opening passages of the *Dialogue with a Jew* (1986: 10–11), the Christian and the Jew discuss the *auctoritas* of the Old Testament and the New, and the place of *ratio* in proofs. For the Jew will accept only the Old Testament. In the *Dialogue with a Gentile* (by whom he means a pagan), Gilbert describes a kind of philosophical club in which the members are discussing Aristotle and Porphyry, and genera and species, and how many branches of the art of argument there are, and how many liberal arts. Once more they have to begin by agreeing which authorities they propose to rely on. "I do not accept your laws and literary works, nor the authorities drawn from them", asserts the 'Gentile', and they are obliged to agree to use reasoning alone (*ibid.*: 62–4). Peter Abelard (2001: 9) addresses the same difficulty in his fictional three-cornered debate of a Jew, a Christian and a Philosopher. Pagans or philosophers will accept only reason; Christians will accept the authority of the New Testament as well as the Old; and Jews will accept only the authority of the Old Testament.

Alan of Lille (*d. c.*1202) adds a further dimension in his treatise against the heretics, where he points out that the dualists (the Manichees of Augustine's day and contemporary Albigensians or Cathars) accept only the New Testament because they deem the God of the Old Testament to be the dark God of matter who is the Principle of Evil. Chapter after chapter in his first book lists "the authorities and reasons" that support a particular position (1855; *Patrologia Latina* 210:307–78).

These considerations all turn ultimately on the distinction Boethius had made between the *theologia*, which is accessible to everyone and is open to pure reasoning, and the study of those parts of Christian theology that rely on the revelation of the Word of God in the Bible and can therefore be known only to those who can read the Bible or hear it read to them.

It was perhaps partly with this distinction in mind, and very probably because he had been discussing the problem with Gilbert Crispin while Gilbert was planning his *Dialogue with a Jew*, that Anselm of Canterbury (*c.*1033–1109) made a bold bid to cross this boundary. In his *Cur Deus homo* (Why God became man) he proposes to try to prove by reason alone that once Adam had sinned the incarnation and all that followed became the only way forward. *Remoto christo* he says, setting aside everything we know about the coming of Christ from Scripture let us see whether we can establish by reasoning what we are told actually happened (Anselm 1940: 42–3).

Alongside this subtle and increasingly complex balancing of *theologia* and *philosophia* are to be found mid-twelfth-century discussions of the syllabus. These are of particular interest because they antedate the invention of the universities and do not relate to any formal requirements with which a student might have to comply before obtaining a qualification or degree. They do, however, help to clarify the way the two disciplines looked at this period.

Hugh of Saint-Victor is again helpful here. Hugh's *Epitome Dindimi in philosophiam* (Dindimus' summary of philosophy) (1966: 189), a partly catechetical, partly Socratic, dialogue between master and pupil, of the sort that was popular at the time, includes an opening definition of philosophy. Hugh takes philosophy to be the study that seeks wisdom (*studium querende sapientie*) and involves the pursuit of truth: indeed, a careful investigation of the truth (*et diligens investigatio veri*). The partners in the dialogue go on to discuss the definitions of wisdom and truth.

Hugh goes on to give a more 'theological' analysis of the 'three things' with which philosophy is properly (*recte*) concerned, as befits a teacher preparing canons for the religious life

> For its first investigation should concern man (*Nam prima investigatio hominis hec esse debet*) so that the philosopher may know himself and be aware that he was created (*ut sciat seipsum et agnoscat quod factus est*). Then, once he begins to know himself, he should reflect on his own creation and contemplate the wonders of the created world he sees all about him.   (1966: 190)

The notion of 'theology' Hugh has in mind here is as much devotional as intellectual. This is a 'mode' of doing theology that he taught in the school at the Abbey of Saint-Victor. It linked the intellectual activities of reading and thinking with the spiritual exercise of meditation. It is in tune with Isidore's definition of *religio* as that through which we turn our souls to God and worship him in service (*Etymologiae* VIII.ii.1–2 [1909]).

'Knowing oneself' was a topic that had a brief fashion in the twelfth century, with some awareness of its meaning in ancient Greek philosophical thought. '*Scito te ipsum*' was the Latin version. "*Gnothi seauton*", know yourself, says Juvenal, explaining that this means 'be realistic about yourself', 'take stock of yourself and describe yourself to yourself as you really are'. Peter Abelard chose the title of his book on the ethics of intention (*Scito te ipsum*) accordingly (Abelard 1971).

The standard introduction to books to be lectured on, the *Accessus ad auctores* (Bernard of Utrecht 1970: 191–3), included in at least some versions "in which part of philosophy" (*pars philosophiae*) the book was to be placed. This implied that 'philosophy' could mean the generality of all disciplines. Hugh of Saint-Victor writes about the syllabus of studies in the spirit of this *partes philosophiae* approach, with the kind of breakdown of the disciplines current in the discussions of the day. They form a tree with branches, with the parts of philosophy being *logica, ethica, theorica, mechanica* (Hugh of Saint-Victor 1966: 191–3). Logic includes *grammatica et ratio disserendi*. 'Reasoning' (*ratio disserendi*) comprises the three branches of 'probable' (syllogistic), 'necessary' (demonstrative, as used by Euclid) and 'sophistical' (fallacious) arguments. The branches of ethics are also listed: *solitaria, privata* and *publica*. Studies classified as 'theoretical' are the three that Boethius lists: *theologia, mathematica* and *physica*, and it is notable that Hugh is happy to leave 'theology' in this corner of the syllabus. Lastly come the 'mechanical' studies, a list derived from Varro, and "scarcely" (*vix*) parts of philosophy at all; Hugh suggests *lanificium, armatura, navigation, agricultura, venatio, medicina* and *theatrica*.

On the evidence we have, not all these could actually be studied, certainly not to the same depth. The textbooks did not exist, for one thing, although some new ones were being written experimentally. The syllabus of the *trivium* and the *quadrivium*, the grammar, logic and rhetoric, and the arithmetic, music, geometry and astronomy of the practical teaching arrangements were, on the evidence of Thierry of Chartres' *Heptateuch*, what Hugh's more comprehensive list of parts of philosophy amounted to in reality in the twelfth-century schools. Grammar and then logic were dominant, the rest tailed off in the detail in which they were treated. In his *Metalogicon*, John of Salisbury gives a lively picture of the way a student, such as he had himself been in Paris when Peter Abelard had been lecturing there, would decide on a whim which book to study next, and choose a master to 'hear' on the subject.

The pragmatic recognition that these arts, especially the arts of language and most particularly the art of argument, were of value whether a student was 'doing' philosophy or theology is noted in passing in Thomas of Chobham's *Art of Preaching*. He is discussing the definition of an 'argument', by which he means a 'topic' or something that can be inserted into a sequence of argumentation. This must be something that could actually happen or exist, even if it does not really exist: "*Argumentum est rerum narratio que si non facta sunt, fieri tamen poterunt*". This kind of thing, he says, neither philosophy nor theology disdains, for both commonly make use of parables and other fictional devices in teaching (Thomas of Chobham 1993: 5).

The Aristotelian synthesis: philosophy and theology change places

It did not take long after the universities began to emerge from the twelfth-century schools for 'philosophy' to take its place in the comparatively lowly arts course while 'theology' became the highest of the higher degree subjects and the queen of all studies. In reality the students of the arts had often made daring raids into the territory of the theologians, for subjects such as contingent futurity (logic) were inseparable from questions about divine foreknowledge and predestination. Aristotle's *De interpretatione*, which ends with this topic, had been available since Boethius had translated it.

But now there was a radical shift from the vague presumption of the previous century that 'philosophy' embraced all other studies and that 'theology' was confined to one section of the study of the Christian faith that it was usual to refer to as the *studium sacrae scripturae*, so solidly founded was it in biblical exegesis and patristic commentary.

The first significant factor in this change was the emergence, from the end of the twelfth century, of universities with syllabuses leading to examinations and the conferment of a degree or *gradus*. It became apparent early on that most students would proceed no further than the study of the *artes*, and the arts became a first-degree course and a foundation for higher studies in medicine, law and theology. There was a certain amount of controversy between the mendicant orders and the universities as to the order of study, for the friars tended to arrive in order to study theology, having taken their preliminary studies in an order determined by their own internal schools.

A second factor was the arrival of the philosophical and natural science works of Aristotle in translation in the medieval West. This made it necessary to revise the syllabus. These books had to be incorporated into a course of study if they were to be admitted to become part of the furniture of educated minds. Albertus Magnus (*c.*1193–1280), one of the masters who taught Thomas Aquinas, was one of the leading synthesizers. Aristotle's 'scientific' and philosophical works, particularly *On the Soul*, quickly became part of the syllabus of the arts course, and were treated as 'philosophical' and as part of a preparation (in the case of those students who were to go on to higher studies) for the study of theology. The regulations of 1268 for the University of Oxford require the study of three of Aristotle's works:

De physica (On physics), *De anima* (On the soul) and *De generatione et corruptione animalium* (On generation and corruption).

The process of assimilation was far from uncontroversial. From 1210 in Paris and at intervals throughout the thirteenth century until the 1270s, lists of banned opinions that were to be found in these books were published in an attempt to prevent them from being mentioned by teachers. Nothing could have been better calculated to stir the interest of students. The kind of problem that could present itself is reflected in a remark of John Blund, writing his own *De anima*:

> Perhaps someone says that it is for theologians to write about the soul (*Foret dicet aliquis quod theologi est tractare de anima*). On the contrary. The theologian's task is to ask in what way the soul may be deserving or undeserving, of salvation or punishment (*Contra. Theologus habet inquirere qua via contingat animam mereri et demereri, et quid sit ad salutem at quid ad penam*). He does not have to enquire that the soul is, *et in quo predicamento sit* and how it inhabits the body.
>
> (Blund 1970: 7)

There were further complications because the new Aristotle came from the Arabic translations that had been made by Islamic scholars as well as directly by translation from the Greek, and it arrived accompanied by works of Arabic scholarship commenting on it. This was learning of great sophistication but it had not, naturally, been shaped by considerations of the compatibility of Aristotle with Christian orthodoxy. The arrival of this stimulating new material meant that the arts course promptly became less lowly; it now included textbooks whose content went far beyond the intricacies of grammar and logic, which had been presenting challenges to theological study since the eleventh century.

All those who emerged from one of the early universities having completed the arts course had learned the skill of disputation, and that was to prove important in the shaping of the late medieval study of theology, especially at Oxford and Paris, the two universities that specialized most notably in this subject. There were, in the later medieval centuries, two strands to the study of theology. The old *studium sacrae scripturae* continued. Every theology student heard lectures on the Bible, and, if he aspired to become a master in his turn, he gave lectures on the Bible himself. But at the end of the twelfth century a systematic theology had begun to emerge, a method of studying doctrine topic by topic. Peter Lombard (*c*.1100–60) had put together a set of *Sentences* (*sententiae* or 'opinions') drawn from the Fathers and arranged in a thematic order, so that the student could see more or less at a glance the range of contradictory opinion he needed to be aware of on any given point. The book was controversial at first, because there was some suspicion that Lombard held unorthodox views on the Trinity, but from early in the thirteenth century it became the standard textbook for students of theology in universities, and remained so throughout the Middle Ages. Within the same tradition emerged the *summa*, for example Thomas Aquinas' *Summa theologiae* and *Summa contra Gentiles*, but no later attempt superseded Peter Lombard's work as the standard textbook. (The significance of Aquinas' *Summa theologiae* began to be felt only in the sixteenth century with the Counter-Reformation.)

The methodology of these collections of contradictory opinions was that of the formal university disputation. A question was put. Arguments were marshalled by the students, citing authorities or reasons. The presiding master 'determined' the answer and proceeded to demolish the arguments that had been advanced against his decision.

Is theology a practical science?

Aquinas argues that in being both speculative and practical, *sacra doctrina* outclasses all other *scientiae*, which are merely one or the other (*Summa theologiae* Ia.1.5). In one sense he was merely showing a sensitivity to the kind of duality Hugh of Saint-Victor insisted on, in which the intellectual and the spiritual both had a place in the study of theology. But he was also well aware, as he shows in his commentary on Aristotle's *Politics*, that there was a fundamental question here. Medieval pedagogy was disposed to consider theory a higher kind of study than practical disciplines. That is why Varro's list of mechanical arts had scarcely (*vix*) deserved a mention in the twelfth century. There was a pervasive separation of the two. *Musica*, for example, was regarded as a different subject from *cantus*. The first was a branch of mathematics, for which Boethius' *De musica* (On music) was the appropriate textbook. The second was the study of actual singing. Geometry, for which Euclid had provided a textbook, was a different study from the skill in measuring fields, for which the *agrimensores* of Roman literature had written guides. The distinction was less easy to maintain in the case of a subject such as politics, since arguably a political science that could not be applied was inherently flawed. The study of politics ought to be useful in the running of states. The same might be said of theology, as Aquinas does in his *Summa theologiae*, but with a consciousness of the Aristotelian dimension of the question that had not been present in the twelfth-century discussions.

The role of Plato and the influence of Pseudo-Dionysius in the medieval West

Hugh of Saint-Victor (1939: 25) explains that the word *theologia* comes from the Greek for the knowledge of God. But knowledge of Greek was sketchy in the medieval West. Partly for this reason, Plato was poorly represented in the West in the medieval 'stage' of the long story of the rebalancing of the relationship of philosophy and theology, at least in terms of the kind of detailed study of the source texts to which the works of Aristotle were progressively subjected.

The most important and distinctive strand in the study of theology in the Middle Ages, which bore the imprint of late Platonism, was represented by the work of Pseudo-Dionysius the Areopagite (*see* Vol. 1, Ch. 20, "Pseudo-Dionysius"), who was probably a writer of the fifth or sixth century and certainly not the much earlier Dionysius who is mentioned in Acts 17:34. He introduced themes that had a different flavour from those that were kin to them within the Western tradition. His concept of mysticism contrasts with the traditional Western mysticism of Augustine and Bernard of Clairvaux. They identified the mystical experience with the rapture described by Paul (1 Thessalonians 4:17). Pseudo-Dionysius, in his *De mystica theologia* (On mystical theology), thought in terms of a 'negative' ultimate 'experience' of God, which reflected what we cannot know about him. To describe God as infinite is, for example, a negative rather than a positive statement. It tells us that God has no boundaries, but it does not tell us what he positively is. The whole question of 'naming God' is made much more difficult by this line of thought.

Maximus Confessor (*c.*580–662) used Dionysian writings, and Johannes Scottus Eriugena (*c.*800–*c.*877), who seems to have been unusual in the West in having a genuine competence in Greek, made use of this work in his own translation and the fragments of his commentary on Pseudo-Dionysius that survive, and also in his huge work on 'nature', the *Periphyseon*. Eriugena was a controversial figure and his endorsement of the Dionysian approach did not assist it to gain currency. Nevertheless, Robert Grosseteste (*c.*1175–1253) compiled a 'corpus' of Dionysian material in the form of translation and commentary. And Aquinas was sufficiently interested in Pseudo-Dionysius to write on the *De divinis nominibus* (On the divine names). Nicholas of Cusa (1401–64) was attracted to the Dionysian paradoxicality of the impossibility of saying anything about God, and his own reflections on this problem underpin the *De docta ignorantia* (On learned ignorance).

The other theme that became partly identified with Pseudo-Dionysius was the concept of a celestial and natural hierarchy. Ideas of hierarchy were familiar and acceptable in the West but it was Pseudo-Dionysius who encouraged the working out of the details, for example, the idea that there are nine orders of angels. These stretched upwards from ordinary angels (messengers) and archangels (who carry special messages such as the Annunciation to Mary) to the cherubim and seraphim of Isaiah 6, who spend eternity in intellectual bliss in the very presence of God. The orders of angels caught the imagination of the medieval West, as did the notion of a detailed breakdown of heaven and earth and hell into their layers. Dante's *Divine Comedy* made use of this in vernacular literature.

As for reading Plato himself and not mere discussions of his ideas, we have seen that Plato's *Meno* and *Phaedo* were available in translation in the twelfth century, as was Chalcidius' rendering of the *Timaeus*, made in the fourth century and available for study in the West as early as the eighth century. The *Timaeus* proved to be the most challenging, because its account of creator and creation seemed incompatible with that of Genesis. Plato envisages a maker who assembles pre-existing matter and form (*see* Vol. 1, Ch. 4, "Socrates and Plato"); Genesis a creator who makes everything from nothing according to ideas he invents himself. Clarembald of Arras, in his *Tractaculus super librum Genesis* (Little treatise on the book of Genesis), wrestled with the task of reconciling the two (1965: 229). Other medieval authors used Genesis as a peg on which to hang discussions of philosophical and scientific problems, optics for example, at the point where Genesis says that God separated light from darkness. Robert Grosseteste wrote on the six days of creation in that spirit in the early thirteenth century, and in the fourteenth century Henry of Langenstein did the same.

This creeping progression towards what would now be identifiable as 'science' was to become important. Among the Platonic notions that chimed with what Boethius had said in his theological tractates was the idea that what seemed right to the reason was likely to be far stronger than anything ascertained in any other way, whether by reading authoritative texts or by attempts at experimental verification. *Per se nota*, the *communes animi conceptions* that Boethius speaks of in the *De hebdomadibus*, were the ultimate intuitively perceived and accepted abstractions. These were essentially Platonic Ideas. As long as it remained the case that all particular exemplifications of such Ideas in the material world must be regarded as inferior to the Ideas themselves, capable of disintegrating and decaying, experimental science could not begin. No experiment could disprove a beautiful idea because its evidence could never be strong enough.

Moreover, there were important implications here for the nature of the boundary between the natural and the supernatural. Modern experimental science confines itself to the study of the physical world on which experiments can be conducted. It does not typically attempt to draw inferences about the supernatural. But to the mind of Plato, that which is above the natural world is the world of Ideas and it bestows on the material things such form as they have and such intelligibility as they possess. Hugh of Saint-Victor, writing on *theologia* in his *Didascalicon* (1939: 25), cites Boethius in his commentary on Porphyry in language that shows how deeply such Platonism penetrated even into early medieval thought.

So the influence of Platonism should not be underestimated just because the works of Plato were not available to be read *in extenso* alongside those of Aristotle in the late medieval universities. Augustine had transmitted a great deal of Platonist thought and assumption, which he had himself imbibed largely second-hand but nevertheless in an age when its implications hung heavy in the air. Platonism was, moreover, a pervasive influence in Eastern Christendom, which had never been cut off from Greek and where the style of Platonic mysticism had proved immensely attractive in the late antique period and after. Also worth mentioning is John Colet (1467–1519), Erasmus' friend and contemporary, who became enraptured with Platonism while studying in Italy as a young man and by the time of his return to England was eloquent on the subject of the hierarchies of Pseudo-Dionysius (Colet 1869).

Philosophy and religion in the sixteenth century

The relationship of philosophy and theology took on a new look once more in the sixteenth century. The study of Greek had now become fashionable, largely driven by the movement to return 'to the sources' (*ad fontes*) in the study of the Bible, to read the Old Testament in the Hebrew and the Septuagint and the New Testament in the Greek. Johann Reuchlin (1455–1522) was one of the leaders in the study of Hebrew, Erasmus of the Greek.

But the pressure to read the Bible itself in Greek was not the result of a wish to read the philosophers whom access to the language also made available, although it was recognized that learning Greek gave access to more than Scripture. Once texts were available in the original Greek, students could read that philosophical literature for themselves.

The call *ad fontes* arose from another quarter altogether. Developments of the later Middle Ages, principally those that concerned the sacraments, ecclesiology, the governance of the Church and the relations of Church and State, had grown contentious because of a perception that the institutional Church of the West had begun to exceed its powers and 'impose' requirements on the faithful that had no divine warrant. In many respects these concerned pastoral rather than intellectual matters. For example, Martin Luther's great bugbear was the system of indulgences. These were remissions of penalties imposed by the Church within the penitential system, and the Church had begun to make a substantial income from selling them, particularly to those who believed they could buy for their deceased loved ones some time off from the period to be served in Purgatory. The Church had undoubtedly exploited the earning potential of indulgences but the system had developed largely in response to popular demand. It met a need, and the theology was cobbled together after the event to justify and explain the practice. Once Luther and others began seriously to challenge the authority of the Church it became important to rethink the whole question of authority. That had led reformers to think afresh about the Bible and to want to examine the text at its 'source', in the original version.

Some of the perennial 'philosophical questions' of Christian theology, such as the doctrine of the Trinity, aspects of Christology and what Anselm of Canterbury had called the 'most famous question' of the relationship of divine foreknowledge, predestination, free will and grace presented themselves afresh for discussion in the sixteenth century in the light of new insights derived from ancient Greek philosophy.

The full range of the Greek Fathers could be read again, and not only small snippets of a few, such as Origen (partly available in the translation of Jerome's contemporary, Rufinus). It was noticed that these Fathers, particularly the Cappadocians – Gregory of Nyssa, Gregory Nazianzus and Basil the Great – were themselves no mean philosophers (*see* Vol. 1, Ch. 17, "The Cappadocians"). They could begin to be given their full context. For the first time Western readers hitherto confined to Latin could appreciate for themselves why Ambrose of Milan had found them so stimulating in composing his sermons on Genesis; and why Augustine's opinion of Christianity had risen so sharply when he heard Ambrose explain creation in terms of the Neoplatonic philosophical ideas with which they were working.

The sixteenth century's changes were also pedagogical. The teaching methodology that had evolved in the medieval centuries with the rise of the universities had included a heavy emphasis on the reading (*lectio*) of set texts with commentary by a 'lecturer' in the form of comparative references to the opinions of earlier exegetes and critics. As this apparatus grew and became more complex and unwieldy, it became usual to defer discussion of particularly knotty questions to a separate session of disputation, in which the pros and cons could be debated and a 'determination' reached, with the master presiding. For this purpose the study of language (at the level of linguistics and epistemology) and logic was of paramount importance, and an immensely sophisticated and demanding syllabus had been constructed. This was now, in the sixteenth century, associated with what the reformers perceived to be the worst excesses of the Church's control of the study of the faith. It was labelled 'scholasticism' and sneered at. That does not mean that its use died away at once. The 'scholastic' syllabus was simplified, but not abandoned altogether until the nineteenth century. But at Luther's University of Wittenberg the disputation was still being used both for teaching and for examination in the late 1530s.

The changes of the sixteenth century, which led to those of the early modern world, were to do with the mechanics of philosophizing and 'doing theology', access to texts, knowledge of languages, understanding of the theory of language and the methodologies of argument. But transformation of those basics presented old questions in an entirely new light and made it possible to ask them from the vantage-point of an assumption that fundamentals could be redefined and human effort allowed to question quite radically what earlier authors had thought.

2

BOETHIUS

John Marenbon

Boethius made two important contributions to the philosophy of religion. In his *Opuscula sacra* (Short theological treatises) (hereafter *OS*; 1983, 2000), he used a method of logically analysing Christian doctrine that would deeply affect the medieval tradition of theology. In his final work, *De consolatione philosophiae* (Consolation of philosophy; hereafter *Consolation*; Boethius 1983, 2000) he devotes most of the last book to discussing the problem of prescience: the question of whether God's foreknowledge of events prevents their being contingent. The solution he proposed was taken up by Aquinas, and this line of argument, as interpreted by contemporary philosophers, is considered to be one of the main ways of tackling the problem. But before these themes can be discussed, they need to be placed into the broader context of Boethius' times, life and works.

BOETHIUS' LIFE AND WORKS

Anicius Manlius Severinus Boethius' life was shaped by the accident of his birth (*c*.476) into a noble Roman family, and his adoption into an even nobler one. His privileged background meant that he acquired fluent Greek and had access to Greek culture and manuscripts. He was able to spend most of his life in learned leisure, devoted to arithmetic, music and, above all, logic. Italy was ruled by the Ostrogoths, and Boethius' social and intellectual eminence led the Ostrogothic king, Theodoric, to choose him as his chief minister. But suspicions among the Goths about his loyalty and rivalries at court led to his fall from favour, imprisonment and (*c*.525) execution on trumped-up charges of treason.

Boethius had taken advantage of his unusually good education to embark on an ambitious scheme of making Greek culture available to Latin speakers. After writing textbooks on arithmetic and music, closely based on Greek models, he turned to logic. Although he proposed to translate all the works he could find of Aristotle and Plato, in fact he confined himself to logic, but not to mere translation of the Aristotelian texts. He composed logical commentaries and textbooks, which would transmit to the Latin thinkers of the Middle Ages many aspects of the logical thinking of late antiquity. Although he was far from being a creative logician, Boethius was not a simple translating machine, putting Greek ideas into Latin words. He had his own distinctive preferences, which led to logic in his presentation having a more genuinely Aristotelian character than many of his contemporaries would have given it.

Although Boethius' culture was formed largely in the pagan Greek Neoplatonic tradition (which also included the study of Aristotle), he and all his Roman contemporaries were Christians – Catholic Christians – as opposed to the Goths, who were Arians. The Greeks were also Catholics, but the 'Acacian schism', a difference over Christology, separated them from the Romans. Boethius, not a priest, but a committed Christian, wanted to use his logical skills to help reunite the Eastern and Western Churches. To this end, he wrote (c.513) a short theological work that proposed a Christological formula that he hoped would be acceptable to both sides: *Against Eutyches and Nestorius* (*OS* V). He then (c.519) wrote two treatises on the Trinity, also designed to heal schism (*OS* I and II, which is just a partial sketch for I). When the *Opuscula sacra* were collected together, two other works were added: a confession of faith (*OS* IV) and a purely philosophical discussion arguing that the goodness that things have in virtue of existing is different from God's goodness (*OS* III).

It was when he was in prison, waiting to be executed, that Boethius wrote his most famous work, the *Consolation*. The *Consolation* was studied throughout the Middle Ages and up to the eighteenth century, and it was the only ancient philosophical work to be translated into a whole variety of medieval vernaculars. The *Consolation* is based boldly on Boethius' own personal situation at the time he was writing it, and it consists of a dialogue between Boethius himself and Philosophy, personified as a woman. Suddenly stripped of his possessions, power and liberty because of a false charge against him, and facing death, Boethius, as portrayed in the dialogue, can no longer believe that human affairs are ordered justly by God: the wicked prosper and the good are oppressed. Philosophy's task is to show Boethius why, despite appearances, the world is ordered by God with complete justice. First, after she has given him the chance to tell the story of his downfall, she shows him that he has lost nothing of value in his change of circumstances. She then introduces the more extreme argument that people go astray by seeking intermediary goods rather than grasping the highest good, which is God himself. She is now in a position to answer Boethius' initial complaint more directly, explaining how the wicked, because they lack a knowledge of the true good, are not really happy but only succeed in punishing themselves. Rather inconsistently, perhaps, she complements this account of the highest good as a final cause with a view of it as efficient cause, a divine providence in which everything, in ways sometimes inscrutable, is planned for the best. But does not the all-encompassing character of God's place, executed on earth by fate, mean that human beings do not act freely? Philosophy argues that the motions of the human mind, at least, are free, but then she is faced by an objection from Boethius. If God foreknows all things, is not even this freedom removed? Philosophy ends the work answering this problem, and her response will be examined in detail below.

Interpretation of the *Consolation* is difficult. Boethius is a Christian, and yet at the end of his life he writes a *Consolation of 'Philosophy'*, in which he carefully excludes any explicit reference to Christianity, and where the authoritative personification clearly belongs to the world of pagan Neoplatonism, although pagan Neoplatonism purged of the elements that clashed openly with Christian doctrine. There is room to ask whether, while showing the respect for pagan philosophy that had shaped his intellectual life, Boethius does not give some hints that Philosophy is not absolutely an authoritative figure, and that the consolation she can offer is limited (see Marenbon [2005: 146–63] for an ill-considered discussion that does, however, set out the issues; and Relihan [2006] for an extreme but interesting view).

THE THEOLOGICAL METHOD OF *OPUSCULA SACRA* I AND V

Boethius was certainly not the first Christian writer to use philosophical and logical tools. In the Latin tradition, Marius Victorinus and Augustine had set an example, and a sophisticated use of logic was a hallmark of much Greek doctrinal writing in his time (Daley 1984). No one, though, at least in the Latin tradition, had developed this use of logical analysis in theology in the two main ways followed by Boethius.

One of Boethius' methods was to try to show that, if scrutinized carefully, and in the light of certain philosophical premises that he considered reasonable to hold, heretical positions were revealed to be incoherent. In *OS* V he is aiming to confute two antithetical heterodox positions: that of Nestorius – that in Christ there was a divine nature and divine person, and a human nature and human person; and that of Eutyches – that in Christ there was just one nature and one person. To Nestorius (*OS* V,4) he objects that the closest relation that the divine-nature–divine-person combination can have with the human-nature–human-person is one of mere juxtaposition: his view leaves the Son of God and Jesus Christ as two separate things and so, instead of explaining the Incarnation, in effect it denies it. Although Eutyches insisted that Christ had one nature, he admitted that it derived from (*ex*) a divine and human nature. It is this admission that allows Boethius to object to him. Boethius argues (*OS* V,6) that none of the ways in which a divine and human nature could, in principle, be combined is possible: the divine nature, which is immutable, could not become human and so mutable; nor could human nature become divine, or divine nature and human nature be combined into a divine-and-human nature, because both sorts of transformation would require (according to the laws of Aristotelian physics) a common matter between divine nature and human nature, and there is none. It remains, then, to conclude that there are two distinct natures in Christ, divine and human, but, as the argument against Nestorius shows, one person: and that, of course, is the orthodox position Boethius set out to vindicate.

Boethius' other method also fits Christian doctrine closely to philosophical argument, but here the aim is to show how far a mystery of the faith can be explained in terms of ordinary logic and to chart the exact point at which such an explanation fails. This is the method he uses in discussing the Trinity (*OS* I). How can the Father, Son and Holy Spirit be the same thing and yet three? They are the same, Boethius argues, because there is no intrinsic predication – a predication that bears on the nature of the thing itself – that can be made about one and not about the others. (Boethius also explains, in Augustinian style, how such predications must be understood differently in the case of God than for created things, because no property outside himself can be attributed to God: to say that God is wise is to say that God is wisdom itself.) They differ (*OS* I,6) just according to the extrinsic predications of paternity, filiation and spiration that can be made about the individual persons. In principle, a thing can be related to itself by a predication of relation: everything, for example, is similar to itself. In the created world, the relations of paternity, filiation and spiration can only hold between things that are also different from each other in other ways besides their differing in these relations. A father cannot differ from his son only in that paternity can be predicated of him and filiation of his son. But in the case of God – and it is here that ordinary logic breaks down – we have to try to imagine that there can be a difference solely in terms of being Father, Son or Spirit in something that is intrinsically one and the same.

The method of the *Opuscula sacra* was imitated and developed by twelfth-century theologians at the beginning of the elaboration of scholastic theology. In particular, in his *Theologia 'summi boni'* of 1120, Peter Abelard (1987b) tried to devise his own extended logic of similarity and difference to explain divine triunity. In his commentary on Boethius' *Opuscula sacra* (*c.*1145), Gilbert of Poitiers set out a whole system of distinguishing ways of speaking about the natural world from what would be appropriate for God, but also of transferring them 'proportionately' so as to provide some way of discussing the divine.

THE PROBLEM OF PRESCIENCE: BOETHIUS' REAL SOLUTION AND THE 'BOETHIAN' SOLUTION

In contemporary philosophy of religion, there is an extensive literature on the 'Boethian' solution to the problem of prescience. But the line of argument attributed to Boethius is not at all what emerges from a careful reading of the *Consolation*. For this reason, Boethius' own arguments (ignoring the dialogue form: the views expressed, usually by Philosophy, that seem to have been endorsed by Boethius the author will be presented simply as his) will be set out in this section; the next section will comment on them and briefly consider their influence; and then, in the final section, the 'Boethian' solution, as it appears in contemporary discussions, will be examined and compared with Boethius' solution.

The problem of prescience: Boethius' real solution

Intuitively, the problem of prescience seems easy to grasp. If God foreknows everything, then it seems that the future must be fixed, since nothing can happen otherwise than as God already knows it is going to happen. I believe that I have the choice whether, this afternoon, I spend my time finishing this chapter, which is already overdue, or cycling in the countryside, but as soon as I reflect that God knows now which choice I am going to make, I see that this belief is false, at least if having a choice implies that there is a possibility of doing otherwise than one does. Suppose God knows that I shall go cycling: I could decide to stay in and work only by making God's knowledge into a false belief, which is impossible.

Putting this intuitive grasp of the problem into a definite form is more difficult, and to a considerable extent the nature of a solution depends on the formal terms in which the problem is set out. In the *Consolation*, the problem is given these two formulations:

(1) "If God sees all things and can in no way be mistaken, then there necessarily happens what he by providence will have foreseen will be" (*Consolation* V.3.4,[1] in Boethius 2000)

and

(2) "If things are capable of turning out differently from how they have been foreseen, then there will no longer be firm foreknowledge of the future, but rather uncertain opinion" (V.3.6).

It may well be that these formulations rest on a logical fallacy, but Boethius seems not to notice this, certainly not when he first puts them into the mouth of 'Boethius' in the dialogue, and arguably not at any time (see below).

Boethius appears to believe that (1) can be answered fairly easily, whereas (2) demands a complex solution, which will also provide a more satisfactory answer to (1). The solution to (1), it seems, lies in the fact that it does not assert that God's foreknowledge *causes* future events (ultimately, Boethius does think that God's knowledge is causative, and this stance presents great problems for interpreting the *Consolation* as a whole (Marenbon 2003: 143–5); but this idea is ruled out of his

---

1. *Consolation* is cited by book, prose and sections numbers (i.e. V.3.4 refers to book 5, prose 3, section 4) and translations throughout are my own.

main discussion of divine prescience). It follows, Boethius argues (V.4.7–13), that, if future events are all necessary, they must be necessary for some reason other than God's foreknowledge. But, if this or other considerations make (1) seem unproblematic, there remains, Boethius acknowledges, the difficulty proposed by (2). For future events to be contingent rather than determined, it must be uncertain now how they will turn out, and this uncertainty prevents them from being objects of *knowledge*. If God foreknows them, then he will be regarding as certain what are not in fact certain: he will be judging something as being other than it is, and that, so it is usually thought, is "foreign to the integrity of knowledge" (V.4.21–3).

At the centre of the long and complex solution to (2) that Boethius now develops is, however, a rejection of precisely this generally accepted and seemingly obvious point: that everything is known as it is. People believe, says Boethius (V.4.24–5), that "everything that is known is known just according to the power and nature of the things that are known". But "the truth is the very contrary. For everything that is known is grasped not according to its own power, but rather according to the capacity of those who know it". What does this assertion – the 'modes of cognition principle' – mean? Since it is supposed to explain how it can count as knowledge to hold that an event that is in itself uncertain (because future and contingent) is certain, it seems to be challenging what is normally held to follow from the definition of knowledge: that

(3) If someone (A) knows something (x), then x is in fact as A knows it to be.

The modes of cognition principle is not, however, arguing for the simple negation of (3), but rather that (3) is an inadequate presentation of what is involved in knowledge. All knowledge must be relativized to the knower, and so, rather than (3), it is more accurate to say

(4) If A knows x, then x is as A knows it to be relative to A's mode of cognition;

and the consequent in (4) is compatible with

(5) x in itself is not as A knows it to be.

In V.4, Boethius sets out a complicated scheme of cognition relativized to knowers, in which each of levels of cognizing – sensing, imagining (common to both humans and non-human animals), reasoning (peculiar to human beings), intellecting (peculiar to God) – grasps the same knowledge through its own special object of cognition in its own special manner.

For the continuation of his argument, however, Boethius relies on a simpler way of applying the modes of cognition principle, which is now stated in a slightly different form: "everything which is known is cognized not from its own nature but from that of those which grasp it" (V.6.1). The suggestion is that, if we want to understand how God has knowledge of future events that are uncertain, we should consider God's nature. And his nature – or the aspect of it relevant to this discussion – is that he is eternal. Being eternal is not, Boethius adds, a matter of existing for an infinite length of time, but rather, he explains (in a definition that became classic) divine eternity is "the whole, simultaneous and perfect possession of unbounded life" (V.6.4). (Many interpreters see this definition as a way of saying that God is atemporal, but it is highly debatable whether this is what Boethius meant; see below). Although this way of eternally living is difficult for human beings to understand, Boethius stresses throughout the discussion in V.6 that it has one important parallel with human experience that helps us grasp it. God lives in an eternal present, which is like our fleeting present, except that our present passes immediately whereas God's remains for ever. For God, all events, past, present and future, are known in this eternal present. If we wish to understand God's knowledge of all things, we should therefore consider our knowledge of the present.

Next, Boethius introduces a distinction that shows how the similarity between our knowledge of what is happening at present and God's knowledge of all things in his eternal present provides the key to solving the problem of prescience. He distinguishes between simple and conditional necessity (V.6.27). Simple necessity is found in natural necessities: it is simply necessary, for instance, that all human beings are mortal and that the sun rises. Conditional necessity is when, for instance, "if you know someone is walking, it is necessary that he is walking". Boethius continues:

> For what each person knows cannot be known and yet otherwise <than it is known to be>, but this condition by no means brings with it that simple necessity. For it is not a thing's own nature which makes this necessity, but the adding of the condition: for no necessity compels a person who voluntarily is walking to be walking, but when he is walking, it is necessary that he is walking. (V.6.28–9)

Boethius, then, is arguing that an ordinary contingent event, such as my walking across the room, is *necessary* when it is relativized to the knowledge of someone who knows it is happening as it is happening in the present, but that this necessity is not like that of a simply necessary event. In the last sentence of the passage quoted, Boethius gives a clue to understanding what is involved in this conditional necessity: it is exactly like the necessity of the present; indeed, the suggestion seems to be that the necessity of the present is a species of it. The necessity of the present is a feature of Aristotle's understanding of modality, which was followed by Boethius, as his commentary on *On Interpretation* shows clearly (cf. Knuuttila 1993: 51–5). Neither Aristotle nor Boethius had a conception of synchronic alternative possibilities. 'I am sitting and it is possible that I am standing' means, for them, that it is possible that at the next instant I stand up. If, at the present moment, I am sitting, then it is necessary that I am sitting at this moment. But this necessity, Aristotle believes, in no sense impinges on freedom.

All Boethius has to do now is to refer back to the parallel between human present knowledge and divine knowledge. When we see something happening, and know it is happening, the event is necessary, but only relative to us and in a way that is entirely unconstraining. "In the same way, therefore", he says, "if providence sees something present, it is necessary that it is, although of its nature it has no necessity" (V.6.30). God does indeed see all things, past, present and future, in his eternal present; relative to him, they have the necessity of the present, but that does not make them simply necessary: things that happen as a result of free will are, in their own nature, free, but in relation to God's vision of them they are necessary "by the condition of God's knowledge" (V.6.32).

To summarize, although some future events – those dependent on free will – are uncertain in themselves, they are certain in relation to God's cognition of them, and so in grasping them as certain, God has knowledge of them. In order to be grasped with certainty, these events must be necessary, but they are conditionally, not simply necessary. Every event is conditionally necessary when it is happening, or when it is known to be happening in the present by human beings, or known to be happening by God (at whatever time relative to us it happens, past, present or future) in his eternal present, but this conditional necessity in no way prevents the events from being the result of free will.

Difficulties with Boethius' solution

It may have struck attentive readers that the way in which Boethius formulates the problem of prescience (in (1) and (2)) seems to be based on a logical fallacy: one concerning logical scope. Boethius seems to be saying (to consider (1); the same point *mutatis mutandis* applies to (2)) that, because God has knowledge of all future events, and because knowledge cannot be erroneous, all future events are necessary. This looks like the following deduction:

(6) God knows all future events.
(7) Necessarily, if someone knows something, it was/is/will be the case.
(8) All future events will happen necessarily (not contingently).

But (8) does not follow from (6) and (7). All that (7) establishes is the necessity of the *connection* between someone knowing something, and that thing being the case (not that thing being necessary). It is true that, necessarily, if God knows that event *x* will happen, it will happen, and it is true that, for every future event, God knows it will happen; but that does not in the least show that any of these events will happen necessarily. What would be needed along with (6) to entail (8) would be the premise

26

(9) If someone knows something, it was/is/will necessarily be the case.

But there is no reason at all to grant (9).

It seems, therefore, that Boethius' statement of the difficulty confuses wide-scope necessity (Necessarily, if *p* then *q*), as found in (7), and narrow-scope necessity (If *p*, then necessarily *q*), as found in (9). (Later medieval logicians would describe this as the distinction between necessity of the consequence and the necessity of the consequent.)

For some modern interpreters (e.g. Sharples [1991] in his generally excellent commentary), when Boethius distinguishes between simple and conditional necessity, he is taking account of precisely this confusion: simple necessity is narrow-scope necessity, conditional necessity wide-scope necessity. But there are three strong reasons not to follow this reading. First, if Boethius finally notices that his initial posing of the problem is based on a fallacious inference, why does he not say so and either declare the problem solved or explain how it can be restated in a way that does not commit the fallacy? So far from such a reaction, he gives no hint that the distinction between simple necessity and conditional necessity reflects back on how he originally stated his views. Rather, his argument proceeds as set out above. Secondly, when necessity is wide-scope and so applies to the whole of an 'if … then …' proposition, not to the antecedent or the consequent, it does not make either the antecedent or the consequent themselves necessary. But in Boethius' account of conditional necessity, he takes it that this necessity *does* make the consequent necessary, but in a special, 'conditional' way.

Thirdly, and most importantly, there is good reason to believe that Boethius could not even have understood the distinction between narrow-scope necessity and wide-scope necessity. In order to notice a scope distinction of this sort, a logician needs to be thinking in terms of propositions and the operations that can be conducted on them individually (negation) or to link them together (conjunction, disjunction, entailment). Following the work of Christopher Martin (1991), it is clear that Boethius had no conception of such propositional operations. He did not even think of conditionals as connecting together propositions, but instead thought of them as proposing a special sort of link between some of their terms.

Still, although Boethius should not be credited with uncovering the scope fallacy, it is an oversimplification to say that he falls into it. He certainly lacked the tools to formulate the problem in such a way as to show that he was aware of and avoiding it, but he did not, as a reading of the opening of his argument in isolation might suggest, think that the problem of prescience consists of inferring (8) from (6) and (7). He recognized, without stating it formally, that time has a central part in the problem: we are not concerned with what God knows about what is happening (for us) now, but with his knowledge of the future. Lying beneath the surface of the apparently invalid inference that he uses to set up the problem is a genuine problem that cannot be resolved by logical disambiguation.

The character of Boethius' position is put into focus by the story of its influence in the twelfth and thirteenth centuries (see Marenbon 2005: chs 3–5). In his *Dialectica* (*c*.1105–15), using the discussion in the *Consolation* as a starting-point, Peter Abelard quickly identified the scope fallacy that a propositional formulation of Boethius' posing of the problem would commit. But Abelard believed that, by unmasking this fallacy, he had solved the problem of prescience, and most of his contemporaries followed him in this belief. It was only gradually, in the course of the thirteenth century, that the temporal dimension of the problem, intuitively grasped by Boethius but ignored by Abelard, was rediscovered. Aquinas, benefiting from the understanding of propositionality that had become common from Abelard's time, was able to formulate this aspect of the problem with a formal precision that entirely eluded Boethius; but his solution proceeds along uncannily Boethian lines.

The 'Boethian' solution

Readers of current literature on the problem of prescience are very likely to be told of the 'Boethian' solution to the problem (sometimes attributed to Aquinas, or to Aquinas and Boethius together) (see e.g. Leftow 1991: 160; Zagzebski 1991: 37–9). It is only loosely related to the line of argument actually proposed by Boethius (and hardly more closely to that advanced by Aquinas). In order to understand this 'Boethian' solution, it is first necessary to see how the problem can be formulated, using the apparatus of propositional logic, in a way that incorporates the temporal element and avoids committing the scope fallacy. If God foreknows all future events, then it is not merely true that now, at time t_2 that he knows what will happen at some future time, t_3, but also that at some time in the past, t_1, he knew what would happen at t_3. We recognize that past events are unchangeable and so in some sense necessary (philosophers speak of their 'accidental necessity'). We can, therefore, say that

(10) It is now, at t_2, (accidentally) necessary that God knew that x will happen at t_3.

It is a principle accepted in the system of modal logic (the transfer of necessity principle) that supposedly best models our common-sense modal intuitions that, if a consequent follows necessarily from an antecedent, and if the antecedent is itself necessary, then the consequent too is necessary. That is to say:

(11) (Necessarily (if p then q), and necessarily-p) implies necessarily-q.

From the disambiguated version of Boethius' posing of the problem of prescience, we can take the (in itself innocuous) statement that:

(12) Necessarily (if God knows p, then p).

But in (10) it has been established that (accidentally) necessarily God knows p (that x will happen at t_3), and so, by (11), it follows that

(13) Necessarily x will happen at t_3.

This formulation of the problem of prescience is called the 'accidental necessity argument' and it formalizes the intuitions about time and knowledge that make the problem intuitively worrying.

The 'Boethian' solution rebuts this argument by rejecting (10) because, according to this solution, God is atemporally eternal. If God is atemporal, then no temporal proposition directly about him is true. It is false, for example, to say that 'God is wise now', or that 'God is good in 2007', or that 'God is good at t_n', where for t_n can be substituted any moment or period of time. (The qualification 'directly' is included because the truth of, for instance, 'In 2007 God is believed to be good by most US citizens' is not challenged by this position.) If, then, God is atemporally eternal, it is not true that he knew at t_1 what would happen at t_3. Rather, it is true that he atemporally knows what will happen at t_3, and this will not provide the premise necessary for the accidental necessary argument to go through. Since the accidental necessity argument depends on the necessity of the past, and none of God's knowledge is past, none of it is accidentally necessary.

Neat though this solution may be, it faces two large problems. First, it can be argued that, if God is atemporally eternal, then the distinction between past, present and future breaks down, not just for God, but for all things. If God is atemporal, then, it is usually considered, his act of knowing in one glance what happens at t_1 and at t_2 and at t_3 must be simultaneous with t_1 and t_2 and t_3. But since simultaneity is a transitive relation, t_1 and t_2 and t_3 will therefore be simultaneous with one another, and time will collapse into a single instant. The counterargument, that the relation of simultaneity between an event in time and a timelessly eternal knower has a special character, and is intransitive (Stump & Kretzmann 1981), just reveals in its apparently *ad hoc* nature the looseness of our grasp on what it might be to be timelessly eternal. Secondly, just as it can be argued that past events are accidentally necessary because unchangeable, so it might be argued that accidental necessity attaches to whatever happens in God's timeless eternity, since it too cannot be changed (Zagzebski 1991: 60–61). In short, even if the 'Boethian' solution does not generate unacceptable consequences – which is doubtful – the problem can easily be reformulated in a way that it cannot solve.

But these criticisms should not be addressed to Boethius, who was not responsible for what is called the 'Boethian' solution. The 'Boethian' solution is directed against a formulation of the problem in terms that he, given his lack of a grasp of propositionality, could not have even understood. And its central principle, that God is atemporally eternal, is arguably not a feature of Boethius's genuine argument at all.

As was made clear in expounding Boethius' argument, he does not think that God's eternity consists in his lacking a beginning and an end to his existence, but rather in having a life that is lived wholly and perfectly at once. There is a distinguished scholarly tradition of interpreting this comment (and a parallel one found in *OS* I,4) to mean that God is timeless, and there do seem to be some earlier ancient authors who had a definite conception of an atemporal type of eternity (Sorabji 1983: 119–20). But there is nothing in Boethius' text to suggest that he considered any temporal proposition about God (such as 'God is good today') to be false. When he talks about divine eternity, Boethius is describing how God lives his life: unchangingly, all at once, so that his knowledge is always the same; his whole life, as he says, is like one of the fleeting instances of our life made permanent and stable (*Consolation* V.6.13). As explained, Boethius builds his solution from this idea, claiming that, since God is eternal in this way, God's knowledge of all things is like our knowledge of what is happening at the present instant. There is no reason, then, to think that Boethius would have wished to reject common-sense claims such as 'God is good today', although he would want to underline that such a statement lacks the usual conversational implicature that he might not be good tomorrow.

CONCLUSION

Boethius' theological methods and his way of tackling the problem of prescience are both examples of a subtlety of mind that shows how mistaken were those scholars in the past who treated Boethius as hardly more than a translator: an intermediary for Greek ideas to pass to a Latin-speaking world. Moreover, his influence on the Middle Ages in both these areas was so profound that no one eager to understand Abelard, Aquinas or even Ockham can afford to neglect him. But Boethius did not speak the language of contemporary philosophy, and he formulated the problem of prescience in a way that obscures what we consider to be its logical substance. The fathering on to Boethius of a solution to the problem, which he neither gave nor even would have understood, is a touching example of the need contemporary philosophers appear to have, at least in philosophy of religion, to wrap themselves in the authority of past thinkers. Since, however, the 'Boethian' solution is all too easily dismissed, it would in all ways be fairer to assess Boethius for what he actually proposed, and not for what it is believed that he should have done.

FURTHER READING

Boethius 2001. *Consolation of Philosophy*, J. Relihan (trans.). Indianapolis, IN: Hackett.
Chadwick, H. 1981. *Boethius: The Consolations of Music, Logic, Theology, and Philosophy*. Oxford: Oxford University Press.

Daley, B. 1984. "Boethius's Theological Tracts and Early Byzantine Scholasticism". *Mediaeval Studies* **46**: 158–91.

Evans, J. 2004. "Boethius on Modality and Future Contingents". *American Catholic Philosophical Quarterly* **78**: 247–71.

Marenbon, J. (ed.) 2009. *The Cambridge Companion to Boethius*. Cambridge: Cambridge University Press.

On ETERNITY see also Ch. 5. On FOREKNOWLEDGE see also Ch. 6; Vol. 3, Ch. 13. On FREE WILL see also Chs 7, 9, 19; Vol. 1, Ch. 18; Vol. 3, Chs 9, 15; Vol. 5, Ch. 22. On LOGIC see also Chs 4, 17; Vol. 3, Ch. 3; Vol. 4, Ch. 19. On THE TRINITY see also Chs 2, 8, 15; Vol. 1, Chs 14, 17, 20; Vol. 3, Chs 3, 9, 17; Vol. 4, Ch. 4; Vol. 5, Chs 12, 23.

3

JOHANNES SCOTTUS ERIUGENA

Dermot Moran

Johannes (*c*.800–*c*.877), known as 'the Irishman' (*Scottus*), who signed one manu-script with 'Eriugena', was a Christian Neoplatonist philosopher and theologian of great originality, and an influential transmitter of Greek Christian theology, notably through his translation of Pseudo-Dionysius the Areopagite. Eriugena is the most outstanding philosopher writing in Latin between Boethius and Anselm and the most significant intellectual from early Christian Ireland during an era known for its scholars, many of whom, as Eriugena himself did, became teachers on the European mainland. While Eriugena's work shows traces of his Irish heritage, there is no direct evidence in his writings of the particular form of Christianity that flourished in Ireland at that time.

Eriugena made a number of important contributions to the history of religion in the West. He stands out because of his considerable familiarity with the Greek language, which allowed him direct access to Greek Christian theologians, several hitherto unknown in the Latin West (e.g. Maximus Confessor). Eriugena trans-lated not only the *corpus* of Dionysius, but also Gregory of Nyssa's treatise on human nature *De hominis opificio* (On the creation of man) as well as Maximus Confessor's *Ambigua ad Iohannem* (Difficulties in response to John). In his own treatises, he enthusiastically advocated Dionysius' negative theological approach and generally sided with Eastern Christianity on a number of issues, including on the nature of the processions within the Trinity and on the nature of the resurrec-tion. His dialogue *Periphyseon* (hereafter *Peri.*) offers a major synthesis of Greek and Latin Christian theologies and promotes a consistent Christian Neoplatonic system that was influential in later centuries.

Although lacking direct knowledge of classical Neoplatonism (Plotinus, Porphyry, Proclus), Eriugena had enormous sympathy for what he thought was the single Neoplatonic framework underlying the Christian writers of the East and West whom he had read: Basil, Gregory of Nyssa, Dionysius, Maximus Confessor, from the East, as well as the more familiar authorities of the Latin West (e.g. Augustine, Boethius). Eriugena's theology centres on the notion of an infinite, incomprehensible, transcendent God – "the immovable self-identical one" (*unum et idipsum immobile*; *Peri.* I.476B)[1] – whose freely willed *theophanies* (divine manifestations) alone can be apprehended by created intellects such as angels and human beings. The One, as highest principle, engenders all things timelessly, allows them to proceed into their genera and species in space and time and then retrieves them back into itself. All things, including human nature, are eternal ideas or causes in the mind of God. Human beings fail to understand their true nature as image of God because they are distracted by created, fleeting temporal appearances (*phantasiai*), which entrap the intellect in the clouded spatiotemporal realm of sense. However, through intellectual contemplation (*theoria, intellectus*) and divine illumination (which is the receiving of a divine self-manifestation, *theophania*), human beings may achieve unification (*henosis*) with God, and the select few will even undergo deification (*deificatio, theosis*). Salvation, or return to the One, involves the corporeal body being resolved into its original incorporeal essence. Both heaven and hell are maintained to be states of mind, not actual places (*loci*). Paradise is nothing other than perfect human nature. Eriugena often quotes Augustine to the effect that God became man (*inhumanatio*) so that human beings can become God (*deificatio*). In this cosmological process, there is a dialectic of outgoing and return, of affirmation and negation.

Part of Eriugena's uniqueness is that he self-consciously adopts the term 'nature' to refer to the whole that consists of both God and the created order. *Natura* is defined as *universitas rerum*, the 'totality of all things' that are (*ea quae sunt*) and are not (*ea quae non sunt*). For Eriugena, the hidden transcendent divine nature does not simply rest in its Oneness but divides or 'externalizes' itself into a set of four 'divisions' (*divisiones*), 'forms' or 'species', which make up distinct levels of the universe: God, the primary causes (or creative ideas in the mind of God), the effects of those causes (the created world of individual entities), and non-being. These four divisions of nature (adapted from similar divisions in Marius Victorinus and Augustine) taken together are to be understood as God, presented as the beginning, middle and end of all things. The four divisions somehow fold back into the divine unity. Creation, then, is a process of divine self-articulation. God (as infinite essence or *ousia*) is understood as having a triadic structure: essence, power, operation (*ousia, dynamis, energeia*). So, in one sense, the entire cosmic drama of expression and return takes place within the Godhead. Human nature, as the image of God, plays a very direct role in the cosmic process of the divine self-manifestation and self-gathering. Eriugena's elevated conception of human nature would subsequently influence Renaissance humanism and its German counterpart.

---

1. Translations throughout are my own.

ERIUGENA: LIFE AND WRITINGS

The exact place or date of Eriugena's birth and the circumstances of his early life are entirely unknown, but circumstantial evidence and some surviving *testimonia* suggest that he was born in Ireland around or before 800. The first certain historical record (around 850/851) is a letter by Bishop Pardulus of Laon that refers to a certain Irishman named 'Joannes' at the palace of the King of France (*Patrologia Latina* [hereafter *PL*] 121:1052A), who was engaged in a theological controversy. It is this reference that has given rise to the appellation 'Johannes Scottus'. The pen name 'Eriugena', meaning 'Irish born', is used to sign his translation of Dionysius (*PL* 122:1236A), offering further confirmation of his Irish origin. A manuscript of biblical glosses attributed to Eriugena includes several Old Irish terms to explain recondite Latin words, offering more evidence of Eriugena's provenance and attesting to other Irish in his milieu. Indeed, Irish scholars had a considerable presence in the Frankish court and were renowned for their learning. Prudentius, however, refers to Eriugena's "Irish eloquence" (*Celtica eloquentia*; *PL* 115:1194A) in a disparaging manner.

Eriugena appears to have spent his life in the ambience of the court of King Charles and in associated ecclesiastical centres, such as Rheims, Laon, Soissons and Compiègne. It is not known whether Eriugena was cleric or lay. His contemporaries regarded him as an erudite liberal arts master, although some challenged his orthodoxy. Thus, Bishop Florus calls him "academic and learned" (*scholasticus et eruditus*; *PL* 119:103A). The learned Anastasius, the Librarian at the Vatican, who improved Eriugena's translation of Dionysius, could marvel at the fact that this *vir barbarus* from the remote ends of the world knew Greek. Two partial commentaries (*c.*840–*c.*850) on *The Marriage of Philology and Mercury*, the liberal arts handbook of Martianus Capella, as well as the aforementioned biblical glosses testify to Eriugena's rich and eclectic knowledge of the liberal arts tradition, including Isidore, Cassiodorus and Cicero. One gloss in the *Annotationes in Marcianum* (Annotations on Martianus Capella) attests "no one enters heaven except through philosophy" (*nemo intrat in celum nisi per philosophiam*); and, indeed, in his mature work, Eriugena continues to see 'true philosophy' as leading to reunion with the divine. Eriugena also wrote some interesting poems that show not only his erudition and fascination with Greek but also his political connections. Some poems specifically praise King Charles, including an important poem, *Aulae sidereae* (Starry halls), which appears to celebrate the dedication of Charles' new church in Compiègne on 1 May 875.

It is probable that Eriugena died some time around 877. An apocryphal tale, recounted by William of Malmesbury, records that he was stabbed to death by his students.

THE CONTROVERSY OVER PREDESTINATION (851)

Eriugena came to the notice of his contemporaries because of his intervention in a theological controversy. He was commissioned by Hincmar, the powerful Archbishop of Rheims, and Pardulus, Bishop of Laon, to rebut a treatise on predestination by Gottschalk of Orbais (*c.*806–868), a priest in Hincmar's jurisdiction. Gottschalk had already been condemned (at synods in Mainz in 848 and in Quierzy in 849) for interpreting Augustine as teaching that God carried out a 'twin predestination' (*gemina praedestinatio*), namely, of the elect to heaven and of the damned to hell. Eriugena's response, *De divina praedestinatione* (On divine predestination; *c.*851; hereafter *De Praed.*), employing rationalistic, dialectical analysis rather than scriptural citation, was a *tour de force* of dialectical argumentation that rejected the doctrine of twofold divine predestination by an appeal to God's unity, transcendence and infinite goodness. It also showed Eriugena's mastery of Augustine whom he quotes against Gottschalk's reading.

Eriugena begins by declaring (following Augustine; *see* Vol. 1, Ch. 18) that true philosophy and true religion are one and the same (*De Praed.* 1.1). He insists that the rules of dialectical disputation be followed and counters Gottschalk's claims by showing them to be counter-sensical. God's nature is one, and so is his predestination. There is a perfectly legitimate sense in which it can be said that God predestines: "There is no doubt that predestination is predicated essentially of God" (3.5). God, being perfectly good and the "willing cause" of all creatures (4.5), wants all human beings to be saved. But God does not predestine souls to damnation; human beings damn themselves through their own free choices. On the basis that contrary effects cannot come from the one cause, Eriugena argues that God cannot predestine both to good and to evil, but only to good. Furthermore, "sin, death, unhappiness are not from God. Therefore God is not the cause of them" (3.3). God cannot predestine to evil since evil is non-being. Following Augustine, to foreknow is not to cause what is foreknown (5.2). Furthermore, not all foreknowledge is predestination. Properly speaking, God, who is outside time and acts all at once (*semel et simul*), cannot be said to *fore*-know or to *pre*-destine (9.6), terms that are transferred from created things (9.7). Eriugena does not fully resolve his claims that predestination both *properly* applies to God and at the same time is attributed *metaphorically*. He does not yet have access to Dionysius' dialectical way of handling divine attribution.

Eriugena's tract was thought by its sponsors to go too far in the opposite direction from Gottschalk. Eriugena was accused of 'Origenism' and 'Pelagianism' by his erstwhile supporter, Bishop Prudentius of Troyes (see his own *De praedestinatione*; *PL* 115:1010c). Ironically, Eriugena himself had placed Gottschalk's heresy of twin predestination somewhere between Pelagianism (which denied the need for grace) and the opposing heresy (which denied human free will). Eriugena's tract was condemned at the councils of Valence (855) and Langres (859), in part for its overuse of dialectic. The phrase 'Irish porridge' (*pultes scottorum*), used in these official denunciations, recalls Jerome's sneer against Pelagius.

THE ENCOUNTER WITH DIONYSIUS

The predestination controversy made Eriugena unpopular with the French bishops but did not affect his standing with King Charles, whose patronage continued. Around 860, Charles invited Eriugena to translate the writings of Dionysius the Areopagite (Pseudo-Dionysius) (*Corpus Dionysiacum*), who was supposedly the convert of St Paul mentioned in the Acts of the Apostles 17:34 ("... a few men became followers of Paul and believed. Among them was Dionysius, a member of the Areopagus ..."). This manuscript had been presented to Charles' father, Louis the Pious, by the Byzantine Emperor Michael the Second in 827. Its author was more likely a late-fifth- or early-sixth-century Christian follower of Proclus (based on the text's language and use of doctrinal formulas from that period). The abbot of the monastery of Saint-Denis, Hilduin, further confused the identity issue when, in his hagiographical life of Dionysius, *Passio sancti Dionysii* (The passion of St Denis), he claimed that Dionysius was not only Bishop of Athens but also the third-century bishop and martyr, St Denis, who was buried in his monastery of Saint-Denis! Eriugena's translation, which drew on Hilduin's earlier attempt (832–5), had a wide circulation through the twelfth century, when it was replaced by the translation of John Sarrazin, who drew on Eriugena's version but had the benefit of other manuscripts.

The importance of Eriugena's discovery and subsequent promotion of Dionysius cannot be overstated. Dionysius' works stood second only to the Gospels and the Letters of Paul in terms of their importance as a source of Christian teaching. Several centuries of Christian apologists (from Justin Martyr to Augustine) had been articulating Christian faith in terms of the intellectual framework of Hellenistic philosophy (primarily Neoplatonic and Stoic), and the discovery of Dionysius' writings finally seemed to provide proof that the synthesis of Greek philosophy and Christian faith was sanctioned by Scripture itself. In fact, later Greek pagan Neoplatonism (from the school of Proclus), with its complex formulations concerning the non-being beyond being and beyond the One, as well as its complex vision of a hierarchically ordered cosmos, had been seamlessly integrated into Christian theology. A new Christian tradition of negative theology had been created and Eriugena was its propagator for the Latin world.

Eriugena enthusiastically adopted Dionysius' negative theology, according to which denials concerning God are 'more true' (*verior*), 'better' (*melior*) and 'more apt' than affirmations. He embraced Dionysius' analysis of the divine names as found in his *Peri theiōn onomatōn* (*De divinis nominibus*; On the divine names). Certain biblical appellations of the divine (God as 'King', 'Life') do not 'literally' (*proprie*) apply to God and must therefore be understood analogically or 'through

metaphor' (*per metaforam, translative*). Such terms are useful for the unin-
structed, but, as St Paul put it, to children milk is given and to adults solid food
(1 Corinthians 3:2). So, higher than these metaphorical statements are the names
and descriptions of the divine that involve negation. Negations are more appropriate to express the divine transcendence. God is more properly not being, not
truth, not goodness and so on. Following Dionysius' *Peri mystikēs theologiās* (*De
mystica theologia*; On mystical theology), God is 'beyond being', 'more than being',
'neither one nor oneness', 'beyond assertion and denial' (*Patrologia Graeca* [here-
after *PG*] 3:1048A). Eriugena reproduces these formulations in Latin to express
paradoxically the nameless transcendent divinity.

Having completed his Dionysius translation (*c.*862), Eriugena went on to trans-
late several other Greek Christian works, including Gregory of Nyssa's *De hominis
opificio* under the title *De imagine* (On the image), and possibly Epiphanius'
Anchoratus: de fide (The anchorite: concerning faith) and Maximus Confessor's
Ambigua ad Ioannem (with commentary) and his *Quaestiones ad Thalassium*
(Questions in response to Thalassius), both important works of Greek Christian
spirituality that offered a more 'Aristotelian' version of several prominent
Neoplatonic themes). He also wrote a long commentary on Dionysius' *Celestial
Hierarchy* (*Expositiones in hierarchiam coelestem*), a fragmentary *Commentary on
the Gospel of John* (*Commentarius in evangelium Iohannis*) and a sermon (*Homilia
in Johannem*) on the Prologue to the Gospel of John, all of which show the influence of the Greek theological tradition.

THE *PERIPHYSEON* (c.867)

Eriugena's main philosophical treatise, *Periphyseon*, also called *De divisione
naturae* (On the division of nature), a dialogue between master and pupil, was
written some time between 860 and 867. Eriugena himself calls it a *physiologia*
("study of nature"; *Peri.* IV.741C), and indeed one manuscript in the British Library
is entitled *Liber phisiologiae Iohannis Scottigenae* (The book on the study of nature
of John Scotigena). It is an extensive treatise on cosmology, anthropology and
theology.

Nature, as defined at the outset by Eriugena, includes both "God and the creature". The first principle of nature is the infinite God, "the cause of all things that
are and that are not" (I.442B). Echoing similar divisions in Augustine (*City of
God* 5.9; *PL* 41:151) and Marius Victorinus (*Ad Candidum*; To Candidus), nature
is divided into four 'divisions' or 'species' (*Peri.* I.441B–442A): that which creates
and is not created (i.e. God); that which creates and is created (i.e. primary causes
or Ideas); that which is created and does not create (i.e. temporal effects, created
things); that which is neither created nor creates (i.e. non-being, nothingness).

Eriugena's original intention (expressed at *Peri.* III.619D–620B) was to devote
one book to each of the four divisions: book 1 deals with the divine nature and

the procession or *exitus* of all things from God; book 2 with the primordial causes and book 3 their created effects, including the nature of *ex nihilo* creation and the stages of the creation of the world. The topic of creation requires Eriugena to address issues connected with the biblical account of creation, and thus, in book 3, he embarks on a Hexaemeron. The creation of human nature on the sixth day of creation called for more extensive treatment, and Eriugena altered his plan, devoting a fourth book to this topic, thus relegating the return of all things to God to book 5.

Dialectic is still to the fore. At the outset Eriugena suggests "five ways of inter-preting" (*quinque modi interpretationis*) the way things may be said to be or not to be (I.443C–446A). According to the first mode, whatever is accessible to the senses and the intellect is said to be, whereas whatever, "through the excellence of its nature" (*per excellentiam suae naturae*), transcends our faculties is said not to be. According to this mode, God, because he may be said not to be, is "nothingness through excellence" (*nihil per excellentiam*). The second mode of being and non-being is seen in the "orders and differences of created natures" (I.444A), whereby, if one level of nature is said to be, those orders above or below it are said not to be: "For an affirmation concerning the lower (order) is a negation concerning the higher, and so too a negation concerning the lower (order) is an affirmation concerning the higher" (I.444A).

According to this mode, the affirmation of humanity is the negation of the angelic order, and vice versa (*affirmatio enim hominis negatio est angeli, negatio vero hominis affirmatio est angeli*; I.444B). This mode illustrates Eriugena's original way of combining the traditional Neoplatonic hierarchy of being with a dialectic of affirmation and negation whereby to assert one level is to deny the others. The third mode (I.444C–45B) asserts that *actual* things are, whereas *potential* things still caught up "in the most secret folds of nature" (a favourite phrase) are not. This mode contrasts things that have come into effect with those things that are still contained in their causes. The fourth mode (I.445B–C) is broadly Platonic: those things contemplated by the intellect alone (*ea solummodo quae solo comprehend-untur intellectu*) may be considered to be, whereas things caught up in generation and corruption, matter, place and time do not truly exist. The fifth mode is theo-logical: those sanctified by grace are, whereas sinners who have renounced the divine image are not. According to this complex and original account, attribution of being or non-being is dependent on the mode of approach and care needs to be taken. Thus, when Eriugena calls God 'nothing', he means that God *transcends* all created being and created modes of existence. Matter, on the other hand, is 'nothing through privation' (*nihil per privationem*). The fluidity of Eriugena's onto-logical attributions must always be borne in mind in analysing his theological claims.

God, as uncreated and creating, transcends everything created; he is the *negatio omnium* (III.686D). The Aristotelian categories do not properly apply to God (I.463D). He is not 'literally' (*proprie*) substance or essence, nor describable in terms of quantity, quality, relation, place or time. He is '*superessentialis*' (I.459D). His 'being' is 'beyond being', or as Eriugena puts it, in his version of a Dionysian saying, God's being is the superbeing (of) divinity (*Esse enim omnium est super esse divinitas*), or "the being of all things is the Divinity above being" (I.443B). Sometimes, Eriugena speaks simply of the "divine superessentiality" (*divina super-essentialitas*; III.634B), or, quoting Dionysius' *Divine Names* I.1–2 (*PG* 3:588B–C), of the "superessential and hidden divinity" (*superessentialis et occulta divinitas*; *Peri.* I.510B). God may also be called 'nothingness' (*nihilum*), since His essence is unknown to all created beings, including all the ranks of angels (I.447C). Indeed, Eriugena argues, God's nature is unknown even to Himself, since He is the 'infinity of infinities' and hence beyond all comprehension and circumscription.

Eriugena defines creation as divine self-manifestation (I.455B) whereby the hidden transcendent God manifests Himself in divine outpourings or theophanies (I.446D). The divine self-manifestation is self-creation, that is, the timeless expression of the Word, which is at the same time the creation of all other things, since all things are contained as primary causes in the Word. All things are always already in God but in a way that respects their otherness: "the Creative nature permits nothing outside itself because outside it nothing can be, yet everything which it has created and creates it contains within itself, but in such a way that it itself is other, because it is superessential, than what it creates within itself" (III.675C). Creatures, as fallen, do not yet know that they reside in God. In cosmological terms, however, God and the creature are one and the same:

> It follows that we ought not to understand God and the creature as two things distinct from one another, but as one and the same. For both the creature, by subsisting, is in God; and God, by manifesting himself, in a marvellous and ineffable manner creates himself in the creature. (III.678C)

Although Eriugena asserts the identity of God and creation, he explicitly rejects the view that God is the 'genus' or 'whole' of which the creatures are 'species' or 'parts'. Only *metaphorically* (*metaforice*) can it be said that God is a 'genus' or a 'whole'. The immanence of God in creation is balanced by God's transcendence above all creation. God is both form of all things and also formless. The creature can never be identified with God.

Periphyseon book 2 discusses the primary causes (*causae primordiales*) or 'divine willings' (*theia thelemata*), a concept that combines the Platonic Forms, Dionysius' divine names and the Stoic–Augustinian notion of eternal reasons (*rationes aeternae*), as well as Maximus' divine willings. These causes are infinite in number and there is no hierarchy or precedence among them; being is not prior to goodness, or vice versa. Each is in its own way a divine theophany. This 'outflowing' (*proodos*; *processio, exitus*) of the causes creates the whole universe from the highest genus to the lowest species and individuals (*atoma*). In his

40

understanding of this causal procession, Eriugena accepts Neoplatonic principles (drawn from the tradition of Proclus) concerning causation: like produces like; incorporeal causes produce incorporeal effects; causes that are immaterial, intellectual and eternal produce effects that are equally immaterial, intellectual and eternal. Cause and effect are mutually dependent, relative terms (V.910D–912B).

The primary causes produce their effects timelessly. The effects, for Eriugena, are also originally timeless and incorruptible, but, as they proceed from their essences through their genera, species and individuals (in a kind of ontological descent through the tree of Porphyry), they become located spatially and temporally but not yet in a corporeal sense. Eriugena seems to postulate two kinds of time: an unchanging time (a reason or *ratio* in the divine mind; V.906A) and a corrupting time. Since place and time are definitions that locate things, and since definitions are in the mind, place and time are therefore in the mind (*in mente*; I.485B). The sensible, corporeal, spatiotemporal appearances of things are produced by the qualities or 'circumstances' of place, time, position and so on, which surround the incorporeal, eternal essence. Following on from Gregory of Nyssa, Eriugena thinks that corporeality and division into sexes are a consequence of the Fall. Indeed, the entire spatiotemporal world (including corporeal human bodies) is a consequence of the Fall. For Eriugena, God, foreseeing that human beings would fall, created a body and a corporeal world for them. But this corporeal body is not essential to human nature, and in the return of all things to God the corporeal body will be transformed into the spiritual body (*spirituale corpus*). The corporeal world will return to its incorporeal essence, and place understood as extension will return back into its cause or reason as a definition in the mind (V.889D).

Book 3 discusses in great detail the meaning of 'creation from nothing' (*creatio ex nihilo*). The term 'nothing' has two meanings: it can mean 'nothing through privation' (*nihil per privationem*), or 'nothing on account of excellence' (*nihil per excellentiam*). The lowest rung in the hierarchy of being, unformed matter, is 'almost nothing' (*prope nihil*), or 'nothing through privation'. Since there is nothing outside God (the transcendent nothingness), 'creation from nothing' does not mean creation from some principle outside God; rather, it means creation out of God himself (*a se*). All creation comes from God and remains within him.

Books 4 and 5 discuss the return (*epistrophe, reditus, reversio*) of all things to God and the role of human nature in the cosmic process, drawing heavily on Maximus Confessor and Gregory of Nyssa. It is natural for effects to return to their causes (since they are only effects because of their dependency on their causes). Corporeal things will return to their incorporeal causes, the temporal to the eternal, the finite will be absorbed in the infinite. As part of this general return, the human mind will achieve reunification with the divine, and then the corporeal, temporal, material world will become essentially incorporeal, timeless and intellectual. Human nature will return to its 'Idea' (*notion*) in the mind of God. 'Paradise' is the scriptural name for this perfect human nature in the mind of God. Human beings who refuse to abandon their 'circumstances' remain trapped in their own fantasies, and it is to this mental state that the scriptural term 'hell' applies. Aside from the general return of all things to God, Eriugena claims there is a special return whereby the elect achieve 'deification' (*deificatio, theosis*), merging with God completely, as lights blend into the one light, as voices blend in the choir, as a droplet of water merges with the stream. God shall be all in all (*omnia in omnibus*; V.935C).

Eriugena's theological anthropology is a radical working out of the meaning of being made in the image and likeness of God (*in imaginem et similitudinem dei*). Interpreting Augustine's *De Genesi ad litteram* (On the literal meaning of Genesis), as well as Ambrose's *De paradiso* (On paradise) and Gregory of Nyssa's *De hominis opificio*, Eriugena argues that paradise is entirely spiritual. He further claims that human nature did not spend time in paradise before the Fall. The entire account refers to what would have been the case had human nature not already sinned. Eriugena follows Gregory of Nyssa's view that sexual difference is a result of the Fall. The Fall is the fall from intellect into sense: *intellectus* distracted by the voluptuousness of sensibility (*aesthesis*). Sexual difference is an external addition: "Man is better than sex" (*homo melior est quam sexus*; *Peri.* II.534A). For Eriugena, human being is neither male nor female: just as "in Christ there is neither male nor female" (IV.795A).

Just as God may be said to be or not to be (*Deus est*; *deus not est*), so too human nature may be said to be animal or not animal. Following Gregory of Nyssa, Eriugena also denies that human nature is a 'microcosm'. Rather, human nature is "a certain intellectual concept formed eternally (*aeternaliter facta*) in the divine mind" (IV.768B). For Eriugena, human nature uniquely mirrors transcendent divine nature. Only of human nature can it be said that it is made in the image and likeness of God. Not even the angels are accorded that honour. Perfect human nature would have possessed the fullest knowledge of its creator, of itself and of everything else had it not sinned (IV.778C). Just as God knows *that* he is but not *what* he is, since he is uncircumscribable, so too human nature knows *that* it is but not *what* it is. Human self-ignorance mirrors the divine self-ignorance and is a mark of the infinite and transcendent nature of the human as of the divine. Human nature, without the Fall, would have ruled the universe (IV.782C). Similarly, perfect human nature would have enjoyed omniscience and other attributes enjoyed by God. Just as God is infinite and unbounded, human nature is indefinable and incomprehensible and open to infinite possibility and perfectibility (V.919C). God's transcendence and immanence are reflected in human transcendence and immanence with regard to its world (IV.759A–B).

Eriugena's account of nature as inclusive of God and creation has been accused of being pantheist, but in fact he wants to preserve both the immanence and the transcendence of the divine. Every statement of divine immanence in creation must be balanced by the recognition of the divine transcendence. There is also the theological worry that Eriugena downplays the significance of the actual Jesus, the crucifixion and so on. But Eriugena in fact makes Christ central to the whole cosmic plan. As Word, he is the manifestation of the divine; he is also "the perfect human" (*vir autem perfectus est Christus*; IV.743B). Christ as the divine idea of human nature is the centrepiece of the entire cosmic procession and return. Christ is actually what all human beings can be and will be, and that is precisely the promise of salvation for Eriugena (II.545A).

For Eriugena, a true image is identical to its exemplar in all respects 'except number' or 'subject' (IV.778A). Neither divine nor human nature is in space or time; both are incorporeal and hence numerical difference, or difference in subject, can only have the Neoplatonic meaning that the first will always differ from what comes after the first. God is creator and humankind is created, but since creation is self-manifestation, that amounts to saying that God manifests himself fully as human nature. Sometimes Eriugena, quoting Maximus Confessor (e.g. V.879C–880A), says that humankind is by grace (*per gratiam*) what God is by nature. On the other hand, all nature is a theophany; nature is the outpouring of grace. Every gift (*donum*) is a given (*datum*), and vice versa. The creation of human nature is both the free outpouring of the divine will and the self-expression of the divine nature. Human nature stands closer to God than any other creature (including the angels, who are not made in the image and likeness of God).

Humanity as a whole in its resurrected and perfected state will be truly illuminated and merged with the divine. Furthermore, the use of the future tense here is somewhat misleading, since time itself is a function of our fallen state and the perfected state is timeless, and so there is a sense in which perfected human nature already is one with God and always has been one with God. Eriugena, then, has a dialectical understanding of the relation of God and humanity that can be viewed as orthodox from one point of view, but which is always transgressing the boundaries of orthodoxy in the direction of a view that has God and humanity mutually contemplating themselves and each other, in an endless, eternal play of theophanies.

Eriugena places extraordinary emphasis on the infinity and boundlessness of both God and human nature. The divine causes are infinite in number and so are the theophanies under which God may be viewed. Human progress to Godhead proceeds infinitely. Holy Scripture too has infinite richness (*Sacrae scripturae interpretatio infinita est*; II.560A), its interpretations are as innumerable as the colours in a peacock's tail (IV.749C). Human capacity for perfection and self-transcendence is also endless (a theme that will reappear in Renaissance humanism).

ERIUGENA'S INFLUENCE

Eriugena's *Periphyseon* had immediate influence in France, notably at the schools of Laon, Auxerre and Corbie. It was very popular in the twelfth century (among Hugh of Saint-Victor, Alan of Lille, and Suger of Saint-Denis, and others) when circulated in the 'edition' of William of Malmsebury and the paraphrase of Honorius Augustodunensis. Eriugena's translations of Dionysius circulated widely during the eleventh and twelfth centuries, as did his *Homily on the Prologue to John* (often attributed to Origen). In the thirteenth century, the *Periphyseon* was somewhat unfairly associated with the doctrines of two Paris theologians, David of Dinant and Amaury of Bène, and was condemned in 1210 and 1225. According to Thomas Aquinas (*Summa theologiae* I.3.8; *Summa contra Gentiles* I.17, I.26), Amaury of Bène was condemned for asserting that God was the formal principle of all things, an accusation of pantheism, which recalled Eriugena's statement that God is the "form of all things" (*forma omnium*). David of Dinant (*floruit* 1210), on the other hand, was supposed to have identified God with prime matter, calling God the *materia omnium*. It is likely that Eriugena's discussion of God and matter as 'nothing' and as transcending sense and intellect according to the first mode of being and non-being contributed to this accusation. Eriugena was also, again unfairly, linked with certain views on the Eucharist associated with Berengar of Tours. In the later Middle Ages both Meister Eckhart of Hochheim (*c.*1260–*c.*1328) and Nicholas of Cusa (1401–64) were sympathetic to Eriugena and familiar with his *Periphyseon*. When Thomas Gale produced the first printed edition of Eriugena's works in 1687, it was soon listed in the first edition of the *Index librorum prohibitorum* (Index of prohibited books), and remained there until the index itself was abolished. Hegel and his followers revived Eriugena as the forefather of German idealism, and process theologians also acknowledged his dynamic conception of the divine. New critical editions of Eriugena's works have spurred a revival of interest in him among those interested in the tradition of negative theology.

FURTHER READING

Beierwaltes, W. 1994. *Eriugena: Grundzüge seines Denkens*. Frankfurt: Vittorio Klostermann.
Brennan, M. 1989. *A Guide to Eriugenian Studies: A Survey of Publications 1930–87*. Paris: Éditions du Cerf.
Cappuyns, M. 1933. *Jean Scot Erigène: Sa vie, son oeuvre, sa pensée*. Louvain: Abbaye de Mont César.
Carabine, D. 2000. *John Scottus Eriugena*. Oxford: Oxford University Press.
Eriugena, J. 1990. *The Voice of the Eagle: Homily on the Prologue to the Gospel of St John*, C. Bamford (trans.). Hudson, NY: Lindisfarne Press.
Gersh, S. 1978. *From Iamblichus to Eriugena*. Leiden: Brill.
Gersh, S. & D. Moran (eds) 2006. *Eriugena, Berkeley, and the Idealist Tradition*. Notre Dame, IN: University of Notre Dame Press.
Marenbon, J. 1981. *From the Circle of Alcuin to the School of Auxerre: Logic, Theology and Philosophy in the Early Middle Ages*. Cambridge: Cambridge University Press.
Moran, D. 1989. *The Philosophy of John Scottus Eriugena: A Study of Idealism in the Middle Ages*. Cambridge: Cambridge University Press.
Moran, D. 1990. "Pantheism from John Scottus Eriugena to Nicholas of Cusa". *American Catholic Philosophical Quarterly* **64**: 131–52.

Moran, D. 1999. "Idealism in Medieval Philosophy: The Case of Johannes Scottus Eriugena". *Medieval Philosophy and Theology* **8**: 53–82.

O'Meara, J. 1988. *Eriugena*. Oxford: Clarendon Press.

Otten, W. 1991. *The Anthropology of Johannes Scottus Eriugena*. Leiden: Brill.

Sheldon-Williams, I.-P. 1970. "The Greek Christian Platonist Tradition from the Cappadocians to Maximus and Eriugena". In *The Cambridge History of Later Greek and Early Medieval Thought*, A. Armstrong (ed.), 425–533. Cambridge: Cambridge University Press.

On CHRISTOLOGY see also Vol. 1, Ch. 10; Vol. 4, Ch. 3. On NEOPLATONISM see also Ch. 4; Vol. 1, Chs 19, 20; Vol. 3, Ch. 9; Vol. 4, Chs 4, 9. On SALVATION see also Vol. 1, Chs 10, 13; Vol. 4, Ch. 19. On THE WORD see also Ch. 9.

4

AL-FARABI

Syed Nomanul Haq

Known as the 'Second Teacher' in the Arabic tradition – second to none other than Aristotle who is recognized as the 'First Teacher' – Abū Naṣr Muḥammad ibn Muḥammad al-Fārābī (al-Farabi) (*c.*870–*c.*950) has received a resounding tribute from a leading contemporary scholar: this philosopher of the Islamic milieu "stands at the head of all subsequent philosophers who made Greek philosophy Western philosophy" (Gutas 1999b: 222).[1] This means that al-Farabi is a personage of global proportions and ought to be repositioned in the context of world civilization, so that he is no longer seen as irrelevant to what we now consider philosophy. Indeed, his works on (Greek) logic and its relationship to the grammar and usages of ordinary language, his political thought, his conceptual enrichment and expansion of Aristotle's notion of God along Neoplatonic lines and above all his overarching theory of intellect, or noetics, with its epistemological and ontological implications, something we find centuries later in Descartes all constitute a milestone in the history of philosophy.

OBSCURE PERSONAL HISTORY

About al-Farabi's personal life we know very little. One does not find any detailed biography until some two hundred years after his death. In fact, a major role in bringing him into focus at a later date is played by the 'Grand Shaykh' Avicenna (Ibn Sina, *d.* 1037), whose works had generated a feverish interest during the heyday of philosophical activity in Islam in the twelfth and thirteenth centuries. Avicenna had presented himself as al-Farabi's follower and successor. Colourful tales about al-Farabi's life were woven subsequently: sometimes depicting him as

---

1. I have drawn heavily in this chapter on the following works in particular: Black (1999), Druart (1999), Gutas (1999a,b). I also owe a special debt to Reisman (2005).

a polyglot who translated Greek texts into Arabic; sometimes as being of Turkish origin with a father named Ṭarkhān;[2] sometimes as a judge who gave up his high position for the love of philosophy, which he read by the light of watchmen's lamps; and sometimes as one who studied in a Christian environment in Constantinople.[3] All of these claims are suspect, and the safest course is to reconstruct elements of al-Farabi's biography out of that small body of data we are able to glean from the earliest manuscript annotations and sporadic biographical information found in his own writings, supplemented by biographical narratives closest to his times that are not contradicted by independent additional evidence.

We learn from al-Farabi himself, as reported in his *Appearance of Philosophy*, that he studied the Aristotelian *Organon* up to the *Posterior Analytics* under the Christian cleric Yūḥannā ibn Ḥaylan in Baghdad, and this must have happened somewhere around the early tenth century (Gutas 1999c). More specifically, al-Farabi is quoted by the biographer Ibn Abi Uṣaybiʿa (*d.* 1270) as having said that Yūḥannā taught him Porphry's standard introduction to Aristotelian logic, the *Eisagoge*, followed by Aristotle's *Categories*, *De interpretatione* and *Prior* and *Posterior Analytics*, in that order (Gutas 1999a: 210). As Yūḥannā's pupil, then, al-Farabi read the logical texts according to the curriculum of the Greek neo-Aristotelian school of the third-century philosopher Ammonius in Alexandria. This Alexandrian neo-Aristotelianism was revived after the Islamic conquests among the Syriac clerics and thinkers in the centres of Eastern Christianity, and it is with this philosophical school that al-Farabi should be associated.[4]

Both politically and socially, al-Farabi's close association with Christian circles is quite certain. Like his mentor in logical studies, his chief student Yaḥyā ibn ʿAdī too was a Christian who is reported by the well-known biographer Ibn al-Qifṭī (*d.* 1248) to have been a Baghdad resident. Then, in Syria, where al-Farabi may have had some association with the Hamdanid ruler Sayf al-Dawla, Yaḥyā's brother Ibrāhīm also became his student; to this Ibrāhīm, according to a manuscript note, he dictated a commentary on the *Posterior Analytics*. Similarly, al-Farabi wrote a text on the defence of astrology for another Christian neighbour of his in Baghdad, the scholar and translator Abū Isḥāq Ibrāhīm al-Baghdādī. Equally certain is al-Farabi's stay in the Abbasid capital until the last quarter of the year 942: he wrote his comprehensive work on music theory *Kitāb al-Mūsīqī al-Kabīr* (The great book of music) for a vizier of the caliph al-Rāḍī (ruled 934–40); and his own notes on some manuscripts of his *Mabādiʾ Arāʾ Ahl al-Madīnat al-Fāḍila* (Principles of the opinions of the people of the excellent city; hereafter *Principles*)

---

2. Gutas (1999a: 209–10) has pointed out that the famous thirteenth-century biographer Ibn Khallikān was at pains to prove that al-Farabi was ethnically Turkish. Ṭarkhān appears as his father's name in the same source. See Ibn Kahallikān (1842–71: vol. 3, 307–11).

3. This was the conjecture of Muhsin Mahdi (1971: 524a), brought to attention by Gutas (1999a: 212).

4. Gutas (1999c) represents a leading piece of research in this regard.

inform us that he began working on this treatise in Baghdad in 942, then interrupted the work and left for Syria at that time.

On the basis of al-Farabi's own testimony and the report of the contemporary historian al-Mas'ūdī (d. 956) it is possible to reconstruct a rough outline of the philosopher's life once he left Baghdad. Thus, we learn from a citation in al-Farabi's *Kitāb al-Milla* (Book of creed) that he continued working on the *Principles* in Syria and completed it in 943 in Damascus. A manuscript note indicates that he also stayed for some time in Aleppo, since according to the note it is here that he taught Ibrāhīm ibn 'Adī. And again, in the notes found in the manuscripts of the *Principles* we learn that he was in Egypt in the years 948–9 writing his six chapters in which he summarized the *Posterior Analytics*. Then, we are informed by al-Mas'ūdī that al-Farabi died in Damascus between 14 December 950 and 12 January 951; there is practically a complete certainty about this piece of information since the reporter, generally reliable as he happens to be, was a contemporary, writing no later than 955–6.

The name 'al-Farabi' would seem to declare in the first instance that his place of origin is in the region of Fārāb on the river Jaxtares in Turkistan. But this is not necessarily the case. For example, his younger contemporary, the redoubtable bio-bibliographer Ibn al-Nadīm (d. end of tenth century) states that al-Farabi's roots lie in Faryāb in Khurasan. Present-day experts are resigned here: they tell us that we do not have sufficient evidence to decide the question of al-Farabi's ethnic or regional origins. And yet, indeed, he is universally referred to by the appellation 'al-Farabi', whatever precisely this might indicate.[5]

GENERAL OBSERVATIONS

Following the lead of contemporary experts, it has already been remarked that the point of departure of al-Farabi's philosophical development ought to be sought in the Greek neo-Aristotelian tradition of the school of Ammonius. One finds in this school a particularly critical preoccupation with the Aristotelian *Organon*, a preoccupation that had placed language studies at the forefront, given that Aristotle's *Categories* and *De interpretatione* both open with linguistic discourses; in fact, these studies practically formed the core of the whole Alexandrian philosophical enterprise. Al-Farabi too is fundamentally preoccupied with language, but his historical context has the additional (and crucial) element of the intellectual milieu of contemporary Baghdad, where among the most powerful philosophical pursuits was one that had its focus on logic, language and grammar. Indeed, it was in the Baghdad of al-Farabi's times that the famous debate between the logician

---

5. Al-Farabi's biography is discussed in detail in Gutas (1999a: 208–12), where the serious reader will find references to the primary sources.

Abū Bishr Mattā and the grammarian al-Sīrāfī took place: a historic debate, studied by Mahdi (1970: 51–83), in which the grammarian argued that (Greek) logic really is Greek grammar, inapplicable to the Arabic language, linguistically limited and without a universal scope.

This brings us to a fundamental feature of al-Farabi's philosophy: his rigorous attempts to establish that logic is, indeed, universal grammar, and that logic is to intellect and intelligibles what grammar is to language and verbal expressions. The outstanding contribution of the Muslim philosopher here is to relate the ordinary grammar of the Arabic language to philosophical logic as this latter was conceived and constructed in the Greek and particularly Aristotelian tradition. This adaptation of Greek logic to a non-Greek linguistic context is a major philosophical and historical breakthrough. In his *Kitāb al-Qiyās al-Ṣaghīr* (Small book of syllogism), al-Farabi declares his intellectual enterprise to be a striving "to express [Aristotelian syllogistic], as much as possible, by means of words familiar to people who use the Arabic language" (Rescher 1963: 49, quoted in Black 1999: 214). As a harvest of this striving, Aristotle's rather unelaborated and dispersed statements on the language–logic relationship were now set on a new, philosophically adventurous path.

Another characteristic contribution of al-Farabi's is his Neoplatonic supplement to Aristotle's metaphysics whereby the scope of Aristotle's notion of God is widened and brought in line with Abrahamic conceptions of deity. Al-Farabi seems to indicate that Aristotle did not pay sufficient attention to the study of ultimate causes of things, that is, the study of God and immaterial beings, something subsequently undertaken by the Neoplatonists. The science of metaphysics was more than what one found in Aristotle's *Metaphysics*, since the latter did not contain a complete enquiry into the beings that were above and beyond natural things in the ontological order (*see* Vol. 1, Ch. 5, "Aristotle"). Such enquiry would lead us to the discovery of a being that was the first principle of all beings. This first principle, al-Farabi teaches, is the divinity: it is the efficient, formal and final cause of all other beings. Aristotle's unmoved mover, which was only the final cause of motion, has now been thrown into an active and creative mode, familiar to the religious believer of al-Farabi's milieu. We note here how al-Farabi extends Aristotle's ideas along Neoplatonic lines. But in fact al-Farabi's Neoplatonism runs deeper in that he fully espouses Plotinian emanationism, and not only that, he makes the theory of hypostases and emanation a foundational element of his grand cosmological system, with all its epistemological implications, innovatively remapping the third-century father of Neoplatonism, Plotinus (*see* Vol. 1, Ch. 15), onto the enduring planetary scheme of the famous astronomer, Ptolemy (*d. c.*168).[6]

---

6. See Druart (1999), where al-Farabi's metaphysics is discussed in the framework of what later became known as general metaphysics and special metaphysics; namely, the study of what is common to all beings, and the study of ultimate causes (i.e. God and other immaterial beings), respectively. This distinction is articulated in Frede (1987).

But it is al-Farabi's all-embracing noetics that serves as the robust anchorage holding his entire philosophical system in place as a coherent integral whole; in fact, it is this anchorage that uniquely defines the very drift and thrust of his thought. For example, logic is not merely a methodological tool for al-Farabi, but hides underneath a governing ontological noetics. This is so since the human mind, he tells us, can think only in the five ways in which the *Organon* divides arguments or propositions: the demonstrative, which he privileges, and the dialectic, sophistical, rhetorical and poetic. Quite remarkably, then, a relationship of bi-implication is made to exist between logic and ontology. Likewise, in al-Farabi's cosmology it is the creative act of *intellection* on the part of the superior sphere that causes the emanation from it of the sphere below in the hierarchical cosmic order of beings. In his practical or political philosophy, also, concerned as it is with individuals and society and with the delicate question of prophecy, philosophy and kingship, his discourses are equally anchored in noetics. We are taught that human beings are made for the sake of their intellect, human happiness lies in the life of the intellect, and the human individual who has reached perfection is the one who has *become* actually intellect (Walzer 1985: 241).

It is for good reasons that al-Farabi received the honorific title of the 'Second Teacher'. He was committed to introducing a comprehensive philosophical curriculum into a non-Greek, Islamic milieu with the latter's own cultural and intellectual dynamics. This curriculum remains neo-Aristotelian in its basic orientation, but it embodies a highly original synthesis that transformed Alexandrian philosophy: a synthesis highly sensitive to the faith of al-Farabi's co-religionists; a synthesis mediated by Neoplatonism, bringing order to the chaos of outstanding philosophical issues of contemporary society and responding directly to the intellectual ferment of Baghdad. Indeed, al-Farabi presents Muslims as the champions of (Greek) philosophy, observing that philosophy was revived in the Islamic period following the restrictions placed on it by Christians: they thought that it would harm Christianity, he writes (Gutas 1999c). We note here a major event in the history of philosophy, namely, al-Farabi's own revival of the study of all of Aristotle's logical writings, the entire *Organon*, including the *Rhetoric* and *Poetics*, thereby extending the later Alexandrian curriculum of Syriac Christian logicians that ended in the middle of the *Prior Analytics*.

Given his curricular ambitions, al-Farabi wrote a large number of introductory works as well as commentaries on, and recastings and paraphrases of, Aristotle's *Nicomachean Ethics* and all parts of the *Organon* – *Categories*, *De interpretatione*, *Prior Analytics*, *Posterior Analytics*, *Topics*, *Sophistical Refutations*, *Rhetoric* and *Poetics* – and also Porphyry's *Eisagogē*. Among his introductory writings are naturally to be counted his *What One Ought to Know before Inquiring into the Philosophy of Aristotle* and his introductions to logic and Plato's teachings. But scholars also include in his introductory corpus the pedagogically conceived trilogy on ethics (*The Attainment of Happiness*, *The Philosophy of Plato* and *The Philosophy of Aristotle*) as well as the three related logical texts: *Directing Attention to the Way to*

Happiness, *Vocables Employed in Logic* (hereafter *Vocables*), and *Paraphrase of the Categories*. Belonging here too is the *Enumeration of the Sciences*, al-Farabi's best-known work which was widely read both in the Arabic and Latin traditions. Note that Marwan Rashed (2008: 58) has recently cast doubt on the authenticity of the tract *Harmony between the Views of the Two Sages, Plato the Divine and Aristotle*, a tract hitherto attributed universally to al-Farabi by modern scholars and generally classified among his introductory works.

Other than (i) introductory works and (ii) commentaries and paraphrases, many (iii) original works are also to be found in the al-Farabi oeuvre. The *Principles*, which has already been referred to, constitutes an example of an original synthesis, as does the *Political Regime* (*Al-Siyāsa al-Madaniyya*), also known by the title *Principle of Beings*. One would likewise classify under al-Farabi's original works his *Conditions of Certitude, Book of the One and Unity*, as well as the *Book of Particles* (the primary Arabic title *Kitāb al-Ḥurūf* is sometimes translated as 'Book of letters'). But this list is far from exhaustive.[7] Also, one should hasten to add that the three categories (i–iii) are not mutually exclusive. Thus, for example, the *Vocables* is both an introductory and an original work. Indeed, al-Farabi's commentaries and paraphrases contain many original insights built around the core text, sometimes integrating outside elements, such as Stoic logic, into the explications. The three categories therefore overlap.

A SURVEY OF AL-FARABI'S LOGIC AND METAPHYSICS

Given both the Alexandrian tradition and the intellectual drift of Baghdad, it is hardly surprising that most of the writings of al-Farabi that have come down to us concern logic and philosophy of language. As noted already, he considers apodeictic demonstration to be the noblest part of logic, and this places a premium on the *Posterior Analytics* (known in the Arabic tradition as the *Kitāb al-Burhān* [Book of demonstration]) as the point of convergence of the entire *Organon*, lying at its centre. Thus four texts of the *Organon* lead to the *Burhān* and the remaining four guard it by showing how apodeictic certainty can be thrown off track by dialectic, sophistic, rhetorical and poetic arguments. With the *Posterior Analytics* occupying the centre, then, the curricular sequential scheme places *Eisagogē–Categories–De interpretatione–Prior Analytics* on its preparatory side, and *Topics–Sophistical Refutations–Rhetoric–Poetics* on its preventive–protective side.

---

7. Rescher (1962) prepared an annotated bibliography of al-Farabi's writings, but many other bibliographies have been compiled before and since. A survey appears in Gutas (1999a: 213). Black (1996: 194–5) has provided a list of modern editions and translations of the al-Farabi corpus. For English translations of the texts, see Hyman (1973: 215–21), Mahdi (1962), Najjar (1963: 31–57), Walzer (1985), Zimmermann (1981). Translations of some of al-Farabi's short logical treatises are listed in Reisman (2005: 71 n.32).

It is in the *Book of Particles* that al-Farabi presents one of his most elaborate disquisitions on his highly original constructs concerning the relationship between philosophical logic and the grammar of ordinary language. We note here Aristotle being naturalized into the Arabo-Islamic matrix, and this marks a process that expanded the scope of Hellenism beyond the Greek sphere in a manner that would prove to be decisive in the history of philosophy. So we see al-Farabi (i) classifying Arabic particles and constructing a system of correspondence to demonstrate how their everyday meanings are transformed into technical logical terms and express ideas related to the ten categories of Aristotle. Then, to this he adds his discourse on (ii) the origin of language and the history of philosophy and, what is particularly relevant here, the relationship between philosophy and religion. The work concludes with (iii) a classification of interrogative particles, again holding Aristotle as the point of reference, since this classification is based on the uses of these particles in philosophical enquiries of an Aristotelian kind as well as the relationship of these particles with Aristotle's four causes (Eskenasy 1988).

At many places we see al-Farabi making demonstration (*burhān*) the *telos* of the whole logical process, and this is one of the many embodiments of the hierarchical nature of his metaphysical thinking whereby the *Posterior Analytics* remains at the pinnacle of all syllogistic arts. His own *Kitāb al-Burhān* opens with two notions, well-known and frequently discussed among present-day al-Farabi scholars, distinguishing what are considered to be the two basic cognitive acts of the human mind: *taṣawwur* (conceptualization) and *taṣdīq* (assent; a verbal noun that literally means 'holding as true'). The former denotes any cognitive act by means of which the human mind knows simple, discrete concepts, the latter, that cognitive act which is complex by virtue of its very nature, involving a judgement of truth and falsehood. Perfect *taṣdīq* is the aim of demonstrative syllogism (Black 1999: 214).

It has already been noted that al-Farabi supplements Aristotle's *Metaphysics* by means of Neoplatonic hierarchical constructs and introduces God and immaterial beings as a proper and not incidental subject matter of metaphysical enquiry. In fact, al-Farabi's *Aims of [Aristotle's] Metaphysics* opens with a discussion on the distinction between *'Ilm al-Kalām* (Science of discourse/enquiry; generally rendered somewhat misleadingly as 'Islamic theology') and metaphysics, but then ends up viewing Aristotle's project as inadequate and so widens the scope of metaphysics to include *kalām*. This is so because "God is a principle of absolute being, not of one being to the exclusion of another" (translated in Gutas 1988: 241). *The Attainment of Happiness* is another of al-Farabi's many writings where his metaphysical teachings are scattered. Here too Aristotle's *Metaphysics* is 'Islamized' so that it becomes theologically fuller and locally recognizable. We read that metaphysics is "the science of what is *beyond* natural things in order of investigation and instruction and *above* them in the order of being" (Mahdi 1962: 22). Metaphysical enquiry leads to the discovery of God, the first principle of being. One notes likewise al-Farabi's metaphysical leap in the *Particles*, where he affirms the existence of beings outside the categories. His *Book of the One and the Unity* is also concerned with questions of divinity.

It is in his *Principles* and *Political Regime* that al-Farabi presents in earnest his integration of Aristotelian logical doctrines with Plotinian emanationism, giving this integral whole a further philosophical treatment by conceiving it in terms of the Ptolemaic order of the motion of celestial bodies taken over from the astronomer's *Planetary Hypotheses*. What we see here is Aristotle's causation of motion that accounts for the revolution of the spheres now becoming causation of being, crossing over from the domain of natural philosophy to that of ontology in a way that causally links the natural with the metaphysical. This was a hierarchical system where the intellection of a superior sphere causes the emanation of the sphere below it along with the latter's intellect and soul. Thus, having begun both works by elaborating the aims of metaphysics – namely, enquiry into beings that are neither bodies nor in bodies, as well as the study of the principles of beings existing in the natural world – al-Farabi affirms his six hierarchical principles of being in the *Political Regime*: (i) the first cause, (ii) the secondary causes (i.e. the first nine incorporeal intellects), (iii) the active or tenth intellect governing the sublunar world, (iv) soul, (v) form and (vi) matter.

The first cause is identified with God; it is also the first mover since the celestial sphere moves out of desire for it. By the creative act of intellecting itself, it emanates the incorporeal being of the first intellect; this is associated with the first heaven, which is considered the outer sphere of the universe. The first intellect intellects doubly: (a) by intellecting the first cause it emanates the second intellect and (b) by intellecting itself it emanates a soul and a body that constitute the celestial sphere of the fixed stars. This creative causal chain of the dual process of self-intellection and intellecting the immediately preceding superior intellect continues its descent: the process emanates seven more successive intellects as well as the ensouled spheres associated with seven heavenly bodies (Saturn, Jupiter, Mars, Sun, Venus, Mercury and Moon), finally emanating the tenth intellect, called the active intellect, which governs the sublunar world (Davidson 1972).

Again, al-Farabi not only engages in Neoplatonizing Aristotle but also restates his cosmological ontology and does so in terms that would be familiar to people of the Abrahamic faith. To begin with, he does not hesitate to say that one ought to call Intellects 'spirits' and 'angels', and the active intellect the 'Holy Spirit';[8] indeed, this latter was subsequently identified in the Islamic tradition with the angel of revelation, Gabriel. Al-Farabi's whole emanationist scheme seems to be grounded in his concern that without such a causal chain of creative generation starting from God, the first cause, there was no way whatsoever of knowing the divine. He tells us that an examination of the first cause reveals that to it belong

---

8. Walzer (1985: III.3, notes) makes some very interesting observations here. This was brought to my attention by Reisman (2005: 58).

primarily and perfectly the universal notions – being and oneness – shared by all other existents, which derive their own being and oneness from it. In this connection, the unique characteristics al-Farabi gives to his active intellect, a construct that enjoyed a long career in Arabo-Islamic philosophy, are to be noted. While all other intellects in his emanationist chain generate in the rung below an intellect as well as the substantiation of a body and soul of a celestial sphere, the active intellect affects only the human intellect in the world of generation and corruption existing below the moon. Al-Farabi's active intellect, then, is a causal agency rather than a source of ontological multiplication; the equivalence with Gabriel thereby becomes highly plausible.

PRACTICAL ETHICS: QUESTIONS OF PROPHECY AND POLITICAL LEADERSHIP

Scholars have considered al-Farabi a major representative of political philosophy in Islam. But the questions al-Farabi addresses ought not to be conflated with our contemporary discipline of political science. While it is true that in his writings he uses the term *siyāsa*, which can legitimately be translated as 'politics', it might be more appropriate to see his project as a practical ethics that covers issues of governance, civil virtues and community leadership: a comprehensive practical ethics that is referred ultimately to his noetics, which we shall examine below. Human beings are not born perfect, we are taught at the outset, nor are they eternally perfect since they are not divine beings. Perfection is a virtue to be achieved: it is to be achieved by leading a life guided by reason and rational understanding of the true nature of things. Ultimate perfection is the perfection of that power of the human soul that is present uniquely in human beings, namely, reason. And ultimate perfection is identical with supreme happiness. To be perfectly happy, then, is to be perfectly rational. So we read in the *Principles*, "Happiness [= perfection of reason] is the good desired for itself, it is never desired to achieve by it something else, and there is nothing greater beyond it that a human being can achieve" (*Mabādi' Arā' Ahl al-Madīnat al-Fāḍila* 1895: 46; trans. in Mahdi 1999: 225).

What is the virtuous regime? It is that regime in which people cooperate and come together with the aim of attaining happiness, that is, they all possess (or follow those who possess) correct similitude of the knowledge of divine and natural beings. Social reality, like metaphysical reality, indeed like all reality, is conceived by al-Farabi hierarchically. Thus, we are told that in practice there will always be a difference among the citizens of the virtuous regime with regard to the character of their knowledge about divine beings, and about the world and civic life, and thereby they will differ in terms of their share of perfection, perfection here meaning intellectual perfection, which is the same thing as happiness. Given this, al-Farabi systematizes the virtuous city as a cooperative collection of a tri-level hierarchy. The highest class of people, the rulers, consists of the wise and the philosophers: these are the supremely virtuous individuals who know the true nature of things by demonstrative proofs or directly by revelation. Al-Farabi's wise, then, include prophets. Below this class are placed those who follow the philosophers and prophets: the class of those who apprehend demonstrative proofs presented by the philosophers, or indirectly grasp the reality of the teachings of a prophet. Finally, the third class is the body of those people who know things only by similitude, by imaginative reconstruction of philosophical truth. The ruler educates these citizens according to their abilities and capacities in a hierarchical manner. On their part, all citizens cooperate and sustain the virtuous regime just as the multiple entities of the cosmos sustain the universe.

We recall here al-Farabi's criticism of Aristotle for paying inadequate attention to divine beings in his metaphysics, beings that transcend the categories. Once again, in his discourses on civil society al-Farabi combines divine and social science to underline the same concern: the need in community life for sound belief about divine beings. Rulers are mediators between divine beings and the citizens, who do not have direct access to the knowledge of these beings. The fundamental qualification of the rulers is that their rational faculty is developed to the highest level: this supreme perfection of rulers consists of the rational faculty's correspondence to or contact with the active intellect. But most people, those lying at the third level, come to know the nature of virtuous social behaviour only through imaginative representation of truth rather than through a rational conception of it; they understand divine things not in themselves but only their imitations. And this is precisely the role of religion: to teach the truth to the common folk in the form of imaginative similitudes and imitations. One may say that for al-Farabi those who are qualified to rule – and this would include both prophet-rulers and philosopher-rulers – know divine beings *primarily* through the active intellect, while those who are ruled over are the ones who know these beings *derivatively* and, in the case of the majority, figuratively (Macy 1986).

It is evident that al-Farabi conceives of an epistemological as well as a political equivalence between the prophet and the philosopher. But there is a difference. While in the general run of things it is only the human rational faculty that has access to the knowledge of divine beings, it may rarely happen that a human individual's faculty of imagination is so powerful, attaining such perfection, that it overwhelms the rational faculty; the imaginative faculty then proceeds directly to the active intellect to receive images of divine beings and knows the nature of things without the mediation of the rational process. This extraordinary phenomenon is prophecy, al-Farabi tells us. Speaking in an emanationist, quasi-theological vein, he writes that imagination and intellect are the two powers by means of which human beings are able to communicate with the active intellect (i.e. the 'Holy Spirit'): when they communicate with it by means of imagination they are prophets; when they do so by means of intellect, they are wise human beings, philosophers.

It is interesting that the Islamic belief in the cessation of prophecy after Muhammad, an issue that became highly sensitive in subsequent centuries, also seems to make its way into the system of al-Farabi. He states that ordinary people are not capable of understanding the rational basis of virtuous behaviour; they are taught social virtues by prophets through persuasion and compulsion, and are prescribed rewards and punishments that they accept as true and eternal. All of this constitutes a necessary requirement for the founding of the virtuous city, but *not* for its survival. The virtuous regime can continue after the absence of the prophets through the teachings, legislation and political rule of philosophers, or by the rule of jurist-rulers who act as shadow philosophers. But al-Farabi also appears to believe that wisdom or philosophy is a necessary requirement both for the founding of the virtuous regime and for its survival.

A NOTE ON NOETICS

All the various streams in al-Farabi's philosophical system, grand as it is in its theoretical proportions and curricular scope, ultimately fall into the ocean of his noetics, as we have been observing above. It is by means of the particular drift of these streams and their final convergence into a single body that the philosopher has managed to construct a coherent *system*, a system in which all else is in the end reducible to one principle, namely intellect. Take, for example, al-Farabi's very notion of being, a notion that flows proximately from his doctrine of certitude. For him it is a cosmic law that certitude is arrived at through the intellectual process of logical demonstration, but he then adds to it a firm cognitive requirement: "Certitude requires both that we know some proposition to be true and that we know *that* we know it". Now comes the core ontological pronouncement, which echoed some seven hundred years later in Cartesian chambers: "Necessary certitude and necessary existence are convertible in entailment, for what is verified as necessarily certain is necessarily existent" (quoted in Black 1999: 215).

We have also seen how noetics lies at the centre of al-Farabi's cosmological emanationist hierarchy, for it was the generative act of the intellection of a superior, logically prior being that caused the emanation of another, logically posterior being to occupy its immediately following rank. So, once again, we note al-Farabi's metaphysical theory of the *intellectual* causation of being. Furthermore, the contact between the transcendental world and the natural world, we are to learn from him, comes to pass by means of the emanation of intelligibles from the active intellect to the human intellect, and it is on receiving these intelligibles that the latter is actualized. Once actualized, the human intellect begins to know the active intellect. Indeed, an identity of the knowing intellect and the object of knowledge is here admitted: an identity of the knower and the known. This epistemological subject–object equation can certainly be traced back to Aristotle, but the centrality and the intense epistemological focus it now acquires is al-Farabi's own contribution, which opened up many a mystical vista for post-Avicennan philosophical developments in Islam.

It would seem that there exists a relation of reciprocal implication between the various strains of al-Farabi's system. His fivefold taxonomy of logical syllogisms –the demonstrative, being the noblest, and the dialectic, sophistical, rhetorical and poetic – is followed by the claim that these are five ontologically fixed modes in which human intellect immutably functions; and further, that the objects of these ways of reasoning conform to the hierarchy of beings. All of this is then linked to psychology: the five logical modes are associated with the faculties of the corporeal human soul. Ontology, then, has implications for logic and psychology. But then one can say with equal legitimacy that it is the other way around: it is logic and psychology that have ontological implications. All of this ultimately culminates in noetics, since the very ground on which being itself is affirmed is nothing other than certainty, the supreme stage of intellection: "what is ... necessarily certain [in the mind] is necessarily existent". It is hard to resist thinking about Descartes here.

Indeed, human beings were made for the sake of their intellect, and the ultimate happiness of the human being consists in the continuous and actual act of knowing. The degree of perfection of human communities, al-Farabi frequently states, is measured by the extent to which they actualize their intellects, receive intelligibles from the active intellect and hold correct opinions regarding divine and natural entities. Dimitri Gutas has brought into focus the noetic basis of the *Opinions*, al-Farabi's major work on individuals and social organizations or, rather, on practical ethics. The *Mabādi' Arā' Ahl al-Madīnat al-Fāḍila* (Principles of the opinions of the people of the excellent city), Gutas explains, "is *not*, as it is often elliptically but misleadingly referred to, the 'excellent city', but 'the *principles* of the opinions of the people of the excellent city'" (1999b: 222). Gutas has also brought to light an interesting passage from Ibn Khaldūn (*d.* 1406) – the "always perspicacious ... conscious originator of political philosophy in Islam" (*ibid.*) – in which the pre-modern sage points out the theoretical nature of al-Farabi's social and political discourses and their fundamental noetic thrust.

Following Gutas, it is worthwhile quoting Ibn Khaldūn again. Opening his section on political leadership by pointing out that all social organizations require a ruler who exercises a restraining influence over people, Ibn Khaldūn also speaks of two types of rule: one based on divine sanction and the other on rational politics. He then goes on to say:

> We do not mean here that which is known as 'political utopianism' [Ibn Khaldūn here employs al-Farabi's book title and term *siyāsa madaniyya*]. By that the philosophers mean the disposition of soul and character which each member of a social organization must have, if, eventually, people are completely to dispense with rulers. They call the social organization that fulfills these requirements the 'ideal city' (al-Farabi's terms *al-madīna al-fāḍila*). The norms observed in this connection are called 'political utopias'. They do not mean the kind

58

of politics (*siyāsa*) that the members of a social organization are led to adopt through laws for the common interest. That is something different. The ideal city (of the philosophers) is something rare and remote. (Ibn Khaldūn 1958: II, 137–8)

And, finally, the writer expressly declares that such an ideal city exists only in the mind: "They discuss it as a hypothesis" (*ibid.*: II, 138).

FURTHER READING

Al-Farabi 1955. "Al-Farabi's Introductory Sections on Logic", D. Dunlop (trans.). *Islamic Quarterly* **2**: 264–82.

Al-Farabi 1957. "Al-Farabi's Paraphrase of the *Categories* of Aristotle", D. Dunlop (trans.). *Islamic Quarterly* **4**: 168–97 and **5**: 21–54.

Al-Farabi 1964. *Al-Siyāsa al-Madaniyya al-Mullaqab bi-Mabādi' al-Mawjūdāt* [Political regime also known as the principles of beings], F. Najjar (ed.). Beirut: Imprimerie catholique.

Al-Farabi 1968. *Iḥṣā al-'Ulūm* [Enumeration of the sciences], U. Amin (ed.). Cairo: Maktabt al-Anjalū al-Miṣriyya.

Black, D. 2006. "Knowledge (*'ilm*) and Certitude (*yaqīn*) in al-Farabi's Epistemology". *Arabic Science and Philosophy* **16**: 11–45.

Daiber, H. 1986. *The Ruler as Philosopher: A New Interpretation of al-Farabi's View*. Amsterdam: Mededelingen der Koninklijke Nederlandse Akademie van Wetenschappen.

Fakhry, M. 2002. *Al-Farabi: Founder of Islamic Neoplatonism*. Oxford: Oneworld.

Kemal, S. 1991. *The Poetics of Alfarabi and Avicenna*. Leiden: Brill.

Lameer, J. 1981. *Al-Farabi and Aristotelian Syllogistics: Greek Theory and Islamic Practice*. Leiden: Brill.

Pines, S. 1997. "The Limitations of Human Knowledge according to al-Farabi, Ibn Bajja, and Maimonides". In *The Collected Works of Shlomo Pines*, vol. 5, W. Harvey & M. Idel (eds), 404–31. Jerusalem: Magnes Press.

On ARISTOTLE see also Chs 10, 11. On COSMOLOGY see also Chs 10, 16; Vol. 1, Chs 6, 8, 14, 17. On ETHICS see also Ch. 8; Vol. 1, Ch. 11; Vol. 3, Ch. 9; Vol. 4, Chs 13, 19; Vol. 5, Chs 12, 15, 21. On HIERARCHY see also Vol. 1, Chs. 15, 20. On LANGUAGE see also Chs 11, 12; Vol. 3, Ch. 14; Vol. 4, Chs 3, 8; Vol. 5, Chs 13, 20. On LOGIC see also Chs 2, 17; Vol. 3, Ch. 3; Vol. 4, Ch. 19. On NEOPLATONISM see also Ch. 3; Vol. 1, Chs 19, 20; Vol. 3, Ch. 9; Vol. 4, Chs 4, 9. On PROPHECY see also Ch. 5.

5

AVICENNA (IBN SINA)

Jon McGinnis

Ibn Sina, the 'Avicenna' of the Latin West, is arguably one of the most significant thinkers and original system-builders in the history of western philosophy. Indeed, his renown in the Islamic world has brought him the title *al-Shaykh al-Ra'īs* ('the leading eminent scholar'). We are fortunate that Avicenna, in an uncustomary fashion, wrote an autobiography detailing his early education. Additionally, one of his students, al-Juzjani, chronicled the later part of Avicenna's life. Thus we are on fairly sure ground concerning the details of much of his personal life.

Abu 'Ali al-Husayn ibn 'Abdallah ibn Sina was born in 980 in the small village of Afshana in what is now part of Uzbekistan and was then part of the Samanid dynasty. His father was the governor of Kharmaythan, an important village in northern Persia outside of Buhkara, the seat of Samanid rule. Avicenna by all accounts was a prodigy; he claimed that by the age of ten he had completed the study of the Qu'ran and a major part of his *belles lettres* and already had surpassed his teacher of logic, Abu 'Abdallah al-Natili'. He continued his own education thereafter, and claimed that by eighteen he had taught himself, and in fact mastered, all the sciences, including Islamic law, astronomy, medicine and, of course, philosophy. It was his knowledge of medicine that provided him an introduction to the Samanid Sultan, Nuh ibn Mansur, who was suffering from an ailment that baffled the court physicians. A young Avicenna, whose skill as a doctor was already recognized, was called in, and he cured the Sultan, who enrolled him into his service. The rest of Avicenna's career was a series of often short-lived associations with such lords. In 1037, on his way to Hamadan in modern Iran, Avicenna died at the age of fifty-eight after apparently overdosing in an attempt to cure himself of colic.

Avicenna's literary outpourings were voluminous with the better part of 300 works being ascribed to him. His *Kitab al-Shifa'* (The cure) appears to be the first philosophical encyclopedia in Islam. He also wrote several other works of an encyclopedic nature such as *al-Najat* (The salvation), *al-Isharat wa al-tanbihat* (Pointers and reminders), the Persian *Danishnamah-yi 'Ala'i* (The book of science for 'Ala' al-Dawla) and an encyclopedia of medicine, *al-Qanun fi al-tibb* (The canon of medicine), which was the major reference work on medicine in both the Islamic East and the Christian West for centuries to come. Other encyclopedic works, only parts of which are still extant, are his *al-Hikma al-mashriqiyya* (Eastern philosophy), which purports to give Avicenna's own judgement and philosophical system rather than following the presentation of earlier thinkers, and *Insaf* (Fair treatment), which comments on a number of influential Aristotelian and pseudo-Aristotelian texts. In addition to these larger works, he penned numerous smaller treatises, ranging from the mathematical to the medical and from phonetics to ethics.

RELIGION AND PHILOSOPHY

It is not clear to what extent, if any, Avicenna had a fully articulated philosophy of religion. He did say, however, that philosophy has two major divisions: theoretical and practical. Theoretical philosophy studies those things whose existence is not a result of our choice or action, while practical philosophy concerns matters that do involve our choice and action (Avicenna 1952: 12). Additionally, he maintained that "divine law or revelation" (*sharī'a ilāhiyya*) provides the details concerning practical philosophy (*ibid.*: 14). Indeed in his monumental work *al-Shifa'*, Avicenna's entire discussion of practical philosophy reads like a summary of dicta derived from the Qu'ran and Islamic law (2005: bk X, chs 3–5). Conversely, he seems to have thought that theoretical philosophy would provide intellectuals with the proper set of religious beliefs about God and divine attributes, creation, the nature and fate of the soul and prophecy. This is not to say that he necessarily discounted the claims of revelation on these and other related issues, or the religious language used to describe them; rather, he thought that philosophy gives the more precise and intellectually satisfying articulation of the truths implicit in the Qu'ran.

GOD AND DIVINE SIMPLICITY

Avicenna's proof for the existence and proper description of God begins with what he considers to be the underlying modal structure of existence: existence can be conceptually divided into necessary existence (*wājib al-wujūd*) (or what is necessary through itself) and possible existence (*mumkin al-wujūd*) (or what is possible in itself). Although, properly speaking, necessary existence and possible existence are primitive notions for Avicenna and cannot be defined in terms of anything more basic, he says we can intuitively grasp the difference between them if we consider what it means for something to exist 'through itself' or 'through another'. Thus he describes the necessary in itself as that whose actual existence is solely through itself and is in no way through another, whereas the possible in itself is that whose existence, when actualized, is through another.

Starting almost solely from this distinction, Avicenna provides a proof that God exists, or to be more precise, that there is something that exists necessarily through itself. His argument (1985: 566–8) is unique in the philosophy of religion and begins with the obvious fact that something exists. Given that the basic conceptual divisions of existence are the necessary through itself and the possible in itself, if that thing which exists is necessary through itself, then there exists something necessary through itself, and the argument is complete.

If the existing thing is possible, then consider it along with every other thing that exists possibly in itself, whether there be a finite or infinite number of such things. In other words, consider the set (*jumla*) of all and only things that exist possibly in themselves. Since this set is an existing thing, and again given Avicenna's conceptual divisions of existence, the set must exist either necessarily through itself or possibly in itself. The set cannot be something existing necessarily through itself; for that which is necessary through itself does not exist through another, and yet a set exists through its members. Thus if the set of all things that are possible in themselves were necessary through itself, then something necessary through itself would be necessary through another, which is a contradiction.

So the set of all and only things possible in themselves must be something possible in itself. Given Avicenna's characterization of the possible in itself, the set, then, must exist through another. Now this other can either be internal or external to the set. If it is internal, and so is one or more members of the set, then again that member exists either necessarily through itself or possibly in itself. Whatever is internal to the set of all and only things possible in themselves could not exist necessarily through itself, since only things possible in themselves were included within the set, and thus something would be both necessary through itself and possible in itself, which is a contradiction. If this member were possible in itself, then since the set and all the members of the set of which it is one, exist through that member, that member's very existence would be through itself, in which case it would be self-necessitating. If something is self-necessitating, though, it is necessary through itself; however, this member was assumed to be possible in itself. So there is again a contradiction. Thus, the existence of the set must be through something external to the set, but all possible existents were included within the set. So this thing external to the set cannot be possible in itself, and the only other division of existence is that which exists necessarily through itself. Therefore, something necessary through itself, namely, God, exists.

Having shown that God exists, Avicenna considers the manner or mode in which something necessary through itself must exist, which he concludes must be as something utterly simple and so wholly without parts. The notion of divine simplicity or unity had become a major factor in philosophical discussions of God – or more precisely the One – since at least the time of the Greek Neoplatonists (beginning around the third century CE), whose influence on Arabic speakers was profound. The centrality of simplicity in describing God took on an even greater urgency in Islam with its doctrine of *tawḥīd*, or profession of the unity of God, which is encapsulated in the Muslim creed 'There is no god, but God'. This profession of faith came to be understood as implying not only that there can be only one eternal God, but also that God could in no way have parts; for if God were to have parts and each of those parts were eternal, there would be a number of eternal things, the divine parts, all worthy of the name 'god'.

Avicenna, then, taking advantage of his conceptual division of the necessary through itself and possible in itself, ardently defends this doctrine of divine simplicity. He argues thus (1985: 549–52): if there were two necessary existents, there would be an aspect that they share in common, namely, necessary existence, and some other aspect by which they differ (for if there truly were more than one, then there must be something that distinguishes *this* one from *that* one). Thus if there were two necessary existents, each would be a whole composed of at least conceptually distinct parts. A whole, again, subsists only through its parts, in which case the necessary in itself would be necessary through another, namely, its parts. Since it is a contradiction for something to be necessary through itself and necessary through another, the assumption that there could be two necessary existents must be false. So given that there is a necessary existent, there can be only one. By an analogous proof, Avicenna argued that the necessary existent must be simple as well.

GOD AND CREATION

The above arguments show that there could be only one thing (God) that exists necessarily through itself, and so all other existents must be possible existents and that whatever exists possibly ultimately requires God to explain its actual existence. In effect, Avicenna's arguments show not only that God exists and is one, but also that God is the cause of the actual existence of everything else, namely, the world. Given that there is a causal relation between God and the world, a significant question at least in the philosophy of Western religions is whether God has been eternally creating the world or began creating it at some first moment in the finite past. In other words, is the world itself eternal or temporally created? Avicenna himself maintains that although the world was created (*ibdā'*) and so is utterly dependent upon God for its actual existence, it is not something that had a temporal beginning (*ḥādith*). For this conclusion, he draws on the entire arsenal of arguments found in the ancient Greek world (for eighteen such arguments see Proclus 2001). In addition to these classical arguments, Avicenna also develops a new argument for the world's eternality based on his own analysis of possible existence.

His argument (see e.g. 2005: 136–41) begins by considering what it means for something to have come to be in time, which he takes to mean that it did not exist and then it did exist. Now it seems obvious that whatever has come to exist must have been possible before it came to exist, and so Avicenna asks, "In what sense does this prior possibility exist before the thing comes to exist?" A presently existing possibility might exist either as a substance in its own right or as something inhering in a substance. In a series of quick, but decisive arguments (see e.g. 1983: 224; 2005: 136), Avicenna puts to rest the suggestion that possibility is a substance in its own right. One of these arguments is that a presently existing possibility is always of or for something that does not presently exist. Thus if possibility were a substance, it would be the substance of something that does not presently exist, in which case the presently existing possibility would not exist, which is clearly false.

Consequently, the possibility of being created must exist in a certain substance, which might be either immaterial or material. If possibility inheres in an immaterial substance, the best candidate would be God, or more exactly God's power (*qudra*) to create. Avicenna objects (2005: 139–40): God's power does not extend to what is impossible, but only to what is possible. Now if something is possible just in case God has the power to do that thing, then when one says that God has the power to do everything that is possible, all one is saying is that God has the power to do everything that God has the power to do. In effect, concludes Avicenna, if there is not some independent notion of possibility, then God's omnipotence becomes vacuous, since everything has the power to do whatever it has the power to do.

Since Avicenna finds all the ways that one might try to make an immaterial substance the substrate of possibility wanting, he concludes that the possibility that precedes those things that come to be in time requires matter in which to inhere if that possibility is to exist. He is quick to add, however, that in as much as that possibility inheres in a subsisting matter, that matter must be made actual, and it is made actual by its having a form, which it ultimately derives from God (albeit through the intermediacy of a chain of separate, immaterial substances stretching to the one that Avicenna dubs the 'Giver of Forms'). The world with all of its possibilities, then, simply is matter actualized by all the various forms we see around us; should every form be removed, the world and matter would cease to be actual, and all possibility would cease to exist.

Avicenna now has all the elements necessary for his peculiar proof for the eternity of the world. It begins: anything that is temporally created must be preceded by the possibility of its existence (for if there were no possibility for its existence, its existence would be impossible). The existence of possibility itself, however, requires matter in which to inhere. Thus, if the material world, that is the composite of forms and matter, were temporally created at some first moment of time before which it did not exist, then the possibility of the material world's existence would have preceded its actual existence, but since that possibility requires matter in which to inhere, matter would have existed before matter was created and so would have existed when it did not exist, but this is a contradiction. Therefore the world could not have been created at some first moment of time in the finite past, but must have always existed and so is eternal.

MIRACLES AND PROPHECY

Avicenna's general deterministic outlook about the cosmos coupled with his doctrine of divine immutability makes his system hostile towards miracles, at least as understood as special acts of divine interference in the natural order at some particular time for some wholly supernatural end. One can appreciate the philosophical justification for Avicenna's reluctance to countenance miracles so described, if one first considers his argument for causal determinism and then his argument for divine immutability.

The notion of causal determinism at play in Avicenna's thought is that whenever something possible comes to *exist as actual* (*ḥāṣil*) it must be necessitated by its causes. His argument for this thesis (1985: 548–9) begins by considering the state of existence when something is merely possible and then the state of existence when it is actual. When that thing is merely possible, it is in a state of possible existence; however, when that possibility has been actualized, there is a change in that thing's state of existence. The existence of that new state must be one of the following: impossible existence, possible existence or necessary existence. Clearly, the new state is not one of impossible existence, since the existence is now actual. As for possible existence, in as much as the possible existence is itself what has changed, the new state cannot also be merely possible existence; for then there would have been no change in the state of existence, and yet that is exactly what did change. Thus it remains, concludes Avicenna, that when anything possible in itself actually exists, the state of its existence is necessary, albeit through another, namely, its causes.

This conclusion alone does not eliminate the possibility that God directly intervenes at some particular moment and that this divine intervention would be a cause of some miraculous event; however, when coupled with the following argument it does seem to preclude such a position. (The following is a generalized version of Avicenna's argument that temporal events cannot cause God's knowledge of them; 1985: 593–9; 2005: 287–90.) If God were not always acting in the same way from all eternity but instead were to act differently at some moment in time so as to bring about a miracle, then God's acting one way at one moment and differently at another would be an event having a temporal beginning (*ḥādith*). When Avicenna considered the world's creation, he noted that all things or events that come to be in time involve a preceding possibility. Yet God is what is necessary through itself and so must be wholly free of possibility; for, as we have just seen, when something possible comes to exist (for example God's performing some special action at this moment, but not before), that event becomes necessary through another, and so what is necessary through itself would be necessary through another, which is a contradiction.

Interestingly, Avicenna does not intend any of the preceding arguments to preclude the existence of prodigies, wonders and even 'miracles', understood as wholly unexpected events, although these events must be understood now as part of a natural, eternal order. One of the best examples exemplifying the 'naturalness' of miracles is prophecy, which for Avicenna is just as real and natural as eclipses.

For Avicenna a human being comes to know and understand something when the intellect receives the intelligible object or concept of that thing. (This point is discussed more fully in the next two sections.) As such the human intellect has a certain natural disposition to receive concepts, where this disposition varies between individuals: some individuals just 'get things' faster than others. Avicenna calls this capacity or disposition to get things 'insight' (ḥads). For some people their insight is so intense that it is as if they know everything on their own without being taught. In these very few, the prophets, their insight so abounds that it over-flows and deluges their imaginations such that they perceive the universal order in the form of images and audible sounds. The prophets are then able to convey to the masses through these images and metaphors the truth about the divine universal order that most people would not otherwise have grasped. Avicenna says that the prophet "blazes with insight" (1959: 249) and so wholly grasps the neces-sary causal order inherent in the world, his or her immediate place in that order and how that causal order must inevitably play out in the future, thus suggesting how prophets can predict future events.

THE IMMATERIALITY OF THE HUMAN INTELLECT

That human beings (and indeed all living things) have a soul is for Avicenna an almost observable fact. Living things clearly are distinct from non-living things as the various actions unique to living things witness. All living things nourish them-selves, grow and reproduce; others sense and choose to move about; still others, namely, human beings, perform acts of the intellect, all of which are absent in non-living things. To explain these unique activities of living things, there must be some principle or cause within them that is absent from the non-living things. Soul, for Avicenna is just "the thing out of which these actions issue and, in short, is anything that is a principle for the issuance of any actions that do not follow a uniform course devoid of volition" (1959: 4).

Virtually all of these living activities require the body or a material organ if they are to occur. Thus, for example, there must be at least some rudimentary diges-tive system if there is to be nourishment, a suitable visual apparatus if there is to be sight and limbs of some sort if there is to be motion. The one exception that Avicenna notes to this general rule is the human act of intellectual perception. For him the intellect, or part of the human soul that accounts for the human ability to acquire scientific knowledge and understanding, must be an immaterial substance independent of the body; however, since the intellect is independent of the body, it can survive the death of the body and indeed is immortal. Before considering Avicenna's proofs that the human intellect is immaterial and immortal, let us first consider the object of intellectual perception.

Unlike sensory or imaginative perception, whose object is always a certain particular thing or individual (whether immediately present, as in the case of sensation or absent as in the case of imagination), intellectual perception has as its object a universal, an idea or concept that holds of every possible instance of a certain kind. For example, if one sensibly perceives a human being, it is always either Peter or Paul or some other particular human being. Similarly, if one imagines a human being, the image before one's mind's eye has a particular shape, colour, gender and the like. In contrast, when one intellectually recognizes what it is to be human, one does not uniquely identify the idea in one's intellect with Peter (for since Peter is not Paul, one would not recognize Paul as a human being), nor does one uniquely identify humanity with any particular image in the imagination (for any person who was not the same shape, colour or in some other way like that image would not be included in one's idea of human). In contrast, when one intellectually perceives what something is, the idea or concept in the intellect is totally devoid of any particularizing traits, such as having some quantity, quality or position, all traits that Avicenna in some way or other associates with being material. Consequently, according to Avicenna the intellectual object, in as much as it is a universal, must be immaterial.

In the activity of intellectual perception, the potential intellect receives an intelligible object. In other words, that aspect of the human soul capable of cognition comes to have or receive a certain concept, for example the concept of 'humanity', and by coming to have or receive that concept, one knows what a human being is. Since the activity of intellectual perception requires that the intellect is a receptacle of immaterial intelligible objects, Avicenna asks whether the intellect could perform this function if it itself were material and argues that it cannot. So assume that the potential intellect, again that part in which one's concepts and ideas reside or inhere, is a material body. That body must either be (i) indivisible or (ii) divisible.

If the body, which is purportedly associated with the intellect, is indivisible, then it must either (a) have no extension (and so is a point) or (b) have some extension (and so is an atom). Now a point is a certain termination of a divisible magnitude and as such a point has no existence independent of that magnitude. In like fashion, whatever inheres in a point does so by inhering in the magnitude of which that point is a limit. So, for example, one might say that a certain colour inheres in some point on a chalkboard because the surface of the chalkboard is coloured and the point is a limit of the chalkboard's surface. Consequently, if an intelligible object were to inhere in the intellect as in a point, it could do so only if it also inhered in a divisible magnitude limited by that point. Consequently, Avicenna defers discussion until he takes up option (ii), whether the purported bodily organ associated with the intellect is a divisible magnitude.

Before that, however, he turns to option (b), namely, that the receptacle of one's intelligible objects or concepts is an atom. In his *Physics* (1983: bk III, ch. 5) he gives a number of arguments to show that atoms, understood as conceptually indivisible minimal magnitudes, are impossible, and he briefly rehearses one of those arguments here (Lettinck 1999). Assume three atoms are in contact with one another so as to form a line ABC. Either B separates A from C, such that A does not touch C, or A does touch C. If B separates A from C, such that none of A touches C, then the conceptually indivisible atom, B, can be divided into the side touching A and the side touching C, in which case what is indivisible would be divisible, which is a contradiction. If B does not separate A from C, and so A touches C, then atoms would interpenetrate one another so as to occupy a single atomic space; however, it was assumed that they formed a line, and so there is a contradiction. Thus the intellect cannot be associated with an indivisible magnitude, whether that magnitude is punctiform or atomic.

Avicenna now considers option (ii), which takes the receptacle of one's concepts, again the potential intellect, to be a divisible magnitude. Whatever inheres in a divisible magnitude is at least accidentally divisible as well; for example, colour becomes divided accidentally when the surface of a chalkboard in which that colour inheres is itself divided. If an intelligible object were localized in some divisible material organ, such as part of the brain, then should that part of the brain be divided into two parts, the intelligible object likewise would be divided accidentally into two parts. The two parts of the divided concept must be either (c) similar or (d) dissimilar.

The two parts of the intelligible object cannot (c) be similar, argues Avicenna, because were one to recombine the two parts so as to make a whole, the whole would be no different from the part, and yet a whole is different from a part. One cannot say that the whole intelligible object is bulkier or larger than either of the purported similar parts; for if the combination of the parts of the intelligible object involved an increase in size, shape or number, then the intelligible object itself would have to be something material, but we have seen that it is intelligible precisely by being immaterial.

If (d), the two parts of an immaterial intelligible object are dissimilar, then these dissimilar parts must correspond with the parts of a definition, namely, genus and difference. So, for example, consider the concept 'humanity'; it can conceptually be divided into 'animal' (a genus) and 'rational' (a difference). Avicenna thinks that many absurdities follow on this hypothesis, one of which is the following. Assuming that the receptacle for concepts is a divisible (non-atomic) magnitude, it would be continuous, and continuous magnitudes are potentially divisible infinitely. Consequently, the intelligible object purportedly inhering in a continuous magnitude would have a potentially infinite number of genera and differences, but Avicenna takes it as an established fact that essential genera and differences are finite. Therefore, if an intelligible object were to inhere in divisible matter, it could not be accidentally divided into dissimilar parts. Since a concept existing in a divisible magnitude must be divisible accidentally into either similar or dissimilar parts, and yet both options lead to absurdities, the intellect cannot be associated with a divisible magnitude.

Avicenna now concludes: if the intellect, that is, the receptacle of concepts, were associated with a body, then that body would have been either indivisible (and so either a point or an atom) or divisible (in which case accidentally divided concepts would have either similar or dissimilar parts). All options have either led to absurdities or contradictions and so the assumption that the intellect is in some way associated with a material body, which gives rise to those absurdities and contradictions, must be rejected. Therefore, concludes Avicenna, the intellect must be immaterial.

THE IMMORTALITY OF THE HUMAN INTELLECT

Having explained that the intellect must be an immaterial substance distinct from the body, Avicenna now argues for its immortality. He begins by observing that if the corruption of one thing, x, entails the corruption of another, y, then x and y must be dependent on one another in one of three ways: (i) x and y may be co-dependent or equivalent with respect to existence (*mukāfi' fi al-wujūd*) (such as in the essential relation between a concave and convex curve or the accidental relation of being 'next to'); (ii) x may be essentially prior to y, and so x is a cause of y; or (iii) x may be essentially posterior to y, and so x is an effect of y.

Avicenna quickly dismisses the suggestion that the immaterial intellect and material body are co-dependent or equivalent with respect to existence. If they were, the co-dependence would be either essential or accidental. On the one hand, if the co-dependence were essential, the existence of the two would be essentially the same, but being immaterial is opposed to being material. So clearly the intellect and body cannot be essentially the same. On the other hand, if the co-dependence were merely an accidental relation, such as 'being next to', then although the destruction of one of the *relata*, for example, the body, would destroy the relation between the two, it would not destroy the other *relatum*, namely, the intellect.

If the body and intellect were related so that the body is the cause of the intellect, continues Avicenna, then the body would be the intellect's (a) material, (b) efficient, (c) formal or (d) final cause. In so far as the intellect is an immaterial substance, it has no material cause and so (a) cannot be the case. Next, matter, according to Avicenna, is wholly inert and as such only acts through the form presently informing it. Thus body *qua* material does not itself act, but what does not act cannot be an efficient cause, and so not (b). Next, the formal cause again accounts for the operations of a thing, but it is the intellect that accounts for the human's operation of knowing and understanding, and so the intellect has a better right to be a formal cause of the body than the other way around, and so (c) must be false. Similarly, the final cause is the end for which a thing functions and it is the operations of the intellect for which the human body functions. So again the intellect is more fittingly the final cause of the body than vice versa, and thus not (d). Since the body cannot stand to the intellect in any of the traditional causal ways, the body cannot be essentially prior to the intellect.

If the intellect is essentially prior to the body then, were it corrupted, the body would be corrupted, but from that fact it does not follow that if the body is corrupted then the intellect is corrupted. Still, it might turn out that the corruption of the body entails the corruption of the intellect if there were no other way to explain the corruption of the body except through the corruption of the intellect. So consider, for example, the proverbial saying, 'Where there is smoke there is fire'. Clearly, fire is essentially prior to smoke and indeed the cause of the smoke. Consequently, should one not see the fire but see the smoke, one could be assured that the fire is still present and, conversely, when one no longer sees the smoke, there is a presumption that the fire has been extinguished. Perhaps, then, the body is essentially posterior to the intellect in the way that smoke is posterior to the fire such that when the body fails to perform the activities associated with life, one can presume that the cause of those activities has passed away. Such an inference would be valid, maintains Avicenna, if and only if the body does not have principles that can explain its own corruption that are unique to it as body and so do not apply to the intellect. The body, so claims Avicenna, does have principles unique to it that explain its corruption, namely, its elemental composition and humoral temperament. More exactly, according to the best science at the time, complex bodies were composites of the four elements – fire, air, water and earth – which themselves form the four humours of animal bodies – blood, phlegm, yellow and black bile – all of which are combined by an innate animal heat. The nature of heat, Avicenna notes, ultimately brings about dissolution and transformation. Consequently, the human body must eventually corrupt owing to its very elemental and humoral nature. In contrast, since this elemental composition and humoral temperament follow on the body's materiality, they cannot apply to an immaterial intellect. Thus while the body must corrupt, the principles that bring about its corruption simply cannot apply to the human intellect as something immaterial.

Thus, concludes Avicenna, the corruption of the body would entail the corruption of the intellect only if the body exists co-dependently with the intellect, or it is either a cause or essential effect of the intellect. Since none of these types of dependence applies to the relation between body and intellect, the death of the body does not entail the destruction of the intellect. Consequently, the intellect can and does survive the body's death, continuing to carry on an intellectual existence wholly dissociated from the body, an existence that Avicenna identifies with true blessedness (sa'āda) and the afterlife.

FURTHER READING

Acar, R. 2005. *Talking about God and Talking about Creation: Avicenna's and Thomas Aquinas' Position*. Leiden: Brill,

Adamson, P. 2004. "On Knowledge of Particulars". *Proceedings of the Aristotelian Society* **105**: 257–78.

Belo, C. 2007. *Chance and Determinism in Avicenna and Averroes*. Leiden: Brill.

Druart, T.-A. 2000. "The Human Soul's Individuation and Its Survival after the Body's Death: Avicenna on the Causal Relation between Body and Soul". *Arabic Sciences and Philosophy* **10**: 259–73.

Janssens, J. 1997. "Creation and Emanation in Ibn Sina". *Documenti e studi sulla tradizione filos-ofie* **8**: 455–77.

Kaukua, J. 2007. *Avicenna on Subjectivity*. Jyväskylä: Jyväskylä University Printing House.

Marmura, M. 2005. "Avicenna's Chapter on Universals in the *Isagoge* of his *Shifā'*". In his *Probing in Islamic Philosophy: Studies in the Philosophies of Ibn Sina, al-Ghazali and Other Major Muslim Thinkers*, 33–59. Binghamton, NY: Global Academic Publishing.

Mayer, T. 2001. "Ibn Sina's 'Burhān al-Siddīqīn'". *Journal of Islamic Studies* **12**: 18–39.

McGinnis, J. 2007. "Logic and Science: The Role of Genus and Difference in Avicenna's Logic, Science and Natural Philosophy". *Documenti e studi sulla tradizione filosofica medievale* **18**: 165–87.

On ETERNITY see also Ch. 2. On EXISTENCE OF GOD see also Chs 6, 13, 14; Vol. 1, Chs 18, 19; Vol. 3, Chs 6, 12, 13, 14, 15, 21; Vol. 5, Chs 11, 16. On IMMORTALITY see also Vol. 1, Ch. 8; Vol. 4, Chs 2, 6, 16. On PROPHECY see also Ch. 4.

6

ANSELM OF CANTERBURY

Thomas Williams

Anselm was born in 1033 near Aosta, in those days a Burgundian town on the frontier with Lombardy. Little is known of his early life. He left home at twenty-three, and after three years of apparently aimless travelling through Burgundy and France, he came to Normandy in 1059. Once he was in Normandy, Anselm's interest was captured by the Benedictine abbey at Bec, whose famous school was under the direction of Lanfranc, the abbey's prior. Lanfranc was a scholar and teacher of wide reputation, and under his leadership the school at Bec had become an important centre of learning, especially in dialectic. In 1060 Anselm entered the abbey as a novice. His intellectual and spiritual gifts brought him rapid advancement, and when Lanfranc was appointed Abbot of Caen in 1063, Anselm was elected to succeed him as prior. He was elected abbot in 1078 on the death of Herluin, the founder and first Abbot of Bec. Under Anselm's leadership the reputation of Bec as an intellectual centre grew, and Anselm managed to write a good deal of philosophy and theology in addition to his teaching, administrative duties and extensive correspondence as an adviser and counsellor to rulers and nobles all over Europe and beyond. His works while at Bec include the *Monologion*, the *Proslogion* and his four philosophical dialogues: *De grammatico* (On the grammarian), *De veritate* (On truth), *De libertate arbitrii* (On freedom of choice) and *De casu diaboli* (On the fall of the devil).

In 1093 Anselm was enthroned as Archbishop of Canterbury. The previous archbishop, Anselm's old master Lanfranc, had died four years earlier, but the king, William Rufus, had left the see vacant in order to plunder the archiepiscopal revenues. Anselm was understandably reluctant to undertake the primacy of the Church of England under a ruler as ruthless and venal as William, and his tenure as archbishop proved to be as turbulent and vexatious as he must have feared. William was intent on maintaining royal authority over ecclesiastical affairs and would not be dictated to by archbishop or pope or anyone else. So, for example, when Anselm went to Rome in 1097 without the King's permission, William would not allow him to return. When William was killed in 1100, his successor, Henry I, invited Anselm to return to his see. But Henry was as intent as William had been on maintaining royal jurisdiction over the Church, and Anselm found himself in exile again from 1103 to 1106. Despite these distractions and troubles, Anselm continued to write. His works as Archbishop of Canterbury include the *Epistola de incarnatione verbi* (Letter on the incarnation of the Word), *Cur Deus homo* (Why God became human), *De conceptu virginali* (On the virginal conception), *De processione Spiritus Sancti* (On the procession of the Holy Spirit), the *Epistola de sacrificio azymi et fermentati* (Letter on the sacrifice of unleavened and leavened bread), *De sacramentis ecclesiae* (On the sacraments of the Church) and *De concordia praescientiae et praedestinationis et gratiae Dei cum libero arbitrio* (On the harmony of God's foreknowledge, predestination, and grace with free choice). Anselm died on 21 April 1109. He was canonized in 1494 and named a Doctor of the Church in 1720.

FAITH AND REASON

Anselm professes to offer proofs – the sorts of proofs that ought to be compelling to any rational and "moderately intelligent" (*Monologion* prol.) person – not only of the existence of God and the divine attributes, but even of the triune nature of God and of the claim that human beings are reconciled to God through the self-offering of a God-man. Although some commentators find it difficult to take this claim at face value, there is abundant evidence in Anselm's works that he took himself to be offering philosophical proofs, rather than merely working out the implications of revealed dogma or defending the coherence of Christian doctrine. Granted, Anselm's claims run foul of the later distinction, familiar from Thomas Aquinas, between the preambles to faith (facts about God, such as his existence and perfection, that can be proved by reason alone) and the mysteries of faith (facts about God, such as his triunity, that must be believed on the basis of revelation). Aquinas based his distinction on his broadly Aristotelian theory of knowledge. For Aquinas, because we come to know God (as we come to know anything) on the basis of sense-experience, we can know philosophically only those things about God that show up somehow in the objects of the senses; and sense objects do not tell us that God is triune, any more than a painting tells us that its creator was married. Since Anselm does not embrace this Aristotelian sort of empiricism, he has no reason to embrace the distinction between preambles and mysteries that Aquinas's Aristotelianism supports, and we can take him at his word when he says that he is offering philosophical proofs of the Trinity (in the *Monologion*)[1] and of the Atonement (in *Cur Deus homo*).[2] For Anselm, the doctrines of the Christian faith are intrinsically rational because they concern the nature and activity of God,

---

1. Contrary to what is suggested in Mann (2004). See also *De incarnatione verbi* 6 and Hopkins (1972: 90).
2. Rogers (2000) defends this reading of Anselm's intentions in *Cur Deus homo*.

who is himself supreme reason (*Monologion* 16, 34) and exemplifies supreme wisdom in everything he does (*Monologion* 16, 32, 33, 34, 44, 48, 53, 60, 64; *Cur Deus homo* 1.15, 2.13). And because human beings are rational by nature, we can grasp those doctrines. Anselm therefore speaks of the *ratio fidei* or "reason of faith": the intrinsically rational character of Christian doctrines in virtue of which they form a coherent and rationally defensible system.

Yet Anselm's confidence in the power of human reason does not mean that he downplays the role of faith, or that the slogan 'faith seeking understanding', long associated with Anselm, gives a mistaken idea of his approach. ('Faith seeking understanding' was the original title of the *Proslogion*.) Anselm holds that Christians are required to begin with faith in order to seek understanding: "a Christian ought to progress through faith to understanding, not reach faith through understanding – or, if he cannot understand, leave faith behind. Now if he can achieve understanding, he rejoices; but if he cannot, he stands in awe of what he cannot grasp" (Letter 136).[3] Faith for Anselm is not simply an epistemic attitude. It involves humility, obedience and spiritual discipline, all of which are useful in curbing the errors to which our reason is prone when it deals with matters that are far removed from our ordinary experience. Humility impresses on us the lowliness of our own minds and the loftiness of divine truth; such a recognition makes us appropriately cautious in our reasoning and saves us from groundless obstinacy in defending our positions. Obedience to Scripture and the teachings of the Church provides a determinate goal at which all our thinking must aim. Spiritual discipline clears our minds of "bodily imaginations" so that we can "discern those things that ought to be contemplated by reason itself, alone and unmixed" (*De incarnatione verbi* 1).

The error of a Christian who "leaves faith behind" because "he cannot understand" is thus at its root a moral error rather than a purely intellectual one. Yet bad reasoning occasioned by sinful conduct is still bad reasoning, and Anselm is confident that it can be counteracted by good reasoning. In arguing against the heresy of Roscelin in *De incarnatione verbi*, Anselm seems to assume that Roscelin is capable of following a rational argument that exposes his mistakes. He also recognizes that an appeal to authority would be useless, since if Roscelin had correctly understood and deferred to the authoritative texts he would not have fallen into heresy in the first place. By contrast, it is perfectly legitimate for *unbelievers* to raise objections to the truth or intelligibility of Christian doctrine, and it is incumbent on the philosophically capable believer to answer those objections. Lacking the guidance of faith, unbelievers cannot discover "the reason of faith" on their own; but a patient, honest and "moderately intelligent" unbeliever can follow and appreciate the demonstration or defence of the reason of faith that is discovered by the faithful believer.

---

3. Translations throughout are my own.

THEISTIC ARGUMENTS

In his first major work, the *Monologion*, Anselm offered several independent arguments for the existence of a self-existent being that is the source of all goodness
and is unsurpassably excellent. It does not appear that Anselm ever came to doubt
the soundness of any of these arguments, but he did become dissatisfied with their
complexity and with the variety of considerations that he had brought to bear in
order to establish his conclusions in the *Monologion*. He became obsessed with the
idea of finding "a single argument" that would establish all those conclusions, or
at least most of them, all at once.

Anselm presented that single argument – really a single form or pattern of
argument – in the *Proslogion*. The argument (baptized by Kant with the curiously
unhelpful name 'ontological argument') is Anselm's most enduring contribution
to the philosophy of religion. It has been interpreted in a bewildering variety of
ways, rejected by some notable philosophers (e.g. Aquinas, Kant) and accepted
or adapted by others (e.g. John Duns Scotus, Descartes, Plantinga, Hartshorne).
Inevitably, any statement of the argument will beg certain interpretive questions;
I will present what seems to be the default or mainstream understanding of the
argument as it appears in chapter 2 of the *Proslogion*.

God, Anselm says, is that than which nothing greater can be thought. But
according to the Psalmist, "the fool has said in his heart, 'There is no God'".
Anselm argues that the conception of God as that than which nothing greater can
be thought is all one needs in order to persuade the fool that he is wrong. For the
fool understands such a being, which means that such a being exists in his understanding. Yet that than which nothing greater can be thought cannot exist only in
his understanding. For what exists in reality is greater than what exists only in the
understanding, so if that than which nothing greater can be thought exists only in
the understanding, we can think of something greater than it: an obvious contradiction. Therefore, that than which nothing greater can be thought exists not only
in the understanding but in reality as well.

The first person to interpret the argument in this way was also the first person to
criticize it. A monk named Gaunilo wrote a "Reply on Behalf of the Fool" in which
he argued that Anselm's argument failed to give the Psalmist's fool any compelling reason to acknowledge the existence of that than which nothing greater can
be thought. Gaunilo's most celebrated objection was the 'Lost Island counter-
example'. Suppose, Gaunilo says, that someone tells me about a Lost Island so
marvellous that no island greater than it can be conceived. I understand the story,
so the Lost Island exists in my understanding. But, Gaunilo continues:

> if this person went on to draw a conclusion, and say, "You cannot any
> longer doubt that this island, more excellent than all others on earth,
> truly exists somewhere in reality. For you do not doubt that this island
> exists in your understanding, and since it is more excellent to exist not

merely in the understanding, but also in reality, this island must also exist in reality. For if it did not, any land that exists in reality would be greater than it. And so this more excellent thing that you have under-stood would not in fact be more excellent." – If, I say, he should try to convince me by this argument that I should no longer doubt whether the island truly exists, either I would think he was joking, or I would not know whom I ought to think more foolish: myself, if I grant him his conclusion, or him, if he thinks he has established the existence of that island with any degree of certainty. (Gaunilo's Reply 6)

Gaunilo clearly thought that the central problem with Anselm's original argument was the premise that it is greater to exist in reality than in the understanding alone, and many subsequent critics have accepted that diagnosis, under the slogan 'Existence is not a perfection'.

In his response to Gaunilo, however, Anselm does not defend the claim that existence is a perfection. Indeed, he denies ever having made the claim: "Nowhere in anything I said can such an argument be found". Instead, Anselm interprets the argument as identifying certain features of that than which nothing greater can be thought that are inconsistent with its being possible but non-existent. For example, when we truly have that than which nothing greater can be thought before our minds – no easy accomplishment, as Anselm emphasizes – we see right away that if it exists, it is a necessary being. Accordingly, if it exists, its existence has neither beginning nor end. For a being that cannot fail to exist is greater than a being that can fail to exist, and a being that has no beginning or end to its existence is greater than a being that comes into being or passes out of being; so a being than which a greater cannot be thought must be necessary and eternal. But when the fool thinks of that than which nothing greater can be thought as non-existent, he is obviously thinking of it as a being that can fail to exist. Moreover, it could come to exist only by beginning to exist. Hence, even if it did exist, it would have a beginning of existence and would be a contingent being; therefore, even if it did exist, it would be less great than that than which nothing greater can be thought. So when the fool thinks of that than which nothing greater can be thought existing in reality, he is thinking something greater than this being whose non-existence he was imagining a moment ago. Hence, the being the fool was thinking of as non-existent was not in fact that than which nothing greater can be thought at all. One cannot coherently suppose that that than which nothing greater can be thought is a possible but non-existent being. (This reading of the argument is developed in detail in Visser & Williams [2008].)

THE DIVINE NATURE

Recall that Anselm's aim in the *Proslogion* was to offer a single argument that would prove not only the existence of God but a wide range of conclusions about the divine nature. Even if Anselm's argument for the existence of God fails, the conception of God as that than which nothing greater can be thought is a useful one, since it means that we can affirm of God "whatever it is better to be than not to be" (*Proslogion* 5; cf. *Monologion* 15). God must, for example, be omnipotent. For if he were not, we could conceive of a being greater than he, which is impossible. Similarly, God must be just, self-existent, invulnerable to suffering, merciful, timelessly eternal, non-physical, non-composite and so forth. For if he lacked any of these qualities, he would be less than the greatest conceivable being, which is impossible.

In theory, the principle that God is whatever it is better to be than not to be allows the 'single argument' to function as a decision procedure for generating a list of divine attributes. In practice, however, the argument produces conclusions about the divine attributes only when conjoined with certain beliefs about what is greater or better. That is, it tells us that God has whatever characteristics it is better or greater to have than to lack, but it does not tell us which characteristics those are. Anselm identifies them in part by appeal to intuitions about value, in part by independent argument.

Anselm's intuitions about value are shaped by the Platonic–Augustinian tradition to which he belongs. Augustine took from the Platonists the idea that what is most fully real, and accordingly what is most fully good, is what is stable, uniform and unchanging. He says in *On Free Choice of the Will*, "And you surely could not deny that the uncorrupted is better than the corrupt, the eternal than the temporal, and the invulnerable than the vulnerable" (2.10); his interlocutor replies simply, "Could anyone?" In keeping with this view, Anselm finds no need to argue that "it is better to be ... impassible than not" (*Proslogion* 6). So God is impassible. That is, nothing can act on him; he is in no way passive. He therefore does not feel emotions, since emotions are states that one undergoes rather than actions one performs.

Yet Anselm would not be at a loss to defend divine impassibility even without appeal to this Platonic intuition about value. The theistic arguments of the *Monologion* all identify God as the ultimate source of goodness and being. That is, God is not merely supremely good, supremely great and supremely existent; he is all those things *through himself*. Everything other than God depends on God to be what it is; God alone depends on nothing but himself. If God were not impassible, he would owe some of his qualities (such as his emotional states) to creatures, in violation of divine aseity.

Notice that Augustine also found it obvious that the eternal is better than the temporal. According to Plato's *Timaeus*, time is a "moving image of eternity" (37d). It is a shifting and shadowy reflection of the really real. As later Platonists, including Augustine, develop this idea, temporal beings have their existence piecemeal; they exist only in this tiny sliver of a now, which is constantly flowing away from them and passing into nothingness. An eternal being, by contrast, enjoys "the complete possession all at once of illimitable life" (Boethius, *Consolation of*

Philosophy V.6). So it seems intuitively obvious to Anselm that if God is to be that than which nothing greater can be thought, he must be eternal. That is, he must be not merely everlasting, but outside time altogether.

In addition to this strong intuitive consideration, Anselm hints at a further argument for the claim that it is better to be eternal than temporal. He opens chapter 13 of the *Proslogion* by observing, "Everything that is at all enclosed in a place or time is less than that which is constrained by no law of place or time". His idea seems to be that if God were in time (or in a place), he would be bound by certain constraints inherent in the nature of time (or place). His discussion in *Monologion* 22 makes the problem clear:

> This, then, is the condition of place and time: whatever is enclosed within their boundaries does not escape being characterized by parts, whether the sort of parts its place receives with respect to size, or the sort its time suffers with respect to duration; nor can it in any way be contained as a whole all at once by different places or times. By contrast, if something is in no way constrained by confinement in a place or time, no law of places or times forces it into a multiplicity of parts or prevents it from being present as a whole all at once in several places or times.

So at least part of the reason for holding that God is timeless is that the nature of time would impose constraints on God, and of course it is better to be subject to no external constraints.

The other part of the reason, though, is that if God were in place or time he would have *parts*. But what is so bad about having parts? This question brings us naturally to the doctrine of divine simplicity, which is simply the doctrine that God has no parts of any kind. Most strikingly, the doctrine of divine simplicity involves the claim that there is no distinction in God between substance and accident or property and bearer. Wisdom, for example, is not a feature of God distinct from the divine essence; nor is it a property that God exemplifies. Rather, God *just is* wisdom; and so on for divine goodness, omnipotence, justice and the rest. As Anselm says, "you are whatever you are, not through anything else, but through yourself. Therefore, you are the very life by which you live, the wisdom by which you are wise, and the very goodness by which you are good" (*Proslogion* 12).

Even for an Augustinian like Anselm, the claim that it is better to lack parts than to have them is less than intuitively compelling, so Anselm offers further arguments for divine simplicity. The passage just quoted suggests an argument from divine aseity: if God's wisdom were something other than God, then God would be wise through something other than himself. The argument of *Monologion* 17 likewise relies on aseity: "Every composite", Anselm argues, "needs the things of which it is composed if it is to subsist, and it owes its existence to them, since whatever it is, it is through them, whereas those things are not through it what they are." In *Proslogion* 18, by contrast, Anselm seeks to relate simplicity to the intuitive considerations that identify what is greatest and best with what is stable, uniform and unchanging. There Anselm argues that "whatever is composed of parts is not completely one. It is in some sense a plurality and not identical with itself, and it can be broken up either in fact or at least in the understanding".

Anselm's success in generating a whole host of divine attributes does present him with a problem. He must show that the attributes are consistent with each other: in other words, that it is possible for one and the same being to have all of them. For example, there seems at first glance to be a conflict between justice and omnipotence. If God is perfectly just, he cannot lie. But if God is omnipotent, how can there be something he cannot do? Anselm's solution is to explain that omnipotence does not mean the ability to do everything; instead, it means the possession of unlimited power. Now the 'ability' or 'power' to lie is not really a power at all; it is a kind of weakness. Being omnipotent, God has no weakness. So it turns out that omnipotence actually *entails* the inability to lie.

Another apparent contradiction is between God's mercy and his justice. If God is just, he will surely punish the wicked as they deserve. But because he is merciful, he spares the wicked. Anselm first tries to resolve this apparent contradiction by appealing to a third attribute, goodness, that entails both justice and mercy. The more extensive God's goodness, the better God is; so it is best for God to be good to the good by rewarding them and good to the wicked both by punishing them and by showing them mercy. But Anselm is not content to resolve the apparent tension between justice and mercy by appealing to some other attribute, goodness, that entails both justice and mercy; he goes on to argue that justice itself requires mercy. Justice to sinners obviously requires that God punish them; but God's justice *to himself* requires that he exercise his supreme goodness in sparing the wicked. "Thus", Anselm says to God, "in saving us whom you might justly destroy ... you are just, not because you give us our due, but because you do what is fitting for you who are supremely good" (*Proslogion* 10). In spite of these arguments, Anselm acknowledges that there is a residue of mystery here:

> Thus your mercy is born of your justice, since it is just for you to be so good that you are good even in sparing the wicked. And perhaps this is why the one who is supremely just can will good things for the wicked. But even if one can somehow grasp why you can will to save the wicked, certainly no reasoning can comprehend why, from those who are alike in wickedness, you save some rather than others through your supreme goodness and condemn some rather than others through your supreme justice.   (*Proslogion* 11)

In other words, the philosopher can trace the conceptual relations among goodness, justice and mercy, and show that God not only can but must have all three;

but no human reasoning can hope to show why God displays his justice and mercy in precisely the ways in which he does.

THINKING AND SPEAKING ABOUT GOD

An unsurpassably perfect being must in some sense be beyond our power to capture in words. The language that we derive from our experience of changeable, composite and imperfect creatures, one might think, cannot apply with its usual meaning to an immutable, simple and perfect God. Unfortunately, this observation seems to undercut the very arguments that establish the existence and nature of God, since those arguments seem to depend on taking words in their usual senses. Anselm sees the difficulty clearly: "What meaning did I understand in all the words I thought, if not their ordinary and customary meaning? So if the customary meaning of words is inapplicable to God, none of my conclusions about him is correct" (*Monologion* 26).

We might state Anselm's problem as follows:

> God has nothing in common with creatures. But if he has nothing in common with creatures, then there is nothing common to the meanings of words that are predicated of both God and creatures. Where the meanings of words are not common, there is equivocation; and where there is equivocation, there is no successful argumentation. Therefore, there are no successful arguments from what we know about creatures to any conclusion about God.

Anselm quite clearly rejects this final conclusion, yet he continues to uphold the first premise, that God has nothing in common with creatures. He must therefore find a way to safeguard divine uniqueness and ineffability while providing an account of the language we use about God that permits successful argumentation.

Anselm distinguishes two ways of saying a thing as well as two ways of understanding a thing. We can say (or signify, or express) a thing 'through its own *proprietas*' or 'through something else' (*per aliud*); we can understand a thing 'through its own *proprietas*' or 'through some likeness or image'. A *proprietas* in this context is what sets a thing apart, what distinguishes it from other things. Since God has nothing in common with creatures, he is, as it were, all *proprietas*. Yet both our descriptions of God and our knowledge of God are derived from creatures. Accordingly, we neither say God nor understand God through his *proprietas*.

Yet this does not mean that we do not say God or understand God at all. Anselm develops a theory of signification *per aliud* in *De grammatico*. A word brings to mind what it signifies. When it signifies something *per se*, it brings that thing to mind directly or straightforwardly; when it signifies something *per aliud*, it brings that thing to mind only in virtue of some additional knowledge or some other feature of the context of utterance. We signify God *per aliud* because all the words we use in speaking about God bring him to mind only indirectly, in light of the knowledge about God derived either from natural theology or from Scripture. What 'wisdom' brings straightforwardly to mind is the perfection that we discern in human beings who order their affairs well or have a grasp of philosophical truth. Yet 'wisdom' does bring God to mind, if only obliquely, because both Scripture and reason tell us that good order and truthful thinking reflect the all-encompassing governance of divine truth, in which they find their ultimate source. In this way the word 'wisdom' "hints at (*innuit*)" divine wisdom "through a certain likeness" (*Monologion* 65).

We also understand God *per aliud* or 'through some likeness or image'. For Anselm, *all* human cognition involves likenesses or images. These likenesses need not be mental pictures; concepts count as likenesses as well. The more accurate a concept is, the more it is 'like' the thing being conceived. For example, I can understand a human being by having a mental image of a human being or by entertaining the concept *rational animal*. The concept *rational animal* is an altogether satisfactory way to understand a human being, since it captures the *proprietas* of human being: what is true of all and only human beings. We can never have such an accurate 'likeness' of God, because we cannot capture God's *proprietas* in our thought in that way. Moreover, the likeness through which we conceive human beings is derived from our experience of human beings, whereas the likeness through which we conceive God is derived from our experience of things other than God. Thus, we understand God *per aliud* in two senses: we conceive God through likenesses that do not reveal God's *proprietas*, and those likenesses get their content from our experience of things other than God.

In this way we do succeed in both signifying and understanding an unsurpassably perfect being who has nothing in common with the objects of our ordinary experience. Yet we always signify or understand God *per aliud*, and in that sense God may be called 'ineffable'. Something that is ineffable in this sense can still be successfully investigated through reasoning: "it is perfectly possible for our conclusions thus far about the supreme nature to be true and yet for that nature itself to remain ineffable, if we suppose that it was in no way expressed through the *proprietas* of his essence but in some way or other designated *per aliud*" (*Monologion* 65). And since there is no successful argumentation where the senses of words are not common, Anselm does not in the end accept the claim that the words used of both God and creatures have a different sense in those two uses. In fact, his account of divine ineffability rests on the assumption that such words are used in their customary senses even when we are talking about God: for it is precisely *because* the senses of our words are derived from, and straightforwardly applicable to, creatures that we can see and say God only *per aliud*. Those words, used in those senses, can establish only a tenuous connection between the human mind and an utterly unique God; but a tenuous connection is still a connection, enough to banish the spectre of equivocation and permit a robust, if always cautious, rational theology.

THE PROBLEM OF FOREKNOWLEDGE AND FREEDOM

An unsurpassably perfect being will also be unlimited in knowledge. And since, as we have seen, Anselm thinks of God as timelessly eternal, all of time is present to him. Therefore, what is future to us is present to God and therefore known by God. Since it is impossible for God to be mistaken, however, it seems that some sort of necessity attaches to the things God foreknows. Yet among the things God foreknows are the free actions of rational creatures and, as Anselm understands freedom, free actions are precisely those that do not come about by necessity. For this reason, Anselm says, "God's foreknowledge seems to be incompatible with free choice, since it is necessary that the things God foreknows are going to be, whereas things done by free choice do not result from any necessity" (*De concordia* 1.1).

Anselm's first solution to the problem is to argue that God's foreknowledge actually *guarantees* freedom. If indeed something in the future will be done freely – that is, not as a result of necessity – then God foreknows that it will be done freely, since God's foreknowledge is complete. And since God's foreknowledge is not only complete but also infallible, it follows that God's foreknowledge of a future free action guarantees that the future action will indeed be done freely and not necessarily. As Anselm puts it, "it is necessary that some future thing is going to be without necessity" (*ibid.*). Therefore, the necessity associated with divine foreknowledge does not threaten, but in fact guarantees, the absence of necessity associated with free action.

If this response is to carry conviction, Anselm must distinguish two kinds of necessity: one kind that characterizes what God foreknows, and a different kind that characterizes unfree actions as such. Anselm calls the kind of necessity that is incompatible with freedom 'antecedent necessity'. An action is antecedently necessary if it can be explained entirely by the nature that God has bestowed on the agent. Antecedently necessary actions are thus "the work and gift of God" (*De casu diaboli* 13), whereas free actions have their ultimate origin in the agent – exercising, of course, the powers inherent in the nature that God has bestowed, but in a way that is not determined by God's action. 'Subsequent necessity', by contrast, is logical necessity of the sort that attaches to statements of the form 'If p, then p' or 'If x is F, x is F' (as argued in Visser & Williams [2008] against Knuuttila [2004]). Such necessity is causally inert, and therefore no threat to freedom.

The necessity that characterizes what is foreknown is subsequent necessity, not the antecedent necessity that is incompatible with freedom. In fact, the necessity of 'If God foreknows x, x will occur' is exactly the same as the clearly trivial necessity of 'If x will be in the future, x will be in the future':

Moreover, if one carefully considers the meaning of the word, merely by saying that something is foreknown, one is saying that it is going to be. For only what is going to be is foreknown, since only what is true can be known. So when I say that if God foreknows something, it is necessary that it is going to be, that is the same as saying that if it will be, it will be by necessity. And that necessity does not compel or constrain anything to be or not to be. (*De concordia* 1.2)

So it is not the case that future free actions will be done because they are (subsequently) necessary; rather, they are (subsequently) necessary because they will be done. Subsequent necessity is an effect, not a cause; and what threatens freedom is *causal* compulsion.

FURTHER READING

Davies, B. & B. Leftow (eds) 2004. *The Cambridge Companion to Anselm*. Cambridge: Cambridge University Press.

Evans, G. 1978. *Anselm and Talking About God*. Oxford: Clarendon Press.

Holopainen, T. 1996. *Dialectic and Theology in the Eleventh Century*. Leiden: Brill.

Hopkins, J. 1972. *A Companion to the Study of St Anselm*. Minneapolis, MN: University of Minnesota Press.

Klima, G. 2000. "Saint Anselm's Proof: A Problem of Reference, Identity and Mutual Understanding". In *Medieval Philosophy and Modern Times*, G. Hintikka (ed.), 69–88. Dordrecht: Kluwer.

Plantinga, A. (ed.) 1965. *The Ontological Argument*. Garden City, NY: Anchor Books.

Southern, R. W. 1991. *Anselm: A Portrait in Landscape*. Cambridge: Cambridge University Press.

Spade, P. 1976. "Ambiguity in Anselm". *International Journal of Philosophy of Religion* 7: 443–5.

Wolterstorff, N. 1993. "In Defense of Gaunilo's Defense of the Fool". In *Christian Perspectives on Religious Knowledge*, C. Evans & M. Westphal (eds), 87–111. Grand Rapids, MI: Eerdmans.

On DIVINITY see also Ch. 8; Vol. 1, Chs 8, 18, 19, 20. On EXISTENCE OF GOD see also Chs 5, 13, 14; Vol. 1, Chs 18, 19; Vol. 3, Chs 6, 12, 13, 14, 15, 21; Vol. 5, Chs 11, 16. On FAITH see also Chs 12, 16, 18; Vol. 1, Ch. 13; Vol. 3, Ch. 8; Vol. 4, Chs 8, 10, 13; Vol. 5, Chs 7, 18. On FOREKNOWLEDGE see also Ch. 2; Vol. 3, Ch. 13. On ONTOLOGICAL ARGUMENT see also Vol. 5, Chs 5, 22.

7

AL-GHAZALI

Michael Marmura

Al-Ghazali (al-Ghazālī), Abū Ḥāmid Ibn Muḥammad Ibn Muḥammad al-Ṭūsī (1058–1111), a towering figure in the history of Islamic religious thought, was trained in Islamic law (*fiqh*) and Islamic theology (*kalām*). A severe logical critic of the philosophers al-Farabi (*d. c.*950) and Avicenna (Ibn Sina, *d.* 1037), condemning them as infidels for some of their philosophical theories, he none-theless reinterpreted some of Avicenna's ideas and incorporated them within his theology. At the age of thirty-seven, he abandoned a prestigious teaching post in Baghdad to follow an ascetic mystic path. He became a noted Islamic mystic, a Sufi, and endeavoured to reconcile Sufism with traditional Islamic belief.

LIFE AND WORKS

Born in the city of Ṭūsī, or its environs, in northeast Persia, al-Ghazali was educated in *madāris* (singular, *madrasa*). He studied first in Ṭūsī, and then in Jurjān on the Caspian Sea. His big educational move took place around 1077, when he went to the *madrasa* in Nīshāpūr, where he studied with Imām al-Ḥaramayn al-Juwaynī, a jurist of the school of al-Shāfiʿī (*d.* 820) and the leading theologian of the Ashʿarite school, named after its founder, al-Ashʿarī (*d.* 935). There are indications that during his study with al-Juwaynī, al-Ghazali had an exposure to philosophy. His intensive study of it, however, came later in Baghdad.

After al-Juwaynī's death, al-Ghazali remained in Nīshāpūr for some six years. He acquired the reputation of being a brilliant scholar of law. His writings in this period were on Islamic law. He was supported by Niẓām al-Mulk (*d.* 1092), the vizier of the Seljuk Turkish sultans. These sultans held the real power in Baghdad, the seat of the Abbasid caliphs. Their power, however, received its legitimacy from the Abbasid caliph. The Seljuk Turks had adopted Islam in its 'orthodox', Sunnī, form, and hence were in conflict with the counter Shīʿite caliphate in Egypt, the Fāṭimid, that took its name from Fāṭima, the daughter of the Prophet

Muhammad and wife of his cousin 'Alī. The Fāṭimid caliphs traced their ancestry to her.

Niẓām al-Mulk was noted for establishing a series of religious colleges, *madrasas*, for the teaching of Shāfi'ī law, partly to counteract Fāṭimid teaching. These colleges were known as the Niẓāmiyyas, after the name of their founder. The most prestigious of these colleges was the Niẓāmiyya in Baghdad. Niẓām al-Mulk appointed al-Ghazali as the professor of Shāfi'ī law at the Niẓāmiyya in Baghdad. With this appointment al-Ghazali became part of the Abbasid–Seljuk establishment and we find that in this period, which lasted from 1091 to 1095, he wrote at the request of the Abbasid caliph al-Muztaẓhir (*d.* 1118) *Faḍā'iḥal-Bāṭiniyya* (The scandals of the esoterics), a theological attack on Fāṭimid theological doctrine.

Probably at the beginning of this period, al-Ghazali underwent a period of scepticism. He tells us in his autobiography, written a few years before his death, that he began to doubt the senses: the shadow's movement, he reminded us, is imperceptible, yet we know that it takes place; again, an object like the sun appears as having the size of a coin, when astronomical proof indicates that it is larger than our earth. If the senses can deceive us, can we trust reason, namely, its primary principles such as the law of excluded middle? For, he observed, one cannot demonstrate the truth of such a principle without circular reasoning: without assuming it. This doubting of reason, he tells us, became a physical affliction that lasted two months. God, he then states, restored to him belief in reason.

It is during this Baghdad period that, despite having a heavy teaching schedule, al-Ghazali applied himself to an intensive study of philosophy, particularly the philosophy of Avicenna. He was impressed by Avicenna's logical writings. Deeming this logic a doctrinally neutral instrument of knowledge, he urged his fellow theologians and lawyers to adopt it. He maintained that it was essentially the same logic they used, but more elaborate and refined. He wrote several expositions of Avicenna's logic. These included *The Standard for Knowledge* (*Mi'ār al-'Ilm*) and *The Touchstone of Theoretical Investigation* (*Miḥakk al-Naẓar*), as well as the first part of his *The Aims of the Philosophers* (*Maqāṣid al-Falāsifa*) (hereafter *The Aims*), which is generally recognized as belonging to this period. In the Introduction and Conclusion of *The Aims*, he states that he composed it to explain the theories of the Islamic philosophers (al-Farabi and Avicenna) as a prelude to his critique of these philosophers in his *The Incoherence of the Philosophers* (*Tahāfut al-Falāsifa*) (hereafter *The Incoherence*), which belonged to this period.

Speaking strictly from the point of view of the history of Islamic and European philosophy, *The Incoherence* is al-Ghazali's most important and influential work. It is an incisive logical critique directed at the philosophies of al-Farabi and Avicenna. Its primary purpose was to show that these philosophers had failed to 'demonstrate' their theories. In this work, his aim was to refute. To this period, however, belonged his most important theological book, *Moderation in Belief* (*Al-Iqtiṣād Fī al-I'tiqād*), a work he continued to regard highly after he became a mystic.

In 1095 al-Ghazali underwent a spiritual crisis that resulted in a physical illness and a temporary loss of speech. As he confessed in his autobiography, he realized that his motivation in his teaching and writing career was worldly success. It was not a genuine religious impulse. Underlying this was a dissatisfaction with the purely intellectual, doctrinal, aspects of religion. These, he realized, bypassed the religiously experiential, the *dhawq*, literally 'taste', the Sufis talked about. He had read the works of the Sufis and realized that it is their mystical experience that yielded the certainty in knowledge that had always been his real quest. Deciding to leave Baghdad and follow the Sufi path, he made appropriate arrangements for the welfare of his family, who were to remain in this city. Moreover, to leave his teaching post at the Niẓāmiyya without opposition from the authorities, he gave as a reason for his departure the intention to go on a pilgrimage to Mecca.

He first went to Damascus, where he secluded himself in the minaret of its great mosque. He then went to Jerusalem, where he secluded himself in the Dome of the Rock, visited Hebron and then travelled to Mecca and Madina. For some twelve years he abandoned teaching, following the path of Sufism. During this period he wrote his magnum opus, the voluminous *The Revival of the Sciences of Religion* (*Iḥyā' 'ulūm al-Dīn*) (hereafter *The Revival*). In this work and shorter works he strove to reconcile traditional Islamic beliefs with Sufi teaching.

In 1106, at the urging of the Seljuks, he resumed teaching law, first at Nīshāpūr and then at Ṭūs, where he died in 1111. During this period he wrote his major work on law, *The Choice Essentials of the Principles of Religion* (*Al-Muṣtasfā min Uṣūl al-Dīn*). He introduced this work with yet another account of Avicenna's logic as a useful tool for legal reasoning. After writing *The Revival*, he wrote a number of important and shorter non-legal works. These include: *The Highest Goal in Explaining the Beautiful Names of God* (*Al-Maqṣad al-Asnā fī Asmā' al-Lāh al-Ḥusnā*); *The Jewels of the Qur'an* (*Jawāhir al-Qur'ān*); *The Book of Forty* (*Kitāb al-Arba'īn*), which sums up some of the main ideas in *The Revival*; *The Just Balance* (*Al-Qisṭās al-Mustaqīm*), a defence of logic and a critique of the Shī'ite theory of knowledge to which the Fāṭimids subscribed; *The Decisive Criterion for Distinguishing Belief from Unbelief* (*Fayṣal al-Tafriqa Bayna al-Islām wa al-Zandaqa*); two mystical works, *The Alchemy of Happiness* (*Kimīa-ye sa'ādat*), written in Persian, and *The Niche of Lights* (*Mishkāt al-Anwār*); his autobiography, *The Deliverer from Error* (*Al-Munqidh min al-Ḍalāl*); and his last work, *Restraining the Commonality from the Science of Kalām* (*Iljām al-'Awām 'an 'Ilmal-Kalām*).

AL-GHAZALI AND THEOLOGY (*KALĀM*)

Background

Kalām, sometimes designated as Islamic 'dialectical' theology, other times as Islamic 'speculative' theology, had its germinal beginnings with the political conflicts that followed the death of the Prophet Muhammad in 632. They centred around the question of who was to succeed the Prophet as leader of the Islamic community. One group insisted that the leadership should be confined to ʿAlī, the cousin and son-in-law of the Prophet, and his descendants. This group was referred to as 'the party', the *shīʿa*, of ʿAlī, from which the term *Shīʿite* derives. Others disagreed on this point, and in time began to be referred to as *Sunnīs*, followers of the customary way of life of the Prophet. The religious and political aspects of the conflict were intertwined. They gave rise to such questions as the nature of true belief, the extent to which human acts are predetermined, and the fate in the hereafter of the unrepentant yet gravely sinful Muslim.

By the middle of the eighth century, we have the beginnings of a school of theology that was to become dominant for a period of time. This was the Muʿtazilite school. The name derives from the verb *iʿtazala*, 'to withdraw'. Some scholars have maintained that it acquired this name because it 'withdrew' or detached itself from the conflict between the Shīʿites and the Sunnīs. This school had two main branches, that of Basra and that of Baghdad, and many sub-branches. It defined itself as adhering to five principles. The first two of these principles, those of divine unity and divine justice, were the most basic.

By divine unity the Muʿtazilites meant that there is no multiplicity in the divine essence. This raised the question of the relation of the divine eternal attributes mentioned in the Qurʾan to the divine essence. Would not affirming their existence introduce multiplicity in God's essence? One answer was that these attributes are identical with the divine essence. This raised two difficulties. The first is the difficulty of distinguishing one attribute from another. A more serious difficulty was that this identification meant that the divine act proceeded from God's nature or essence. This meant that God by his very nature was compelled to act. But would this not mean the denial of the attribute of will? To resolve this difficulty, the idea that the divine will itself was created was proposed. But then such a will would have to be preceded by another will that created it and this latter by yet another will and so on *ad infinitum*. Other Muʿtazilites strove in ingenious ways to interpret the divine attributes mentioned in the Qurʾan in a manner that would not violate the principle of God's unity.

Their second cardinal principle, that of divine justice, entailed the doctrine of free will. A just God cannot reward or punish people for acts they are predetermined to do, or for acts that are beyond their capacity. Hence they maintained that human beings are morally accountable only for those acts they could do and can choose to do. Related to this is their belief that reason, independently of revelation, discerns in the moral acts their intrinsic 'goodness' or 'badness'. Hence, it is because an act is in itself morally good that God commands it and because it is in itself an evil act that God prohibits it. It is neither good nor bad simply because God either commands or prohibits it.

Al-Ghazali's Ash'arism

Ash'arism can perhaps be best understood as a reinterpretation of these two principles. Its founder al-Ash'arī, originally a Mu'tazilite of the school of Basra, rebelled against it, maintaining that it deviated from the traditional Islamic belief. He, however, sought to defend the more traditional belief by the use of reason. Al-Ghazali's position, basically that of al-Ash'arī, introduced certain refinements to it and is noted for reinterpreting some ideas of Avicenna, adapting them to his Asha'rite world perspective.

This perspective relates to the Ash'arite doctrine of the eternal divine attributes. As al-Ghazali explains it, such attributes as life, knowledge, will and power, although intimately related to the divine essence, are not identical with it. They are 'additional' to it. This does not violate the concept of divine unity. Just as ordinarily speaking a human does not become 'many' because of having life, knowledge, will and power, the divine essence does not become 'many' by the 'additional' divine attributes. These attributes, not being identical with the divine essence, do not impose any limitation on the divine act. Such an act is not the necessary consequence of the divine nature or essence. It is a free act, chosen by the eternal will. True enough, what the eternal divine will chooses is necessary in the sense that it must come to be. But the divine will could have chosen a different act or not to act at all. Once it chooses an act – and al-Ghazali reminds us that this language is metaphorical – what it chooses must come to be.

If such eternal attributes as life, knowledge, will and power are co-eternal, how do they relate to each other? There can be no knowledge without life, no will without knowledge, and no power without will. Life is a necessary condition for the existence of knowledge, knowledge a condition for will, and will a condition for power. To say that the existence of one attribute is a necessary condition for the existence of another does not mean that it is its cause. All these divine attributes are uncaused and co-eternal.

What God eternally wills is brought about by divine power. The attribute of divine power, which again is 'additional' to the divine essence, is pervasive. It does not consist of individual powers. It is an eternal power that brings about each and every existing entity and event, including the human act. In line with this occasionalist view, al-Ghazali holds that existents other than God have no causal efficacy. Rather, it is divine power that is the direct cause of all created existents and events. For al-Ghazali and the Ash'arites, the world consists of transient atoms and their transient accidents, that is, transient qualities all of which are the direct creation of divine power.

Al-Ghazali's main Ash'arite objection to the second cardinal Mu'tazilite doctrine, the principle of divine justice, is that it contradicts the concept of divine omnipotence. It imposes values extraneous to God to which God must adhere. For al-Ghazali, there are no moral values that belong intrinsically to acts. An act is morally good if God commands it, bad if he prohibits it. Moreover, the

Mu'tazilite view that human beings initiate or, as they expressed it, 'create' those acts for which they are morally responsible makes these acts impossible for God to perform. By definition, these acts are 'creaturely' acts, outside the province of direct divine power. God can create similar acts, but not identical ones.

If al-Ghazali, then, denies the Mu'tazilite claim that people choose and 'create' those acts for which they are morally accountable, how does he account for human moral responsibility? This brings us to his defence of the Ash'arite doctrine of *kasb*, 'acquisition'. According to this doctrine the human act, like any event in the world, is the direct creation of divine power. To create such an act, divine power must also create the necessary conditions for it, namely, life, knowledge, will and power, each of these attributes being also the direct creation of divine power. Does this mean that the created power in human beings is efficacious? Al-Ghazali maintains that it is not. He holds that what we ordinarily regard as the effect of our own power is also created for us by divine power. It is an 'acquistion' God creates for us. Moreover, human power is created with the creation of the human act that accompanies it. It does not precede the act.

Al-Ghazali holds that this theory is a compromise between extreme determinism and the doctrine of free will. But if human power is not efficacious, how do we differentiate the spasmodic movement from the one we regard as due to our own power and will? The answer to this is that both movements are created by divine power. The spasmodic movement, however, is created without the created power, while the movement we regard as being by our own doing is created simultaneously with the creation of human power. We ourselves experience the difference between the two movements. Al-Ghazali does not deny that this theory poses difficulties, particularly in relation to the question of moral responsibility. But the difficulties, he maintains, arise because we are thinking on the mundane level. It is through mystical vision (*al-mushāhada*) that the true nature of the doctrine of acquisition becomes comprehensible to us.

AL-GHAZALI AND PHILOSOPHY

In *The Incoherence*, al-Ghazali subjects twenty theories of the Islamic philosophers al-Farabi and Avicenna to logical criticism. Both philosophers had formulated closely related but not identical emanative metaphysical systems. Al-Ghazali's main criticisms are directed against Avicenna, but many of his criticisms apply to al-Farabi as well. The motive for al-Ghazali's criticism is religious. His approach, however, is logical: to prove that, contrary to the claims of these philosophers, they have failed to demonstrate their theories. Of the twenty theories he criticized, he regarded seventeen as heretical innovations, to some of which one Islamic sect or another had subscribed. Three, however, he regarded as utterly contrary to Islamic teaching, charging those who upheld them with infidelity (*kufr*).

The first of the three theories he condemned is the theory of the world's pre-eternity. According to Avicenna, the world emanates from God as a necessary consequence of the divine essence. In other words, it is by God's very nature or essence that God must bring about the existence of all other beings. For Avicenna, the essential cause does not precede its effect in time. It coexists with it. God is eternally in act. The world is the necessitated coexisting effect of an eternal essential cause. It must hence be eternal. For al-Ghazali, this meant a denial of the divine attribute of will. This also meant the denial of the eternal attributes presupposed by the eternal will: the divine attributes of life and knowledge. The second theory he rejected is Avicenna's theory that God knows only the universal aspects of the particulars in the terrestrial world. This meant, as al-Ghazali pointed out, that God does not have particular knowledge of individual human beings and their individual actions. It is thus a denial of divine omniscience, of the divine attribute of knowledge, as understood in traditional Islam.

Al-Ghazali then argues against Avicenna's theory of the individual immortality of souls according to which there is no bodily resurrection. While he agrees with Avicenna that there are spiritual rewards in the hereafter that are higher than the physical, the Qur'anic descriptions of physical rewards and punishments in the afterlife can only be rejected if the impossibility of bodily resurrection is demonstrated. But, argued al-Ghazali, none of Avicenna's arguments to prove such an impossibility have been demonstrated.

In the seventeenth Discussion of *The Incoherence*, al-Ghazali offers his famous critique of natural causation. The main concern behind this critique is the question of the miracles reported in the Scriptures. Avicenna maintained that some of these reports are literally true because they can be explained in terms of his theory of natural causation. Some reports, however, contradict such a theory. Hence, they cannot be true, and the language reporting them must be interpreted by the philosophers as metaphorical. With this, al-Ghazali strenuously disagrees.

He begins with a declaration of the Ash'arite position, namely, that the connection between what we habitually believe to be a cause and effect is not a necessary one. With any two things, where the existence of one does not entail the existence of the other, each can exist separately from the other. Some of the examples he gives are drinking and the quenching of thirst, satiety and eating, burning and contact with fire. All these are concomitant events, that God creates 'side by side'. God could create any of these without the other. He could, for example, create death without decapitation and a continuation of life after decapitation. Consider a piece of cotton when in contact with fire. What you actually observe is the occurrence of burning *with* the contact; you do not observe the burning *by* the fire. It is God, al-Ghazali then states, who enacts the burning.

Al-Ghazali then raises a possible objection an opponent may raise: if this is the case and the causal disconnection of natural things is deemed possible, then chaos would ensue. Al-Ghazali responds that such chaos does not ensue, for these are possibilities rather than necessities, and God in his goodness does not create for us a disorderly course in nature. But even if we grant the opponent that there are necessary causal connections in nature, provided one does not deny God voluntary action, the miracles deemed impossible remain possible though divine intervention. This does not mean that al-Ghazali subscribes to this theory. On the contrary, in the *Moderation* and the *Revival* he gives explicit endorsement to the Ashʻarite doctrine that denies necessary causal connection in things, attributing all action to divine power.

It is, however, al-Ghazali's endorsement of Avicenna's logic that once again raises the causal question. Al-Ghazali held that this logic is a philosophically neutral tool of knowledge. This includes for him Aristotelian demonstration. But for Avicenna, who follows Aristotle in this, scientific demonstration is based on the causal theory al-Ghazali rejects. For a resolution of this difficulty, al-Ghazali invokes the Ashʻarite doctrine of *irjāʾ al-ʻāda*: God's ordaining events to proceed in a habitual, uniform way. This uniformity is not necessary in itself and hence can be disrupted. This disruption occurs when God creates a miracle on behalf of a prophet. When such a miracle occurs, God removes momentarily from the believer knowledge of this uniformity, creating in its stead knowledge of the miracle. Ordinarily, the world follows the uniform pattern ordained by the divine will, a pattern that includes those events we normally regard as causes and effects. Such events behave as though they are real causes and effects, when in fact they are not. Rather, they are concomitant events that have no causal efficacy. But they follow an order that parallels the cause–effect sequences in Avicenna's philosophy. It is on this basis that al-Ghazali advocates causal reasoning and scientific demonstrative inference. In other words, al-Ghazali accepts the reasoning pattern of demonstrative logic, substituting for its underlying Aristotelian causal theory his own Ashʻarite theory.

MYSTICISM

In approaching al-Ghazali's mysticism a first question that arises is its relation to his Ashʻarite *kalām*. For although he was an Ashʻarite in theology, he was critical of this discipline and his criticisms of it are related to his mysticism. A second question concerns the relation of his mysticism to his attitude towards philosophy.

In his autobiography he tells us that he had contributed works to *kalām*, yet it did not satisfy his quest after certainty. He held that the main function of *kalām* – by which he intended *Ashʻarite kalām* – is the defence of Sunni Islamic belief against heretical innovations. This defence is certainly needed. But the teaching of *kalām* should be confined to the few; the masses should not be exposed to it. They will not understand its arguments, which will simply confuse them, leading them to a loss of faith. There are Muslims who can follow its arguments, and if afflicted by doubts about their faith *kalām* could provide a remedy. It could restore to them their faith. *Kalām*, for al-Ghazali, is thus a means to an end. It is an error to take it as an end in itself, to believe that indulging in it constitutes what is experientially religious. In *The Revival*, he indicates that some ardent, sincere theologians have committed such an error. Their dogmatic defence of Islamic belief has often acted as a veil preventing them from the apprehension of 'realities'.

What, then, are these 'realities'? These, for al-Ghazali, belong to the realm of the unseen, to the world of the divine kingdom (*'ālam al-malakūt*). Glimpses of this world are attained through direct mystic vision (*mushāhada*), leading to the knowledge that the only reality is God and his acts. This is experiential knowledge, *ma'rifa*, gnosis, and it varies in degrees of intensity as the mystic wayfarer advances in the spiritual journey towards the divine.

However, traditional belief, as defended by *kalām*, and gnosis are related. Al-Ghazali illustrates this by an example. The belief that a certain individual is in the house may be due to the fact that the one who informs us about this is a person we have always known to be truthful. This belief is analogous to the belief of the common people, who accept the truths of religion on faith. They would have heard such truths from their parents and teachers. These truths become firmly established in their hearts. But this does not guarantee total immunity to error. If, however, in addition to being informed by a reliable witness about the existence of the individual in the house, one also hears his voice, the certainty that such an individual is in the house increases, although again error may take place. This level of knowing is akin to that of the theologians who add to traditional belief some evidential proof (*dalīl*). It is, however, when one gets into the house and actually sees the individual that one attains certainty. This is analogous to the gnosis of the mystic. Al-Ghazali then explains that cognitions of the Gnostics vary in degree of intensity and clarity and even in the number of the things apprehended. This knowledge, however, remains certain because it represents what is directly experienced.

Some of our thoughts on the mundane level often lead us to paradoxes. This is particularly the case when struggling with such questions as determinism and the freedom of the will. It is through mystical insight, which provides access to the realm of the divine kingdom, that such paradoxes are resolved. For the mystic would then have a vision of things in their true light.

Turning to al-Ghazali's attitude towards philosophy, even though he was a severe critic of the Islamic philosophers, he was also infuenced by them. There are particularly two areas of his thinking where this influence is seen, namely, in the realms of moral philosophy and metaphysics. Al-Ghazali adapts to his mystical thought certain moral concepts that are largely Aristotelian. He also develops a metaphysical framework (inspired by the famous verse of light, Qur'an 24:35, to be discussed below), wherein he expresses his mystical thought. In this there is a discernible Avicennan influence.

The most conspicuous of the Aristotelian moral concepts that al-Ghazali embraces and adapts is the doctrine of the mean. He introduces it in terms of the Aristotelian/Avicennan theory of the division of the human rational faculty into the theoretical and the practical. In summing up Avicenna's theory of the soul in the eighteenth Discussion of *The Incoherence*, he indicates that this theory can be interpreted in terms of the Ash'arite doctrine of *irjā' al-'āda* (defined earlier in discussing al-Ghazali's endorsement of Avicenna's logic). The doctrine of the mean developed in other writings by al-Ghazali is introduced in discussions of the practical faculty. The task of this faculty is to control and manage the lower faculties. This involves developing those dispositions that are termed virtues. These consist of the mean between excess and deficiency. The typical example al-Ghazali gives is Aristotle's definition of courage as the mean between cowardice and rashness. Al-Ghazali, however, introduces a religious, Islamic, element to this concept of the mean, as he maintains that it is arrived at through both reason and the revealed law. Divine help is needed for arriving at it. This doctrine entails habituating the soul to act in moderation and to subdue the animal passions. It is an act of purification, a requirement of piety for Muslims in general and a necessary prerequisite for the mystic wayfarer in his journey towards gnosis. Pursuit of the mean leads to a hierarchy of virtues, the highest of which is the love of God.

Turning to metaphysics, the most philosophically metaphysical of al-Ghazali's works is his *The Niche of Lights* (*Mishkāt al-Anwār*), an interpretation of the beautiful verse of light (Qur'an 24:35) which begins, "God is the light of the heavens and the earth". Avicenna had given a philosophical interpretation of this verse in terms of his emanative worldview. One discerns here the influence of Avicenna's emanative metaphysics and epistemology on al-Ghazali's interpretation. The two interpretations, however, remain different.

For al-Ghazali, the true light is God. Physical light is only light in a metaphorical sense. This does not mean that it does not have real existence on the mundane level. It has this mundane reality and experiencing it is a first step in the process leading to mystical knowledge. We know physical light through sight. Sight, however, has its limitations: a higher form of knowing that overcomes these limitations is through reason. It involves the act of intellectual apprehension on the philosophical level. This is knowledge of the elect (*al-khawāṣṣ*). There is, however, a higher level of intellectual apprehension, confined to "the elect of the elect" (*khawāṣṣ al-khawāṣṣ*), the mystics, which can bring about a gradual access to the realm of the divine.

All creation is an effusion of a series of lights, descending from God. These represent levels of light that are hierarchically arranged, the closest to God, the source of all the lights, being the highest. There are some parallels here between this view and Avicenna's emanative system. But these parallels must be drawn with caution. For in the third Discussion of *The Incoherence*, al-Ghazali subjected Avicenna's emanative scheme, as expressed in the *Metaphysics* of his voluminous *The Healing* (*Al-Shifā'*), to severe criticism. Avicenna's explanation of how the world emanates from God, al-Ghazali points out, is arbitrary and involves absurd non sequiturs. There is nothing in *The Niche of Lights* to indicate that al-Ghazali no longer subscribes to the criticism of Avicenna's emanative system in *The*

Incoherence. What seems to be a more basic difference between his metaphysics and that of Avicenna is that in *The Niche of Lights* al-Ghazali is speaking of a level of apprehension, that of "the elect of the elect", that is higher than Avicenna's philosophical level, at least as the latter expresses it in the *Metaphysics* of *The Healing*. On the other hand, when it comes to Avicenna's description of the mystic's spiritual journey in his late work, *Directives and Pointers* (*Al-Ishārāt wa al-Tanbīhāt*), we discern an affinity between the mystical views of these two thinkers.

FURTHER READING

Fakhry, M. 1958. *Islamic Occasionalism and Its Critique by Averroes and Aquinas.* London: Allen & Unwin.

Hourani, G. 1976. "Ghazali on Ethical Action". *Journal of the American Oriental Society* **96**: 69–98.

Marmura, M. 1965. "Al-Ghazali and Demonstrative Science". *Journal of the History of Philosophy* **111**: 183–209.

Marmura, M. 2002. "Ghazali and Ash'arism Revisited". *Arabic Sciences and Philosophy* **12**: 91–111.

Marmura, M. 2004. *Probing in Islamic Philosophy: Studies in the Philosophies of Ibn Sina, al-Ghazali and Other Major Muslim Thinkers.* Binghamton, NY: Global Academic Publications.

Shehadi, F. 1964. *Ghazali's Unique Unknowable God.* Leiden: Brill.

Watt, W. 1963. *Muslim Intellectual: A Study of al-Ghazali.* Edinburgh: Edinburgh University Press.

On CAUSATION see also Vol. 5, Ch. 17. On DIVINE UNITY see also Ch. 13. On FREE WILL see also Chs 2, 9, 19; Vol. 1, Ch. 18; Vol. 3, Chs 9, 15; Vol. 5, Ch. 22. On MYSTICISM see also Ch. 7; Vol. 5, Chs 2, 3.

8

PETER ABELARD

Constant J. Mews

Peter Abelard (1079–1142) introduces a new perspective into the philosophy of religion in the Latin West through his emphasis on the common source of pagan and religious philosophical insight. Although not the first person to argue that pagan philosophers shared some understanding of truths manifest through divine revelation to Jews and then to Christians, Abelard was one of the first teachers to create a coherent synthesis of *theologia* in which this insight was the driving principle. Boethius (*c.*476–*c.*525) had pursued philosophical enquiry into orthodox Christian doctrines relating to the Trinity, but never reflected explicitly on the relationship of pagan philosophy to Christian revelation. Rather than commenting on the *Opuscula sacra* (Sacred works) of Boethius, Abelard decided to create his own independent synthesis on the subject, a treatise about the Trinity, now known as the *Theologia 'summi boni'* (hereafter *TSum*). After the work was condemned as heretical at the Council of Soissons in 1121, he revised it in the early 1120s as his *Theologia Christiana* (Christian theology; hereafter *TChr*), transforming it yet again into his *Theologia* (the *Theologia 'scholarium'*; hereafter *TSch*) by the early 1130s. This final version was identified by the famous Cistercian abbot, Bernard of Clairvaux, at the Council of Sens, held on 25 May 1141, as containing many heresies (Mews 2002).

In responding to Abelard, Bernard of Clairvaux created a powerful image of Abelard as a rebellious thinker who would continue both to horrify the Christian faithful and to fascinate those sympathetic to anyone persecuted for questioning ecclesiastical authority, down through the centuries:

> We have in France a former teacher turned new theologist, who from his earliest youth has dabbled in the art of dialectic and now raves about the Holy Scriptures. He tries to raise teachings, once condemned and silenced, both his own and others, and added new ones besides. He who deems to know everything in heaven above and on earth below apart from "I do not know," lifts his face to heaven and gazes on

the depths of God, bringing back to us words that cannot be spoken, which is not lawful for a man to speak. While he is ready to supply a reason for everything, even those which are beyond reason, yet he presumes against reason and against faith.

(Bernard, *Omnia opera* 1953–80: 8:17–18)

Any attempt to present Abelard's philosophy of religion must question the influential stereotype evoked by Bernard. Was Abelard making audacious claims about the capacity of philosophical reason to understand the nature of religious truth? To appreciate the significance of his ideas, we must first consider how they evolved out of an awakened interest in the late eleventh and early twelfth centuries in the philosophy and literature of the ancient world, as well as out of a desire among many scholars to draw connections between the insights of pagan antiquity and the truths of Christian faith.

THE GROWTH OF INTEREST IN PAGAN WISDOM: 1080–1120

Abelard, born in 1079 at Le Pallet, near the border between Brittany and Anjou, was inspired to study the Peripatetic tradition in logic, as far as it was then known in the Latin West, by Roscelin of Compiègne (*c.*1050–*c.*1125), under whom he studied during the 1090s at Loches, the ducal palace of the Counts of Anjou. Roscelin had come to Anjou after having been accused of expounding heresy by disciples of Anselm of Canterbury at a Council held at Soissons (*c.*1092). The charge laid against Roscelin was that in describing the three persons of the Trinity as three things, he opened himself to tritheist heresy. In fact, Roscelin insisted that he was simply pursuing the same broad agenda, as opened up by Anselm, of explaining Christian belief through the use of reason, in the same way that 'pagans' (i.e. Muslims) and Jews both defended their religious traditions. While Anselm had set a precedent for exploring faith through reason alone (*sola ratione*), Roscelin wished to go further in identifying the particular meaning or 'thing' (*res*) of each of the words, Father, Son and Holy Spirit, predicated of God. He was interested in the way theological categories were applied to God through human imposition, but retained a semantic theory influenced by Augustine, which identified words as signs of things.

Under Roscelin, the young Abelard absorbed a vocalist interpretation of dialectic that emphasized how categories were words (*voces*) rather than things in themselves. Even though he did not engage in the formal study of theology under Roscelin, Abelard would have known of his teacher's broader project of relating rational reflection to Christian faith in ways that went beyond the specific synthesis offered by Anselm. At the same time, Abelard became increasingly aware of limitations in his teacher's perspective, and thus sought to explore educational opportunities further afield.

Around 1100, Abelard went to Paris to study under William of Champeaux, famous for teaching both dialectic and rhetoric at the cathedral school of Notre-Dame as well as for his involvement in the ecclesiastical reform movement. Abelard, on the other hand, seems to have been supported by William's rival, Stephen of Garlande, also an archdeacon of Paris, but more closely aligned to royal control over the Church. In dialectic, William emphasized continuity with the teaching of Boethius, and took for granted that universals were indeed real things, in which individuals participated. Abelard challenged this perspective, most famously during a course of lectures on rhetoric that William was giving, perhaps soon after Easter 1111, when William resigned from the cathedral to create a community of Augustinian canons at Saint-Victor, just outside the city. While unable to inherit William's position at Notre-Dame, Abelard was able to establish himself as the pre-eminent dialectician at the schools of Sainte-Geneviève.

In 1113, following William's appointment as Bishop of Châlons-sur-Marne, Abelard spent a short time studying divinity under Anselm at Laon, before acquiring the position he coveted at Notre-Dame. He took particular exception to the way that records of Anselm's *sententie* or teachings were revered by disciples as authoritative when he found that they never addressed the questions that he wished to pose. Even though he reports that he did compose certain glosses on Ezekiel, Abelard was not particularly comfortable with biblical exegesis as a genre during these years, or with what he saw as an excessive reliance on arguments from patristic authority.

The episode for which Abelard is perhaps most well known is his love affair with the young Heloise, niece of Fulbert, one of the cathedral canons at Notre-Dame, where he taught at the cathedral school, from 1113 to 1117. While Abelard plays up the erotic nature of their early relationship in the *Historia calamitatum* (History of my troubles), there seems no doubt that his discussion with Heloise broadened his reading to embrace a wide range of pagan classics, in particular the poetry of Ovid and the writing of Cicero about friendship. A collection of over one hundred love letters (*Epistolae duorum amantium* [Letters of two lovers]), exchanged in the first half of the twelfth century between a controversial dialectician, excited by love as erotic passion, and a brilliant young woman, keen to reflect on the ethical demands of love, records voices very similar indeed to those of Abelard and Heloise (Mews 1999). Although these letters are not concerned with religious themes as such, they reveal a young woman convinced of the spiritual authenticity of her love and deep friendship for a teacher, who is awed by her capacity to reflect on ethics and friendship.

In the *Historia calamitatum*, Abelard presented his early relationship to Heloise as driven by lust rather than by love or philosophical concerns, so as to present what happened subsequently as ordained by providence, turning all things to the good. He contrasted what he presents as his false passion for Heloise with his gradual recognition of the consoling love of God, manifest through the Holy Spirit. He explained the development of the affair as the living out of a classic fable. After their relationship was discovered, Heloise gave birth to a child, and only reluctantly accepted Abelard's proposal that they marry. The secret marriage failed to placate her uncle, who had Abelard castrated in reprisal for the way he had treated Heloise. He became a monk at Saint-Denis, a wealthy abbey with close links to the Crown, while she took vows as a nun at Argenteuil, the abbey where she had been raised. The child was sent to be looked after by Abelard's sister, back in Brittany. Abelard was not happy, however, at Saint-Denis, and criticism about his teaching activity from fellow monks drove him to establish a school at a site some distance from the main abbey.

THE *THEOLOGIA 'SUMMI BONI'* AND ITS INSPIRATION

This was the context in which Abelard first started to draft his treatise on the Trinity. He would later explain that he was responding to the demand of his students for convincing reasons to accept Christian faith:

> It happened that I first applied myself to the foundation of our faith through analogies from human reasoning and composed a certain treatise of theology about the divine Unity and Trinity for our students, who were asking for human and philosophical reasons, and demanded more what could be understood than simply recited. They said indeed that proclaiming words that understanding did not follow was redundant, nor could anything be believed unless it was first understood, and that it was ridiculous for anyone to preach to others what neither he nor those he was teaching could grasp in the intellect, the Lord himself saying that such people were like the blind leading the blind.
>
> (1978: 82–3)

Abelard conceals here a more specific task by which he was preoccupied when writing the first version of his treatise on the Trinity, namely, to refute the theological error imputed to Roscelin of teaching that the three divine persons were as distinct as three things (*res*). His larger goal, however, was to provide a rational account of the foundations of Christian belief, but not necessarily in the way that Anselm had presented this.

Abelard's central theme in the *Theologia 'summi boni'* is that the names 'Father', 'Son' and 'Holy Spirit' are each applied to the supreme good, "which Christians call God" for a specific reason: to signify a particular attribute (*proprietas*) of the supreme good, namely divine power, wisdom and goodness (*TSum* 1.1). While he emulates Roscelin in analysing terms, he refuses to identify each name as signifying a particular thing (*res*). In the first of its three books he presents arguments from authority, identifying these attributes as discerned by both ancient philosophers and the prophets of the Old Testament. The second and third books are devoted to arguments from reason, showing how these concepts relate to each other in ways that parallel orthodox Christian doctrine about the three persons of the divine Trinity. Taking for granted the truth of the Christian religion, his concern is more hermeneutic in character: to explain the meaning of familiar terms in Jewish and Christian discourse by relating them to arguments evident through philosophical enquiry as well as from the testimony of Scripture.

The doctrine that Christ is the embodiment of divine wisdom, the Word of God, and that the Holy Spirit revealed itself both in the creation of the world and through the history of the Jewish people, is rooted in the New Testament itself. Early Christian writers, however, always tended to contrast the inadequacy of pagan philosophical insight compared to the truth of God's revelation in Christ. Abelard attached central importance to Paul's statement in Romans 1:20 that the invisible things of God (*Invisibilia Dei*) have always been evident to philosophers through the created world (*TSum* 1.30). Augustine had used this Pauline comment to acknowledge that Socrates and Plato had come closer than any other philosopher to understanding aspects of divine truth, but he did so only to contrast their understanding to the divine revelation offered to Moses and the Jewish people. By contrast, Abelard maintained that both philosophers and prophets were witnesses, each in their own way, to aspects of the supreme good, fully manifest only in the person of Christ.

Prior to 1120 there had been a few isolated attempts to argue that ancient philosophers had glimpsed the same truths as articulated by Christian doctrine. At Chartres, Bernard of Chartres (*d. c.*1126) was celebrated in the early decades of the twelfth century for his exposition of Plato's *Timaeus*, as translated by Chalcidius. While Bernard never himself explicitly identified Plato's World Soul with the Holy Spirit, Thierry of Chartres (*d. c.*1150) does briefly venture this claim in a commentary on the Hexaemeron (1971: 567), or six days of creation, that seeks to combine the authority of the first chapters of Genesis with Plato's account of the cosmos and its soul in the *Timaeus*. Because Abelard questions a literal identification of the Holy Spirit with the World Soul in his *Dialectica*, completed perhaps 1117/18, he may be referring directly to arguments made by Thierry (under whom he reportedly tried to study natural science, but unsuccessfully), as well as by the young William of Conches, also a disciple of Bernard of Chartres.

Rather than attempt any simplistic identification of Platonic and Christian doctrine, Abelard drew attention to the way different words could identify different attributes of the same truth. Thus he described the concept of the World Soul as a beautiful "covering" (*involucrum*) to explain that it could not be interpreted literally, but was rather a poetic image to describe the effect of God's goodness in the world. Much of the first book of the *Theologia 'summi boni'*, retained in all subsequent versions of the work, is an exposition of those passages in Plato's *Timaeus* and Macrobius' *Commentary on the "Dream of Scipio"* in which he explores how Plato's understanding of goodness infusing the entire world echoes what Christians believe about the effect of the Holy Spirit within creation. Eschewing the traditional Augustinian understanding of the Holy Spirit as the mutual love of the Father and Son, Abelard prefers to focus on divine benignity towards creation as a whole. By comparison, he gives much less attention in the earliest version of his treatise to justifying from philosophical authority his claim that 'Father' was the name given to divine power, and that the Son was divine wisdom (cf. *TSum* 1.35–6).

Abelard's identification of Father, Son and Holy Spirit as the attributes of power, wisdom and benignity was not controversial in itself. In one of his earliest writings, Hugh of Saint-Victor (*d.* 1141) invoked the triad of divine attributes in his *De tribus diebus* (On the three days), as part of a larger argument that the physical world (*mundus sensilis*, a term used by Chalcidius in his translation of Plato's *Timaeus*) is like a book, through which we can learn about divine power, wisdom and benignity of good. His treatise is not about the Trinity as such, but rather about how God reveals himself as a trinity of attributes, revealed in three allegorical 'days' or phases of creation. Abelard develops this triad very differently from Hugh in being much more concerned to explore the meaning of the words, 'Father', 'Son' and 'Holy Spirit'. Whether Abelard is here drawing on Hugh's version of the triad as has been argued (Poirel 2002) is not certain. Much depends on the precise dating of particular works. Both Abelard and Hugh of Saint-Victor may be responding to the use of the triad by Thierry of Chartres as part of his desire to connect Platonist teaching to Christian doctrine (Mews 2008). The triad of divine power, wisdom and goodness was a Middle Platonist theme invoked by Basil in his commentary on the Hexaemeron and thus by Ambrose. Augustine had himself preferred more psychological analogies to the Trinity, notably in comparing the three divine persons to memory, understanding and will in the human soul. Abelard never questions the Platonic notion that there is a supreme order to the cosmos, and was sympathetic to the broader project of linking the *Timaeus* and Scripture, but was critical of assuming that Platonic Forms had an independent reality of the subjects that they informed.

Unlike Thierry of Chartres, Abelard focused on the meaning of the words used to define Christian doctrine. He devoted the second and third books of his *Theologia 'summi boni'* to the issue that had so troubled Roscelin: how could one speak of three distinct persons, all sharing one essence? By suggesting that Father, Son and Holy Spirit were names given to signify divine attributes (*proprieties*) rather than specific things, he hoped to escape the implication, raised by Roscelin's argument, that they were ontologically separate entities. Abelard defended the role of reason to explore Christian doctrine, but rejected the narrowness of "false dialecticians" like his own teacher. While Abelard turned to the central argument of Augustine's *De Trinitate* (On the Trinity) that there was a trinity of relations within God, identified in Latin as *personae* (or invented characters), he transformed the Augustinian argument by applying this notion to the relationship between three attributes, namely power, wisdom and benignity. In his discussion of possible objections that can be made to orthodox Christian doctrine, he considers possible ways of considering identity and difference to conclude that there is no real distinction between the three persons, other than of signifying distinct attributes in the divine nature, the supreme good. In the core section of the third book in the *Theologia 'summi boni'* (3.52–87), Abelard presents his idea that wisdom, or the power of discernment, is related to power in the same way as species is to genus, or a wax image and wax itself. Central to his analysis is a conviction that words in particular phrases often operate metaphorically (as when we say 'the fields smile', to mean that they bloom), and not according to the literal meaning of individual words. This was a notion that Abelard may have picked up from the theological writing of William of Champeaux, who had also attempted to provide a philosophical account of Trinitarian doctrine. Yet whereas William gives only a brief suggestion about how the three persons may signify distinct attributes, Abelard explores at length the philosophical relationship between species and genus. In a short subsequent section (3.88–93), Abelard considers how the Holy Spirit or divine benignity proceeds from both power and wisdom through operating in the world.

There were clearly many inadequacies in Abelard's account, notably in the imbalance in identification of authorities (more philosophical than patristic) and in the limited attention given to God the Father as divine power. These weaknesses were exploited by his critics at the Council of Soissons, where former disciples of Anselm of Laon (Alberic of Reims and Lotulph of Novara) accused him of expounding heresy. The official charge that Abelard mentions as raised against him was that he attributed power to God the Father alone, but not to the Son or the Holy Spirit. Abelard understood God's power to be manifested in his potentiality as source for all that could come to be, not in his capacity to act. His understanding of religion, at least when he initially drafted his treatise on the Trinity, was based on the perception of a divine order to creation rather than on revelation over and beyond the created world.

Soon after the burning of his treatise at Soissons and (after a brief incarceration at Saint-Medard) his return to Saint-Denis, troubles with other monks of that abbey led Abelard to escape to the territory of Champagne, where he found a place to live not far from the city of Provins, on an estuary of the Seine. Here he built an oratory that he dedicated initially to the Holy Trinity, but then rededicated to the Paraclete or Holy Spirit, reflecting the particular emphasis of his theology. Abelard continued to modify his treatise on the Trinity, giving it the title *Theologia Christiana*. Although *theologia* would become common currency within scholastic discourse during Abelard's generation, the term was not used by traditionally minded writers such as Bernard of Clairvaux, except to refer to that work, which he labelled *Stultilogia* or 'Stupidology'. The title *Theologia Christiana* was itself a controversial one, presenting his arguments as a Christian version of a pagan philosophical practice. Abelard seems to have understood *theologia* in a traditional sense of purely abstract reflection about God rather than about Christ or the Church.

In this much enlarged version, Abelard supplied more written authority for his argument, both from pagan and patristic authors. He found many of these texts while compiling the *Sic et non* (Yes and no), an evolving anthology of patristic texts collected over a long period. He organized them around a range of subjects, not just the Trinity, but also the person of Christ, the sacraments and charity as the foundation of all ethical behaviour. This anthology, which he may have begun while still at Saint-Denis, was introduced by a Prologue laying out his conviction that the foundation of all critical enquiry, and thus the first key to wisdom, lay in the questioning of texts. Abelard recognized that often doctrinal statements were shaped by rhetorical technique and thus prone to human error. Rather than simply accepting authority, one had to subject all written claims to the scrutiny of reason. In the *Theologia Christiana* he responded to the questions that he had raised at the outset of the *Sic et non* about the nature of faith in God. Public criticism forced him to find greater written authority to defend his arguments.

In addition to doctrinal comment, he added a great deal of polemical material deriving from Jerome about the ethical example set by the ancient philosophers (perhaps drawn from a lost *Exhortation* to his fellow monks), incorporated into a completely new second book. He also improved core aspects of his central philosophical argument comparing the interrelationship of three attributes to that between three persons of the Trinity. These attributes were not things in themselves, he argued, but only abstractions predicated of God, who was beyond all form. Whereas Roscelin had been very literal in his understanding of terms predicated of God, Abelard drew on Aristotle's *On Interpretation* to reflect on how the same word could generate different meanings (*TChr* 3.162; cf. *TSum* 2.103). In the case of the Trinity, this meant that statements about God the Son being generated from God the Father needed to be understood as analogous to the relationship between wisdom and power (or potentiality) in general, and statements about the Holy Spirit proceeding from the Father and the Son need to be understood to be about God's goodness proceeding from his power and wisdom to the world. In a final fifth book, Abelard started to develop ideas about the nature of divine power itself. In particular, he started to expand the notion, implicit in his original thought, that God's power did not refer to God's ability to act in any way that he wished, but only in the way that he did act, namely, through wisdom and goodness.

Abelard's philosophy of religion, as he articulated it during the 1120s, when he was teaching at the Paraclete, was based very much around an ideal of imitating ancient philosophers in their commitment to an ideal of reflection on the supreme good. A remark that he makes in his *Soliloquium* (Soliloquy), probably from the early 1120s, about another treatise that has not survived, crystallizes his conviction during these early years:

> Whoever reads this exhortation will see that the philosophers are greatly in fellowship with Christians not so much in name as in actual

fact. For Greece, equipped with so many philosophical arguments, would not have submitted to the yoke of the Gospel so quickly had she not been prepared for this in advance by the writings of the philosophers, just as Judaea had been prepared by those of the prophets.

(1984: 893)

Although this short interior monologue, between Petrus and Abaelardus, does not get very far in reflecting on the fundamental identity of the philosophical pursuit of wisdom and the preaching of Christ, it does articulate his fascination with exploring the common ground shared by philosophy and the Gospel.

There is greater depth of analysis in Abelard's *Collationes* (Conferences), written perhaps in the early 1130s (although its date has been much disputed). In the first of its two dialogues, between a philosopher and a Jew, Abelard debates the positive role of Jewish law in establishing a moral code with a degree of sympathy not often found in Christian literature, which usually asserts the superiority of Christian over Jewish revelation. The philosopher articulates his regret that too often there is no progress in matters of faith, because people do not investigate faith rationally (2001: 11). While the Jew defends the regulatory function of the Law in restraining acts of wickedness, the philosopher argues that there were many who lived before Moses simply in accordance with natural law, without any rituals such as circumcision. By implication, the precepts of the Law are not in themselves essential to a virtuous life. Abelard presents the philosopher as one who worships one God, has been circumcised as a descendant of Ishmael, but relies simply on natural law. Abelard may not have had a specific Muslim in mind in presenting this philosopher, but he uses this figure to debate a broader issue: the intention behind acts of religious duty. The Jew puts forward eloquent testimony that "the law extends the feeling of love both to people and to God, and you will realize that your law too, which you call 'natural', is included within ours, then for us just as for you those which concern perfect love would be enough for salvation" (*ibid.*: 55). Although Abelard does not formally resolve this part of the debate, he leaves the reader to conclude that even if the philosopher respects the purpose of the Law, he is not bound by its obligations.

In the second dialogue, between a philosopher and a Christian, Abelard explores the theme that their common goal is identified as ethics by the philosopher, but as divinity by the Christian. One focuses on the journey, the other on the goal (*ibid.*: 83). The debate enables him to develop ethical concerns based on philosophical teaching (mediated in particular through Cicero; *see* Vol. 1, Ch. 8), and to consider how they may relate to Christian theological reflection. It begins with the philosopher and the Christian setting the ground rules for such a debate, in particular with both accepting that reason has to precede authority (*ibid.*: 93), an inversion of the argument that Anselm had put forward, that one had to believe in order to understand. They then present their respective teachings about the supreme good for man and how it can be reached. The philosopher sees virtue (distinguished by Cicero as prudence, justice, courage and temperance) as the only way of leading to happiness, while the Christian identifies *caritas* (love) as the foundation of the virtues, which may not be equal in all people. The Christian argues that although justice, courage and temperance (in all of which prudence is present) are central to human perfection, positive laws, such as the commandments in Scripture, encourage growth in virtue. Specific actions, however, are not good or bad in themselves. They conclude by debating the highest good, by which a person is made better. Abelard's driving argument is that the vision of God, the supreme good, should not be interpreted in physical terms, but rather as a spiritual awareness, in the same way as the suffering of hell should not be interpreted as a physical fire (*ibid.*: 195). Although he never gives the Christian the opportunity to explain how the supreme good should be acquired, Abelard does have him reflect on what might seem a supreme evil, Christ's death, could yet be something good. Everything that happens is done for a good reason: exactly the same theme as underpins the *Historia calamitatum*.

While Abelard's arguments in the *Collationes* are strongly philosophical in character, he seems to have devoted more of his attention in the 1130s to his theological writing as well as to Scripture, a shift that may be linked to a change in his personal situation. In 1129, after having spent two years in relative exile at Saint-Gildas, in Brittany, he decided to transfer control of the Paraclete to Heloise (presumably at her request), as she and her nuns had been expelled from the abbey of Argenteuil. This was the context in which Abelard wrote the *Historia calamitatum*, in theory for a fictional friend, but quite possibly for Heloise and her nuns as a way of outlining the origins of their oratory. In response to the subsequent demand of Heloise that he attend to the spiritual needs of the community, Abelard was obliged to create homiletic and liturgical writings that responded to the needs of the women. He was obliged to draw much more on Scripture than on the philosophical writings familiar to his students in the early years of the Paraclete.

Soon after 1131, Abelard also resumed teaching at the schools of Sainte-Geneviève, Paris, where his friend Stephen of Garlande was still dean. Abelard organized his theological teaching into a tripartite structure, based around faith, the sacraments and charity, already laid out in the *Sic et non*. Although he never wrote a complete synthesis of his teaching on all these subjects, collections of *sententiae* taken down by students reveal that Abelard did develop a mature body of theological teaching during these years. He transformed the *Theologia Christiana* into a much more tightly argued work, the *Theologia 'scholarium'*. Here he simplified a complex philosophical discussion about identity and difference into a presentation of his core image of the Trinity as like a bronze seal, in which the seal issued from the bronze (like the Son from the Father) but became sealed on wax in the same way as the Holy Spirit imprinted the divine image in man (*TSch* 2.112–16). While the core of his argument about the divine persons as names for divine attributes had not changed, he now defended much more clearly the need for rational discussion of all religious doctrine. As he argued at the outset of his treatise, faith was "the estimation (*aestimatio*) of things unseen", and there-fore could never be defined in any particular form of words. In the third book of the *Theologia 'scholarium'* Abelard also took much further his thinking about the nature of divine power, wisdom and goodness. God could only act in the way that he did, always shaped by wisdom and goodness in ways that sometimes went above human understanding.

In his commentary on Paul's Epistle to the Romans, also written during the 1130s, Abelard developed his thinking about the act of Christ's redemption of humanity. Refuting the argument that humanity had fallen through original sin to a legitimate yoke to the devil, Abelard insisted that humanity needed to be shown the example of divine love, manifested by Christ through his life, death and resur-rection. Inevitably such ideas moved him far away from the thinking of Augustine about original sin and our need for grace. Abelard did not deny grace, but insisted that only through a free act of the will could humanity turn towards God.

One of Abelard's last major writings was his *Ethics*, always called in manuscripts *Scito teipsum* (Know thyself). Only the first book, on vice, survives complete, as he may never have finished the second, about virtue. Here he picks up his emphasis on intention, initially raised in the *Collationes*, but takes it to a new degree of sophistication, with awareness that a wrong will or thought may not be sinful in itself. Sin, he now argues, consists in consent to that wrong will in contempt of God. Such thinking may well have been in response to Heloise's insistence that her intentions to Abelard had always been pure, and that simply having a lustful thought was not in itself a sign of sinning against God.

Abelard's outspoken way of presenting what he considered to be the values of true religion, as distinct from false superstition, generated hostility from his critics. William of Saint-Thierry and Bernard of Clairvaux were alarmed, not just at Abelard's questioning of traditional notions of original sin, but at his apparent rejection of traditional notions of divine omnipotence. They accused Abelard of minimizing the omnipotence of God the Son and rejecting it completely in the case of the Holy Spirit. They did not appreciate that Abelard's theological system was based on a desire to reformulate the standard definitions of Christian belief in ways that were more fully in accord with the precepts of philosophical reason.

FURTHER READING

Brower, J. & K. Guilfoy (eds) 2004. *The Cambridge Companion to Abelard*. Cambridge: Cambridge University Press.

Clanchy, M. 1997. *Abelard: A Medieval Life*. Oxford: Blackwell.

Jolivet, J. 1969. *Arts du langage et théologie chez Abélard*. Paris: Vrin.

Luscombe, D. 1969. *The School of Peter Abelard*. Cambridge: Cambridge University Press.

Marenbon, J. 1997. *The Philosophy of Peter Abelard*. Cambridge: Cambridge University Press.

Mews, C. J. 2001. *The Legacy of Abelard*. Aldershot: Ashgate.

Mews, C. J. 2002. *Reason and Belief in the Age of Roscelin and Abelard*. Aldershot: Ashgate.

Mews, C. J. 2005. *Abelard and Heloise*. Oxford: Oxford University Press.

Sweeney, E. 2006. *Logic, Theology, and Poetry in Boethius, Abelard, and Alan of Lille*. Basingstoke: Palgrave Macmillan.

On DIVINITY see also Ch. 6; Vol. 1, Chs 8, 18, 19, 20. On ETHICS see also Ch. 4; Vol. 1, Ch. 11; Vol. 3, Ch. 9; Vol. 4, Chs 13, 19; Vol. 5, Chs 12, 15, 21. On JUDAISM see also Vol. 1, Chs 9, 10; Vol. 3, Ch. 15; Vol. 5, Chs 8, 15. On LAW see also Ch. 10; Vol. 3, Ch. 12. On PAGANISM see also Vol. 3, Ch. 2. On THE TRINITY see also Chs 2, 15; Vol. 1, Chs 14, 17, 20; Vol. 3, Chs 3, 9, 17; Vol. 4, Ch. 4; Vol. 5, Chs 12, 23.

9

BERNARD OF CLAIRVAUX

Brian Patrick McGuire

Bernard of Clairvaux (1090–1153) was not a philosopher in the strict sense of the word. His writings, however, have an epistemological foundation and belong to a perennial discussion within Christian thought about the relationship between faith and reason. Thus the great historian of medieval philosophy, Etienne Gilson, had no qualms about including Bernard in his *History of Christian Philosophy in the Middle Ages*. In a chapter called "Speculative Mysticism", Gilson showed how Bernard described a process by which the human soul seeks the love that God offers: "Ecstasy is nothing else than the extreme point of this union of wills and this coinciding of a human love with the divine" (Gilson 1955: 167).

Bernard was born into a family of the lower nobility at a castle just outside of Dijon, Fontaines-lès-Dijon, in Burgundy. He was educated by canons in the town of Châtillon-sur-Seine. They seem to have encouraged the great love of Latin letters that is reflected in his writings. He apparently intended to continue his education in the manner of the wandering scholars of his era. According to a story included in his hagiography, Bernard was on his way to study in Germany, but the recollection of his mother, who had recently died, made him turn back and become a monk (William of Saint-Thierry, *Sancti Bernardi vita prima* [The first life of Saint Bernard; hereafter *Vita prima*] 1.3.9, in *Patrologia Latina* [hereafter *PL*] 185:231–2).

At the age of twenty-two or twenty-three Bernard entered what was then called the New Monastery, which later came to be known as Cîteaux. It had been founded in 1098 by breakaway monks from Molesme. Its monks were seeking a stricter way of life in accord with the *Rule of Saint Benedict*. Bernard was attracted to what we can call heroic monasticism, emphasizing strict asceticism but also fostering the enjoyment of close bonds among the monks. According to his legend, he arrived at the gate of Cîteaux with more than thirty friends and relatives, who also wanted entrance into the monastic life (*Vita prima* 1.4.19, in *PL* 185:327).

We know very little about Bernard's first years as a monk, but by 1115 the Abbot of Cîteaux, Stephen Harding, was ready to send him to Champagne to found a daughter house. According to his first hagiographer, William of Saint-Thierry, Bernard said that what he learned about the Scriptures came from meditation on them while he was "in forests and fields" and that "he had had no masters except the oaks and the beeches". They were, he said "in a gracious joke", his friends (*Vita prima* 1.4.23, in *PL* 185:240). This idea of learning from nature reappears in a letter of Bernard to the monk Aelred of Rievaulx. Bernard had asked Aelred to write a work about charity in monastic life, and Aelred had replied that he was not sufficiently learned to compose the required exposition. Bernard replied that Aelred's learning came from hard physical work in the outdoors. According to Bernard, Aelred had gone to the school of the Holy Spirit, a far superior teacher than "some grammarian" (Aelred of Rievaulx, *Opera omnia I*, 1971: 3).

Bernard was not just playing with words here. Regardless of his aristocratic background, which would have looked down on manual labour, Bernard as a monk came to terms with the physical environment that every new Cistercian foundation had to transform in order to make it a suitable place for a monastic community. For Bernard the trees and streams of Clairvaux were part of a learning process in which he combined his deepening knowledge of biblical and patristic texts with the challenges and inspiration of the world around him.

Bernard's philosophical foundation was thus based on what might be called the school of nature. Besides participating in the hard manual labour required by the Cistercian life, he also made extreme demands on his body in terms of ascetic deprivation. When his health collapsed, Bernard had to cut back on such observances (*Vita prima* 1.7.32, in *PL* 185:246). But the intensity of his penetration of biblical language is connected to an ability to concentrate his attention on the spiritual or interior dimension.

BERNARD'S PRE-SCHOLASTICISM

Bernard's ascetic regime in no way prevented him from involving himself in intellectual questions. A good indication of his activity is a letter dated around 1125 in reply to a request from Hugh of Saint-Victor, a distinguished house of canons in Paris. Hugh (*d.* 1141), one of the leading scholars of his day, turned to Bernard for advice. The fact that he wrote to the still young Bernard shows that the abbot of Clairvaux already had a reputation that had reached the schools of Paris.

Bernard's reply is listed as his Letter 77, but is sometimes given the title of a treatise, *On Baptism*. As the Benedictine scholar Hugh Feiss has shown, Hugh was asking Bernard to respond to three propositions that were associated with the school of Peter Abelard (Feiss 1992: 358). Much of what Bernard argues in his response is based not on scriptural authority but on reason. In many passages he was expressing himself not as a theologian but as a philosopher. He claimed, for example, that it would be wrong to condemn the non-baptized who lived prior to the command of Jesus that everyone must be baptized in order to be saved: "Is it congruent for the author of life, who had come to root out death, to make use of death at the very beginning of his ways, to the disadvantage of a world which was still ignorant of the latest heavenly decree?" (*ibid.*: 361; *Sancti Bernardi opera* [The works of Saint Bernard; hereafter *SBO*], 1957–77: vol. 7, 185). Bernard concluded that prior to Christ's promulgation of the command to be baptized, there would have been other ways by which people could have been saved.

But what about people who lived after Christ? Bernard formulated what later would be called the doctrine of baptism of desire. He referred to authorities from the writings of Church Fathers such as Ambrose and Augustine. But he also continued his argument on the basis of reason. First of all, the martyrs were saved by their faith and blood. Secondly, children are saved by faith: not their own but that of those who love them (Feiss 1992: 366–8; *SBO* vol. 7, 190–92).

In the course of this brief but concentrated exposition, Bernard argues on the basis of thesis and counter-thesis. His basic assumption is that it befits a God of love to save as many as possible. Just as many Christians today, he points out, know little about the future life but still believe in it, so too believers before Christ had hope in salvation but did not know how it would take place. They were saved on the basis of their faith, even though they were not baptized.

Hugh of Saint-Victor made good use of Bernard's arguments and included them in his landmark theological work, *De sacramentis* (On the sacraments) (Feiss 1992: 355). Hugh turned to Bernard because the Abbot of Clairvaux did not just list authorities to back his point of view. As Feiss has shown, Bernard "uses reason to solve apparent contradictions among authorities, to create dilemmas, to drive home arguments, and to rebut objections" (*ibid.*: 359).

Bernard here can be seen as following the theology of the twelfth-century schools, where logic was used in order to solve intellectual questions. In this sense he went beyond the practice of monastic theology attributed to him by Jean Leclercq (1982: 222–5). According to Leclercq, this approach to learning meant close meditation on the language of Scripture and the Fathers. The contemplative and experiential element is contrasted with the logical and speculative approach of scholastic theology.

In this letter-treatise, however, Bernard immersed himself in the argumentative procedure that characterized the schools. He was thus able in his mid-thirties to deal with the theological questions of his day in a manner that matched the intellectual argumentation then current in Paris. Bernard was clearly influenced by William of Champeaux, who had been Abelard's teacher. William and Bernard became friends and in 1115 William ordained Bernard. It is possible that William endowed Bernard with his enthusiasm for the writings of St Augustine.

Besides Bernard's letter on baptism, another product of the 1120s that indicates his singular ability to reason in the manner of the schools is his treatise *On Grace and Free Choice*, usually dated to 1128. Although Bernard here was very much aware of the ideas of St Paul, especially in the Epistle to the Romans, the Abbot of Clairvaux provided his own agenda for reconciling God's grace with human free will. His purpose was to show free choice as cooperating with grace. He defined voluntary consent as "a self-determining habit of the soul" (*On Grace and Free Choice* II.3, in *SBO* vol. 3, 167; 1977a: 55). Consent is a necessary point of departure for human responsibility. Bernard argues carefully for a threefold freedom: of nature, of grace and of life in glory (III.7). He asks about the freedom that belongs to the saved and considers what is special for God and what is found in all rational creatures (IV). Freedom of choice belongs to all who have the use of reason (V.15). At the same time, however, grace is a necessity so that the person can will that which is good: "Created, then to a certain extent, as our own in freedom of will, we become God's as it were by good will" (VI.18, in *SBO* vol. 3, 179; 1977a: 73).

The references in these pages are to Paul, especially to the Corinthians and to Romans, but the form of argumentation is Bernard's own. He insists that free choice remains even after the person has sinned (VIII). The existence of free choice in the creature reflects the image of the creator (IX). Grace does not take away free choice (XI). In sin we still have free choice and are responsible for our acts (XII). Bernard thus argues for human responsibility, but he also considers human merits to be gifts of God (XIII).

Bernard concludes that our consent and our actions derive from God but are our own (XIV). He claims that he has remained close to St Paul and has returned "to almost his very words" (XIV.48, in *SBO* vol. 3, 200; 1977a: 107). But the Abbot of Clairvaux has gone beyond Paul: he has made a systematic presentation of human free will in its relation to God's grace. He has done so in a rigorous and discursive manner different from what we find in the Epistles of Paul.

Approaching one of the central questions of Christian theology, Bernard defines human choice in terms of grace. His key concept is the good will that the individual must manifest in order to receive the grace offered by God (XIV.46–7). Bernard balances his concepts on a knife-edge in order to include both grace and free will: "Grace does the whole work, and so does free choice – with this one qualification: that whereas the whole is done *in* free choice, so is the whole done *of* grace" (*totum quidem hoc, et totum illa, sed ut totum in illo, sic totum ex illa*; XIV.47, in *SBO* vol. 3, 200; 1977a: 106).

BERNARD'S EXPERIENTIAL REFLECTIONS

Bernard's reputation as a solid theological thinker meant that the masters of the Paris schools turned to him for advice. Far more important for his reputation in monastic circles, however, was his ability to combine meditation on the language of Scripture with personal insight. Here Bernard followed the practice of Anselm of Canterbury (*d.* 1109) in linking his theological reflections to his own interior life (Southern 1966: 34–47). Anselm did so in his prayers and meditations, while Bernard chose the vehicle of the eighty-six *Sermons on the Song of Songs* (*Sermones in Cantica*; hereafter *SC*) that he preached for the monks of

Clairvaux. These sermons are masterpieces of twelfth-century Latin prose and reveal Bernard's talent for linking language with thought (Casey 1988).

Here is Bernard addressing the monks about how it was for him to receive spiritual insight:

> I want to tell you of my own experience, as I promised. Not that it is of any importance. But I make this disclosure only to help you, and if you derive any profit from it I shall be consoled for my foolishness; if not, my foolishness will be revealed. I admit that the Word has also come to me – I speak as a fool – and has come many times.
>
> (*SC* 74.5, in *SBO* vol. 2, 242; 1980: 89)

Bernard could allow himself to speak about his inner life in order to help his monks. Paul had done the same thing, and Bernard was thus able to draw on a Christian practice of revealing the movements of the heart and soul in order to provide consolation, encouragement and help to others.

The passage here is a long exposition about how the coming of the Word cannot be described in any physical terms. The Word is full of paradoxes. Bernard says that he has no way of knowing how and when the Word entered into him, and yet he knew the Word was there. In his own innermost being, Bernard could rejoice in the coming of the Word: "Only by the movement of my heart, as I have told you, did I perceive his presence and I knew the power of his might" (*SC* 74.6, in *SBO* vol. 2, 243; 1980: 91).

The meditation continues, making up the better part of this sermon. One can wonder whether Bernard actually preached it to the brethren at Clairvaux. What matters, however, is that he considered it appropriate for all who read him to hear about some of the most profound experiences of his life. In this sense he was much more than a conventional master of the schools of his age. He offered his own interior life as food for thought and spiritual sustenance for his audience.

In a much earlier sermon Bernard shared himself with his monks not in terms of mystical experience but in relation to his trials and doubts (*SC* 14.6, in *SBO* vol. 1, 79; 1977b: 102). He spoke of the "coldness and hardness of heart" that he had felt. In seeking the love of God, he had found only a sense of numbness. At the same time he missed having a friend to help him out. Bernard felt there was no consolation to be had. Then suddenly he became aware of the presence of a good man or the memory of a dead or absent friend, and this experience would open up the gates of emotion and bring tears.

Bernard described how the happiness caused by such an event could leave him feeling depressed. This reaction he could also experience in his present life: "even now, if a similar experience should happen to me, I eagerly grasp at the proffered gift, I am grateful for it, even though I feel sad beyond words that I have not won it by my own merits" (*SC* 14.6, in *SBO* vol. 1, 80; 1977b: 103). Bernard interpreted such a reaction as indicative of the human longing for the vision of God. He took it for granted that many of his monks had similar experiences, and he saw these as fostering love among the brethren. Such moments could be medicine that helps cure the sick and strengthens the convalescent.

The language here is Bernard's way of conveying his own interior life to his monastic community and of telling its members that he assumed his experiences were theirs. Bernard legitimized self-doubt and hesitation, while at the same time encouraging the brothers to share their deepest feelings with each other. He allowed them to emphasize their need for each other in friendship and consolation. In such sharing, he accepted tears as a way of manifesting the inner life.

What do such descriptions have to do with philosophy? Bernard told his monks that he sought a "more refined and interior philosophy, to know Jesus and to know him crucified" (SC 43.4, in SBO vol. 2, 43; cf. 1 Corinthians 2:2). Bernard was looking for ways of reconciling his inner life with that of his fellow monks in relating their existence to the crucified Christ. This was his philosophy, one that was not taken "from the school of rhetoricians and philosophers" (SC 36.1, in SBO vol. 2, 4). Bernard warned against their pride, but he also considered the arrogance of his own heart. This awareness brought about in him the *acedia* or dryness of soul that was the fear of every monk: "The psalms are stale, reading is disagreeable, prayer is devoid of joy, the accustomed meditations irretrievable" (SC 54.8, in SBO vol. 2, 107; 1979: 76–7).

Again, Bernard made use of his own interior life in order to describe what he assumed his fellow monks were experiencing. He spoke of inability to work, fits of anger and lack of restraint in speaking. Instead of talking down to the monks, his method was to speak of his own dilemmas in order to describe theirs. Such experiences, according to Bernard, are the way by which God manifests himself for our good (SC 36.6, in SBO vol. 2, 8). It is then that a person will cry out to God who will hear him.

A further dimension of this inner life is the link between Bernard the authority figure and Bernard the friend. Many of Bernard's letters are expressions of friendship, and it would be right to say that Bernard could not imagine monastic life without the bonds of friendship. This fact cannot be taken for granted. The Desert Fathers had in general warned against friendship as a distraction from or even a danger to monastic discipline (McGuire 1988: 25–34). Bernard, in contrast, was so confident about the benefits of friendship in the monastery that he did not even feel called on to defend its practice.

The claims of friendship and love in the monastery are apparent in Bernard's remarkable lament on the death of his brother. He interrupted one of his sermons to describe his sense of shock and loss on the news of the death of Gerard. Here he defended his right to shed tears of sorrow: "Our weeping is not a sign of a lack of faith, it indicates the human condition" (SC 26.13, in SBO vol. 1, 180; 1976: 72).

It can be argued that such a passage is a complex literary construction and by no means reflects spontaneous feeling. Without dealing with the question of the relation between written and spoken text in these sermons, I think it still possible to claim that Bernard wanted his audience to know how much he loved his brother and suffered from his death. In expressing his own lament, he legitimized close bonds among the brothers. In speaking of his tears, he allowed the brothers to weep for their own losses.

Bernard thus offered his audience what we can call a philosophy of personal experience. He was not an individualist in the modern sense, for his sense of self and identity was tied to his belonging to the collective of a monastery and a monastic order. But for Bernard the monastic life was made deeper and richer through an awareness and sharing of the inner lives of his monks. Close bonds grew up in the admission of faults, the pursuit of contemplative experience and the love of the language of the liturgy. Bernard's *Sermons on the Song of Songs* reflect these dimensions in his life and manifest his desire to share himself with others. In this way Bernard is *magister spiritualis*, a spiritual teacher, who through his writings made himself available not only to other monks but also to anyone able and willing to read his magnificent Latin prose.

THE POSSIBILITIES AND DANGERS OF LEARNING

Bernard of Clairvaux does not always come across in medieval studies as a master of enlightenment. He has in fact often been described more as the enemy of learning than its friend (Grane 1970: 121–2). This interpretation can stem from an opposition made between Bernard and Abelard: the first is seen as the advocate of authority and blind faith, while the second is interpreted as manifesting a new emphasis on reason that is the harbinger of modern times. Bernard is thus the dark Middle Ages, while Abelard brings the light of reason.

Such an opposition, however convenient, is not only deceptive but also wrong. Bernard did not oppose learning, whether in the cloister or outside, and the way he responded to his opponents shows how much time and effort he invested in study and thought. We do him a disservice to suggest that his primary recourse was to issue decrees against his opponents in the faith.

At the same time, however, it is right to see Bernard as having been sceptical about the benefits of learning for its own sake. This scepticism was based on a concern that highly educated people become infatuated with themselves. In one of his *Sermons on the Song of Songs* he defended himself from the charge "that I have cast aspersions on the learned and proscribed the study of letters" (*SC* 36.2, in *SBO* vol. 2, 4; 1976: 174). He insisted that he was aware of how scholars benefit the Church, "both by refuting her opponents and instructing the simple". The problem, however, is that knowledge inflates (cf. 1 Corinthians 8:1).

Bernard here begins a long reflection on the limitations and possibilities of learning. So far as he was concerned, "all knowledge is good in itself, provided it be founded on the truth" (*SC* 36.2, in *SBO* vol. 2, 5; 1976: 175). Knowledge, however, is like food. It has to be consumed in the right order. All the foods that God made are good, but health is harmed if due order is not observed.

Here, as elsewhere in his writings, Bernard is close to St Paul, whom he quotes: "If anyone imagines that he knows something, he does not yet know as he ought to know" (1 Corinthians 8:2). The benefit and usefulness of knowledge depend on the manner in which one knows. There must be order, application and purposefulness in approaching the object of study. Bernard warns against the misuse of knowledge for shameful curiosity, vanity or material gain. Thankfully there are people who want knowledge in order to be of service. They perform an act of charity: *Sed sunt quoque qui scire volunt, ut aedificent, et caritas est* (*SC* 36.3, in *SBO* vol. 2, 6).

From here Bernard continues in emphasizing the importance of self-knowledge. We must be aware of our own sinfulness and seek the vision of God: "if I look up and fix my eyes on the aid of the divine mercy, this happy vision of God soon tempers the bitter vision of myself" (*SC* 36.6, in *SBO* vol. 2, 7; 1976: 179). In this manner self-knowledge provides a point of departure for coming to the knowledge of God. Bernard was concerned with the experience that the individual acquires in facing himself and at the same time seeking God.

Sermon 36 provides insight into Bernard's scheme for the good use of knowledge, in which the individual makes use of his own self-understanding in advancing to a meeting with God. Knowledge (*scientia*) is in itself neutral. It can be used for good or evil. Bernard is by no means afraid of it: he sees the knowledge that comes from experience and learning as a possible path to God.

At the same time, however, he warned against the "windy chatter" of philosophers (*ventosa loquacitas*; *SC* 58.8, in *SBO* vol. 2, 131). Bernard spoke of their utterances as a bad kind of rain that caused sterility in the earth instead of fruitfulness. Even worse were the rains brought by heretics, who produced thorns and thistles rather than good fruits.

Bernard was here speaking in general of philosophers and heretics. He does not go into detail. But it is interesting that he places the two categories of people so close together. The same is the case in another sermon, where he again points to the wordiness of philosophers, and then places them next to heretics in their wranglings: *nec verbositate philosophorum nec cavillationibus haereticorum* (*SC* 79.4, in *SBO* vol. 2, 274).

Such a juxtaposition indicates a great deal of reserve on Bernard's part towards the learning of philosophers. In the one place in the *Sermons on the Song of Songs* where he mentions a specific heresy, however, he was careful to make it apparent that he believed in the value of persuasion and learning. Describing dualist heretics and asking what to do with them, Bernard asserted that faith is a question of persuasion and not of force: *quia fides suadenda est, non imponenda* (*SC* 66.12, in *SBO* vol. 2, 186–7). Heretics, however, were often beyond such persuasion. They could not be convinced by logical reasoning, which they did not understand. Nor could they be won over by references to authorities they did not accept. Also, persuasive arguments were useless (*SC* 66.12, in *SBO* vol. 2, 286).

Bernard here laid bare his own argumentative method: *ratio, auctoritas* and *suasio*. For him it was right and necessary to do more than quote authorities. As a philosopher of Christ, he had use of reason and persuasion.

In reviewing Bernard's correspondence in trying to get Abelard condemned as a heretic at the Council of Sens in 1141, it is clear that he also made use of *ad hominem* arguments and did whatever he could to blacken the man's reputation. Bernard's behaviour is an indication of a holy zeal that can forget charity. In the end, however, Bernard apparently did accept the settlement arranged for Abelard by the Abbot of Cluny, Peter the Venerable (Clanchy 1999: 319–24). However much Bernard considered Abelard to be a heretic, he was willing to believe in the latter's good will.

A PHILOSOPHY OF MONASTIC LIFE

Bernard's vitriol against Abelard was due to his conviction that his opponent misused philosophy and theology. The Abbot of Clairvaux, however, spent much more energy in trying to establish the rightful boundaries of the monastic life. His monument to this vocation, *On Precept and Dispensation*, was probably written in the early 1140s, and was the fruit of Bernard's own life as a monk over several decades. He took as his point of departure the *Rule of Saint Benedict* and asked whether its precepts are commands or counsels. This question led him to consider the types of necessity: stable, firm or fixed (II.4). The first covers rules that were established by human beings and can be changed. The second refers to God's own laws: these cannot be changed, except by God. The third type of necessity has to do with what has been established by God from all eternity and cannot be changed, even by God himself (III.7).

With this distinction in mind, Bernard can return to the specific case of the rules observed by monks. They belong to the first category. They cannot be changed arbitrarily, however, and his first point is that the abbot himself is subject to the *Rule of Saint Benedict* (IV.9). The monk promises obedience not according to the will of his superior but according to the Rule. At the same time obedience must be kept within the limits of monastic profession (V.11): "Let not the commands or prohibitions of the superior over-step these bounds. They cannot be stretched farther nor cut shorter. Let no superior forbid me to fulfill my promises, nor demand more" (*SBO* 3, 261; 1970: 113).

Point by point Bernard goes through the categories of obedience and considers its limitations. He makes it clear that there are different degrees of disobedience, just as there are different authorities and precepts (VII.13). Similarly there are degrees of obedience. Some actions are allowed when there is no specific prohibition against them, as in the case with conversation and laughter (VIII.17).

Sometimes it is necessary to refuse obedience, in the case when an order is given that is opposed to the law of God (IX.19). Normally, however, what superiors order is to be looked on as what God has commanded (IX.21).

Bernard then considered the punishment for disobedience: it was to be in proportion to the fault. Sometimes even breaking silence in the monastery can be a serious sin. Bernard asked whether what he required was asking too much of the individual monk. He replied on the basis of what he had seen in monastic life. As so often, experience was his teacher (XIII.32). Bernard allowed for different customs according to different monastic professions (XVI.48). He visualized monastic life as a second baptism. He asked whether a monk should remain in his own monastery in a state of anger or seek peace elsewhere (XVIII.56). In an age when men and women were seeking new forms of monastic life, this was a burning issue.

Bernard made clear in this treatise how much faith he had in the possibility of reflecting on human experience and logical distinctions in order to find meaning and order. The monastic life that he described was based on self-sacrifice but also on self-preservation. There was no place for excessive devotions that killed the body. As Bernard wrote towards the end of *On Precept and Dispensation*: "we are partly bound to our bodies and partly to the Lord: bound to our bodies by bonds of life and feeling, and bound to the Lord by faith and love" (XX.60, in *SBO* vol. 3, 292; 1970: 149). The love that the monk expresses towards God brings him to God in direct relation to that love: *Praesens igitur Deo est qui Deum amat in quantum amat* (XX.60, in *SBO* vol. 3, 293). The epigram is typical for Bernard: a linguistic *tour de force* that expresses a deep theological truth.

THE AFTERMATH

The abbot and monastic writer who had involved himself so intimately with the teachings coming from the twelfth-century schools of Paris did not become a central figure at the scholastic university that was established there after about 1200. In the thirteenth century Bernard's works more or less drop out of sight, except for his *On Grace and Free Choice* (Elm 1994: 53). His way of expressing himself was perhaps not sufficiently rigorous for the generations that built up theology according to *summae*.

In the later Middle Ages, however, Bernard's theology made a comeback to the schools of Paris. His presence can especially be seen in the writings of the theologian Jean Gerson (1363–1429), who dealt with the question of vows by turning to Bernard's *On Precept and Dispensation* (McGuire 2005: 156). Bernard is one of Gerson's favorite authors, and Gerson even gave a sermon on Bernard on the saint's feast day, 20 August, at the College of Saint-Bernard, the Cistercian house of studies in Paris (1998: 128–48). This had been established in the 1240s in order to make it possible for the Cistercians to participate in the scholastic theology of their age (Lekai 1977: 81). In naming the college after Bernard, the Cistercians indicated their belief in learning in relation to the life and writings of Bernard.

Gerson saw in Bernard a man who combined learning with affectivity. The term *affectus* is a key concept in describing what it is that characterizes Bernard's teaching. The saint believed that by investigating the interior life of the human person, he would find the trace of God. Human emotion and attachments were not threats for Bernard, as they had been for the Desert Fathers. Emotional bonds provided a point of departure for reaching out for God. Bernard was convinced that the monastic life was the best way to make this journey. His successors, such as Bonaventure, would point elsewhere. But both Bonaventure in the thirteenth century and Gerson in the fifteenth bear witness to the durability of what we can call Bernard's Christian philosophy. Through a union of thought and feeling the human person can return to the foundation of their being. In love and friendship with other persons the human person makes their way to the font of love.

Bernard was confident that Christ as the Word of God makes his visitations in the human soul. As Bernard described his own experience: "I perceived his presence, I remembered afterwards that he had been with me; sometimes I had a presentiment that he would come ..." (*SC* 74.5, in *SBO* vol. 2, 242). Thought and feeling unify in the unity of God's son.

FURTHER READING

Gilson, E. 1990. *The Mystical Theology of Saint Bernard*. Kalamazoo, MI: Cistercian Publications.
James, B. 1957. *Saint Bernard of Clairvaux: An Essay in Biography*. London: Hodder & Stoughton.
McGuire, B. P. 1988. *Friendship and Community: The Monastic Experience, 350–1250*. Kalamazoo, MI: Cistercian Publications.
McGuire, B. P. 1988. *The Difficult Saint: Bernard of Clairvaux and His Tradition*. Kalamazoo, MI: Cistercian Publications.
Sommerfeldt, J. (ed.) 1992. *Bernardus Magister*. Kalamazoo, MI: Cistercian Publications.
Southern, R. 1996. *Scholastic Humanism and the Unification of Europe, Volume 1: Foundations*. Oxford: Blackwell.

On FREE WILL see also Chs 2, 7, 19; Vol. 1, Ch. 18; Vol. 3, Chs 9, 15; Vol. 5, Ch. 22. On THE WORD see also Ch. 3.

10

AVERROES (IBN RUSHD)

Gerhard Endress

Abū-l-Walīd Muḥammad ibn-Muḥammad ibn-Rushd, known in the Latin West under the Hispanicized name 'Averroes', was, like his ancestors, a jurist in Islamic Andalusia. He became Chief Judge of Cordoba and Seville, court physician to the Almohad princes of Morocco and Spain, counsellor and courtier in the orbit of power. He belonged to the three worlds of intellectual culture in his age: he was brought up in the world of the *ʿulamā*, learned exegetes and administrators of the *Sharīʿa* (the revealed law of Islam); he mastered the world of the rational sciences – applied in medicine and astronomy, and crowned by the universal wisdom of philosophy that was taken to lead the way to true wisdom and ultimate happiness; and he rose to high station in the world of court, where the Commander of the Faithful ruled as absolute king. He embodied the sum of intellectual excellence and active experience a person could gain in his time and place.

The religious community, and the political conditions, of Muslim Spain underwent deep changes in Averroes' lifetime. His project – to give a rational foundation to the Muslim doctrine and in the long run to vindicate the work of philosophy as a rule of reason governing all of society – with its progress and its setbacks, was closely connected with the social condition, the spiritual outlook and the dialectic of power and authority in the Andalust.

When Averroes was born in Cordoba in 1126, the Maghrib and Andalusia were governed by the Berber dynasty of the Almoravids (al-Murābiṭūn, 'warriors of the faith'), who had entered North Africa from south of the Atlas. These were followed by the Almohads (al-Muwaḥḥidūn: proclaiming God's unity, *tawḥīd*), a fundamentalist reform movement led by the Berber Ibn Tūmart, the Mahdī ('The Rightly Guided'). After years of study in the East, he returned to North Africa and, proclaiming a spiritual reform of Muslim society, conquered Morocco. The entry of the Almohads into Andalusia (from 1145) was followed by two decades of unrest and revolt. Only years after the access to power of the amīr Abū Yaʿqūb Yūsuf (1163, taking the caliphal title of Commander of the Faithful, *amīr al-muʾminīn*, in 1168), the country was pacified. The submission, in 1169 and 1171, of the insurgents contending with the Almohads for power in central Andalusia and threatening Cordoba and Seville initiated the heyday of Almohad power in Andalusia.

In the course of the 1160s, Averroes conceived his project, the long-term project of his life, defined ever more clearly in the course of a prolonged struggle with the epistemic paradigm of the religious community, and brought to fruition in his years of maturity: establishing demonstrative science, the law of reason, as the basis of thought and action in the whole of human society, thus uniting the religious, scientific and intellectual communities under the authority of the philosopher–jurist. This project seems to have consciously developed when he was qadi of Seville, in the years from 1169 until at least 1171, the year of the earthquake at Cordoba. Waiting for peace to return to Andalusia, Averroes wrote his epoch-making manual of the principles of legal reasoning, and his three works on rational theology, the defence of reason versus the religious community and the refutation of al-Ghazali's *Incoherence of the Philosophers*, the famous theologian's attack on the validity of demonstrative philosophy.

The legal and theological doctrine of the founder of the Almohad movement, Ibn Tūmart, the Mahdī, could be read as a support of rational theology and independent legal reasoning. In law, he condemned the rigid, traditionalist casuistry exercised by the dominant Mālikī schools of law, and demanded a return to the sources of the revealed law, the Sharīʿa, and to the principles of sound reasoning; in theology, he insisted on the rational necessity of the creator and his unicity. Indeed, Averroes closely followed his creed in his own exposition of the articles of faith, while showing that philosophy, not the theology of traditionalist Ashʿarism, was the true defence of the purity of *tawḥīd*.

The consent of society to this attitude is signalled by an anecdote about the encouragement given to Averroes by the Almohad Abū Yaʿqūb Yūsuf, who in 1163 had succeeded the caliph ʿAbd-al-Muʾmin: the prince himself prompted the Muslim jurist and Aristotelian scientist to interpret this philosophy from its authentic sources. After a decisive breakthrough, Averroes perceived Aristotle as the exemplary man – an example given to humanity by divine Providence – who, in his encyclopedia had encompassed all science, and who by his method of demonstration had proved the coherence of rational knowledge with the reality of the intelligible cosmos (*see* Vol. 1, Ch. 5, "Aristotle"). After the re-pacification of the Andalus, Averroes returned to Cordoba, where he became great qadi, and also court physician to the Almohad prince.

In 1194, an indictment of unbelief was brought against him, born from the enmity of traditionalist jurists and the adherents of Sufi mysticism. In 1197 he was exiled; in 1198 he returned to favour. A few months later, on the night of 11 December, he died.

ARISTOTLE AND ARISTOTELIANISM

The project of Averroes evolved in the course of a dialogue with the philosophical and religious authorities of the Hellenistic and the Muslim Arabic traditions. The increasing and, in the final analysis, paramount importance that is accorded to Aristotle is a primacy given to the absolute authority of reason. The project of instituting demonstrative philosophy as a general basis of the epistemic community – embracing the religious institutions a well as the scientific community of mathematicians, astronomers and physicians – was to be realized through a commentary of the Aristotelian encyclopedia of the sciences.

Since the first reception of his works in Arabic translation, Aristotle was regarded by his Arabic followers (the *falāsifa*) as the guarantor of the way towards demonstrable truth, for the rational sciences as well as for the religious disciplines: the First Teacher, so called by Avicenna (Ibn Sina, *d.* 1037). Avicenna set out to rewrite the Peripatetic canon of readings according to the order and under the titles of the Aristotelian works: *Logica*, *Physica* and *Metaphysica*, supplemented by the mathematical quadrivium, and by the *Canon* of theoretical and practical medicine. His *Summa* of philosophy was based on a new metaphysics, which was to supersede Aristotle's. It is Aristotelian in that the universals are bound up with real substances, but can be abstracted by intellectual analysis, relying on self-evident principles and on demonstrative reasoning. It is (neo-)Platonic in that the divine mind is placed at the origin of an emanative series of intellects descending from the first cause, origin of the first intellect, over the celestial spheres down to the agent intellect. As a cosmic entity, the agent intellect (or 'active' intellect, in Aristotle's *On the Soul* III.5, an entity that makes actual what is potentially known in the soul's material) bestows the forms of the terrestrial world: the sublunary world of form-in-matter. The emanation of the forms from the 'Giver of Forms', the agent intellect, into the genera and species of the material substances, corresponds to the movement of cognition: the return of the soul to its origin, to the vision of the intelligible cosmos. In the process of cognitive reversion, the agent intellect, making actual what is potential in the mind, confers the divine illumination required for every true and necessary act of knowledge. Departing from the concepts of substance and accident, essence and existence, matter and form, potentiality and actuality, Avicenna specified the concept and proof of the divine cause under the terms of *kalām* theology (Wisnovsky 2003). He established the first cause as the necessary existent that alone has being essentially, is necessary by itself and is not a composite of essence and existence; all contingent, temporal being needs a first cause, which is necessary and eternal and confers being on the creation but, together with its eternal cause, the whole of the world coexists eternally.

This hierarchy of creation, modelled on Avicenna's cosmology, is still reflected in Averroes's early *Epitome* of Aristotle's *Metaphysics*. For the religious community, however, this Aristotelian Neoplatonic model – which implied the eternity of the world – remained a stumbling block even for those theologians who adopted Aristotelian logic as a basis of rational discourse. The refutation written by the jurist and theologian al-Ghazali (d. 1111), who was well versed in philosophy and a formative influence on the young Averroes through his summaries of Avicennian *falsafa* (i.e. *philosophia* in its Arabic adaptation), provoked the Andalusian's response. Al-Ghazali contested the philosophers' claim that human reason was consistent with God's wisdom, but nevertheless placed Aristotelian logic and hermeneutic into the service of the religious disciplines. Through al-Ghazali's adoption of Aristotelian concepts, systematized by the schools of Sunnī *kalām* developing in his wake, Avicenna's new interpretation of Aristotelian metaphysics shaped the scholasticism of later Islamic theology. In consequence, the defence of philosophy – of a philosophy to be further developed, refined and made immune – was undertaken by members of the same community who regarded rational demonstration as indispensable as a firm basis of sound argument in the service of Islam, and prepared the way for an Islamic scholasticism, adopted as a propaedeutic and methodology by the teachers of theology and law.

AVERROES AND HIS PREDECESSORS IN THE MUSLIM WEST

Meanwhile, the Aristotelians of the Muslim West – Andalusia and North Africa – took up the challenge of al-Ghazali. Averroes' first predecessor in the field of philosophy, Ibn Bājja (d. 1139), who introduced al-Farabi into Andalus, had despaired of applying the remedy of philosophy to the Almoravid state of his day; the hope that the few 'weeds' (an expression coined by al-Farabi for the seeds of corruption, now used in a reverse sense) of philosophy would spread out in the field dominated by narrow-minded jurists (*fuqahā'*) remained vague. If the emigration (*hijra*) from the corrupt state, which al-Farabi had recommended (and practised), proved impossible, the philosopher must lead the life of the solitary, of those "whom the Ṣūfīs call the strangers", strangers in this world "who travel in their minds to other abodes, which are their true homes" (Ibn Bājja 1968: 42ff.).

Ibn Ṭufayl (d. 1185) was the author of the famous philosophical romance of the Philosophus Autodidactus, *The Living Son of the Wakeful*: that is, the human intellect, brought to perfection by the divine active intellect. In the preface, he makes an attempt to mediate between Avicenna's and al-Ghazali's concepts of intellectual and religious knowledge: While the 'intuition' (*ḥads*) of Avicenna is the ultimate perfection of demonstrative reasoning, providing the accomplished philosopher with the result of a perfect syllogism in one immediate operation, the *ḥads* of mystical theology – like al-Ghazali's, grafted on Avicenna's *falsafa* by Ibn Ṭufayl – is the irrational inspiration accorded by divine grace. It was Ibn Ṭufayl, personal physician to the Almohad prince Abū Yaʿqūb Yūsuf, who presented Averroes at the court to be his successor, and it was Abū Yaʿqūb who encouraged the Muslim jurist and Aristotelian scientist to interpret the philosophy of the ancients from its authentic sources.

ALMOHADISM AND RATIONAL THEOLOGY

In keeping a cautious distance from such philosophical studies as would involve the controversial principles of physical and metaphysical doctrine, in his earlier works Averroes conforms to the material, social and intellectual restrictions imposed by the community in a time of crisis. The final victory of the Almohad dynasty opened chances for rational philosophy to join rational theology in the defence of the *Sharīʿa* and of the purity of the monotheistic creed. While militant and intolerant in the imposition of their ideology of *tawḥīd*, the confession of the unicity of God, the Almohads brought an ideology not legalistic but intellectual. 'Almohadism', as defined by recent studies on the background of Averroes (Urvoy 1991; Geoffroy 1999), is originally the spiritual outlook of the founder of the movement, Ibn Tūmart. In the articles of faith of his *Creed*, laid down on his return from Baghdad to the Maghreb, he evinced the firm conviction that each of the basic articles of faith is a truth demanded by reason: the existence of God the creator, the unicity of God, the necessary attributes of God and the transcendence of the divine – his essence, symbolized by the divine names in the revelation, must be accepted "without anthropomorphism, and without [asking the question] 'how'" (attrib. Averroes, Almohad Creed, my translation). The religious and moral content of the Sharīʿa follow from the knowledge of God, known through his creation (Urvoy 1978). These very principles were applied in Averroes' early works on jurisprudence and on the positive theology of Islam (Geoffroy 2005).

The Distinguished Jurist's Primer is a handbook of the methodological principles of legal reasoning (*ijtihād*), based on analogy; in its very first sentences, it opposes those schools of Muslim law that decline independent reasoning, and insists on the jurist's authority to choose from the decisions of the schools of law, and to make independent deductions.

In his exposition of the positive Islamic theology of Almohadism, *Clarifying the Methods of Proof Concerning the Beliefs of the (Religious) Community*, Averroes makes use of the tools of non-demonstrative discourse, poetical metaphor (*tashbīh*) and rhetorical persuasion (*iqnāʿ*), true to the paradigm established by al-Farabi, that is, to the ancillary task of instruction of the community, not trained in demonstrative method, but of necessity controlled by the masters of demonstration. Averroes proceeded to demonstrative argument in his commentary on Plato's *Republic*, where he duly eliminated from 'scientific' discourse the myth of the tenth book as containing "dialectical argument" and "remote imitations", "not necessary to a man's becoming virtuous" (Averroes 1974). While the religious law may provide guidance to the people, the community will be corrupted if it fails to seek guidance from the philosophers' demonstrative science (*ibid.*: 3ff., 145ff., 148ff.). Even though his purpose in the *Methods of Proofs* is different, Averroes will never compromise his philosophical creed, and will adduce not only the Scripture but also the works of Aristotle in order to prove his point. The *Mutakallimūn*, the speculative theologians (especially those of the Ashʿariyya, al-Ghazali's school of thought), using allegory to preserve the transcendence of God in the face of the anthropomorphism of the Scripture, fall short of the criteria of certitude that only valid demonstration can meet. Thus Averroes turns to Aristotle in order to show that the notions of material body, space and time do not apply to God. Even though God is omnipotent, he is not the creator of evil, but (against the determinism of al-Ghazali) human beings have full responsibility for their actions. Even though God is self-contained, remote from knowing the particulars of his creation and exercising providence towards them, Averroes admits of a teleological argument; in his demonstrative expositions, he will say that God the Prime Mover, being most perfect, will draw the world towards perfection, being their final cause. (For Averroes' further development of this topic, see Kukkonen 2002; Taylor 2007.)

Initially inspired by the attitude of al-Ghazali, perceived as spokesman of a religion purified and enlightened by reason, Almohadism arrived at sustaining a philosophy that, contrary to the *kalām* of al-Ghazali, held up the essential coherence between the divine will and the reason bestowed on humanity: a coherence demonstrated on the evidence of the physical creation. Now, abandoning the synthesis between Avicennian *falsafa* and the Ghazalian paradigm of religious knowledge, Averroes returned to the universal claim of absolute reason, which, in the Islamic community, had been first raised by al-Farabi: assuming for demonstrative science the authority of true exegesis, and relegating theology to an ancillary role where non-demonstrative methods would serve to convey the truth to the multitude.

This he took on with his great polemic against the *kalām* of al-Ghazali. As a motivation of his effort in defence of philosophy, he would state from the outset that the discourse of the theologians (*al-mutakallimūn*) was contrary to the explicit evidence of the *Sharī'a*. In order to avert error and heresy from religion, the philosopher assumes the authority of true exegesis.

In the first place, he wrote a legal pronouncement (a *fatwā*) in his *Decisive Treatise on the Nature of the Relation between the Religion* [Sharī'a] *and Philosophy*), asserting that the *Sharī'a* "has rendered obligatory the study of beings by the intellect, and reflection on them, … and has urged us to have demonstrative knowledge of God the Exalted and all the beings of His creation" (1967: 50), and showing that demonstrative truth and scriptural truth cannot conflict. What is more: true philosophy, based on demonstrative reasoning, is the safeguard of the true religion (*ibid.*: 70). Only "Those who are well grounded in science" (Qu'ran III: 9) are able to reconcile apparent contradictions in the Scripture.

> Now since this religion is true and summons to the study which leads to knowledge of the Truth, we the Muslim community know definitively that demonstrative study does not lead to [conclusions] conflicting with what Scripture [or Religious Law] has given us; for truth does not oppose truth but accords with it and bears witness to it. (1967: 50)

Averroes discarded the *kalām* paradigm of hermeneutic knowledge in his reckoning with Ghazali, clearing the way for his ultimate purpose: the final emancipation of reason from the strictures of scriptural exegesis and traditionalist literalism. In defence of philosophic rationalism, he wrote his large-scale, systematic refutation of Ghazali, the *Incoherence of the Incoherence* (*Tahāfut al-Tahāfut*), which is accompanied by a new interpretation of the true Aristotle, and is at the same time a critique of Avicenna's system. The main points of al-Ghazali's attack against Aristotelian philosophy in its Avicennian interpretation were the doctrines of the eternity of the world, and the denial of individual immortality; more generally, the 'incoherence' of philosophical demonstration, not valid for resolving the aporias set before human understanding of God's transcendence.

It is true that these treatises were restricted to 'dialectical' arguments, using non-technical language, to be used towards those who are "not men of scientific learning" in order "to establish virtuous opinions in their souls", and hence defended for this purpose in political science. The philosopher was bound to obey the structures of reasoning and its consequences, which Aristotle had arrived at uncompromisingly. Under this condition, the harmony between legal reasoning based on the revelation and the absolute truth based on demonstrative reasoning from universal premises, which the early school of philosophy founded by al-Kindī pretended to provide, did not hold. Thus the ancient cosmology, the doctrine of the eternity of the world, was transmitted to the early *falāsifa* and adapted by them, in a form simplified and made acceptable for the adherents of a monotheistic and creationist religion: of belief in a God who was both first cause and first intellect, and who had willed at the beginning of time to create the physical world from nothing. But the true philosopher was bound to the strictures of demonstrative reasoning. This is conceived as a higher dimension of rationalism where reason is not just an ancillary tool, and is unhampered by restrictions imposed by a divine will contrary to its inherent necessity. "According to the philosophers, the meaning of 'will' in God is nothing but that every act proceeds from Him through knowledge" (Averroes 1954: 257).

DEMONSTRATIVE SCIENCE

The primary purpose of Averroes was determined by a philosophic tradition that sustained the method of demonstrative logic and the encyclopedia of the rational sciences in the framework of the Peripatetic canon. This was presented as a system – including, and at the same time subordinating, the religious disciplines – by al-Farabi, refounded and rewritten by Avicenna, put into the service of religious learning by al-Ghazali and reduced to the role of an ancillary by al-Ghazali's successors. Accordingly, the initial project of Averroes was limited to "what is necessary for the first perfection of man" (*Epitome de anima*, cf. Alaoui

1982: 53ff.), starting with concise compendia of logic and the physical sciences, but from the very beginning taking Aristotle as supreme guide.

The same limitation is pronounced in the Epitome of Aristotle's *On the Soul*. The 'first perfection' (entelechy) refers to the grades of actuality, as described by Aristotle in his treatise on the soul (II.1): Soul is the perfection of the ensouled body, its entelechy – the essential form of the living being. Aristotle distinguishes the first from the second degree of perfection by the example of the degrees of knowledge; the first is the degree of acquired knowledge, the second is knowledge employed in an actual cognitive operation or contemplation. In the soul, reason is active, at first potentially, and then actually, and as the eye is in need of light making seen the visible, reason is in need of an activating principle that "makes all things" (*De anima* III.5). To clarify the process of cognition and, through this, to ascertain the possibility of the perfection of humanity through reason was to become the main objective of Averroes' project, turning with an increasing and exclusive devotion to Aristotle as an example of such perfection of the first seed implanted in the nature of humankind.

THE COMMENTATOR: THE RETURN TO ARISTOTLE

Around 1169, Averroes was presented to Abū Yaʿqūb Yūsuf, who engaged him in a disputation about the philosophers' doctrine of the eternity of the world, and encouraged him to undertake a detailed explanation of Aristotle's books. Abandoning the restraint of his early works, launching the new series of 'Middle Commentaries' (*talkhīṣ*, commentary-paraphrase) of no less than fifteen works of Aristotle, he follows Aristotle's text much more closely and meticulously than in the early epitomes. Returning to the text of Aristotle, and approaching the true meaning of his words, he gains an ever increasing confidence in the validity of demonstrative science: if Aristotle could be proved true, pursuing his method would assert the authority of his followers. Repeated statements in praise of Aristotle present Averroes on his way to an attitude of eager optimism; the newly won insight into the true meaning of Aristotle permits him to put his commentators, ancient (Alexander of Aphrodisias, Themistius, Johannes Philoponus) and 'modern' (al-Farabi, Avicenna, al-Ghazali) into place.

COSMOLOGY

The ambivalence of Averroes' esteem of his predecessor, and his new self-confidence, can be observed in his cosmological treatises of this 'middle' period: the "Middle Commentary on Aristotle's *On the Heaven*", and the treatise *On the Substance of the Sphere* (written in 1178–9), on the nature of the celestial body: being eternal and possessing infinite force, can the celestial body be composed of matter and form?

The basic issue is the relation of matter and form in the celestial soul: if the celestial sphere is a composite, it is susceptible to corruption and so, given an infinite amount of time, would in fact corrupt, in which case it could not be eternal, and yet for Averroes (and most Arabic-speaking philosophers after al-Kindi) the celestial sphere is eternal. Averroes argues that the moving form in the celestial body is a separate form, not a form-in-matter. If this body were composed of form and matter, it would be eternal by accident only. The intellect and the intelligible in the celestial body being one and the same, the form towards which the sphere is moved and the form by which it is moved are one and the same. The celestial body functions as matter for this incorporeal form, but exists in actuality, not requiring the form for its existence; it constitutes a matter, or rather a subject (*mawḍūʿ*), only for the purpose of receiving the celestial form, which is giving it eternal duration (Endress 1995). As long as the definition of soul as the form of a bodily substrate was upheld in the case of the celestial body – as in Averroes' Alexander – the aporia remained unsolved. Only his own proposal would take account of all the problems involved. Both John Philoponus and Avicenna had exposed philosophy to criticism and abuse: Philoponus, the Christian Alexandrian who in his refutations of Aristotle and the Neoplatonists (especially of Proclus' *On the Eternity of the World*) tried to prove the world's creation in time, erred through his faulty understanding of the motive force in the heaven. Avicenna went wrong with his conception of the first principle. He built his proof of the existence of a first principle on an analysis of the concepts of necessary and possible being: there must be a divine first cause which alone is necessary in virtue of itself; but then the celestial body, which in itself has a finite force, would be necessary and infinite only in virtue of another, immaterial principle; and it would be absurd to posit a contingent being having a possibility of being destroyed which is never actualized (Averroes 1986: 104ff.). Averroes contends that only a physical, not a metaphysical, proof based on the motion of natural substances can provide a valid demonstration of God's existence. Only the true understanding of Aristotle's doctrine – and this is the task Averroes had set for himself – could redeem true philosophy from error and blame. He never tires of invoking the testimony of his forebears. But in the final effort, he is on his own.

While still in the course of his defence of philosophy against Ghazali's *kalām*, Averroes embarks on the last and most ambitious phase of his project: the Great Commentary (*sharḥ*, *tafsīr*) of the five works of Aristotle he deemed central with regard to his purpose: the books on demonstration (*Analytica posteriora*; hereafter *An. post.*), on natural processes (*Physica*), on the soul (*De anima*), on the celestial sphere and the superlunary and sublunary universe (*De caelo*), and the principles of being (*Metaphysica*). At the very time when he finished the *Incoherence of the Incoherence*, he started on the *Great Commentary on the Book of Demonstration* (completed in 1180), the fundamental work on the conditions, and limits, of the acquisition of rational knowledge through demonstration. Taking up the method of the ancients, the literal commentary of late Hellenism, which for Peripatetic and

Neoplatonist alike had become the principle vehicle of philosophic argument and innovation, Averroes returns to re-establishing the true sense of Aristotle's text from the bottom up. The work of Aristotle is living proof of the highest perfection of the human species, an encouragement taken by the author to pursue his final aim (*Great Commentary on De anima*; Averroes 1953: 433).

METAPHYSICS

Among the principal points Averroes raised against Avicenna is the subject and scope of first philosophy. The Aristotelian concept of the science of *Meta ta physika* as a science of being *qua* being had been focused by the Neoplatonist commentators on the specification of first philosophy, looking into the first and noblest beings: eternal, intelligible and unmoved essences (as opposed to physics, which looks into mobile beings, eternal or corruptible). Early Islamic philosophy – al-Kindi and his school – had adopted this from the Alexandrian school as a model of rational theology, but identified the One and first cause and the first intellect, legitimizing demonstrative science as a vindication of monotheism. Then al-Farabi, and following him Avicenna, in redefining the Aristotelian metaphysics of being *qua* being, brought the Platonic subject matter of philosophy – the immaterial transcendentals – under the sway of this science. Averroes followed suit, but in his early *Epitome*, he already contends with Avicenna about the autarchy of demonstration in metaphysics. He agrees that it is the task of the metaphysician to examine the ultimate causes of being with regard to the deity and the divine, that is, the immaterial things, but only after the physicist has dealt with the material causes and those of motion and has proved the existence of an immaterial first cause of motion. No other science was able to prove this point. Only then could metaphysics go on to determine the efficient and final causes as first principles. In interpreting Aristotle's statement "that one cannot demonstrate the proper principles of everything" (*An. post.* I.9, 76a16–17), Averroes explains that this does not mean that any of the particular nether sciences is not able to demonstrate the causes of its subject matter at all. Aristotle meant that it cannot provide proof of its subject *simpliciter*, that is, of both its existence and cause. Since "it is impossible to know what a thing is if we are ignorant whether it is" (*An. post.* II.8, 93a20), each science must ascertain the existence of its matter from immediate evidence or deduction based on the lower domains of knowledge. But it can infer the causes of its particular matter only from induction: valid if the underlying sign (*dalīl*, σημεῖον) is a valid *causa cognoscendi*, but lacking absolute necessity. Only from the perspective of the higher *genus* will the *causa cognoscendi* and the *causa essendi* coincide, but the higher science, while it can demonstrate the reason why, often does not know the fact. This holds for metaphysics *a fortiori*. The first philosophy does not demonstrate *simpliciter* the principles of the sciences, but can demonstrate such principles only in as far as they are of existents (being *qua* being), not in so far as they are proper to the particular subjects of the sciences. Metaphysics explains absolute being in as far as this is the highest *genus* common to all subjects of the particular sciences. But these particular sciences, and only these, yield the specific causes for the existence of their proper subjects, and the reasons specific to the subject of a particular science are the concern of that science. Avicenna failed to understand this when he maintained that physical science takes the concepts of prime matter and the first cause from metaphysics: physics explains prime matter and the first cause (the Prime Mover) 'through signs' in that these are causes of motion, not in that they are classes of being.

The existence of matter and the laws of motion are presupposed, not demonstrated by metaphysics, and there is no way to prove the existence of the Prime Mover but through the arguments of this science; *pace* Avicenna, this is not within the grasp of metaphysics. By relegating his proofs of the first cause to metaphysics, he exposed his argument to the critique of al-Ghazali. By disregarding existence as a criterion of demonstrable truth, he disavowed reason.

Whereas the Aristotelian tradition argued for the first cause *qua* first mover by way of motion, Avicenna established the existence of the first cause *qua* necessary existent (*wājib al-wujūd*), a concept occurring in the works of some of his predecessors, but developed by him to become a cornerstone of metaphysics. In his later writings, Avicenna rejected outright the cosmological argument:

> It is nonsensical to arrive at the First Truth by way of motion and by way of the fact that it is a principle of motion, and [then] to undertake from this [position] to make it into a principle for the essences, because these people [Aristotle and his commentators] offered nothing more than establishing it as a mover, not that it is a principle for what exists.   (Avicenna, *Book of Fair Judgment*, trans. in Gutas 1988: 264)

The ontological distinction between necessary (uncreated) and contingent (created) being is based on the principal difference between essence and existence, existence being accorded to the essences by the necessary being – the One and First – in which both coincide. But this very distinction offered a convenient handle to al-Ghazali, who postulated the intervention of the divine will to confer existence on the possible essences: creation.

Avicenna's mistake – in the eyes of Averroes' meta-critique – is the mistake of a philosopher pretending to pull himself up by his bootstraps. The possible (*versus* actual) into which Avicenna divides existence is "a quality in a thing, different from the thing in which the possibility is", "not an entity actually outside the soul" (Averroes 1954: 118ff.). Hence it could be denied altogether to exist outside the human mind in the external world, as al-Ghazali argued in his *Tahāfut*: as universals exist only in the mind, "it can be said that possibility is a form which exists in the mind, not in the actual substances [of the external world]" (Averroes 1954: 64).

In reality, Averroes replies, the possible can be truly said only of things that are potentially actual, that is, of substances: "The possible existent in bodily substance must be preceded by the necessary existent in bodily substance" (*ibid.*: 254). There is no realm of pure form, nor a realm of pure matter; the bodily form is the dimensionality of first matter – a potentiality in act. It is not possible, as Avicenna says, "that there should be something contingent by its essence but necessary on account of something else", but:

> *motion* [in the case of the motion of the heavens] can be necessary by something else and contingent by itself, the reason being that its existence comes from something else, namely the mover; if motion is eternal, it must be so on account of an immovable mover, either by essence or by accident.　　(Comm. on *Metaphysics* XII, in Averroes 1984: 165)

This is said in connection with the problem of the eternity of the world, the principal point of contention between physical philosophy and the religious worldview. The metaphysician must stick to physics – to the external world – for incontrovertible arguments based on reality. Metaphysics cannot prove its own principles, but can only deduce from signs (*dalā'il*); we cannot proceed except from what is best known to our minds to what is certain by itself.

SOUL AND INTELLECT

In order to perceive the true subjects of metaphysics, the separate intelligences that move the celestial spheres, and the pure entelechy of the Prime Mover, the philosopher is, again, dependent on the psychological and physical parts of natural science. The only way, then, to arrive at the highest degree of cognition, and thus at the ultimate happiness available to humanity, is through the theoretical sciences: demonstrative reasoning founded on, and directed towards, real substances, essence undivided from existence.

The universal is not (as in the theory that al-Ghazali presumed to refute) the object of knowledge: through it, the things become known. The principles of demonstration are not themselves acquired through demonstration, but are known through the agency of the intellect (*tu'lam bi-l-'aql*), since only the intellect is a stronger safeguard of truth (*akthar tahqīqan*) than demonstration: contrary to the successive assemblage of data in discursive thinking, the agent intellect opens the mind's speculation, through the universals illuminating the mind's images as light does to the objects of vision among the sensibles, to the contemplation of God: the separate intellect thinking himself in eternally actual thought.

Whenever this happens – and this results from the highest activity of reason – the active intellect informs the material intellect, the expression (or 'place') in human beings of this universal and eternal intellective principle, and thus constitutes the speculative intellect in the individual human being; the intelligible is the eternal form of the material intellect universally, and at the same time the transitory form of the speculative intellect individually, and in either respect a self-thinking subject identical with its intelligible object in the act of thought. It is the act of an eternal principle, but in substance different from its own, generated and corruptible. "In this way only" the incorruptible, separate forms may be thought of as conjoining with the corruptible, contingent nature of human beings, and, "as Themistius said, man will become similar to God in that he is all beings in some way and knows them in a way; because beings are nothing but His knowing [them], and the cause of beings is nothing but His knowing" (1953: III 500ff.).

But the final *assimilatio Dei* of human beings through reason is conceived metaphorically (*quoquo modo*) and obliquely in a citation from Themistius, as the final goal of humanity's movement towards universal knowledge, to be realized, if at all, in a transitory moment of truth. It is not a union of humanity with God; the union to which the Ṣūfiyya pretends or at which the Ṣūfiyya aims cannot reach even this degree, but only the demonstrative sciences will open the way towards this "natural perfection", which may yield "a quasi-divine perfection of man". It is not possible that a generated and corruptible substance should conjoin substantially with the separate, eternal forms in the union of self-thinking thought; in this the human soul – the form of a corruptible body – is different from the separate intellects moving the celestial bodies. This led al-Farabi, in a famous passage of his commentary on the *Nicomachean Ethics* (now lost, but quoted by Ibn Bājja and Averroes), to deny the possibility of a conjunction between the separate forms or intelligences with the intellect in human beings. Ibn Bājja objected, but with faulty arguments. In several stages, Averroes found his final analysis of the intellect, referring to the true understanding of Aristotle. The material intellect is not subject to generation and corruption, but is the eternal and universal counterpart of the agent intellect; the agent intellect is not the form, but the agent of the intellect in humans (otherwise, al-Farabi's argument would hold): acting in us as 'form for us' in the process of abstracting universals from the material forms and their representations in the mind. The speculative intellect in human beings, under this agency, projects images onto the receptacle of the mind. The material intellect, then, is not subject to generation and corruption: not a material intellect of each individual (*pace* Alexander), but one unique and eternal principle, eternally and universally prepared to conjoin with the Forms.

But this conjunction is actualized in the speculative intellects of individual minds: individual not *qua* matter (which is universal), but *qua* form (the *intentio intellecta*) in the multiple images of thought. The material intellect, one and singular with respect to the one and singular agent intellect, cannot be separated from the corporeal forms in the imagination, the origin of its becoming actual, of the individual. At any given time, however, human beings will think and will thus provide forms to this universal intellect: the universal matter of the universal species of humanity. In this, that is, in studying the speculative sciences, human beings will "help each other", and it can be assumed that the intelligibles, being eternal, will at all times be informing a philosopher's thought, "for, since it is the case that wisdom exists in some way proper to human beings ... it is deemed impossible that the whole habitable world should abandon philosophy" (Averroes 1953: 408).

Philosophy, the highest activity of reason in human beings, participates in the eternity of the human species. In this, "when the human perfection is reached, the intellect is bared of potentiality", and "since it is impossible that at any one time we should not be thinking by it, it remains that when this intellect is free from potentiality, we are thinking by it in that this is an act of its very substance, and this is the ultimate felicity" (Averroes 1932, 1942, 1948: 1490).

The ultimate happiness is in ultimate knowledge; but the highest perfection to be conceived will obtain "when this intellect is free from potentiality, and we think by it through the activity of its own substance: this is the ultimate happiness" (*ibid.*), and this is not the way of thinking in an individual mortal human. The philosopher is on his way, by engaging in the activity proper to human beings, to accomplish this "movement toward conjunction". Demonstrative philosophy is not just a method to an end; it is a way of life that makes human beings worthy of the divine gift of reason. But Averroes divides severely between the divine intellect, constituting reality by its knowing, and humanity's quest for the comprehension of the separate intelligibles, depending for its science on the material of sense-perception: not a divine, but a human, perfection. There is no way to asserting, in this critique of pure reason based on demonstration, the immortality of the individual soul; only the human species is eternal, as are the separate, Agent and Material, eternal intellects.

Convinced that philosophy, representing the totality of rational science, will accept only the evidence of the principles deduced by reason, and that he must exercise the demonstrative method (the *burhān*) alone, Averroes excludes revelation from his quest for absolute truth. Religion is true; religions are "obligatory, since they lead towards wisdom in a way universal to all human beings, for philosophy leads only a certain number of intelligent people to the knowledge of happiness" (Averroes 1954: 360); but religion is just a metaphor of the absolute truth open to the philosopher.

Aristotle, the greatest of philosophers, led humanity on the way to a truth beyond the limit of any individual human being: the final assimilation to God, and the ultimate bliss to be pursued, although never attained by an individual reason embodied in a mortal vessel.[1]

---

1. For a survey of the works of Averroes, their medieval Latin and Hebrew versions, editions and modern translations, see Endress (1999b). A current bibliography is offered by the project Averroes Latinus, of the University of Cologne, on its internet site: www.thomasinst. uni-koeln.de/averroes/index.htm (accessed May 2009).

FURTHER READING

Alaoui, J.-E. 1986. *Le Corpus Averroicum* [in Arabic]. Casablanca: Toubkal.

Daiber, H. 1999. *Bibliography of Islamic Philosophy*. Leiden: Brill.

Davidson, H. 1992. *Alfarabi, Avicenna, and Averroes on Intellect: Their Cosmologies, Theories of the Active Intellect, and Theories of Human Intellect*. New York: Oxford University Press.

Davidson, H. 1997. *Proofs for Eternity, Creation and the Existence of God in Medieval Islamic and Jewish Philosophy*. New York: Oxford University Press.

Endress, G. 1987–91. "Die wissenschaftliche Literatur". In *Grundriss der arabischen Philologie*, vol. 2, 400–506, vol. 3, 3–152. Wiesbaden: Reichert.

Geoffroy, M. & C. Steel 2001. *Averroès: La béatitude de l'âme*. Paris: Vrin.

Gutas, D. 1988. *Avicenna and the Aristotelian Tradition*. Leiden: Brill.

Urvoy, D. 1991. *Ibn Rushd (Averroes)*. London: Routledge.

Wisnovsky, R. 2003. *Avicenna's Metaphysics in Context*. Ithaca, NY: Cornell University Press.

On ARISTOTELIANISM see also Chs 4, 11. On COSMOLOGY see also Chs 4, 16; Vol. 1, Chs 6, 8, 14, 17. On ISLAM see also Vol. 3, Ch. 15. On LAW see also Ch. 8; Vol. 3, Ch. 12. On METAPHYSICS see also Vol. 3, Ch. 8. On REASON see also Chs 11, 12, 16, 18; Vol. 3, Chs 8, 12, 16, 21; Vol. 4, Chs 4, 8.

11

MOSES MAIMONIDES

Charles Manekin

Moses Maimonides (1138–1204; known also by the Hebrew acronym 'Rambam') is a paradoxical figure in the history of the philosophy of religion. He is thought by many to be the greatest Jewish philosopher who ever lived, yet he did not consider himself to be a philosopher. When he refers to "the philosophers" and "the men of speculation", he generally intends those who wrote books on philosophy, thus separating himself from them. Born in Cordoba, Spain, Maimonides lived an active life in Egypt as rabbi, judge, communal leader and, in the later years of his life, as a physician in the Ayyûbid court in Cairo. His major work, *The Guide of the Perplexed* (hereafter *Guide*; *c*.1185–90), is widely regarded as a masterpiece in the philosophy of religion, yet its subject matter concerns the fundamentals of the religious Law (*shariʿa*/*Torah*), and its primary aim is the explanation of some difficult terms and parables in Scripture. Most of his early writings deal with Jewish law, including the *Mishneh Torah* (completed 1178–80) and his commentary on the *Mishnah* (completed 1168–70), the third-century law code that forms the basis of rabbinic Judaism. In the last decade of his life he primarily wrote medical books. Only one purely philosophical work, a short glossary of logical terms, is attributed to Maimonides, and that attribution has recently been questioned (Davidson 2004: 313–22). Nonetheless, his philosophical treatment of the fundamentals of Judaism – he was the first Jewish thinker to draw up a list of such fundamentals – and his largely Aristotelian outlook earned him the designation "the divine philosopher" by the Provençal savant, Samuel ibn Tibbon, who translated the *Guide* from its original Judaeo-Arabic into Hebrew.

Maimonides lived his entire life in Jewish communities around the Mediterranean and within the Islamic world. Like others who were born into Andalusian rabbinical families, the young Maimonides studied traditional Jewish texts along with the works of secular learning available in Arabic. While it is difficult to know with certainty what those works included, we can infer that by the time he was an adult he was quite familiar with the Muslim religious theology known as '*kalām*', and that he had a good grounding in the works of Aristotle and his commentators that were available in Arabic. Scholars have found influences of al-Farabi, Avicenna (Ibn Sina), al-Ghazali and Ibn Bājja in his writings, although the nature and extent of such influence has been debated.[1] Maimonides was also familiar with earlier Jewish philosophers, but he rarely refers to them, and the unmistakable impression is that they are less authoritative for him than the Muslim philosophers. His supreme religious authorities were, of course, the biblical prophets, followed by certain rabbinic sages whom he considered to possess eternal truths of physics and metaphysics. While not strictly speaking 'philosophers', prophets and sages often held similar doctrines, even though they expressed them in figurative and parabolic language.

One of the tasks of Maimonides in the *Guide* is to uncover the deep meaning of Scripture and its rabbinic interpretations concealed by the surface meaning of the text. The words of Scripture are likened to "apples of gold in settings of silver" (*Guide* 1.Int., 11);[2] their external meaning, although beautiful and beneficial, conceals an internal meaning, namely, the eternal truths of science and philosophy. For Maimonides, Scripture is to be interpreted according to the underlying principles of religion, most of which are consonant with the doctrines of the true, that is, the Aristotelian, philosophers. Reason uncovers, rather than determines, the true meaning of Scripture. Revelation and reason are two sources for the same truth, provided they are understood properly.

RELIGIOUS LANGUAGE

Some of Maimonides' most distinctive doctrines in the philosophy of religion emerge from his attempts to interpret the Torah or, more accurately, the foundations of the Torah, in light of what he holds to be philosophically demonstrated truths. The Torah teaches that God is one, for example, but it is the task of the philosophically trained sage to tell us what that implies. For Maimonides, divine unity is interpreted both as simplicity of essence and uniqueness. Simplicity of divine essence rules out multiplicity of any kind, which, according to Maimonides, has implications for religious language and one's conception of God. It is his thesis that the affirmative predication of attributes generally implies divine multiplicity, and hence he holds that no attributes can be predicated affirmatively of God. The *no affirmative attribute* thesis was certainly not original with Maimonides; on the contrary, it was virtually a commonplace among his philosophically trained predecessors, both Jewish (Abraham ibn Da'ud) and Arab (Avicenna). The same

---

1. For an exhaustive discussion of Maimonides' sources in philosophy, see Davidson (2004: 86–118).
2. References to Maimonides' *Guide of the Perplexed* will be given in the text by listing part number, introduction or chapter number, and then the page number of the Shlomo Pines translation in Maimonides (1963). Occasionally the translation in the text is my own.

is true with another thesis often associated with Maimonides, the *desirability of employing negative attributes* when speaking of God. Both the 'no affirmative attribute' thesis and the 'desirability of employing negative attributes' thesis should be distinguished from a third thesis held by Maimonides, namely, that attributes predicated of God and creatures are *completely equivocal* in meaning.

Of the three theses Maimonides is the most insistent about the 'no affirmative attribute' thesis because of his view that predications of affirmative attributes generally carry with them existential import: that is, they imply the existence of separate notions (*ma'āni*) within, or added to, the divine essence, which is incompatible with divine simplicity. Maimonides' chapters on divine attributes in the *Guide* are written chiefly as a counter to the *kalām* theologians, who either accept that affirmative predicates signify separate things in God, or who hold doctrines that, according to Maimonides, imply multiplicity. He does not discuss the view of some *kalām* theologians that a small set of unavoidable essential attributes (e.g. living, powerful, knowing), although not synonymous, refer to one single notion, and hence do not undermine divine unity.[3] Nor does he give an independent argument against affirmative predication as implying *per se* a dualist ontology of subject and predicate, and hence as inadmissible with reference to God.[4] On the contrary, he implies that were two putative attributes, for example knowing and living, to signify the same notion, then predicating them of the divine essence would not imply multiplicity (1.53, 122), provided that they were considered identical with God's essence, rather than notions within it, or superadded to it.

Why, then, does Maimonides take such an uncompromising stance on the predication of affirmative attributes? He believes that such predication is systematically misleading. While it *can* be given an interpretation that does not logically imply multiplicity, people generally employ affirmative attributes imprecisely. Similarly with respect to the implications of affirmative predication for divine uniqueness, that is, incomparability: since the divine essence is wholly unique, to predicate a predicate of God and of us in anything less than a completely equivocal sense misleads us into thinking that the difference between God and his creatures is merely quantitative, and not qualitative. One could avoid this implication, presumably, by saying something like, "In the predication, 'God is living', I do not intend that 'living' signifies a notion separate from, or internal to God's essence, or that his life is comparable in any way to ours". That is basically Maimonides' advice when dealing with certain biblical predications, as well as predications of perfection, which he allows, provided they are not taken as referring to real attributes or damaging God's incomparability (1.61, 148). Later on in the *Guide* he explicitly licenses such affirmative predications as 'God is knowing' when he claims that 'knowledge' is said of God and other knowers with complete equivocation.

---

3. In Saadia Gaon, *Book of Belief and Opinions* 2:5; see Saadia Gaon (1948: 103–4).
4. See Stern (2000) for the contrary view.

But, on the whole, Maimonides cautions against affirmative predication because it contains "an element of deficiency and associationism", that is, associating something not divine – in this case the conventional meaning of the attribute 'knowledge' – with God.

The 'completely-equivocal attributes' thesis was criticized by later philosophers such as Aquinas and Gersonides as forestalling the possibility of any knowledge about God. If the 'completely-equivocal attributes' thesis were true, then "from creatures nothing could be known or demonstrated about God; for the reasoning would always be exposed to the fallacy of equivocation".[5] Scholars have taken the thesis as reflecting Neoplatonic tendencies, or theological scepticism, or, at least, an emphasis on the limitations of human knowledge. These interpretations, although possible, are difficult to reconcile with Maimonides' positive theological statements. No less an Aristotelian than Averroes (Ibn Rushd) holds that knowledge is predicated of God and other knowers with pure equivocation. Both Maimonides and Averroes maintain that there is an essential difference between God and his creatures, and hence that the divine essence cannot be understood. But this does not rule out the possibility of real theological knowledge arrived at through philosophy and revelation. The issue is not so much the limitations of human knowledge concerning God, but rather the *limitations of theological language* in expressing truths about God, given that the divine essence cannot be apprehended by any creature, even the angels. This is not a particularly radical doctrine for a medieval philosopher.

In fact, it is not even clear that 'complete equivocation' rules out for Maimonides some resemblance in meaning between terms referring to God and to creatures. We see from several passages in Maimonides' writings that there can be some *functional resemblance* between things that are signified by equivocal terms. For example, when discussing the faculties of the soul in his *Commentary on Mishnah*, Maimonides claims that the term 'nutritive' is said equivocally of the nutritive faculty in man, eagle and donkey, and that the term 'sentient' is said equivocally of man and other animals because the souls of different species differ essentially. Nevertheless, he argues, because there is a functional resemblance we can apply the same names. To illustrate this, Maimonides cites as an example the phrase 'lit place' when said of three places in which the source of light varies. The phrase is said to signify "with only the name in common" because the cause of the light, as well as its activity, differs in each place (Maimonides 1964: 374). But surely Maimonides does not mean to say that 'lit place' *means something entirely different* in each case, at least in our everyday sense of meaning. Of course, the no-likeness thesis will be stronger in the case of God than in the case of lit places, but not necessarily strong enough to rule out the sort of functional resemblance we are suggesting here. After all, Maimonides does not create a *new* category of significa-

---

5. Aquinas, *Summa theologiae* I.13.5; Gersonides, *Wars of the Lord* 3, 3.

tion to denote terms referring to God and to others ('hyper-equivocation'?), but rather relies on the notion of complete equivocation.

If this interpretation is correct, then a tacitly assumed *functional resemblance* in the signification of attributes could do the same work for Maimonides that analogous predication does for Aquinas, and that primary and secondary predication (where terms such as 'being' and 'knower' are said primarily of God and secondarily of creatures) do for Aquinas and Gersonides; it would allow for some sort of shared meaning between terms predicated of God and creatures. Maimonides never considers analogous or primary and secondary predication, although he rejects amphibolous predication (where two things denoted by a single term are said to resemble each other in their non-essential properties) on the grounds that God has no non-essential properties (1.56, 131). Analogous predication is somewhere between amphibolous and purely equivocal predication; it is difficult to know what Maimonides would have thought of it, had he been aware of the concept.

In any event, Maimonides' official doctrine is that "the description of God ... by means of negations is the correct description" (1.58, 135). This is often known as Maimonides' 'negative theology', which is nothing more than the view that it is more appropriate, and less misleading, to describe God by what he is not than by what he is. Given that God's essence is unknowable – a non-controversial assumption for most medieval philosophers – how is one to arrive at a concept of God, one that picks out the God of our beliefs and prayers? The problem is particularly acute because "the Torah is written according to the language of men" (1.26, 56) and so its literal meaning cannot be relied on for teaching philosophical truths. Maimonides' answer is something like the following: by demonstrating philosophically that God is incorporeal or infinite, for example, we are not told what God is like, but only what he is unlike. Yet through these demonstrations we are able to construct a concept that: (i) picks out, by a process of exclusion, the entity that we refer to as 'God'; and (ii) does not explain to us anything about this entity's essence, that is, why it is what it is. Thus we can prove that this entity's existence is necessary, *without knowing what it is about the entity that renders its existence necessary*. We can prove that it is not corporeal, *without knowing what it is about this entity that renders its existence not corporeal*. To use Maimonides' formulation, we can learn things about God's *thatness*, his existence, but not about his *whatness*, his essence, which explains why he is the way he is. Negative attributes "conduct the mind toward that which one should believe with regard to Him ... [and] ... toward the utmost reach that man may attain in the apprehension of Him" (1.58, 135).

Maimonides' theory of divine attributes is intended to purify the believer's concept of God, which has been corrupted by a literalist reading of Scripture, the imagination and the weak and sophistical arguments of the theologians. All people are capable of possessing a concept that genuinely picks out the entity named 'God'. After only a small amount of philosophical training it is possible to believe that one should negate of God attributes that entail corporeality, potentiality, likeness to creatures, and change (1.35, 81). The doctrine that God possesses no likeness to creatures is taught in the Bible, and everyone already is aware of it. But if the believer does not know these doctrines through philosophy, that is, through the rational demonstrations of their correctness, then she possesses true belief but not certainty. Without philosophy, the concept of God is vague and unfocused, and can be easily directed away from its referent. Ultimately, what appears to constitute an accurate concept of God, according to Maimonides, is the apprehensions of the intellect about God, which, if arrived at through the process of philosophical demonstration, are certain. However, they are difficult to formulate in language, and, as we have seen, such formulations may be systematically misleading.

Although philosophy fine-tunes for us our concept of God, it does not provide us with knowledge of God's 'true reality', his essence. God is unknowable in the sense that his essence is not fully comprehensible or scientifically explicable. Like his contemporary Averroes, Maimonides believes that in order to understand the nature of the divine cognition we would have to be God (3.21, 485). So the chapters on divine attributes teach us about the strengths and the weaknesses of philosophy, the religious mandate for the pursuit of scientific knowledge and the limitations of such knowledge. Above all, they point out to us the limitations of human language, which means not only verbal speech but also mental conceptualization with reference to God, and they provide us with the strategies to circumvent, as much as is humanly possible, those limitations.

NATURAL NECESSITY AND DIVINE WILL

Maimonides' theology appears to undergo a development from his earlier writings to his later writings, although the core remains the same. In the first book of the *Mishneh Torah* we see God described as the First Existent that brings into existence all other existing things; their existence is dependent on God's existence, but God's existence is not dependent on theirs. The First Existent is the Mover, who conducts the outermost celestial sphere with an unlimited force, for the sphere rotates perpetually, and as a body it cannot itself contain an unlimited force. To demonstrate that this Existent is one and incorporeal, Maimonides also appeals to the premise that the sphere rotates perpetually.

Maimonides does not tell us in the pre-*Guide* writings *how* the world proceeds from God, specifically, whether it is a product of God's choice and will, or whether it proceeds of natural necessity. In fact, the divine will–natural necessity distinction, which plays such a key role in the *Guide* and in subsequent writings, does not appear in the pre-*Guide* writings. Nor do we learn anywhere from the pre-*Guide* writings that God created the world *ex nihilo* or that time has a beginning. On the contrary, by assuming the perpetual rotation of the outermost sphere in the first book of the *Mishneh Torah*, Maimonides assumes the eternity of the heavens. He himself tells us this when he relates in the *Guide* that in his books of jurisprudence, whenever he establishes the existence of God, he employs the premise that the world is eternal. This is not, he says, because he accepts the premise, but rather because he wishes to establish the proofs of God's existence "through a demonstrative method as to which there is no disagreement in any respect" (1.71, 182). However, this after-the-fact explanation seems unconvincing.

By the time we reach the *Guide*, and in subsequent writings, the doctrine of creation has been promoted to a foundation of the Law of Moses, second in importance only to belief in divine unity (2.13, 282). For Maimonides, the theological significance of creation lies in its implications for divine omnipotence, specifically, God's ability to perform miracles, and in general, the voluntariness of divine agency. Divine actions such as the collective reward and punishment for the Jewish people's observance and transgression of the Law, or the miraculous withholding of prophecy from a prophet who is prepared to receive prophecy, are connected with a robust notion of divine will that is lacking in the earlier writings. Miracles, for example, are understood in the *Guide* as involving a temporary change in the natural way of things; in the pre-*Guide* writings, Maimonides appears to hold that they are embedded within the nature of things (Kasher 1998; Langermann 2004). With the exceptions of miraculous providence and the miraculous withholding of prophecy, Maimonides adopts the naturalistic interpretation of these phenomena found in the Muslim philosophers. God's activity is eternal and his essence immutable, and so God does not *respond* to events. Rather, God governs or supervises the world via intermediaries, for example the celestial spheres, intellects and, in general, the natures of things. Also, biblical descriptions characterizing God as a person are to be interpreted metaphorically. These assumptions are enough to rule out both literal biblical conceptions of a personal God who *intervenes* in history, and deist conceptions of a God whose activity is limited to the creation of an autonomous, mechanistic system of nature. Instead, nature should be seen as God's ongoing activity through intermediaries, and indeed Maimonides glosses the phrase "divine actions" with the phrases "natural actions" (3.32, 525) and the "stable nature of things" as decreed by God's eternal will. He even allows the affirmative predication of attributes of *action* to God, since these do not pertain to the divine essence, nor posit a comparison between God and creatures, but only describe the natural way of things.

In a similar fashion, general and individual providence are interpreted, for the most part, naturalistically, as are divine reward and punishment. Even God's granting a petitionary prayer can be understood naturalistically: if the petition is on a spiritually appropriate plane, it will receive its share of the constant divine overflow, and the prayer will be 'answered'. Moreover, since God is supreme intellect, that divine overflow is intellectual. The late Hellenistic Aristotelians already gave a naturalistic interpretation of God's general providence; some of the Muslim philosophers, as well as Maimonides, extend that interpretation to include individual providence, which is effected through the conjunction of the human intellect with the celestial agent intellect, the last of the celestial intelligences (the movers of the spheres, described in the Bible as 'angels'). Prophecy is also interpreted intellectualistically and naturalistically: when the prophet, who possesses a highly capable imagination and perfected intellect, has achieved the requisite preparations, "the holy spirit immediately descends upon him", that is, he immediately receives the intellectual overflow from the agent intellect. In the *Guide*, Maimonides allows that prophecy can be miraculously withheld by God. Human happiness requires intellectual perfection, for which moral perfection is a necessary, but not sufficient, condition (3.53, 635).

Maimonides' intellectualist reading of traditional theological doctrines was the subject of more criticism in later generations than was his naturalistic reading, especially since he had tempered his naturalism with an emphasis on God's mastery of nature. The claim that providence, prophecy, reward and punishment, ultimate human happiness and immortality depended mostly on intellectual perfection rather than solely on faith or obedience to the Law was rejected by Jewish thinkers in the late Middle Ages, some of whom, living in Christian lands, were influenced by the scholastic rejection of Arab Aristotelian naturalism and intellectualism (Manekin 2000: 263–81).

The identification of the natures of things with God's ways, and the assumption of divine beneficence, raise the question of the existence of natural evils such as floods, earthquakes, illnesses and so on. Maimonides adopts the view that all God's actions are good, and so God does not produce evil essentially but rather accidentally through the creation of matter, which is limited in its capacity to receive good. Even the existence of matter is a good, because through it the cycle of generation and corruption can continue. Human evils, like natural evils, are privations of the good; they come about through ignorance of the good and the right (3.12–13, 484–97). Maimonides places blame for the evils that human beings inflict on themselves on the poor choices people make through ignorance and through vicious dispositions. He dismisses as false and tantamount to idolatry the idea of astral fatalism (although not the Aristotelian idea that the movements of the heavens influence the sublunar elements), and he claims that the human ability to act autonomously is taught by both philosophy and Scripture. Maimonides' emphasis on the human ability to act unconstrained by astral influences does not mean that he adheres to a libertarian conception of free will. Like Aristotle, he emphasizes the importance of voluntariness for the appropriateness of praise and blame (and reward and punishment), but no more than that. On the contrary, he states that in some cases it is extremely difficult for people to act against their native temperament.

As for reconciling divine omniscience with the human ability to act freely, Maimonides claims that both principles are taught by philosophy and Scripture. If philosophy cannot provide an adequate explanation of how God can know particular actions without rendering those actions necessary, that is hardly surprising; God's knowledge is identical with his essence, and just as philosophers have demonstrated that God's essence is incomprehensible, so too they should accept the demonstration that his knowledge cannot be fathomed (3.20, 481–2).

RELIGIOUS EPISTEMOLOGY

According to Maimonides, the highest epistemic status that a belief can have is certainty (*yakīn*), and the possession of certain beliefs and certain knowledge are within our grasp. He defines 'belief' as "the affirmation that what has been represented is outside the mind just as it has been represented in the mind". He then adds: "If, together with this belief, it is realized that a belief different from it is in no way possible and that no starting point can be found in the mind for a rejection of this belief or for the supposition that a different belief is possible, that is certainty" (1.50, 111). This understanding of certainty probably derives from the Muslim philosopher al-Farabi, who replaced the Aristotelian model of *epistēmē* (scientific or explanatory knowledge) with that of certainty (Black 2006). This is an important move for theology, for it implies that we can have certain knowledge, such as the knowledge that God exists, without explanatory knowledge, such as why God must exist.

Maimonides holds throughout his writings that God's existence, unity and incorporeality can be demonstrated, but beginning with the *Guide* he rejects the sufficiency of the Aristotelian proofs, since they rest on the premise that the world is eternal. Rather, he argues for God's existence on the basis of the following constructive dilemma: either the celestial sphere is eternal or created *de novo*; if the former, then God's existence, unity and incorporeality are demonstrable according to the ways of the Aristotelians (several of which are cited); if the latter, then the world's requiring a creator is a primary intelligible, "for everything that exists after having been nonexistent must have of necessity someone who has brought it into existence" (2.2, 232; cf. 1.71). Maimonides does not seem entirely consistent in his attitude towards the Aristotelian demonstrations: he occasionally accords them a greater status than is warranted, given his rejection of the eternity of the world (cf. 1.71, 180). Some have seen this as evidence that he secretly accepts the Aristotelian premise, but it seems more likely that his conflicting statements are the result of his desire to harmonize his new-found emphasis on divine will and creation with his previous near-total acceptance of the Aristotelian scientific worldview.

In addition to demonstrations, miracles also provide certainty, but only for those who witness them (3.50, 615–16). The teachings of the Torah are considered certain; however, if they are known merely on the basis of tradition, then they are not certain. The prophetic vision is known by the prophet with certainty, even though prophecy is acquired in a dream or through the imaginative faculty (3.24, 501). In the small *Treatise on Logic* attributed to Maimonides, knowledge of the sensibles, the primary and secondary intelligibles, and knowledge achieved through critical experience, are all considered certain (Maimonides 1938: 17–18). And finally, one:

> who has achieved demonstration, to the extent that that is possible, of everything that may be demonstrated; and who has ascertained in divine matters, to the extent that that is possible, everything that may be ascertained; and who has come close to certainty in those matters in which one can only come close to it – has come to be with the ruler [i.e. God].
> (3.15, 619)

Why does Maimonides place such emphasis on the attainment of certainty? It may be that, for him, certainty provides a reflexive awareness that prevents the mind from doubting or disbelieving even the possible falsity of an 'intelligible', that is, an eternal truth. Certain knowledge of an intelligible provides, as it were, a lock on it that cannot be shaken or dislodged. Doubting one's beliefs involves breaking the psychological–ontological bond between the knower and the agent intellect (cf. 3.51, 625). As mentioned previously, this bond is essential for Maimonides' explanation of special providence, prophecy, the immortality of the soul and the granting of petitionary prayer. In the *Mishneh Torah* Maimonides had warned against philosophical speculation by those who are not adept, who can easily be led astray by doubts and false beliefs; in the *Guide* he extends this to those who wish to know things beyond the limitations of human knowledge (1.31, 65–7). The quest for certainty, then, is essential to Maimonides' religious epistemological project.

While certainty safeguards the knower from falling into doubt, and hence from breaking the bond between the believer and the agent intellect, achieving certainty does not appear to be a necessary condition for creating or preserving that bond. If it were, then the attainment of human happiness and immortality of the soul (i.e. survival of the acquired intelligibles, the so-called 'acquired intellect') would be limited to those believers who possess certain knowledge. Although some of Maimonides' statements appear to imply this conclusion, others suggest that merely possessing true beliefs on eternal matters is sufficient for immortality. A resolution of this question is important for determining whether believers who assent to theological truths on the basis of traditional authority, rather than on the basis of demonstrative arguments, attain any measure of immortality. For ordinary knowers, demonstration appears to be the only way to achieve certain knowledge of eternal truths. "Primary intelligibles ... and things that come near to them in respect to their clarity", such as the existence of motion and the ability of human beings to act, are indeed "clear and manifest" (1.51, 112). But since "strange opinions" are capable of raising doubts even for these, demonstration is necessary to render them indubitable.

Not all eternal truths, however, can be demonstrated. There is a whole category of truths, including much of celestial science and metaphysics, that cannot be known with certainty, but only with a degree of epistemic status that ranges from conjecture to near certainty. The most important proposition in this category is that the world was created "after having been purely and absolutely non-existent ... time itself being one of the created things" (2.13, 281). The truth of this proposition can be established, not by demonstration, but by proofs approximating demonstration that provide the believer with near-certainty. To understand Maimonides' strategy in these proofs, one must first appreciate the awkwardness of the position in which he finds himself. His most admired authority, Aristotle, holds that the world always existed in the way it does now. Aristotle's position apparently follows from the principles of his science, such as the view that the continual, unending motion of the celestial spheres governs the continual, unending cycle of generation and corruption down below. On the other hand, the *kalām* theologians whose premises and methodology Maimonides often belittles provide him in this case with an argument for creation that he fashions into his chief proof for creation, once he has made it 'philosophically respectable'.

That argument is called the argument from particularization and goes something like this: assume that the world is eternal. This means that it eternally emanates from or is produced by God in a uniform, stable manner. This uniformity and stability enables it to be an object of scientific knowledge, which, according to Aristotle, is of what is permanent and not of what is non-essential. But suppose that the world contains phenomena that cannot be explained with reference to the stable nature of things. Suppose, also, that such phenomena cannot be understood as accidental, in the Aristotelian sense that they occur infrequently and without purpose. If such phenomena exist, they could only be explained as indicative of a divine purpose that cannot be ascertained by human beings.

Maimonides claims that he has found examples of such phenomena, for example the differing speeds and directions of the motion of the spheres, the number and position of the stars in the spheres, and in general the diversity of celestial phenomena (2.24, 326). He is able to appeal to authorities who question the adequacy of Aristotelian scientific explanation with respect to the heavens. With respect to Aristotle's terrestrial science, says Maimonides, matters are different. There the variety of phenomena is understandable, since sublunary material substances are composed of the four elements (earth, air, fire and water) in various proportions, which enables these substances to receive a variety of forms. But celestial material substances are composed of one homogeneous matter, which would lead one to expect at the very least a greater uniformity than is the case.

Moreover, Aristotelian physics cannot account for, and indeed conflicts with, basic concepts of Ptolemaic astronomy, a conflict that was well known to Maimonides' philosophical authorities. This conflict, we are told, is of no consequence to the astronomer, for he makes no existential claims about the system he posits in order to explain the observed movements of the celestial bodies (2.24, 326). But the fact that the heavens are not observed to operate according to the principles of Aristotle's natural science (without much tinkering, anyway) raises serious doubts about the adequacy of Aristotle's theory. Because these celestial phenomena cannot be given a satisfactory natural explanation, and because they do not appear to be random or accidental, Maimonides concludes that they are best attributed to the will of an intelligent deity who particularizes them to be as they are for its own purpose, as its wisdom dictates. This conclusion, Maimonides argues, does not accord well with the thesis of the eternity of the world. Hence, it is highly probable that the world was created.

Maimonides does not claim that the particularization argument demonstrates conclusively that the world is created, nor does he claim that on the basis of such an argument one may hold with certainty that the world is created. He does argue that the Aristotelian arguments for the eternity of the world are not conclusive demonstrations, and that the creation thesis occasions fewer significant doubts than the eternity thesis. What motivates him to accept the creation thesis is his belief that only the world's creation "after absolute nonexistence" is compatible with a robust notion of divine voluntary agency. In the absence of a demonstration to the contrary, it is rational for him to accept the well-established evidence of Scripture that God's will can overcome nature: indeed, that the natures of things are subject to a divine will that can will otherwise.

Maimonides' acceptance of a somewhat more robust notion of will does not sit easily with his Aristotelianism. For example, he generally holds that it is the intellect and not the imagination that determines what is necessary, possible and impossible. But whereas the Aristotelian considers creation *ex nihilo* impossible, the creationist considers it to be possible. What, then, is the operative criterion that distinguishes the possible from the impossible? To say that the distinction is determined by the intellect does not help, if one is unable to distinguish the intellect from the imagination. To these and other questions, Maimonides replies simply, "All these are points for investigation, which may lead very far", but he, himself, offers no answers (3.15, 461). While he accepts the Aristotelian principle that all real possibilities will be actualized at some time, he exempts God from its application; for God, there are unactualized possibilities – those things that he could create but does not. In later authors such as Scotus, emphasis on divine will and omnipotence will lead to a different conception of modal notions than in Aristotle. Maimonides, and Aquinas after him, begin on that road but do not get very far.

FURTHER READING

Altmann, A. 1987. "Maimonides on the Intellect and the Scope of Metaphysics". In his *Von der mittelalterlichen zur modernen Aufklärung*. Tübingen: Mohr.

Butterworth, C. & R. Weiss (eds) 1975. *Ethical Writings of Maimonides*. New York: Dover.

Davidson, H. 2004. *Maimonides: The Man and His Works*. Oxford: Oxford University Press.

Kreisel, H. 1999. *Maimonides' Political Thought: Studies in Ethics, Law, and the Human Ideal*. Albany, NY: SUNY Press.

Maimonides, M. 1963. *The Guide of the Perplexed*, S. Pines (trans.). Chicago, IL: University of Chicago Press.

Manekin, C. 1990. "Belief, Certainty, and Divine Attributes in *The Guide of the Perplexed*". *Maimonidean Studies* **1**: 117–42.

Manekin, C. 2005. *On Maimonides*. Belmont, CA: Wadsworth.

Pines, S. & Y. Yovel (eds) 1986. *Maimonides and Philosophy*. Dordrecht: Martinus Nijhoff.

Seeskin, K. 2000. *Searching for a Distant God: The Legacy of Maimonides*. New York: Oxford University Press.

Seeskin, K. (ed.) 2005. *The Cambridge Companion to Maimonides*. Cambridge: Cambridge University Press.

Twersky, I. (ed.) 1972. *A Maimonides Reader*. New York: Behrman House.

On ARISTOTELIANISM see also Chs 4, 10. On KNOWLEDGE see also Ch. 18; Vol. 1, Ch. 6. On LANGUAGE see also Chs 4, 12; Vol. 3, Ch. 14; Vol. 4, Chs 3, 8; Vol. 5, Chs 13, 20. On NEGATIVE THEOLOGY see also Vol. 5, Ch. 21. On PREDICATION see also Chs 13, 16; Vol. 5, Ch. 18. On REASON see also Chs 10, 12, 16, 18; Vol. 3, Chs 8, 12, 16, 21; Vol. 4, Chs 4, 8. On REVELATION see also Ch. 11; Vol. 1, Ch. 14; Vol. 3, Chs 7, 11, 16; Vol. 4, Chs 5, 11; Vol. 5, Chs 8, 23.

12

ROGER BACON

Jeremiah Hackett

Unlike his younger contemporaries, Aquinas and Bonaventure, Roger Bacon (*c*.1214–1292) did not write a treatise on the existence and nature of God, nor did he leave us a series of *Questiones* on topics related to the philosophy of religion. Moreover, he does not fit neatly into a modern 'analytic' understanding of philosophy of religion where the latter is often understood to be a justification of religion before the bar of argument alone. It is not that argument is lacking in Bacon's account, but that argument occupies a place that is clearly subordinate in Bacon to experience and to revelation. Bacon presents a view of a universal revelation of all knowledge beginning with the Hebrews and continued by the Greeks, Romans, Islam and Christianity that was to be common teaching until the European Enlightenment. This entails a universal revelation of all knowledge, both sacred and secular.

My account will emphasize the views of the mature Bacon (1260–92), since it is in this period that Bacon most explicitly discusses the relationship of philosophy and religion.

PHILOSOPHY AND THEOLOGY: THE HISTORICAL CONTEXT

Before presenting Bacon's account of the relation of philosophy to theology in *Opus maius* (Major work), part 2, I shall present the historical context outlined in part 1 of the *Opus maius* for Bacon's belief that philosophy as the search for wisdom must begin as a negative criticism of the impediments to knowledge. These are: submission to faulty and unworthy authority, influence of custom, popular prejudice and the concealment of one's own ignorance by means of ostentatious rhetoric. In regard to knowledge, Bacon is no egalitarian. "For many have been called but few are chosen for the reception of divine truth and philosophical truth as well" (*Opus maius* 10–11).[1] He holds that the way of the gifted few (the *Sapientes*) in philosophy and theology is superior to methods of the *vulgus philosophantium* (the common herd of philosophers).

From the beginning, Bacon introduces an unexpected element. He does not see the debate between philosophy (science) and religion as one between reason (argument) alone and religious faith. Rather, all epistemic activity involves the following: authority, reason, experience and belief. In Bacon's view, the omission of any one of these four elements leads one to an artificial epistemic situation.

Bacon is convinced that worthy and tested authority is preferable to faulty authority. He thinks that bare reason alone without experience can lead to unfounded theory. And so, for Bacon, it is never the case that philosophy of religion involves just a bare argument alone without experience. In fact, for him at every level – from the physical to the psychic to the mental to religious experience – a bare argument, without the requisite experience, is blind.

Bacon's own understanding of truth and revelation is conservative. Following the example of Aristotle, whom he regards as the leading philosopher, and of Seneca, Bacon holds that one must respect one's predecessors. Bacon looks to Avicenna (Ibn Sina), "the chief authority in philosophy after Aristotle", and to Averroes (Ibn Rushd) as his own predecessors. One must not underestimate the enormous influence these Islamic thinkers have on Bacon, specifically in terms of philosophy of religion. We shall see this specifically in Bacon's *Moralis philosophia* or "*Moral Philosophy*" (*Opus maius*, pt 7). This dependence on his predecessors enables Bacon to sketch out a progressive history of the appropriation of wisdom. "Just as Averroes, the greatest after these [Aristotle, Avicenna] refuted Avicenna, so also our men of science correct him in more instances, and rightly so, since without doubt he erred in many places, although he spoke well in others" (*Opus maius* 15). This critical open-mindedness on Bacon's part is not limited to his reading of the philosophers. He also argues that "not only the philosophers but even the sacred writers have been subject to some human infirmity in this respect" (*Opus maius* 15). As examples of theological disagreement and necessary criticism as a constituent part of a religion, Bacon cites the examples of Paul against Peter and Augustine against Jerome.

Moving to his own times, Bacon states that despite past condemnation of "the Philosophers" between 1210 and 1265, the wise thinkers (*Sapientes*) at Paris *c.*1266:

> approve of the abovementioned [Islamic thinkers] *as both philosophers and sacred* writers, and we know that every addition and increase in wisdom they have made are worthy of favour, although in many other

---

1. References to *Opus maius* (Bacon 1900) are to section numbers. Translations throughout are my own.

matters they have suffered a lessening of their authority and in many matters they are superfluous, and in certain need correction and in some explanation.   (*Opus maius* 21)

From this it is clear that twelve years before the Parisian Condemnation of 1277, Bacon defends the integration of Greek, Roman and Islamic philosophy into Christian learning, and he condemns those theologians and canon lawyers who had condemned "the philosophers and the scientists". Indeed, it has been shown that as a professor of philosophy in the 1240s, Bacon had anticipated the main issues in philosophy of religion that arose owing to the reception of Aristotle in the Latin West (Hackett 2005). Much of his 'philosophy of religion' is an attempt to secure the learning of these important thinkers for the *Res publica Christiana*. Bacon integrates this learning by introducing 'science/philosophy' as *the hand-maiden of theology* (Lindberg 2003: 7–32). Naturally, this might seem strange to a modern reader, but in fact it was by means of this device that Bacon, like Albertus, Bonaventure, Aquinas and many others, managed to build a permanent place within the Christian religion for scientific practice and philosophical reflection. Significant in this respect is the fact that Bacon is worried that some theologians and canon lawyers have unfairly and blindly attacked both the great philosophers and theorists of natural science. His 'philosophy of religion' is largely an effort to recover these domains within the Christian world of the Middle Ages. One might see the *Opus maius*, then, as a synthesis of human experience, science, philosophy and religion. But unlike his younger contemporaries such as Bonaventure and Aquinas, Bacon did not write a treatise on this topic. Rather, he developed a long '*persuasio*', that is, a rhetorical argument, for this new synthesis of philosophy, science and religion, based, according to Bacon, on the example of the two impor- tant English theologians and scientists Robert Grosseteste and Adam Marsh.

PHILOSOPHY AND THEOLOGY AS MODES OF WISDOM

Bacon's understanding of the relation of philosophy to theology depends on his understanding of truth. For him, the revelation given in the sacred Scriptures is the one and only source of truth. He states:

> I wish, in this second distinction, to point out that there is but one perfect wisdom contained in Sacred Scripture from whose roots all truth branches out. I say, therefore, that one science is the mistress of the others, namely, theology, to which the remaining sciences are completely necessary and without which it is not capable of reaching its fulfilment. Theology claims the strength of these sciences for her own law, to whose nod and rule the other sciences subordinate them- selves. Or better, there is perfect wisdom, which is totally contained in

Sacred Scripture, and which ought to be unfolded by means of Canon
Law and Philosophy.   (*Opus maius*, pt 2, 36)

For Bacon, moral philosophy is the branch of philosophy that is closest to
theology. Indeed, for Bacon, the natural moral law is contained in and originates
from Scripture, and thus its origin is essentially theological. Modern presenta-
tions of natural law as the self-sufficient produce of practical reason would be
an absurdity for Bacon. It would be a foundationalism without an explicit theological origin. For him, even the common law is both divine and human. From a
modern viewpoint, it would appear that philosophy as an independent, autonomous activity has been totally subordinated to theology.

Indeed, Bacon is writing explicitly as a Christian theologian who looks to
Augustine as his model (*see* Vol. 1, Ch. 18, "Augustine"). The doctrine of divine
illumination is given as the foundation for Bacon's understanding of the discovery
of truth. Whereas in his early works Bacon spoke of an agent intellect within the
human being, he now (post-1265) holds that God alone is the agent intellect:

> The agent intellect is the one which flows into our minds, illuminating
> them in regard to virtue and knowledge ... And thus the agent intel-
> lect, *according to the greater philosophers*, is not a part of the soul, but
> is an intellectual substance different and separated essentially from
> the possible intellect. And since it is necessary for the persuasion of
> my position to show that philosophy exists through the influence of
> divine illumination, I desire to prove this point conclusively, especially
> since a grave error has invaded the rank and file of philosophers in
> this particular matter, and has also invaded a large number of theolo-
> gians. For what a person is in philosophy that he is proved to be also
> in theology.   (*Opus maius*, pt 2, 45)

What does he mean by "the greater philosophers"? They constitute all great thinkers
from Moses through the Greeks up to Bacon's own times (Hackett 2000).

Bacon places Aristotle, the greatest philosopher, in the tradition coming from
Plato as expounded by Plotinus and others. He takes over Aristotle's language in
stating that it is better to speak of the illuminating "agent intellect as a substance
separate from the soul in essence" (*ibid.*). In Bacon's view, the leading Islamic philosophers such as Avicenna and al-Farabi as well as leading Christian philosophers
such as William of Auvergne and Grosseteste defended this synthesis of ancient
wisdom as handed on by al-Farabi and Avicenna. Moreover, since "God has illumined the minds of those men in perceiving the truths of philosophy, it is evident
that their labor is not opposed to the divine wisdom" (*Opus maius*, pt 2, 49).

One might ask: if philosophy is foundationally illumined by God, what is the
task of philosophical reflection and knowledge? Put simply, the history of philosophy for Bacon has the task of leading the human being from knowledge of

creation towards knowledge of the creator. "For speculative philosophy attains knowledge of the Creator through knowledge of creatures, and moral philosophy establishes the honesty of morals, just laws and worship of God" (*Opus maius*, pt 2, 51). Indeed, the latter enables the human being to seek ultimate happiness in this life and in the next. *Philosophy, therefore, is an introduction or preamble to theology*. Philosophy and science disclose the material, formal and efficient causes of natural or created events. Illumined divine wisdom reveals the ultimate goal of natural and human events. For example, science and philosophy identify the material, formal and efficient causes of the rainbow; sacred Scripture in the book of Genesis identifies the final cause of the rainbow. As a consequence, philosophy occupies a necessary but lower position than theology in the search for ultimate wisdom. "And philosophy considered only in itself has no usefulness … And so philosophy cannot have anything of dignity except in so far as it has something that is required by Divine Wisdom" (*Opus maius*, pt 2, 69). The highest goal of knowledge, therefore, consists in a "Reduction of the Arts to Theology" (*ibid.*).

Bacon presents his understanding of the historical unfolding of wisdom based on Jewish, Islamic and Christian sources in the context of this theory of the origin of truth. For him, there are two traditions of truth and wisdom, one constructive, the other destructive. The constructive tradition is that of the great philosophers and theologians from Plato to Grosseteste. It is important to note that medieval writers like Bacon think of philosophical authorities much as they thought of religious authorities. And so, just as Paul is given the authoritative title of 'Apostle', Aristotle is given the authoritative title of 'Philosopher' (*Philosophus*).

The destructive tradition is the anti-philosophical mythological tradition that Bacon associates with Nemroth, Zoroaster, Atlas, Prometheus, Mercurius Trismegistus, Aesculapius, Apollo and Minerva, "who were worshipped as Gods on account of their own wisdom" (*Opus maius*, pt 2, 67–8). Nimrod the Giant is both the one who destroyed the unity of language and the figure from the *Liber nimroth* who is to be worshipped because of his knowledge of the heavens.

For Bacon, then, his contemporaries stand on the shoulders of giants, that is, philosophical giants, but they are continually lured away from philosophy by the false self-important mythical claims of the followers of Nemroth. And in Bacon's view, pagan philosophers such as Aristotle or Seneca, Jewish and Islamic philosophers as well as Christian philosophers are in agreement in opposing this self-centred mythical wisdom. And he states:

> For this the unbelieving philosophers do, compelled by the truth in so far as it was granted to them; for they refer all philosophy to divine wisdom, as is clear from the books of Avicenna on *Metaphysics and Morals* and from al-Farabi, Seneca, Cicero and Aristotle in the *Metaphysics* and *Ethics*. For they refer all things to God as an army to its chief, and draw conclusions regarding angels and many other substances. (*Opus maius*, pt 2, 70)

Bacon's account of non-Christian philosophical discourse on God was not limited to the texts of the 'great' philosophers available to him. He had read William of Roebruck's account of a staged religious dialogue before the Great Kahn and had spoken with the author about his experiences (see Southern [1962] for an account of this event). Indeed, for Bacon, "the principal articles of (Christian) faith are found in these thinkers" (*Opus maius*, pt 2, 70). *God has illumined these great philosophers.* According to him, these philosophers are aware of the limitations of critical questioning in philosophy. Critical questioning was essential to human flourishing. Yet, these thinkers claim that philosophy as sceptical enquiry alone may not be self-sufficient. "And for this reason, philosophy advances to the discovery of a higher science, and proves that it must exist, although philosophy cannot unfold it in its special function. And for this reason, Philosophy transcends itself into the science of divine things" (*Opus maius*, pt 2, 75). One can see how Bacon can derive this understanding of philosophy from his predecessors: all of the ancient philosophers with the possible exception of the sceptics and Epicureans held to some such position, namely, that philosophy led the questioner through critical thinking to some form of union with the divine.

Philosophy, then, has the task of being a preamble to religious belief. The arguments within philosophy in this task are internal to philosophy; they do not belong to this higher theological knowledge. Still, Bacon expects more from his philosophical predecessors than bare philosophical argument alone. For him, the ancient and medieval philosophers "were anxious to inquire about the verification of a school of wisdom in which the salvation of humankind could be found, and these philosophers give clear methods of proof about this as will be shown in our *Moralis philosophiae*" (*Opus maius*, pt 2, 76). And so, for Bacon, philosophy is intimately linked with the discovery of the 'care of the self' in which a *way of salvation* can be discovered. Bacon's treatise on moral philosophy examines natural theology, virtue and religion in the context of the claims of Western religions, including Islam, in order to identify such a universal path to salvation.

In presenting this search, Bacon, reacting to the practice of Crusades, is quite optimistic in his belief that if great philosophers from the great world religions could engage in rational discourse as philosophers, they could achieve a measure of common agreement about human well-being. And in this manner, 'philosophy of religion' could become the basis for inter-cultural understanding. For Bacon, 'philosophy of religion' is a constituent part of moral philosophy, and in this sense even metaphysics becomes a part of moral philosophy.

Bacon expresses this view forcefully:

> But with Christian students of Philosophy, moral science apart from the other sciences and made perfect *is* theology. And this moral science adds the faith of Christ and divine truths to the theology of the pagans. This moral science has its own speculative part prior to the moral-practical part. But the end, namely, the Christian Law, adds

to the Law of the Pagan Philosophers the formulated articles of the faith, by which means it completes the law of moral philosophy so that now one can have *one complete* law. For the Law of Christ takes and assumes the laws and morals of philosophy, as we are assured by the Sacred Writers and by the practice of theology and the Church.

(*Opus maius*, pt 2, 77)

It would appear, then, that Bacon has so taken up philosophy into religion as to render *philosophy as a foundational discipline* redundant. Still, he can claim that both philosophy and religious wisdom can address "the many common rational truths, which every wise person would easily accept from one another" (*Opus maius*, pt 2, 78). The means for addressing these common truths is nothing other than careful use of rational logic and grammar. In this way, Bacon has managed to build the tradition of rational argument and grammar into the heart of a religious determination of the meaning of life, but he would seem to do so at the cost of a radical self-limitation of the powers of philosophy.

Before proceeding directly to an explicit treatment of these concerns in his *Moralis philosophia* (*Opus maius*, pt 7), Bacon will take up the issue of the applications of philosophy and the liberal arts (the linguistic arts and the natural sciences) to religion and theology. It is in this application that Bacon will develop some of his significant and novel approaches to the relationship between 'philosophy and science' and religion.

THE APPLICATIONS OF PHILOSOPHY (ARTS AND SCIENCES) TO RELIGION

Writing as an emeritus professor, Bacon regards the *sentence-method* of theology as being linguistically defective (see *Opus minus* [Minor work] 322). Hence, a complete reform of language study is recommended as the starting-point of philosophy. This study is much wider than the bare introduction to languages that is normal for most students of philosophy in the medieval university.

First, students should be grounded in the Wisdom languages (Hebrew, Greek, Chaldean). The proper study of language at all levels is fundamental for Bacon's philosophy of religion. These levels include vernacular, technical linguistics (technical Latin) and semiotics. In Bacon's judgement, the philosophy and theology of his contemporaries fails because of its lack of a critical theory of language. Drawing on Augustine and Aristotle, Bacon presents a novel semiotic theory that has the effect of changing the traditional relation between sign, concept and thing in ways that would eventually lead in the fourteenth century to a nominalist semantics. For most of Bacon's contemporaries, the relation of sign to thing signified was primary, and that of sign to perceiver of the sign was secondary. For him, however, a sign is not a sign unless it is perceived. "The sign is in the predicament of relation and is spoken of essentially in reference *to the one for whom it signifies*" (*De signis* [On signs] 81). In Bacon's view, words refer immediately and directly to present things and indirectly to concepts. Reference to past things and future things is made by way of analogy. For him, the traditional view allowed ambiguities to enter philosophical discourse, and also theological discourse. Thus, for Bacon, the complete speech act involving both speaker and hearer needs much logical and grammatical analysis. Bacon's late work (*c.*1292) deals with the difficulties about *ambiguity* in philosophical and religious discourse.

In parts 4–6 of the *Opus maius*, Bacon examines the uses of mathematics in the sciences and addresses the importance of mathematics for religion. His doctrine of the multiplication of species presents a physics of nature in which the notion of a universal multiplication of forces is presented. This physics of light is connected to the metaphysics of light. Bacon presents the ways in which religion can benefit from the study of mathematics: calendar reform, geographical study, study of astrology. In *Opus maius*, part 5, Bacon presents the rudiments of a philosophy of mind and a treatise on *Perspectiva*. At the end of the treatise, he argues that the language of optics can be used as a suitable metaphor for moral and religious persuasion. Indeed, Bacon is the one, under the influence of Grosseteste, who introduced this perspectivist analysis of moral discourse into the Latin West as an aid to preaching and teaching in religion. It was taken up and developed in the *Tractatus moralis de oculo* (The moral treatise on the eye), the influential treatise by Peter of Limoges (*c.*1285) (see Newhauser 2001). These major parts of Bacon's works dealing with *physical change* should not be overlooked. They are relevant for Bacon's understanding of religion. The doctrine of the multiplication of species and the doctrine of *perspectiva* are an essential part of his physical doctrine of light, which in turn is related to moral philosophy (theology) and to the background Neoplatonist 'metaphysics of light' in Grosseteste and Marsh. They would provide Bacon, Peter of Limoges and others with new metaphors for explanation in religious and moral teaching.

BACON'S *MORALIS PHILOSOPHIA*:
PHILOSOPHY OF RELIGION AS MORAL DISCOURSE

Bacon's treatise on moral philosophy is divided into six parts. Part 1 deals with the task of philosophy with regard to proof and testimony in religion. Part 2 is a very brief summary of Avicenna on law and social life. Part 3, the largest part, is a summary of Aristotelian and Latin Stoic teaching on the primacy of virtue and the virtuous sage. Part 4 deals with the forms of religious life known in the Middle Ages; it is astrological and sociological in nature. Part 5 deals with the role of rhetoric and poetics in regard to persuasion in religion. Part 6 is a one-page summary on forensic rhetoric. Thus, the scope of moral philosophy includes: (i) metaphysics in relation to morals, (ii) social life, (iii) the care of the self,

(iv) religious groups, their goals and methods of proof, (v) persuasion and religion and (vi) forensic rhetoric.

Metaphysics, the foundation of morals

In Bacon's view, moral philosophy is essentially practical in nature. "This science is preeminently active, that is operative, and deals with our actions in this life and the other" (*Moralis philosophia* 3). The object of this science is human action. These actions are concerned with the practical intellect as it leads to actions that are good or evil. Practical matters of the artificial or natural kind are products of the speculative intellect. For Bacon, practical matters of the moral kind (*operabilia*) are more difficult to know than are the objects of the speculative intellect. In fact, the corruption of the human will and our natural irascible nature make it difficult for human beings to perform these moral actions. According to Bacon, the main *operabilia* consist of "the highest truths concerning God and divine worship, eternal life, the laws of justice, the glory of peace and the sublimity of the virtues" (*Moralis philosophia* 247). The 'eternal matters' are difficult for human beings owing to sin, the body and the immediacy of sensible things.

Moral philosophy has two parts. The first deals with the speculative aspect of moral questions such as the nature of God and the Good, that is, the ultimate goals of human life and whether we can know those goals. The second examines the processes of moral persuasion. Bacon's example is instructive: one may know much theory from books on medicine but such knowledge does not give one any adequate experimental/experiential knowledge of medical matters. In this, Bacon is presenting the argument that experience of actual phenomena is more important than mere argument or book knowledge (knowledge on the basis of scribal authority). In moral matters, according to Bacon, one has appeal to the following: *authority*, *experience* and *reason*. Bacon is opposed to any moral theory that would base itself on bare *reason alone*. And so for Bacon, "The practical half [of Moral Philosophy] is related to the first half as the curing of the sick and conservation of health that is treated in the practical part of medicine is to that part of medicine where one teaches about the nature of health" (*Moralis philosophia* 248). Just as there are professors of medicine who know medical theory but are terrible practitioners, so too there are professors of moral theory who know about the works of human action (*operabilia*) but who are themselves morally reprobate.

This moral and civil science of the human being in relation to God, to others, to itself and to the laws, has the task of persuading us to moral well-being. Moral philosophy, to the extent that it can, is essential to this task and is therefore the noblest science. It is the internal goal of all the sciences. Indeed, it deals with the same objects as theology; the latter simply considers these objects in the light of the Christian faith. In fact, moral science as the end or goal of the other sciences takes up the conclusions of these sciences as premises in moral science. And in a certain manner, the principles of moral philosophy are verified in the

159

other sciences so that they can be gathered from those sciences in so far as they are guided to a moral goal. Philosophers have spread moral matters throughout their speculative endeavours in order to move human beings to wisdom. These remarks should be collected and used in moral philosophy. Moral philosophy is therefore the queen of all the preceding sciences. This allows the moral philosopher to draw on the authors of these sciences such as Aristotle, Avicenna and Averroes.

As a result, Bacon concludes that "It ought to be known that there is a deep agreement between Metaphysics and Moral Philosophy" (*Moralis philosophia* 7). They both deal with topics such as God, angels and eternal life.

> For Metaphysics properly investigates by means of the common concepts of all the sciences, and inquires about spiritual matters on the basis of knowledge of corporeal matters, and from the latter reaches a knowledge of the Creator, and from our present life it learns about the future life. In this, it offers many preambles (*preambula*) to Moral Philosophy. (*Moralis philosophia* 7)

What follows consists of the *testimonies* of the ancient philosophers concerning knowledge about God and the immortality of soul. Bacon will argue that ancient philosophers spoke not only about the bare fact of the existence of God but that they anticipated significant internal Christian doctrines such as the Trinity and the Incarnation.

Metaphysics according to Bacon can demonstrate that God exists and can be naturally known by human beings; that "God is infinite in power and goodness"; that God in essence is One and not a multiplicity, and that though he is One in essence he is threefold in another manner; that God created and governs all things in the "being of nature"; that in addition to corporeal beings he has created the "spiritual substances" that we call "intelligences or angels", and that apart from these he created other spiritual substances, namely "the rational souls present in humans", and that he created them immortal; that there is the happiness (*felicitas*) of the afterlife, namely, the highest good, and that the human being has a capacity for this happiness; that God governs the human race on the path of life just as he does other things in the "being of nature"; that God promises eternal life to those who live rightly in this life according to the rule of God, and that those who live an evil life deserve a wretched future as Avicenna teaches in the tenth book of his *Metaphysics*; that God ought to be worshipped with due reverence; that just as one is directed to God in due reverence, so too one must be directed to one's neighbour in justice and peace, and to one's self in a virtuous life; that the human being on the basis of his own knowledge cannot ultimately know the will of God but must depend on the truth of a revelation; and that there is but one revealer, a mediator between God and human beings, and the Vicar of God on earth to whom the whole human race is subject. This law-giver and highest priest, who "in spiritual and temporal matters has fullness of power", is, in the words of Avicenna's *Metaphysics* book 10, "a human God, who is allowed to be worshipped after God. And thus Metaphysics continues into Morals and descends into Morals as towards its own end, as Avicenna so beautifully conjoins them at the end of his *Metaphysics*" (*Moralis philosophia* 9; see 211–23 for development of this theme). Having understood the limitations of metaphysics with regard to morals, the '*Legislator*' ought to turn to those topics such as 'the attributes of God in particular, angels and eternal life', issues that metaphysics as a discipline is not able to examine in depth. Metaphysics can ask 'Does God exist?', but while it can discourse about 'a being and being', it is not able to enter into any depth about the nature of God. But moral philosophy can examine all the secrets of God and angels and other matters in so far as these need to be explained to the masses of human beings, lest they fall into heresy as Avicenna teaches in *The Foundations of Moral Philosophy*. Elsewhere, Bacon expands on this latter theme:

> For the multitude is too imperfect, and for this reason a plea for the faith that is within its grasp is crude, undigested and unworthy of the learned. I wish therefore to proceed on higher ground and to present a persuasion concerning which the learned can judge. For in every nation there are some industrious people who are fitted for wisdom, who can be persuaded by the force of reason so that when these men become enlightened, the persuasion through them of the multitude becomes easier. (*Moralis philosophia* 196–7)

THE TESTIMONY OF THE 'GREATER PHILOSOPHERS' ABOUT THE SUBJECT MATTERS OF MORAL PHILOSOPHY

Bacon notes that he has already (in *Opus maius*, pt 2) shown how and why philosophers can discourse about God, that is, the "greater philosophers" had a "revelation" that they had received from the ancient "Patriarchs and Prophets" who wrote about matters not only "theologically and prophetically, but also philosophically, since they discovered and taught all of philosophy" (*Opus maius* 72). However, although the metaphysician can speak of the unity and trinity of God, he needs access to moral philosophy (theology) to proceed in any depth.

What follows is a list of philosophical anticipatory testimonies about the truths of Christian belief. Plato and Aristotle are taken to have taught about the unity and trinity of God. This material is taken from Augustine's history of philosophy in *De civitate Dei* (On the city of God) and from other writers. Aristotle is interpreted here on the basis of Bacon's reading of the *Politics*, and on the basis of Averroes and Avicenna. Bacon examines the infinite power and goodness of God and then turns to testimony about an 'Incarnate God'. This consists of examining elements in previous writers, ancient and medieval, who spoke about an 'Incarnate

God'. These include Porphyry and Abu Ma'shar. He then turns to the topic of 'the Antichrist', and mentions the testimony of Pliny and Solinus. He then uses the *Secretum secretorum* (The secret of secrets), Abu Ma'shar, Avicenna, Ethicus and Trismegistus to argue for the doctrine of the creation of the world, and he uses Aristotle and Avicenna to argue for the creation of angels and human beings as ones having 'voluntary motion'. Using the *Liber de causis* (The book of causes) and Ethicus, he argues for the generation of individual human beings as members of one species, and that an angel constitutes a species. He finds further information on angels in Plato as handed on by Apuleius. He argues that there is much in these 'pagan' philosophers that is suitable for Catholic Christians. The sections that follow concern the immortality of soul, future happiness and religious worship.

Bacon's account of the immortality of soul turns out to be an argument for the resurrection of the body on the basis of the philosophers. For Bacon, following Aristotle, virtue is not due to a soul inhabiting a body. It is the product of the union of both soul and body, that is, the human being by means of the soul. Thus, happiness (*felicitas*) is the result of this union of both soul and body. The composite of soul and body is there for the benefit of the one individual human being, and so happiness accrues to both parts of the composite (*Moralis philosophia* 23–4).

Moral philosophy can examine "the happiness of the other life" in a more particular manner than metaphysics. Owing to sin, corporeal preoccupation, attachment to the world and the lack of a revelation, the human being is impeded in the knowledge of future happiness. In this, Bacon depends greatly on Avicenna. In this world, the human being is spread out into earthly delights and, as Avicenna points out, we neglect "insensible and spiritual" being. Following Avicenna, Bacon recommends a purification of the mind from sin, earthly desires and a separation of the mind from the sensible world. In this way, the self will reach and become attached to "the intelligible world". Further, one is enabled to know these things that are beyond human comprehension by means of "a verification by means of a revelation and prophecy". In regard to these, we believe the testimony of "the prophets and law-givers, who have received a law from God". Those who follow this path will agree with Aristotle, Theophrastus and Avicenna that the practice of contemplation, in so far as that is open to human beings, provides the way to future happiness (*Moralis philosophia* 27). These philosophers have had a revelation from God.

Bacon links up this spiritual interior illumination with Aristotle's account of wisdom as the fulfilment of happiness in the *Nicomachean Ethics*. He argues that *wisdom* is not the same phenomenon as "bare argument", but is a kind of "intellectual power" that also perfects the affective self. This is the beginning of future happiness and coincides with the knowledge and love of God. This leads to the "beatitude of the whole human being both in body and in soul". Complete happiness consists in participation in the supreme good.

In all of this, it is clear that Bacon advocates what one might call a 'traditionalist' understanding of wisdom. The philosophical elite organize the teaching and cult practices for the multitude. They veil the true teaching and practice from the normal superstitious rites. Further, the philosophers dissimulate in their teaching and acknowledge public religion only because of public law and common practice, not on account of the truth of the matter. In this, Bacon is following the advice of Seneca.

Part 2 of the *Moralis philosophia* consists of Avicenna's quasi-Platonic organization of society into three parts: "*dispositores, ministros et legis peritos*". This is a blueprint for a social organization of society.

Part 3 of this work is a set of 'selected texts' with comment from the Latin philosophers, especially Cicero and Seneca. This account acknowledges the unity of virtue and the primacy of virtue as exhibited by the Stoic sage. For Bacon, "Virtue is the life of the human being". Bacon presents a brief account of the Aristotelian virtues and then proceeds to extol the Stoic sage as the ideal of the human moral agent. He defends the notion of the unity of all the virtues. A major section of this part deals with the vice of anger (wrath) in relation to leadership in society. Drawing largely on Seneca's *De ira* (On wrath), Bacon argues for a moral contempt of the world in which self-restraint and guided moral action will overcome the destructiveness of wrath (Hackett 1995). What follows is an extended account of the virtues and vices.

Part 4 of the *Moralis philosophia* examines the different kinds of religion known to Bacon, and attempts a classification of religions on the basis of the history of religion and astrological design. He gives an account of the religion of the Saracens (Islam), Tartars (Buddhism), pagans, idolators, Jews and Christians (*Moralis philosophia* 189), and uses the Aristotelian doctrine of the end of political life to describe each group. Bacon has the typical medieval Latin view that members of Islam are given to things of this world and to lust, owing to having many wives. He sees the Tartars as being guided by a desire for domination, and the pagans as a group who carry over their earthly goods to the next as seen in the heroic funeral pyre. In a similar way, the idolators in the East are dedicated to things of this life. The Jews seek both goods in this life and the goal of eternal life. Christians tolerate temporal goods so as to practise spiritual discipline in this life, so that in body and soul they will reach eternal life. This classification is set in the context of an astrological world. Bacon, like his contemporaries, acknowledges astrological influence and believes that nations can be described in astrological terms. Yet, he does hold strongly to a doctrine of the freedom of the will.

Part 5 of the *Moralis philosophia* deals with the 'rhetoric and poetics' of persuasion in religion. Since our speculative intellect can be weak in regard to moral actions (the *operabilia*), one has need of forms of persuasion. "The highest truths about God, divine worship, eternal life, laws of justice, the glory of peace and sublimity of virtue" are concerned with matters that transcend "bare rationality" (*Moralis philosophia* 247). These matters involve deep motivation, desire, inclination, hope and will. In brief, they belong to affective life and practical reason. It follows, therefore, that the dialectical and demonstrative arguments outlined by Aristotle in his *Logic* are not sufficient for this purpose. "Hence, Aristotle in book one of his *Ethics* resolves that moral science does not have to use demonstrations but instead requires rhetorical arguments" (*Moralis philosophia* 250). In this way, speculative truth does not automatically lead to virtue and the practice of moral goodness. For Bacon,

> Therefore, it is necessary that we have strong inducements in moral matters since the practical intellect is more noble than the speculative. Further, the practical intellect is related to what is good in a more difficult and less delightful manner than the speculative intellect is related to truth ... (*Moralis philosophia* 251)

This is his most explicit statement on the primacy of the practical intellect. The latter is induced to action primarily by means of rhetorical arguments. Still, any old rhetoric will not suffice. Bacon makes a sharp contrast between the mere forensic rhetoric of Cicero and the deeper moral rhetoric of Aristotle. "We need the complete doctrine found in Aristotle and his commentators." This is a kind of argument based on truth that avoids fraud and sophistry. It is directed to the production of belief, right action and right judgement. Teaching, of course, is necessary but is not a sufficient means to move human beings to moral and religious actions. Oratory aimed at moving to action is required.

Bacon presents a threefold division of rhetoric corresponding to the threefold division of practical philosophy. The first kind deals with persuasion in religion. This is concerned with what is provable and with the levels of assent in religious truth. There are six forms of proof: the testimony of the Church, sacred Scripture, the witness of the saints, the abundance of miracles, the power of reasons and the consensus of Catholic teachers. The second kind of rhetorical argument deals with forensic rhetoric as seen in part 6 of the *Moralis philosophia*. The third kind of rhetoric is concerned with things that move us towards moral actions. He calls the first two kinds of persuasion, "rhetoric as such".

According to Bacon, the third kind is labelled "poetic argument" by Aristotle and other philosophers. That is, truth-bearing poets sway us towards honest virtue. The example he gives is Horace, who provides noble and beneficial direction, as opposed to Ovid, who prevents mere frivolity.

In Bacon's view, the ordinary student and teacher at the medieval university does not know this "poetic argument". Diligent scholars who know the works of Aristotle and his Arabic commentators can know this argument. They can draw on al-Farabi, Avicenna, al-Ghazali and Averroes (see Black 1990; Rosier-Catach 1998). Here, we can see the extent to which Bacon's ideas on religion and philosophy are determined by his great interest in these major Islamic thinkers. Bacon, at the end of part 5, links up these thinkers with major Roman and Christian thinkers. He takes Augustine's *De doctrina Christiana* (On teaching Christianity) as his model for the use of language and interpretation in religion (see Maloney 1995). But the baseline in all of this is that rhetoric and poetics are not something secondary, a kind of frill added on to the obvious speculative truth of theoretical reason. Rhetoric and poetics in religion provide the only kind of argument that can move people to the practice of virtue and to religious practice. It helps to understand this when one sees that Bacon like Augustine links rhetorical/poetic persuasion to the appreciation of music, perhaps the most forgotten of the medieval quadrivium. Above all, it becomes clear that Bacon represents a different kind of philosophy of religion than that commonly found in Western philosophy. In the latter, the whole religious phenomenon is often reduced to a function of logical argumentation alone. Bacon appreciates the role of logic but he does not forget that in regard to human moral action, logic without the requisite moral experience is blind.

It will be clear from this account that Bacon belongs to a Christian culture in the Middle Ages that was profoundly influenced by various aspects of Jewish and Islamic religious and moral practices. He draws strongly on the tradition of truth and secrecy initiated by al-Farabi and developed by thinkers such as Maimonides (Hackett 2002). Above all, he is strongly influenced in his philosophy by Avicenna, al-Ghazali and Averroes. To characterize Bacon's position as an "Augustinisme-Avicenniant", as Etienne Gilson did, is not mistaken. But it is clear that the names al-Farabi, al-Ghazali and Averroes must be added. Bacon succeeded in linking up the concerns of these philosophers with the tradition of Augustine, especially with the doctrine of truth as illumination and the doctrine of the primacy of moral actions over bare arguments.

FURTHER READING

Bacon, R. 1983. *De multiplicatrione specierum, De speculis comburentibus*, D. Lindberg (ed.). Oxford: Clarendon Press.

Bacon, R. 1988. *Compendium studii theologiae,* Studien und Texte zur Geistesgeschichte Des Mittelalters 20, T. Maloney (ed.). Leiden: Brill.

Bacon, R. 1996. *Perspectiva (= Opus maius, part five)*, D. Lindberg (ed.). Oxford: Clarendon Press.

Boadas, I. & A. Llavat 1996. *Roger Bacon: Subjectivitat i ètica*. Barcelona: Editorial Herder.

Hackett, J. 1987. "Moral Philosophy and Rhetoric in Roger Bacon". *Philosophy and Rhetoric* **20**: 18–40.

Hackett, J. 1988. "Averroes and Roger Bacon on the Harmony of Philosophy and Religion". In *A Straight Path: Studies in Medieval Philosophy and Culture: Essays in Honor of Arthur Hyman*, R. Link-Salinger *et al.* (eds), 98–112. Washington, DC: Catholic University of America Press.

Hackett, J. 1991. "Philosophy and Theology in Roger Bacon's *Opus maius*". In *Philosophy and the God of Abraham: Essays in Memory of James A. Weisheipl O.P.*, R. Long (ed.), 55–70. Toronto: PIMS.

Hackett, J. 1997. *Roger Bacon and the Sciences: Commemorative Essays,* Studien und Texte zur Geistesgeschichte 57. Leiden: Brill.

Maloney, T. 1995. "Is the *De doctrina Christiana* the Source for Bacon's Semiotics?". In *Reading and Wisdom: The De doctrina Christiana of Augustine in the Middle Ages*, E. English (ed.), 126–42. Notre Dame, IN: University of Notre Dame Press.

Molland, A. 1974. "Roger Bacon as Magician". *Traditio* **50**: 445–60.

Molland, A. 1983. "Roger Bacon and the Hermetic Tradition in Medieval Science". *Vivarium* **31**: 140–60.

Newhauser, R. 2001. "Inter scientiam et populum: Roger Bacon, Pierre de Limoges and the *Tractatus moralis de oculo*". In *Nach der Verurteilung Von 1277: Philosophie und Theologie an der Universität Paris im letzten Viertel des 13. Jahrhunderts: Studien und Texte*, J. Aertsen, K. Emery Jr. & A. Speer (eds), *Miscellanea Medievallia* **28**: 682–703.

Power, A. 2006. "A Mirror for Every Age: The Reputation of Roger Bacon". *English Historical Review* **121**: 657–92.

Rosier, I. 1994. *La Parole comme acte: Sur la grammaire et la semantique au xiiie siècle*. Paris: Vrin.

Rosier-Catach, I. 1998. "Roger Bacon, al-Farabi et Augustin: Rhètorique, logique et philosophie morale". In *La Rhétorique d'Aristote: Traditions et commentaires de l'antiquité au XVIIe siècle*, G. Dahan & I. Rosier-Catach (eds), 87–110. Paris: Vrin.

On FAITH see also Chs 6, 12, 16, 18; Vol. 1, Ch. 13; Vol. 3, Chs 8; Vol. 4, Ch. 8, 10, 13; Vol. 5, Chs 7, 18. On IMMORTALITY OF THE SOUL see also Ch. 16; Vol. 1, Chs 2, 4; Vol. 3, Chs 10, 19. On LANGUAGE see also Chs 4, 11; Vol. 3, Ch. 14; Vol. 4, Chs 3, 8; Vol. 5, Chs 13, 20. On MORALITY see also Vol. 3, Chs 2, 8, 12, 14, 21, 22; Vol. 4, Chs 4, 12, 18; Vol. 5, Ch. 6. On REASON see also Chs 10, 11, 16, 18; Vol. 3, Chs 8, 12, 16, 21; Vol. 4, Chs 4, 8. On SCIENCE see also Vol. 3, Ch. 17; Vol. 4, Chs 7, 11, 12, 15, 17, 19; Vol. 5, Chs 4, 19.

13

THOMAS AQUINAS

John F. Wippel

Thomas Aquinas was born in 1224/25 in his family's castle at Roccasecca, Italy. After receiving elementary schooling at the nearby Benedictine abbey of Monte Cassino, in 1239 he began to study liberal arts and philosophy at the newly founded *studium generale* at Naples. While a student there, he joined the Dominican Order in 1244, much to the chagrin of his family who wanted him to become a Benedictine. At the request of his mother, he was forcibly taken from the Dominicans by soldiers and detained at the family castle for a year or more; but all efforts on the part of his family to persuade him not to become a Dominican failed. In 1245 his family permitted him to rejoin the Dominicans, who promptly sent him to Paris for further studies. There he came into contact with Albert the Great, and after some years in Paris, journeyed to Cologne with Albert, under whom he studied from 1248 until 1252. From 1252 until 1256 he studied theology at the University of Paris and fulfilled the requirements for becoming a *magister* in theology, including lecturing on the *Sentences* of Peter Lombard, which resulted in his Commentary on the *Sentences*. At this time he also published his first two philosophical opuscula: *De ente et essentia* (On being and essence) and *De principiis naturae* (On the principles of nature). In 1256 he delivered his inaugural lecture as *magister*, and during 1256–9 served as Master in Theology at the University of Paris and produced some of his major writings including, among others, his Disputed Questions *De veritate* (On truth) and five public Quodlibetal Disputations. From 1259 until late 1268 Aquinas served as lecturer or as Regent Master in different Dominican houses of study in Italy and continued to write at a prodigious pace, producing his *Summa contra Gentiles* (begun in Paris and completed in Italy), the First Part of his *Summa theologiae* and many other writings too numerous to mention here. In late 1268 he returned to the University of Paris to resume his duties there as Regent Master in Theology. His writings during this period included many of his twelve commentaries on Aristotle, seven more Quodlibetal Disputations, other major Disputed Questions, subsequent parts of the *Summa theologiae*, and many other works (Torrell 2005: 330–59). In 1272 he was recalled to Italy to set up a Dominican *studium generale* in Naples, and continued to publish until December 1273, when he ceased writing. On his way to take part in a general Council of the Church at Lyons early in 1274, he became seriously ill and died on 7 March. Apart from four or five philosophical opuscula, his commentary on the *Book of Causes* and twelve commentaries on Aristotle, most of his writings are theological rather than philosophical in literary genre; but many of these are also important sources for his philosophical thought (Wippel 2000: xvi–xxii).

Viewed as a distinct discipline within its own right, the philosophy of religion was unknown in the time of Aquinas. While this discipline may be understood as the philosophical study of religious phenomena, many contemporary philosophers of religion focus heavily on examining and evaluating philosophical truth-claims that are pertinent to religion and religious belief. Much within the writings of Aquinas is relevant to such an effort. For Aquinas himself two human disciplines are dedicated to the study of God and his relationship to human beings. One is a theology based on revelation in which the motive for accepting something as true is religious belief in the authority of God revealing. The other is included within metaphysics and hence is strictly philosophical. The present chapter will concentrate on what, in Aquinas' eyes, metaphysics can contribute to truth-claims pertinent to religion and religious belief.

In accord with Aquinas' theory of knowledge, we discover the subject of metaphysics – being as being – by beginning with our experience of individual objects at the level of sense-perception. By freeing our understanding of being from restriction to any given kind of being through an intellectual process, a negative judgement known as separation, we can discover being as being and investigate whatever falls under this notion (*Super Boetium de Trinitate* [On Boethius' 'On the Trinity'] q. 5, a. 3; Wippel 2000: 35–62). As one of its tasks, indeed as its end or goal, metaphysics should ultimately arrive at knowledge of the cause of its subject, that is, at knowledge of God or divine being.

For Aquinas, like most of his thirteenth- and fourteenth-century contemporaries, divine being itself is not the subject of metaphysics (*Super Boetium De Trinitate* q. 5, a. 4). But unlike almost all of his contemporaries, Aquinas holds that divine being or God is not included under being as being: the subject of metaphysics (Zimmermann 1998: 210–33; Wippel 2000: 17–18). This means that purely philosophical knowledge of God can only be indirect, based on a process of reasoning from effects that are readily known to us, to knowledge of him as the cause of such effects. While this position effectively protects Aquinas from falling into what is currently referred to as 'ontotheology', at the same time it has important implications for his views about the kind of philosophical knowledge human beings can have about God's nature or essence, or about God as he is in himself.

Consequently, the following discussion will examine Aquinas' views concerning: (i) philosophical evidence for the existence of God; (ii) the possibility of quidditative knowledge of God, that is, knowledge of God's essence; (iii) analogical predication of the divine names; (iv) God's goodness; (v) God's knowledge; (vi) God's will; and (vii) God's freedom to create.

PHILOSOPHICAL EVIDENCE FOR THE EXISTENCE OF GOD

Regarding human knowledge of God, Aquinas distinguishes: (i) truths about God that unaided (philosophical) reason can discover, for instance, God's existence, God's unity (uniqueness), and other truths of this kind concerning God or his creation that, Aquinas says, are proved in philosophy and presupposed for faith, and which he refers to as preambles of faith (*Super Boetium De Trinitate* q. 2, a. 3); (ii) truths about God that are not accessible to philosophical discovery and proof but can be known only through revelation (e.g. the Trinity or the Incarnation); (iii) truths that, while open in principle to philosophical discovery, are also contained in revelation. For Aquinas knowledge that God exists is an illustration of the first type of truth concerning God, that is, a preamble of faith, but it also falls under the third type. He argues that even though this truth can be, and in fact has been, demonstrated philosophically, it was most fitting for God also to reveal it to human beings. Otherwise, the vast majority would never in fact arrive at knowledge of it; those who did succeed in this effort would do so only after a long period of time had elapsed; and even then, some error might be intermingled with the truth they had discovered (*Summa contra Gentiles* [hereafter *SCG*] I.3–4).

As regards philosophical argumentation for the existence of God, Aquinas maintains throughout his career that the fact that God exists is not self-evident (*per se notum*) to human beings. This follows from his theory of knowledge according to which all of our knowledge, even of immaterial beings, must be derived from our perception of sensible things. It is in his discussions of the more general claim that God's existence is self-evident to human beings that Aquinas also considers on several different occasions Anselm's argumentation as presented both in *Proslogion* c. 2 and in *Proslogion* c. 3.[1]

In refuting various arguments in support of the claim that God's existence is self-evident, Aquinas makes an important distinction between propositions that are self-evident in themselves but not to us, and those that are self-evident in

---

1. Some recent critics of his treatment of Anselm's argumentation have not fully appreciated this, for instance, Hartshorne (1965: 154–64). In his earliest consideration of this in 1252 in his Commentary on *I Sentences* d. 3, q. 1, a. 2 (Aquinas 1929: vol. 1, 93–4), Aquinas presents the version from *Proslogion* 2 as a fourth argument in support of the claim that God's existence is self-evident. In *De veritate* q. 10, a. 12 (*c*.1257) he again presents reasoning based on *Proslogion* c. 3 as a version of argumentation in support of the same claim. In *SCG* I.10 (*c*.1259) he presents the argumentation found in *Proslogion* c. 2 and then in c. 3 as two versions of arguments intended to prove that God's existence is self-evident. But in *Summa theologiae* (hereafter *ST*) I.2.3 (1266) Aquinas considers only the version found in *Proslogion* c. 2.

themselves and to us. As for the proposition 'God exists', Aquinas holds that it is self-evident in itself because God's essence is identical with his act of existing (*esse*). Hence anyone who could understand the essence of God would then also understand that he exists. But in this life human beings cannot understand God's essence or quiddity. Therefore the proposition 'God exists' is not self-evident to us (*De veritate* q. 10, a. 12; *SCG* I.10; *ST* I.2.1). Human beings can only reason to knowledge that God exists by beginning with effects that are accessible to human cognition, and by reasoning from knowledge of them to knowledge of him as their uncaused cause (Wippel 2000: 388–99).

Not surprisingly, therefore, both in his earlier presentation of arguments for God's existence and in his better known 'five ways' from *ST* I.2.3, Aquinas always proceeds from some kind of effect that is accessible to human beings to a knowledge of God as their cause (for earlier arguments see Van Steenberghen [1980: chs 1–7]; Wippel [2000: 400–41]). Among the earlier arguments, only that offered in Aquinas' *De ente et essentia* (hereafter *De ente*) will be presented here, followed by the 'five ways' themselves.

In his *De ente* c. 4 (Leon. ed., 43.375–7), Aquinas proposes to examine how essence is realized in separate substances, that is, in the soul, in intelligences (separate substances other than God) and in the first cause. Against those who would attribute some kind of matter–form composition to intelligences and to the human soul, Aquinas argues that their nature as intelligences precludes their being composed of matter and form. But given this position, he must explain how such beings can be distinguished from the perfect simplicity of God. In his effort to show that such beings must still be composed of act and potency, he introduces argumentation in support of a distinction and composition in them of essence and *esse* (act of existing). It is in the course of developing a three-stage argument to make this point that he presents a metaphysical argument for the existence of God. In the first stage of the general argument, he reasons that whatever is not included within the intelligible content of an essence or quiddity comes to it from without and enters into composition with it. But every essence or quiddity can be understood without anything being understood about its actually existing. Thus one can understand what a human being is or what a phoenix is and not know whether it exists in reality. Therefore, he concludes this first stage of the argument by stating that in any such being *esse* is distinct from (literally, 'other than') essence or quiddity.

Perhaps because he realizes that this argument might be criticized for moving illegitimately from the order of thought to the order of reality, he immediately adds an all-important second stage: "Unless perhaps there is some thing whose quiddity is its very act of existing" (*ibid.*). But, he continues, such a thing can only be one and first. Here he does not assume that such a being exists, but argues that if such a being does exist, it can only be one. To prove this point he distinguishes three ways in which something might be multiplied: (i) by the addition of some difference, as a generic nature is multiplied in species; (ii) by the reception of a given form in different instances of matter, as a specific nature is multiplied in different individuals; (iii) by the fact that in one case it exists in absolute and unreceived fashion in itself, and in all other cases it is received in some subject. But if there is something that is pure and subsisting *esse* (act of existing), it cannot be multiplied in either the first way (for then it would be *esse* plus some differentiating form) or in the second way (for then it would not be pure subsisting *esse*, but *esse* plus matter). He concludes stage two by accepting the third way and reasons that, by process of elimination, there could at most be one instance of subsisting *esse*. Hence, by contrast, in every other thing there must be a distinction between the nature or quiddity or form (i.e. the essence) of that thing and its act of existing.

In stage three Aquinas attempts to prove that the one possible exception – self-subsisting *esse* – does actually exist. Whatever pertains to something either is caused by the principles of that thing's nature (as the ability to laugh follows from the essence of a human being), or comes to it from some extrinsic principle. But *esse* (the act of existing) cannot be caused efficiently by the form or quiddity of a thing, for such a thing would then also be the efficient cause of its own existence, which is impossible. Therefore, everything whose *esse* (act of existing) is other than its nature (or essence) must receive its *esse* from something else. In other words, it must be efficiently caused. And because that which exists only by reason of something else must ultimately be traced back to something that exists of itself as to its first cause, some thing must exist that is the cause of existing for all other things by reason of the fact that it is pure *esse* in and of itself. Otherwise one would regress to infinity in caused causes of *esse*. The argument concludes by noting that whatever receives something from something else is in potency with respect to what it receives and, therefore, that even a pure form or intelligence is in potency to the *esse* that it receives from God, its uncaused cause. Hence in any such being there is a composition of *esse* and of essence as of act and potency.[2]

In this text there is a certain ambiguity in interpreting the Latin term *esse* because at times Aquinas uses it simply to refer to the actual existence of a thing, that is, to the fact that it exists. At other times he uses it to refer to an intrinsic principle of actuality present in every distinct entity by reason of which that thing exists, and which is the ultimate intrinsic source of its perfection, actuality and actual existence. In stage one of this argument Aquinas uses *esse* in the first sense (as facticity) when he refers to one's ability to understand what something is without understanding that it is. But then he quickly concludes to the intrinsic presence of *esse* taken in the second sense as an intrinsic perfecting principle (act of existing) that is distinct from the essence of every existing thing. Throughout

---

2. For some other interpretations, see Owens (1965, 1981, 1986), MacDonald (1984), and Wippel (1984, 2000).

stage two, however, he consistently uses it in the second way, thereby overcoming this weakness in the first stage.

In *ST* I.2.3, Aquinas presents his well known 'five ways' or arguments for the existence of God. The first "and more manifest" way is based on motion. It is certain and evident from sense-experience that some things in this world are moved. But whatever is moved is moved by another. Not content merely to cite this Aristotelian principle, however, Aquinas attempts to justify it by basing it on the distinction between act and potency. Something is moved only in so far as it is in potency to that to which it is moved. But something moves only in so far as it is in act, since to move is nothing other than to reduce something from potentiality to actuality. But something cannot be reduced from potency to act except by something that exists in actuality. Thus what is actually hot such as fire renders something that is hot only in potency actually hot, and thereby moves (alters) it. But, he continues, it is not possible for something to be simultaneously in act and in potency in the same respect but only in different respects. For instance, what is actually hot cannot simultaneously be potentially hot (with respect to the same degree of heat, one should understand), although it is potentially cold. Therefore it is impossible for one and the same thing by reason of the same motion to be both mover and moved, or to move itself. Therefore whatever is moved is moved by something else. But suppose that that by which something is moved is itself moved by something else, and that in turn by still something else. Here Aquinas rejects such a regress to infinity of moved movers as an ultimate explanation because then there would be no first mover and, consequently, no other movers; second movers (i.e. moved movers) do not move unless they are moved by something else. Hence one must arrive at some first (unmoved) mover which is not moved by anything else, which everyone understands to be God.[3]

Aquinas' second 'way' is based on the nature of efficient causality. On the strength of sense-experience he concludes that we find that an order obtains between efficient causes. By this he means that certain efficient causes cannot produce their effects without themselves being caused by a higher cause. But it is impossible for something to be the efficient cause of itself, because it would then be prior to itself. Again he considers and rejects the possibility of a regress to infinity in caused causes without the admission of a first (or uncaused) cause. In the case of ordered efficient causes, that is, a situation in which one efficient cause

---

3. In *SCG* I.13, Aquinas had offered two much longer and more complicated versions of the argument for God's existence based on motion, which he had developed from Aristotle's argumentation in *Physics* VII and VIII. The present argument is more metaphysical, with its key principle justified by appeal to the distinction between act and potency. Even so, dispute remains concerning whether or not this same key principle has been undermined by Newtonian physics and the principle of inertia. For fuller discussion, see Kenny (1980: ch. 2); Weisheipl (1985: chs 4–5); MacDonald (1991); Kretzmann (1997: chs 2–3); Wippel (2000: 444–59, 413–31).

cannot produce its effect without itself being caused by a prior cause, the first is the cause of the intermediary (or intermediaries), and it/they are the cause of the last cause, that is to say, of the starting-point in the order of discovery. In light of Aquinas' remarks about intermediaries here and elsewhere, it seems that he would hold that even if the intermediaries are infinite, the same point will follow.[4] He concludes that in such a series of ordered causes, if there is no first efficient cause, that is, no uncaused efficient cause, there will be no intermediary cause or causes, and hence no ultimate effect. Because this is false, a first efficient cause must be admitted, which is God.

Aquinas' third 'way' has generated much controversy on the part of Thomistic scholars, primarily because of two statements that appear in his presentation of it. The argument begins with a distinction between the possible and the necessary. Among the things we experience we find that certain things are possible (capable of existing or not existing), and this is because they are subject to generation and corruption. Hence, as Aquinas uses the term 'possible' here, he simply means that which is capable of being generated and corrupted and therefore, as he puts it, capable of existing or not existing. But, he continues in the first problematic sentence, it is impossible for all things that exist to be such because "what is capable of not existing at some time does not exist". (Many critics have asked why this follows: Could not something capable of not existing or capable of being corrupted actually never undergo corruption simply because another cause or set of causes keeps it in existence?) One may perhaps salvage this sentence by taking it to mean that a possible being by definition is capable of being generated and, assuming that it did arise by generation, it began to exist after having not existed. But the next problematic sentence states: "If all things are possible (capable of not existing), at some time nothing whatsoever existed". This is more difficult to defend because it seems to commit the fallacy of composition, that is, it moves from the claim that every possible being at some time was not existent to the universal claim that all possible beings would therefore have been non-existent at one and the same time (Wippel 2000: 462–9; Davies 2001 [who defends the argument]). If one grants the truth of this, then the rest of the argument's first part follows. If it were true that at some time nothing whatsoever existed, then nothing could have begun to exist and so now nothing would exist. Given the falsity of such a consequence, the argument concludes that not all things are possibles, and that there must be some necessary being, that is, a being not subject to generation and corruption.

In its second part the argument reasons that every necessary being either has a cause of its necessity from something else, or it does not. But regress to an infinite series of caused necessary beings will not account for anything, just as Aquinas

---

4. See his Commentary on *Metaphysics* II, lect. 3, 86–7, n. 303; Wippel (2000: 421–4, esp. n.63).

earlier reasoned about such a series of caused efficient causes. Therefore, Aquinas concludes, one must posit the existence of a being that is necessary in and of itself that does not depend on something else for its necessity. (In a somewhat parallel argument in *SCG* I.15, Aquinas establishes the conclusion of the first part of this argument in a less problematic way.)

Aquinas bases his fourth and most Platonic 'way' on the different degrees of perfection one finds among things in the external world. Some things are more or less good, more or less true, more or less excellent, and so too with respect to other perfections of this type. But more and less are said of different things in so far as they approach in differing degree something that is such to the maximum degree. Therefore there is something that is truest and best and most excellent, and which therefore is being to the maximum degree; for those things that are true to the maximum degree also enjoy being to the maximum degree. Here Aquinas appeals to the transcendental nature of ontological truth, that is, truth of being, and its convertibility with being. In referring to degrees of goodness, he is again referring to ontological goodness, not moral goodness.

In the second stage of this argument, Aquinas reasons that what is supremely such in a given genus is the cause of all other members of that genus. Therefore there is something (that which enjoys being to the maximum degree) which is the cause of being (*esse*) and of goodness and of every perfection in all other beings. While Aquinas clearly has efficient causality in mind in the argument's second stage, the kind of causality he envisages in the first stage is disputed by his interpreters: is it solely exemplar causality or also efficient causality? It seems that, as the argument stands, its first part is based only on formal exemplar causality but, in order to be convincing, it needs to be rephrased so as to include efficient causality (Wippel 2000: 469–79).

Aquinas introduces his fifth 'way' by noting that it is based on the governance of things. He appeals to our awareness of the fact that certain things that lack any kind of cognitive power (natural bodies) nonetheless act for the sake of an end. In support he cites the fact that they always or at least more frequently act in the same way so as to obtain that which is best, and hence concludes that such consistent behaviour cannot be accounted for by appealing to chance. But things that lack cognitive ability cannot act for an end unless they are directed to it by some intelligent being (just as an arrow must be directed to its target by an archer). Therefore, he concludes, there is some intelligent being by which all natural things are ordered to an end. While this argument is sometimes presented as one based on order and design, its starting-point is really finality in nature.

It is sometimes asked whether Aquinas thought that any of the five ways, if taken individually, would suffice to establish the unity (uniqueness) of God. There is no doubt that he thought that this can be demonstrated philosophically since he has listed it as another preamble of faith (*Super Boetium de Trinitate* q. 2, a. 3). In the argument Aquinas presents in *De ente* c. 4, the fact that there can be only one instance of subsisting *esse* (God) is built into the second stage of his overall argumentation. But in *ST* I, it is only somewhat later, in I.11, that Aquinas explicitly addresses and argues philosophically for the uniqueness of God.

THE POSSIBILITY OF QUIDDITATIVE KNOWLEDGE OF GOD

In *ST* I, immediately after his presentation of the five ways, Aquinas introduces his discussion in I.3 with the comment that once we have recognized that a given thing exists, we must determine how it is in order to arrive at knowledge as to what it is. But in the case of God we cannot know what he is but only what he is not, and so we cannot know how he is, but rather how he is not. Given this, in the immediately following questions Aquinas endeavours to show by using philosophical argumentation how God is not by denying of him that which is incompatible with his very nature. And so he will establish God's simplicity by denying all composition of him (I.3), his perfection (I.4), his goodness as following from his perfection (I.5–6), his infinity (I.7), his presence in things as following from his infinity (I.8), his immutability (I.9), his eternity (I.10) and, as already noted, his unicity (I.11).

In his earlier discussion of this in *SCG* I, after offering a series of arguments for God's existence in I.13, Aquinas notes in I.14 that in thinking about the divine substance (essence) one must use the way of negation (*via negationis*). This is because the divine substance surpasses each and every form that the human intellect can grasp, thereby making it impossible for it to know "what God is". But we can arrive at some knowledge of him by knowing what he is not. And in so far as we negate more things of him, we advance in our knowledge of him. For example, by denying that he is an accident, we distinguish him from all accidents. By adding that he is not a body, we distinguish him from some substances. And so by negating more and more things of him, we can distinguish him from everything else. This knowledge will not be perfect, however, since what God is in himself will remain unknown.

In I.15–27 in this text Aquinas endeavours to show that God is eternal (not subject to time because he is immutable), that there is no passive potentiality in him, that there is no matter in him, that he is perfectly simple (not composed in any way), that he can undergo no violence, that he is not a body, that he is his essence because he is not distinct from it, that in him essence and act of existing (*esse*) are identical, that there is no accident in God, that nothing can be added to the divine being that would enable him to be defined, that he falls into no genus, that the divine existence is not the formal act of existing of other things, and that God himself is not the form of any body.

And then, while still using this method of succeeding negations, in I.28 Aquinas argues that God is completely perfect, that is, that no excellence of any kind is lacking to him. In the first of a series of arguments he reasons that if there is something to which the total power of existing (*virtus essendi*) belongs, no perfection of any kind can be lacking to it. But this is true of that being which is identical with its act of existing (*esse*), which in I.22 he has shown God to be. Hence God is all-perfect. The conclusion that God is all-perfect, although reached by negating any lack of perfection of him, now opens the way for Aquinas to begin predicating certain names of God with positive content. As a necessary step in this development, in I.29 he argues that the vast difference between God and any and all creatures notwithstanding, there must still be some minimum degree of likeness between them and God. This is because a form found in any effect must in some way (i.e. either formally or virtually) be present in a cause that surpasses it in perfection, but in a different way and with a different meaning (*ratio*). This is expressed by the axiom that every agent produces something that is like itself.

ANALOGICAL PREDICATION OF DIVINE NAMES

This in turn leads Aquinas to take up the issue of the kinds of names that can be predicated of God (*SCG* I.30). Certain names that signify pure perfections without any deficiency may be predicated of God and of other things, such as goodness, wisdom, being (*esse*), and so on, although even in such cases this applies only to that which such names signify (their *res significata*), and not to the way in which they signify (their *modus significandi*). Their creaturely mode of signifying must be denied of them when they are applied to God. Moreover, such names cannot be predicated of God univocally (so as to have exactly the same meaning when applied to creatures and to God), or equivocally (so as to have completely different meanings when said of both), but only analogically (which names include some factor that unifies their diverse meanings).

In *SCG* I.34 and in *ST* I.13.5 Aquinas distinguishes between two kinds of analogical predication: that of many to one and that of one to another. In the first case a name may be applied to different things because each of them involves some kind of relationship to a first or primary instance (e.g. medicine, food and urine are all said to be 'healthy' because each has some relationship to the health of the body). In the second case the same name can be applied to two different things and yet have different meanings in the two cases because one of them is directly related to the other (e.g. 'being' is said of accident and of substance in different ways because of the relationship of accident to substance). Names cannot be applied to creatures and God in the first way because then something would be prior both to God and to creatures, for instance, being or goodness, in which both God and creatures would share. Only the second kind of analogy (of one to another) is appropriate in this case. In spite of the different meanings the name of a pure perfection has when it is applied to creatures and to God, the relationship of the created effect to God as to its cause provides sufficient unity to overcome purely equivocal predication.

Among the names of pure perfections Aquinas assigns to God, a few will be singled out here that are of special interest to students of the philosophy of religion, namely, that God is good, that he is intelligent, that he wills and that he creates freely.

Divine goodness

In *SCG* I Aquinas connects his argumentation for God's goodness with his conclusion that God is all-perfect. Thus in I.37 he explicitly states that God's goodness can be shown to follow from God's perfection. In the first of a series of arguments he reasons that that by reason of which something is said to be good is its own excellence (*virtus*). As Aristotle says in *Ethics* II (1106a3), the excellence of each thing is that which makes that which possesses it good and renders its work good. But an excellence is a kind of perfection, since each and every thing is good in so far as it is perfect. Hence each and every thing desires its own perfection as its proper good. Since God is perfect, he is good.

In *ST* I, after showing in I.4 that God is perfect, Aquinas devotes I.5 to a general discussion of the nature of the good (see Aertsen 1996: ch. 7; Velde 1999). Then in I.6.1, he reasons that goodness pertains above all to God. Something is good in so far as it is an object of appetite. But every thing desires its own perfection. And the perfection and form of an effect is a certain likeness of its agent, since every agent produces something that is like itself. Therefore the agent itself is an object of appetite and has the nature of the good. What is desired of an agent is that its likeness be participated in by others. Because God is the first efficient cause of all things, it follows that the nature of the good and of that which is an object of appetite pertains to him. And so Dionysius attributes goodness to God as to the first efficient cause of everything else (*see* Vol. 1, Ch. 20, "Pseudo-Dionysius"). In a. 4 Aquinas writes that each and every thing is said to be good by reason of the divine goodness *as* it is good by reason of the first exemplar – and first efficient and final cause – of all goodness.

God is intelligent

Among a series of arguments Aquinas offers in *SCG* I.44, to show that God is intelligent, a brief but important one is based on divine perfection. Aquinas recalls that he has shown (in I.28) that God is all-perfect because no perfection present in any kind of thing can be lacking to him. The presence of perfection in God does not compromise the divine simplicity, as he has shown in I.31; for God is identical with his perfection. But among the many perfections found in creatures, the most powerful (*potissima*) is for something to be intelligent. This is so because by means of its intellect a cognizing being becomes, in a certain way, all things. Therefore Aquinas concludes that God is intelligent (Kretzmann 1997: 173–96). For a similar argument, see his *Compendium theologiae* (Compendium of theology), c. 28 (Leon. ed., 42.9:1–7).

God's will

In *SCG* I.72, Aquinas presents a number of arguments intended to show that the fact that God possesses will follows from the fact that he possesses intellect. In the first of these Aquinas reasons that because a good that is understood is the proper object of will, it follows that a good that is understood, in so far as it is understood as good, is willed. But what is understood implies one who understands. Therefore one who understands the good as good is one who wills. Since God understands perfectly (as Aquinas has shown in chapters 44, 45), it follows that in so far as he understands being he also understands it as good. (Implied here is Aquinas' view that the good is a transcendental property of being and therefore convertible with it.) Hence he concludes that God possesses will (literally, that God wills [*volens*]). (Also see *Compendium theologiae* I, c. 32.)

God's freedom to create

Basing himself on the metaphysically dependent and participated existence (*esse*) of every being other than God, Aquinas maintains that God is the creative and conserving cause of all things other than himself (*ST* I.44.1; *De potentia Dei* [On the power of God] q. 3, a. 5; q. 5, a. 2; Velde 2006: 125–46). Moreover, he argues at length that God freely creates such things. Some scholars have challenged Aquinas' success in defending this last point. Arguing from Aquinas' view that God necessarily wills and loves his essence and his usage of an axiom taken from Pseudo-Dionysius to the effect that the good is diffusive of itself, they maintain that Aquinas should have concluded that God necessarily wills and produces things other than himself (Lovejoy 1965: 73–81; Kretzmann 1983, 1997: 218–25, 1999: 120–26, 132–6). Aquinas does maintain that God necessarily wills and loves his own goodness and his own being and that this is the reason for his willing other things, that is, in so far as they are ordered to the end of imitating and manifesting his own goodness. However, because the divine goodness can be realized without the existence of anything other than God and receives no increase in perfection from the fact that other things are created, the divine will is not necessitated to will other things. Because no individual creature or totality of creatures could ever be equal to or add to the intensively infinite divine perfection, Aquinas argues that God does not need creatures in order for his goodness to be manifested. He is free to create or not create at all, and he is free to create this creature rather than that. As for the axiom taken from Pseudo-Dionysius, Aquinas insists that it should not be interpreted in terms of efficient causality (which would mean that the good had to diffuse its goodness by causing other beings as their efficient cause), but only that the supreme Good or God diffuses his goodness by serving as a final cause for his creating other beings (*De veritate* q. 23, a. 4; *SCG* I.81; Wippel 2007: ch. 9, 218–39).

While much more could be said about Aquinas' philosophical discussion of the divine nature (see Further Reading), enough has been presented here to show that he maintains that sound philosophical reasoning can establish the existence of God, along with his unicity, simplicity, perfection, goodness, intellection, volition and freedom to create, and that all other beings depend on God for their very existence.

FURTHER READING

Davies, B. 2002. *Aquinas*. London: Continuum.

Montagnes, B. 2004. *The Doctrine of the Analogy of Being according to Thomas Aquinas*, E. Macierowski (trans.). Milwaukee, WI: Marquette University Press.

Rocca, G. 2004. *Speaking the Incomprehensible God: Thomas Aquinas on the Interplay of Positive and Negative Theology*. Washington, DC: Catholic University of America Press.

Shanley, B. 2002. *The Thomist Tradition*. Dordrecht: Kluwer.

Stump, E. 2003. *Aquinas*. London: Routledge [chs 2–5].

On PREDICATION see also Chs 11, 16; Vol. 5, Ch. 18. On DIVINE UNITY see also Ch. 7. On EXISTENCE OF GOD see also Chs 5, 6, 14; Vol. 1, Chs 18, 19; Vol. 3, Chs 6, 12, 13, 14, 15, 21; Vol. 5, Chs 11, 16. On THOMISM see also Vol. 5, Chs 9, 20.

14

JOHN DUNS SCOTUS

Richard Cross

John Duns Scotus was born *c*.1266 in the small town of Duns, just north of the border between England and Scotland, and some time early in his life became a Franciscan friar. By inference from the place of his ordination in 1291 (Northampton), we learn that he was studying at Oxford by that date. Scotus remained in Oxford until at least 1301, and in the last couple of years of the thirteenth century started lecturing on Peter Lombard's *Sentences*, a necessary step for a Bachelor of Theology on the way to becoming a Master of Theology. We know that Scotus was in Paris, lecturing on the *Sentences*, during the academic year 1302–3, in order to qualify as Master of Theology in the pre-eminent of the two great medieval theological centres. He became Master of Theology at Paris in 1305, and was moved to Cologne in 1307. Known from very soon after his death in 1308 as the 'subtle doctor', Scotus wrote the first systematic treatise dedicated to a proof for God's existence, the *De primo principio* or *On the First Principle*. As his nickname might suggest, the treatise – as with most of Scotus' works – is not an easy read. In what follows, I shall try to summarize some of the moves that Scotus makes in this treatise, and add some further relevant material from other works of Scotus'.

THE EXISTENCE OF A FIRST CAUSE

Scotus' aim, in *De primo principio*, is to try to find a proof for God's existence that rests not on contingent premises but on necessary ones. Scotus chooses three such necessary premises:

(1) Some producible nature exists (Scotus, *De primo principio* [hereafter *DPP*] 3, n. 1; Scotus 1982: 43).
(2) Some nature able to be directed to a goal exists (*DPP* 3, n. 8; Scotus 1982: 59).

(3)   Some nature able to be exceeded in perfection exists (*DPP* 3, n. 9; Scotus 1982: 61).

At first sight, these premises seem to be contingent, not necessary. But an item in the domain of interpretation of all three premises is a *nature*: not an individual in the world, but something more akin to a universal – as Scotus puts it, "a being understood quidditatively" (*DPP* 3, n. 1; Scotus 1982: 43). And the existential claim made in the premises amounts to no more than that such natures can be instantiated in the real world. The quantification ranges over properties, not individuals. In this sense, the first premise, for example, really means that there 'is' a (property/universal) *being producible*, and 'exists' should be understood in this specialized sense. So (1)–(3) amount to the following:

(1*)   Something of a producible nature is possible.
(2*)   Something of a nature able to be directed to a goal is possible.
(3*)   Something of a nature able to be exceeded in perfection is possible.

This is not the only odd feature of the three premises. For Scotus understands the modalities (i.e. 'able to be') as somehow parasitic on the constitution of the actual world: if there 'is' a *being producible*, for example, this is because the following two conditions are satisfied: *being producible* is internally coherent, and its instantiation is compatible with the world as constituted. Given this understanding of the modalities in (1)–(3), Scotus argues that these three premises imply the following three conclusions, respectively:

(4)   Some nature able to produce exists (*DPP* 3, n. 1; Scotus 1982: 43).
(5)   Some nature able to be a goal of activity exists (*DPP* 3, n. 8; Scotus 1982: 59).
(6)   Some nature able to exceed in perfection exists (*DPP* 3, n. 9; Scotus 1982: 61).

And these amount to the following necessary claims:

(4*)   Something of a nature able to produce is possible.
(5*)   Something of a nature able to be a goal of activity is possible.
(6*)   Something of a nature able to exceed in perfection is possible.

Scotus puts the inference from (1) to (4) as follows, and argues similarly for (5) and (6), *mutatis mutandis*: "There is among beings a nature that can produce an effect. Which is shown thus: some [nature] can be produced, therefore some [nature] can produce an effect. The consequence is clear by the nature of correlatives" (*DPP* 3, n. 1; Scotus 1982: 43). Scotus here appeals to a standard argument form, that from relative opposites, and such arguments are necessary when concerning possible situations; here, if something can be produced, then something can produce. The relation between the inference and the relevant understanding of modality is that, for example, nothing could be such that it is producible unless there is something that has the power to produce it. Possibility here is dependent on the constitution of the actual world. Analogously, the property of *being producible* is correlative to the property of *being able to produce*: the one property requires the other. There is no *being producible* without a *being able to produce*. Still, Scotus has not made any claims about individuals in the world; his point is merely that the causal constitution of the actual world is not such as to block the existence of causes, goals and things more perfect than other things.

Scotus argues at considerable length for the impossibility of an infinite regress of causes, at least in cases where the causal relations are transitive ("essentially ordered", as Scotus puts it); the key argument is the first: "The totality of essentially ordered causes is caused: therefore [it is caused] by some cause that does not belong to the totality (for then it would be its own cause), for the whole totality of dependent things depends, and [does so] on no member of the totality" (*DPP* 3, n. 3; Scotus 1982: 47).

The first cause of any essentially ordered causal series is not itself a part of that series. Every member of an essentially ordered series is dependent; by removing the first member from the series in this way, Scotus can ensure that, since every member of the series is dependent, the whole series is, and thus requires some first cause.

Given the impossibility of an infinite causal series, (4) entails

(7)   Some simply first nature able to produce exists,

which amounts to the following necessary claim:

(7*)   Something of a nature that is simply first and able to produce is possible.

As Scotus puts it:

> Something able to produce an effect is simply first, that is, neither able to be produced, nor able to produce in virtue of anything else. It is proved from the first [conclusion]: something is able to produce an effect. Let it be A. If [A] is the first, understood in this way [viz., in the second conclusion], the proposal is shown. If not, then it is a producer later [than some other producer], for it can be produced by another, or is able to produce in virtue of something else (for if a negation is denied, the affirmation is posited). Let that other be given, and let it be B, about which it is argued as it was argued of A. Either we will proceed to infinity in producers (of which each will be second with respect to a prior), or we will reach something not having anything prior. An

infinity in an ascending [order] is impossible. Therefore primacy is necessary, for whatever has nothing prior is not posterior to anything posterior to it [given the impossibility of] ... a circle in causes.

(DPP 3, n. 2; Scotus 1982: 45)

(Again, Scotus holds similar principles that yield analogous conclusions from (5) and (6), too, but for the sake of simplicity I focus here on the cosmological proof.) Scotus' next move is to argue that

(8)   Any simply first nature able to produce is uncausable.

His reasoning is that if such a nature were causable, it would not be simply first. So (7) amounts to the claim that some uncausable nature exists:

> Anything that is able to produce an effect, and that is simply first, is uncausable, because it cannot be produced as an effect and is independently able to produce an effect. This is clear from ... [(7)], for if it were produced as an effect, or causative in virtue of anything else, there would be a regress to infinity, or a circle [of causes], or else we would reach something that cannot be produced and is independently productive. And I call this the first, and it is clear that the other is not the first, from what you grant. It is further concluded that if the first cannot be produced, it is uncausable.

(DPP 3, n. 4; Scotus 1982: 51)

The next stage of the argument establishes (Scotus believes) the actual existence of an individual that instantiates such a first nature:

(9)   Something simply first, able to produce, exists.

Scotus' argument runs as follows:

> Something simply first, able to produce an effect, is actually existent, and some actually existing nature is thus able to produce an effect. It is proved: anything with whose nature it is incompatible to have the possibility of existence from another (*cuius rationi repugnat posse esse ab alio*), has the possibility of existence from itself, if it can be. But it is incompatible with the nature of anything simply first, able to produce an effect, that it have the possibility of its existence from another (from [(8)]); and it can exist (from [(7)]) ... Therefore anything simply first, able to produce an effect, has the possibility of existence from itself. But what does not exist of itself does not have the possibility of existence from itself, for then non-being would produce something in

being, which is impossible; and furthermore the thing would then cause itself, and thus would not be entirely uncausable.

(*DPP* 3, n. 5; Scotus 1982: 51–3)

The gist of (7) is that the existence of something instantiating the first nature is possible (in the sense of being compatible with the causal constitution of the actual world), and the gist of (8) is that such a thing, if it exists at all, cannot be caused by anything else: it "has the possibility of existence from itself". By itself, the conjunction of (7) and (8) does not amount to showing that there is a first being. But Scotus subscribes to a further principle, which I shall label the 'actuality principle', which explains why he thinks himself entitled to conclude to the existence of such a first being. The principle is this: "Nothing can not-be unless something positively or privatively incompossible with it can be" (*DPP* 3, n. 6; Scotus 1982: 53). What the actuality principle means, in effect, is that it is non-existence, rather than existence, that requires explaining: actuality is in every sense primary, and a nature is actual – is instantiated – unless something in the actual world prevents it. Putting it crudely, if there is nothing about the causal constitution of the actual world that prevents something from existing, then that thing exists. This claim relates precisely to the modal assumptions that Scotus makes in this argument (indeed, as far as I can see, it entails them, although it is not entailed by them). If something can be, at some time it is, and this is because its possibility is precisely the result of the causal constitution of the actual world. This is closely related to the so-called 'principle of plenitude', and shows how in this context Scotus' understanding of the modalities is far removed from the innovative one that he develops elsewhere, which I discuss below. If there is nothing incompatible with the existence of a first being, then that being exists. The key point about the earlier stages in the argument – particularly (7) – is to show that the existence of such a being is not incompatible with the causal features of the actual world.

Scotus argues similarly for the instantiation of an ultimate goal of existence and a maximally excellent being, and goes on to show that anything that instantiates one of these attributes (*being a first cause, being an ultimate goal, being maximally perfect*) instantiates the other two as well: the attributes are coextensional. He argues that any being satisfying any one of the attributes is uncausable (*DPP* 3, nn. 9–10; Scotus 1982: 59–61), and that anything uncausable is a necessary existent (*DPP* 3, n. 6; Scotus 1982: 53). But, he reasons, there can only be one kind of necessary existent. So only one kind of thing can instantiate the three relevant attributes (*DPP* 3, n. 10; Scotus 1982: 63). Scotus argues that the possession of the property of necessary existence is supposed to provide in some sense an explanation for the existence of the substance: a necessary existent cannot fail to exist. But different kinds of necessary existent would require additional attributes, necessary for their existence. This seems, however, to generate a contradiction: the attributes fail to be required (because necessity is sufficient);

the attributes are required (to differentiate the kinds of necessary existent) (*DPP* 3, n. 6; Scotus 1982: 55–7). At first glance the argument seems to prove too much, because it would entail that necessary existence is the only attribute that could be had by a necessary existent – something that Scotus does not accept – God has many other attributes too. But Scotus does believe that God's attributes are somehow 'contained in', or intrinsic to, his being in a way in which the attributes of other beings fail to be, and that this containment relation cannot obtain between necessary being and any kind of attribute other than the ones that God has, as we shall see.

ATTRIBUTES OF THE FIRST CAUSE

Scotus is aware that none of this entails that there is just one instantiation of these coextensional attributes, and at a later stage in his argument tries to come up with some reasons for there being just one such instantiation. But these reasons are parasitic on the most famous feature of Scotus' account of God: his attempt to show that any instantiation of the three coextensional attributes must be *infinite*. The most important argument for infinity begins from the notion of omniscience. There are infinitely many objects of knowledge; any intellect that simultaneously knows these objects – such as God's – is infinite (*DPP* 4, n. 15; Scotus 1982: 103). Infinity entails perfection:

> Let us change the idea of the potentially infinite in quantity into the idea of the actually infinite in quantity, if it could be actual. For if the quantity of the [potentially] infinite necessarily grew by taking part after part, so too we could imagine taken at once (or to remain at once) all the parts that can be taken, and we would have an actually infinite quantity, for it would be as great actually as it is potentially … If we were to understand there to be, among beings, something actually infinite in entity, that should be understood proportionately to the imagined actual infinite in quantity, such that that being is said to be infinite that cannot be exceeded in entity by anything, and that truly will have the feature of a whole, and of something perfect: whole, for although the whole actually infinite in quantity lacks none of its parts, or no part of such a quantity, nevertheless each part is outside the other, and thus the whole is from imperfect things. But a being infinite in entity has nothing entitative 'outside' in this way, for its totality does not depend on things imperfect in entity: for it is whole in such a way that it has no extrinsic part (for then it would not be totally whole). So although the actually infinite could be perfect in quantity – for it is lacking nothing of the quantity, according to itself – nevertheless each part is lacking some of the quantity, namely, that which is in another

[part]: neither is it perfect in this way [namely, quantitatively] unless each [part] of it is imperfect. But an infinite being is perfect in such a way that neither it nor any of its [parts] lacks anything.

(Quodlibetum 5, n. 2; Scotus 1639: 12:118)

Modelling God's infinity on the mathematical infinite is radical in an Aristotelian universe in which actual infinities are held to be impossible. The thought experiment involves too the thought that degrees of qualities can be somehow quantified, a move that proved very important in the history of science. But more important for our purposes here is the argument that there cannot be two perfect infinite minds. The question is how such minds would know each other. If directly, then each would be dependent on the other, and thus not wholly perfect. If by means of a representation, then each would understand itself better than it understands the other mind, and thus would not have wholly perfect knowledge of the other (*DPP* 4, n. 38; Scotus 1982: 149).

Still, all this presupposes that the first being has knowledge. Why should we accept this? Scotus' argument begins from the thought that the universe appears to be contingent, and to include events that occur contingently. Such an event is one "whose opposite could have happened when it did" (*DPP* 4, n. 6; Scotus 1982: 85); note here Scotus' innovative understanding of the modality in the modern way, as broadly logical, not the world-dependent nomological modality of the argument for God's existence. The contingent events that Scotus has in mind are particularly the results of human free will. If there is genuine contingency, then the first cause must be able to cause contingently. But Scotus, in common with his broadly Aristotelian age, holds that there are no random events: "There is no principle of acting contingently other than will, or something requiring the will, for everything else acts by the necessity of nature, and thus not contingently" (*DPP* 4, n. 5; Scotus 1982: 83). But voluntary activity requires that there are goals of activity that are known, and thus requires a mind (*DPP* 4, n. 5; Scotus 1982: 83).

As we shall see below, Scotus holds that God cannot have accidental properties. In line with this, he holds that God's knowledge of contingent truths cannot be the result of anything external to himself, or the result of God's 'seeing' things external to himself (*Reportatio* [hereafter *Rep.*] 1A.38.1–2, n. 24; Söder 1999: 230). So his knowledge of free creaturely actions is the result of his being a (partial but presumably irresistible) cause of such actions (*Rep.* 1A.38.1–2, n. 37; Söder 1999: 233–4). Scotus spends a great deal of time attempting to show that this view of God's knowledge is compatible with genuine creaturely freedom (*Ordinatio* [hereafter *Ord.*] 2.34.7.1–5, nn. 143–50; Scotus 1950– : 8:429–32). Although Scotus believes God to be timeless (for the evidence, see Scotus, *Ord.* 1.8.2.un., nn. 294, 297; Scotus 1950– : 4:322, 4:324) – which I think he takes to be an inference from God's immutability – he is unable to resolve the issue of the compatibility of human freedom with divine knowledge. His view that God cannot 'see' things external to himself entails that it is not open to him to claim that God timelessly 'sees' all time and thus knows future contingents without having to cause them.

Scotus' view of God's unconditioned nature leads Scotus to a strong emphasis on divine supremacy. God's ideas of unreal but possible objects are themselves the result of some minimal kind of causal activity on God's part: he cannot simply 'inspect' his essence to gain knowledge of such things (*Ord.* 1.35.un., nn. 47–9; Scotus 1950– : 6:264–6); and God's knowledge of modal truths likewise depends on God's causing those truths: not that God could cause the contents of such truths other than he does, or that he could avoid causing such truths at all, but that there would be no such truths at all were it not for God's causal activity (see the discussion in Cross 2005: 69–77). Equally, the infinite perfection of God, coupled with the fact that all his external causal activity is contingent, has some curious results on Scotus' ethical theory. God has no obligations other than to himself. If he had obligations to creatures, or were in some way constrained to act in accordance with what would count as obligation were he a moral agent, then (some of) his external acts would be necessitated, which is false (*Lectura* 1.39.1–5, n. 43; Scotus 1950– : 17:492). A consequence of this is that natural law extends only as far as the first table of the decalogue: those commands governing the 'Godward' aspects of creatures' moral duties. God can command creatures as he will (*Ord.* 3.37.un., n. 6; Scotus 1639: 7:645).

DIVINE SIMPLICITY AND THE FORMAL DISTINCTION

Classical theism of the kind defended by Scotus maintains that God is simple: that he lacks any kind of part. This doctrine is, according to Scotus, entailed by divine infinity. Suppose the relevant parts are finite. Then, as Allan Wolter has put it, "According to Scotus' definition of infinity the infinite exceeds the finite by a non-finite measure. Thus, no matter how many the parts, they do not add up to infinite" (Scotus 1982: 353). Suppose the relevant parts are infinite. Then, absurdly, the parts would not be less than the infinite whole (*DPP* 4, n. 31; Scotus 1982: 135). Divine infinity likewise entails that God cannot have any contingent or accidental properties. The infinite cannot lack anything; so it always has whatever properties it can have (*DPP* 4, n. 33; Scotus 1982: 139). (It is a hard matter for Scotus to square this with his belief that God's external willing and action are contingent, but let that pass, since Scotus at least recognizes the problem: see Cross [2005: 86–7].) This view, incidentally, further entails that God is immutable (see *Ord.* 1.8.2.un., n. 228; Scotus 1950– : 4:281).

More distinctive is Scotus' view on the relation between the various divine attributes, and between these attributes and God's substance (God himself). Many versions of classical theism maintain that there is no distinction between the various divine attributes, and likewise no distinction between the divine attributes and God's substance. On this view, God does not have properties or attributes (I use the two terms synonymously here): not only is he just properties, but he is just one property – his own nature or self. Scotus is vehemently opposed to this way of thinking of God. He has little problem with the thought that God could be just properties. But he strongly disagrees with the view that God is just one property: that there are no distinctions between the various divine attributes. As Scotus understands the view that he opposes, when we talk about different divine attributes, we are merely talking about different ways in which God can be resembled by creatures, or represented to them. These different ways do not correspond to anything real in God other than just God himself (see Scotus' summary of the position he opposes at *Ord.* 1.8.1.4, n. 162; Scotus 1950– : 4:233–4). All that the position asserts is that we can correctly think of God in various different ways. Scotus opposes this view by arguing that there must be some kind of distinction in God, and thus that the things so distinguished must have some kind of reality independent of our way of thinking about them. To defend this position, Scotus develops an elaborate account of various different kinds of distinction, because, as we have seen, he rejects the view that God could be composed of really distinct parts, so whatever his doctrine about the divine attributes amounts to, it cannot entail that God is composed, or that the attributes are really distinct from each other. The key passage is worth quoting in full:

> There is therefore a distinction [between essential divine perfections] preceding in every way the intellect, and it is this: that wisdom really exists in reality (*est in re ex natura rei*), and goodness really exists in reality, but real (*in re*) wisdom is not real goodness. Which is proved, for if infinite wisdom were formally infinite goodness, then wisdom in general would be formally goodness in general. For infinity does not destroy the formal notion of the thing to which it is added, for in whatever degree some perfection is understood to be (which degree is a degree of the perfection), the formal notion of that perfection is not removed by the degree, and thus, if [this perfection] *as in general* does not formally include [that perfection] *as in general*, neither [does this perfection] *as in particular* [include that perfection] *as in particular*.
>
> I show this, because 'to include formally' is to include something in its essential notion, such that if there were a definition of the including thing, then the thing included would be the definition or a part of the definition. Just as, however, the definition of goodness in general does not include wisdom, neither does infinite [goodness include] infinite [wisdom]. There is therefore some formal non-identity between wisdom and goodness, inasmuch as there would be distinct definitions of them if they were definable. But a definition indicates not only a concept caused by the intellect, but the quiddity of a thing: there is therefore formal non-identity from the side of the thing, which I

understand thus: the intellect forming this [sentence] 'wisdom is not formally goodness' does not cause, by its act of combining, the truth of this combination, but it finds the terms in the object, and a true act is made by their combination.

> (*Ord.* 1.8.1.4, nn. 192–3; Scotus 1950– : 4:261–2)

Halfway through the second paragraph here, Scotus claims that there is some "formal non-identity between wisdom and goodness". This is Scotus' (in)famous 'formal distinction': very roughly, the kind of extramental distinction that exists between two inseparable properties of one and the same substance (on the assumption that properties are in some sense real features of things, and not merely linguistic or mental items – predicates or concepts – an assumption to which I shall return in a moment). But why suppose that God's wisdom and goodness (for example) are distinct in this kind of way? The argument is that the relevant creaturely attributes – wisdom and goodness – are not coextensional, and thus that there must be some sort of distinction between them. But if the intelligible content of the relevant divine attributes overlaps with the intelligible content of the corresponding creaturely attributes (as Scotus supposes to be the case), then there must be some sort of distinction between the relevant divine attributes too (even if the relevant divine attributes are coextensional with each other).

Still, why suppose that properties are in some sense real features of things? The end of the passage makes some preliminary suggestions: for at least certain sorts of property, statements about the identity or distinction of different properties require truth-makers, and these truth-makers must be (somehow) real, entailing that the properties themselves are somehow real. But this argument as it stands is hardly decisive (since it does not provide a principle for distinguishing cases such as this from those in which no extramental truth-maker is required), and elsewhere Scotus develops what he has in mind at greater length. Fundamentally, Scotus maintains that there are some concepts under whose extensions both divine and creaturely attributes fall. The concept of *wisdom*, for example, includes in its extension both divine and creaturely wisdom. And if creaturely wisdom and creaturely goodness are distinct in Socrates, then they must be somehow distinct in God too. As Scotus puts it in the passage just quoted, "if infinite wisdom were formally infinite goodness, then wisdom in general would be formally goodness in general".

RELIGIOUS LANGUAGE AND UNIVOCITY

Now, I have shifted from speaking of properties to speaking of concepts, and the reason for this is that Scotus is fundamentally appealing to a certain *semantic* theory to secure his conclusion here, albeit, a material conclusion with important theological consequences of its own. The semantic theory involves conditions for univocity, for employing the same *concept* in different contexts. Scotus states the conditions as follows:

> I call that concept univocal which is one in such a way that its unity is sufficient for a contradiction when affirmed and denied of the same thing, and also is sufficient for a syllogistic middle term, such that the extremes are united in the middle term which is one in such a way that they can be united between themselves without the fallacy of equivocation. (*Ord.* 1.3.1.1–2, n. 26; Scotus 1950– : 3:18)

The issue here is sameness of *concept*, and the criteria for such sameness are syntactic. But what is at stake is, nevertheless, a *semantic* matter: identity of informational *content*. For, accepting standard Aristotelian medieval semantic presuppositions, concepts are meanings of words. And one of the grounds for syllogistic validity is that the terms mean the same things in the premises and conclusions. Thus, Scotus maintains that theological reasoning requires that God and creatures fall under (some of) the same concepts:

> Every metaphysical inquiry about God proceeds by considering the formal notion of something and removing from that formal notion the imperfection that it has in creatures, retaining the formal notion, attributing to it utterly the highest perfection, and then attributing it to God. Example of the formal notion of wisdom (or intellect) or will: for it is considered in itself and according to itself, and from the fact that this notion does not formally entail imperfection or limitation, the imperfections which follow it in creatures are removed from it, and, retaining the same notion of wisdom and will these are attributed to God most perfectly. Therefore every inquiry about God presupposes that the mind has the same univocal concept which it receives from creatures. (*Ord.* 1.3.1.1–2, n. 39; Scotus 1950– : 3:26–7)

What Scotus is wondering about is this: how could we argue from one perfection to another unless the meanings of the words that signify the various perfections were the same – exactly the same – in the premises and the conclusion? How could we (e.g.) infer from God's wisdom that God knows many facts unless we knew that all things that are wise know many facts? Once we know (on whatever grounds) that the inference is sound, we know that the various words are being used univocally. I do not think that Scotus or his contemporaries would have regarded as in any way controversial the thought that theological arguments that are *prima facie* sound are in fact sound; thus, as Scotus puts it in a much-quoted passage, "Masters who write of God and of those things that are known of God, observe the univocity of being in the way in which they speak, even though they deny it with their words" (*Rep.* 1.7.1, n. 7; Scotus 1639: 11:43).

Given that there is some kind of distinction between the various divine attributes, what account does Scotus give of their unity? And how does he distinguish these formally distinct attributes from really distinct parts? The answer to both questions relies on Scotus' controversial account of real identity. For Scotus maintains that formally distinct attributes can be really identical with each other and with the whole that emerges from the union of such attributes (i.e. that emerges from their real identity with each other). These claims require careful construal, for Scotus' account of real identity is not exactly as the accounts of modern philosophers presuppose. Fundamentally, real identity, at least between different properties, is most closely related to the modern philosophical notion of *compresence*, a relation that ties together distinct properties, and which has the formal properties of symmetry and (unlike real identity) intransitivity. Intransitivity allows two sets of compresent properties to overlap without thereby being identical with each other, a requirement that turns out to be vital in Scotus' defence of the doctrine of the Trinity (see Cross 2005: 169–70, 237–40). Scotus maintains that divine infinity automatically explains the real identity of his various attributes with each other:

> If we abstract wisdom from anything which is outside the notion of wisdom, and likewise if we abstract goodness from anything which is formally outside its notion, each quiddity will remain, understood precisely, formally infinite. From the fact that the cause of their identity in this very precise abstraction is infinity, the cause of the identity of the extreme terms [in a sentence such as 'divine wisdom is divine goodness'] remains. For these were precisely the same not on account of their identity with some third thing from which they are abstracted, but on account of the formal infinity of each.
>
> (*Ord.* 1.8.1.4, n. 220; Scotus 1950– : 4:275)

The idea is that if a divine attribute could be part of a composite, it would not itself be infinite. The reason for this goes back to those arguments that derive simplicity from infinity, mentioned earlier. Things that can enter into composition are finite, since being a component entails being less than the whole made up of components. Infinite attributes are such that they cannot be exceeded, and therefore such that they cannot enter into composition with each other. They are therefore really identical. Thus, considered even in complete abstraction from their subject (in this case, the divine essence), divine attributes can be predicated of each other "by identity", as Scotus puts it. Infinity guarantees numerical identity, and thus occupies a key role in the most characteristic Scotist teaching on divine simplicity, namely the real identity of, and formal distinction between, the various divine attributes. And this explains how God's attributes are somehow 'contained in' his infinite being, as mentioned above, and why the argument for divine unicity is not undermined by the presence of distinct attributes in God.

FURTHER READING

Craig, W. 1980. *The Cosmological Argument from Plato to Leibniz*. Basingstoke: Macmillan.

O'Connor, T. 1993. "Scotus's Argument for a First Efficient Cause". *International Journal for Philosophy of Religion* **33**: 17–32.

Vos, A. 2006. *The Philosophy of John Duns Scotus*. Edinburgh: Edinburgh University Press.

Williams, T. (ed.) 2002. *The Cambridge Companion to Duns Scotus*. Cambridge: Cambridge University Press.

Wolter, A. 1990. *The Philosophical Theology of John Duns Scotus*, M. Adams (ed.). Ithaca, NY: Cornell University Press.

On EXISTENCE OF GOD see also Chs 5, 6, 13; Vol. 1, Chs 18, 19; Vol. 3, Chs 6, 12, 13, 14, 15, 21; Vol. 5, Chs 11, 16. On FIRST CAUSE see also Ch. 14; Vol. 1, Chs 15, 16; Vol. 3, Ch. 6.

15

WILLIAM OCKHAM

Gyula Klima

William Ockham (*c*.1287–1347) was an English Franciscan friar, famous for his *nominalism* (Klima 2006), whose name is preserved in the commonly used designation of the methodological principle called 'Ockham's razor' (Adams 1987: 156–7, 281). This chapter will focus primarily on Ockham's nominalist doctrine and its impact on his theology.

William Ockham was born around 1287 in a little village called Ockham, twenty-five miles from London. He received his elementary education in London in the convent of the Franciscan order (the Greyfriars). At the time, the London House of the Greyfriars was a distinguished intellectual centre for not only elementary but also higher education, although it was not a university. Thus, having completed his studies in grammar, logic and natural philosophy, Ockham began studying theology there around the age of twenty-three, but soon moved on to Oxford. Probably in 1317, he began lecturing on the *Sentences* of Peter Lombard in Oxford, which was a general requirement for getting one's licence as a Master of Theology. However, in 1321, Ockham returned to the Franciscans in London before completing the programme at Oxford; thus he never became a Master of Theology (hence his honorific title, *Inceptor Venerabilis*, the venerable *inceptor*; that is, one who began work on, but has not received, his degree). Accordingly, it is only book I of his *Commentary on the Sentences* that exists in the form of an *ordinatio* (a text revised by the author himself for copying); the remaining three books exist only in the form of *reportationes* (unrevised lecture notes). He stayed three more years at the London Greyfriars, where he was involved in important philosophical and theological debates with his confreres, such as Walter Chatton and Adam Wodeham. It was during this period that he produced, among a number of minor theological and philosophical works and some important commentaries in logic and natural philosophy (see Spade 1999: 5–11), his groundbreaking *Summa logicae* (hereafter *SL*; *c*.1323), laying out his nominalist logic, and his *Quodlibetal Questions*, presenting his mature philosophical and theological views. The disputations recorded here took place in London, in the years 1322–4, but Ockham revised and edited them in Avignon, in 1324–5, where he was summoned to the papal court to answer charges of heresy. Or so the traditional story goes.

Recently it has been questioned whether Ockham was indeed 'summoned' to Avignon, or whether he was assigned by his order to teach there, or whether he went voluntarily to answer the charges, in hope of a positive outcome (Shogimen 2007: 2–3). In any case, it is certain that there was a formal enquiry into his teachings, and out of fifty-six questionable propositions collected from his doctrine, fifty-one were indeed censured (i.e. deemed erroneous), although not formally condemned (Pelzer 1922). It is also quite certain that completing the *Quodlibetal Questions* was the last act of Ockham's purely academic career. But it was not the outcome of the inquisition into his nominalist doctrine that eventually ended his academic activity. In 1327, during his stay in Avignon, the master general of his order, Michael of Cesena, was summoned to Avignon because of the ongoing controversy between the order and the pope over the idea of 'apostolic poverty' (the idea that Christ and the apostles owned no property and lived on alms, whence the mendicant order's similar practice was considered as a special form of imitating Christ). In 1328, at the request of Michael of Cesena, Ockham reviewed the pope's relevant bulls for their orthodoxy. Apparently much to his own surprise, Ockham found that John XXIII held heretical views and thus was in fact a heretic. As a result, on 26 May 1328, Ockham, along with Michael of Cesena and some other Franciscans, fled the papal court to seek the protection of Ludwig of Bavaria, who was staying at the time in Pisa. Ludwig had been excommunicated earlier, in 1324, over the issue of the succession to the throne of the Holy Roman Empire. On the strength of military success, Ludwig challenged the view that the emperorship was a gift from the papacy, and, having occupied Rome in 1328, had the Roman people declare him Holy Roman Emperor. On 6 June 1328, Ockham was formally excommunicated for leaving Avignon without permission. Thus, along with the other fugitive Franciscans, he followed Ludwig to the imperial court in Munich, where he stayed for the rest of his life, being involved in political controversy over issues ranging from apostolic poverty to heresy, in particular papal heresy, and papal authority, until his death in 1347.

OCKHAM'S NOMINALISM

The term 'nominalism', especially in the context of medieval philosophy, is usually taken to designate a metaphysical position, consisting in the denial of the existence of universal entities or 'real universals', as opposed to the 'realist' position, endorsing the existence of such universals, and to the 'conceptualist' position, positing that universals exist only in the mind. Indeed, based on this sort of classification, nominalists tend to be described as *conventionalists*, for whom the only universals are words (*nomina*) and thus would take our universal terms to apply to things grouped together arbitrarily or conventionally and not on the basis of anything inherent in the nature of things (as 'realists' would have it) or in the nature of our minds conceiving of them (as 'conceptualists' would take it to be the case). Thus, nominalists also tend to be taken to be *sceptics*, who would claim that we can never get to know the inherent natures of things, if they have anything like that at all.[1]

Under these descriptions, these terms are nearly useless in classifying the much more sophisticated views of medieval thinkers, whose disagreements simply lay elsewhere. Still, with the proper clarification of their *genuine* disagreements, it will still make sense to classify Ockham as a nominalist, as opposed, say, to Thomas Aquinas, John Duns Scotus or Walter Burley as (more or less 'moderate') realists, disregarding in this comparison *their* more subtle differences.

To be sure, Ockham did deny the existence of mind-independent universal entities existing in their universality in the nature of things, such as the Platonic Forms of Man or Horse 'in itself'. But after Boethius, so did nearly everybody else. Medieval realists would rather claim that individual substances, such as rocks, trees, horses or human beings, are sorted into their natural kinds (species and genera) on account of their inherent individualized natures, which, however, can be recognized by the abstractive intellect as instances of the same common nature. That common nature itself, nevertheless, is not an entity existing on a par with its instances: the actual real entities are only the individualized instances themselves, just as copies of a book are the only actually existing entities, whereas 'the book itself' can only be discerned by those who are able to read the copies. Although this conception is not open to the usual objections of inconsistency marshalled against Plato's 'naive' theory of Forms (such as the Third Man argument, recognized already by Plato himself in his *Parmenides*), Ockham still finds it unacceptable for several reasons.[2]

In the first place, he takes it to lead to several sorts of absurdities, especially in connection with Scotus' conception of the relationship between the common nature taken in itself and what individualizes it in its instances. In the second

---

1. Cf. Gracia: "If the universal has only mental existence, the objectivity and scientific validity of our concepts is undermined" (1994: 23). Interestingly enough, this sort of reasoning, tying the denial of real universals to scepticism, is present already in Scotus (for whom a real universal is an entity having what he calls "less than numerical unity"):

    If every real unity is numerical unity, therefore every real diversity is numerical diversity. The consequent is false. For every numerical diversity, in so far as it is numerical, is equal. And so all things would be equally distinct. In that case it follows that the intellect could not abstract something common from Socrates and Plato any more than it can from Socrates and a line. Every universal would be a pure figment of the intellect.   (Quoted in Spade 1994: 62)

2. For a more detailed exposition of the medieval problem of universals, see Klima (2000). For Ockham's detailed discussion, including a point-by-point response to Scotus' arguments, see Spade (1994: 114–231).

place, and perhaps more importantly, he argues that there is no theoretical need whatsoever to posit such universal entities.

Ockham's arguments in favour of the first conclusion here are intended to rule out universal entities by means of *reductio ad absurdum*. For instance, he argues that if Socrates and Plato shared the same common essence without which neither could exist (which would have to be the case if there were common natures), then it would be impossible even for God to create or annihilate them independently, which is clearly absurd, since they were actually born and died independently of one another (*SL* I, 15: 51, ll. 29–38).[3] But this sort of argument assumes a rather crude conception of a universal, according to which it is an entity that is numerically one in all of its distinct instances, and numerically distinct from each of them. So, in another set of arguments, Ockham addresses Scotus' much more sophisticated account, according to which universals, possessing a less-than-numerical unity, are *merely formally*, but not numerically, distinct from what individualizes them in their particular instances: their so-called *individual difference*, or 'haecceity'. In particular, he argues against what he takes to be the fundamental absurdity in Scotus' notion of a formal distinction:

> [I]n creatures,[4] there can never be any distinction outside the mind unless there are distinct things; if, therefore, there is any distinction between the nature and the difference, it is necessary that they be really distinct things. I prove my premise by the following syllogism: this nature is not formally distinct from itself; this individual difference is formally distinct from this nature; therefore, this individual difference is not this nature. (*SL* I, 16: 54)

Scotus and his followers were more than prepared to handle such and similar 'absurdities', by for instance distinguishing between different types of predication. But for Ockham, that sort of strategy would simply amount to 'adding epicycles' to save a generally useless and ill-founded doctrine. Thus, his second strategy consists in showing not so much the absurdity of the opposing position as the possibility of a consistent system of thought without any commitment to the ontological extravagances of the realist position. Based on the heuristic principle bearing his name (which nevertheless had been in use by earlier scholastics as well), he can eliminate from his ontology not only 'real universals', but all sorts of 'weird entities' posited by his realist opponents.

For according to Ockham, nearly all of the *metaphysical* troubles of the 'realist' position stem from a radically mistaken conception of the fundamental *semantic* relationships between language, mind and reality. As he wrote: "And this is the

---

3. This is a simplified presentation of Ockham's somewhat more complicated argument.
4. It is significant that Ockham restricts his argument to creatures; see the section on his doctrine of the Trinity below.

root (*principium*) of many errors in philosophy: to want that to a distinct word there always correspond a distinct *significate*, so that there is as much distinction between the things signified as there is between the names or words that signify".[5] Actually, it would be hard to find among Ockham's genuine opponents someone who would have held such a simple-minded 'isomorphistic' view (however, see (Pseudo-)Campsall 1982). But it is true that the semantic conception Ockham challenges does posit several semantic values for each term of our language in various categories, which then inevitably raises the metaphysical problems of the distinctness and identity of these semantic values. Ockham's radical solution is the simple *elimination* of many of these *metaphysical* problems by challenging the *semantic* assumptions that gave rise to them in the first place.

For instance, an obviously emerging problem for the traditional framework was whether relations are identical with or distinct from their foundations: if Socrates is equal to Plato in height, is his height the same as or distinct from his equality to Plato? Apparently both answers would lead to absurdities. If they are the same, then it would seem that if by Plato's growth Socrates' equality to him ceases to exist, then so should his height, which is absurd. But if they are distinct, then it would logically, and hence by divine omnipotence, be possible for Socrates and Plato to be equal even if they are not of the same height, if God preserves their equality, even if one of them outgrows the other, which is also absurd. Again, the realists Ockham criticizes had their own *metaphysical* solutions to these problems (Henninger 1989; Brower 2005). However, Ockham argues that the problem itself emerges only on the basis of a mistaken *semantic* conception, and, therefore, on the right conception it should not emerge at all.

For the reason why the question emerges for realists in the first place is that they would take the term 'equal to' in the predication 'Socrates is equal to Plato' to signify an inherent property, Socrates' equality to Plato, the existence of which is what verifies the predication. Thus, when the predication ceases to be true on account of Plato's change, the question as to what happened to this alleged entity is just inevitable. By contrast, on 'the right' account, that is, Ockham's own, there is no need to posit such an entity at all. For on this account, just as the term 'man' does not signify some common nature, humanity, existing individualized in all human beings, but merely signifies human beings absolutely, yet indifferently, so the term 'equal' does not signify a common nature, equality, existing individualized in things that are equal, but merely signifies these things themselves indifferently, yet not absolutely, but *connoting* the things to which they are equal.[6]

---

5. "Et hoc est principium multorum errorum in philosophia: velle quod semper distincto vocabulo correspondeat distinctum significatum, it quod tanta sit distinctio rerum significatarum quanta est nominum vel vocabulorum significantium" (Ockham 1984: 270); cf. *SL* I, 51: 169–71.

6. Connotation is usually explained as secondary signification: a connotative term primarily signifies things it can stand for in a proposition, and secondarily signifies or connotes all

Thus, Socrates' becoming unequal to Plato on account of Plato's growth need not involve the mysterious perishing of any inherent entity in Socrates, but merely a change in the connotation of the term, on account of which it no longer applies to the thing, Socrates, to which it formerly did with this connotation. On the other hand, the absolute term 'height' still signifies Socrates' unchanged height, without any change whatsoever. Therefore, on this account, the mystery of the possible vanishing of Socrates' height with his equality to Plato, or the possible persistence of this equality without Socrates' being as tall as Plato, simply does not emerge.

Indeed, Ockham does not stop here. Applying his novel analysis to how our terms, whether absolute or connotative, apply to the things they signify, he argues that there are only two really distinct categories of entities, namely, those of substance and quality. It is only abstract terms in these two categories and concrete terms in the category of substance that are simple absolute terms, signifying singular substances and their particular qualities indifferently, yet absolutely. All other terms in the other logical categories distinguished by Aristotle (namely, quantity, relation, action, passion, time, place, position and habit), signify substances or qualities, variously connoting other substances or qualities. It is these various types of connotation, explicable in their nominal definition, that sort these terms into these different logical categories, and *not* the different types of entities they supposedly signify in the same way, as it was conceived on the realist conception.

Thus, for instance, quantity terms, whereby substances are said to be (this) big or small or tall or short or wide and so on do not apply to substances on account of signifying their distinct inherent dimensions, but rather signify these substances or their parts themselves, variously connoting their parts or other substances or their parts. Accordingly, the predication 'Plato is tall' is not rendered true because of the existence of an inherent entity, Plato's tallness, which then would have to be accounted for in one's metaphysics and physics (causing all sorts of headaches in these disciplines); rather, this predication is true because Plato is identical with one of the things signified by the predicate, namely, tall human beings (i.e. human beings who would stick out in a crowd of all other human beings). How this intuitive idea can be made more precise is a further issue, to be taken care of in Ockham's programme of 'ontological reduction' of the categories (for further details, see Klima [1999]). But those details need not detain us here. The point of this sort of analysis is that Ockham's new semantics is capable of accounting for the semantic properties of the terms we use in describing reality, yet without having to account for these *logical* properties in terms of the *ontological* properties of the peculiar entities these terms are supposed to signify. Thus, he ends up

---

other things, in relation to which it signifies its primary significata. For example, 'father' primarily signifies men having children in relation to their children: thus, the primary *significata* of the term are these men, and its *connotata* are their children.

with a perfectly functioning logic, yet without many of the traditional ontological problems generated by the realist framework.

OCKHAM'S NOMINALISM IN HIS THEOLOGY

The demonstrability of God's uniqueness

As was noted earlier, nominalists are often accused of scepticism on the grounds that if there are no real common natures in the things themselves, as they claim, then it seems that our grouping things together into species and genera may be completely arbitrary or at best pragmatically conventional. This charge certainly does not hold for Ockham's nominalism, or indeed for late medieval nominalism initiated by Ockham in general.[7] For Ockham, things are mind-independently sorted into their natural kinds. However, this is not because of some common nature distinct from and inherent in them, but on account of the things themselves. For him, essential similarity of co-specific or co-generic individuals is a 'brute fact', not needing any further explanation. The same goes for the essential dependencies of things, that is, their natural causal relations.

Therefore, Ockham's nominalism does not have any direct epistemological implications concerning his natural theology. In fact, he is happy to go along with Scotus' arguments as far as he finds them plausible without begging the question. Thus, he argues that according to the two possible nominal definitions one can provide for the common term 'God', one can provide two different answers to the question of the demonstrability of the existence and uniqueness of God (Ockham 1980: I, q. 1). Using the first nominal definition, according to which the name applies to a being that is more perfect than anything else, it is easy to prove the uniqueness of God. For if we assume that there are two beings satisfying the description, then we at once arrive at the impossibility that one of them is more perfect than the other and *vice versa*. However, according to Ockham, there is no evident, non-question-begging proof that there is such a being. On the other hand, on the other nominal definition, according to which the name 'God' applies to a being than which nothing is more perfect, it is possible to prove

---

7. For an interesting rethinking of these customary charges, see Lee (2001). See also:

> Buridan was a committed Nominalist. He was, in other words, on the philosophically wrong side of the major metaphysical controversy of the Middle Ages. Like Ockham, he believed there were no universals: strictly speaking, no colours, only coloured things; no virtue, only virtuous people; no circularity, only individual circles. The rest was all just hot air (*flatus vocis*). The Nominalists ended up poisoning the well of sound philosophy with scepticism, relativism, agnosticism and even atheism. Fortunately, Realism was not sent to rout and has many exponents in present-day analytic philosophy.   (Oderberg 2003)

For a discussion of this sort of charge in the case of Buridan, see Klima (2005).

that there is such a being from the impossibility of an infinite regress in the series of essentially dependent conserving (as opposed to merely productive) causes of necessarily increasing perfection. But according to Ockham, we do not have a non-question-begging proof for the uniqueness of such a being. He commends Scotus' arguments to this effect as ones that are plausible; he just cannot accept them as demonstrative. However, these considerations do not directly stem from Ockham's nominalist doctrine; they merely reflect a strict application of a high standard of scientific demonstration. Ockham's nominalism has a more direct impact on his metaphysical treatment of traditional theological topics than on his views on the natural cognition of God.[8]

Divine simplicity

In fact, there are certain parts of medieval Christian theological doctrine that are actually easier to handle in Ockham's nominalist framework than in the earlier (and also contemporary) realist framework. An obvious example is the doctrine of divine simplicity. According to this doctrine, divine perfection demands God's absolute simplicity, that is, the denial of any sort of composition in God. Thus, God cannot be composed of matter and form as material creatures are, as this involves the obvious limitations of existence in space and time, which certainly cannot apply to the creator of space and time, who has to exist both everywhere in space at every time and beyond all space and all time. He cannot be composed of substance and accident either, as this would involve mutability, and so a possible decrease or increase of perfection, which is impossible in the case of absolute perfection. There cannot be a composition of nature and *suppositum* (i.e. the thing that has this nature) in God, because that would entail the possibility of the multiplication of the same nature in several *supposita*, that is, there could be several Gods, which is impossible, because there cannot be more than one absolutely perfect being, one that is more perfect than anything else.[9]

In the realist framework opposed by Ockham, this conception inevitably posed the problem of the apparent irreconcilability of the multitude of distinct divine attributes with the simplicity of the indivisible, simple divine essence, with which each of these attributes is supposed to be identical. For instance, since God is wise, God has wisdom, and since he is powerful he has power, but on account of divine

---

8. Since this chapter focuses primarily on the impact of Ockham's nominalism on his theology, and not on the finer details of his natural theology or of his take on the relationship between faith and reason in general, for those details I refer the reader to Freddoso (1999).

9. Thomists would also add, most importantly, that in God, as opposed to all creatures, there is no composition of essence and existence. But that is peculiar to the Thomistic conception. Medieval 'Augustinians', such as Henry of Ghent or Scotus, would not acknowledge that sort of composition in creatures either.

simplicity both divine wisdom and divine power have to be identical with divine essence, that is, with God himself. But how is this possible? After all, wisdom and power are distinct attributes, as is testified by the existence of powerless wise and powerful stupid people.

Medieval realists, such as Aquinas, were able to claim that since we gain our concepts of perfections from creatures, in which these perfections are distinct, our concepts of these perfections are distinct as well, but to the extent that these concepts grasp anything of divine perfection they apply to the same simple divine essence. So our terms expressing these concepts are non-synonymous. The attributes considered in general, in abstraction from their instances, are not the same. Still, in the case of divine perfection they are just different, imperfect expressions of one and the same infinitely perfect reality. The idea is often illustrated by an analogy of vision: our concepts derived from the multitude of creaturely perfections provide us with imperfect representations of their single, absolutely perfect source, just as our sight of the various colours of the stained glass windows of a cathedral gives us an imperfect glimpse of their unique source, the sunlight; indeed, just as we cannot directly gaze into the sun and can get a glimpse of it only through some coloured glass, so our intellect in its natural state is incapable of directly apprehending the divine perfection, except through its natural apprehension of creaturely perfections.

However, this idea seems to cause further problems for the realist account on a 'higher level'. For our concepts, being acquired through abstraction from the forms of creatures we encounter in experience, do represent distinct forms in creatures; indeed, the concepts are distinct on account of that distinction; so how can these distinct concepts, representing by their nature distinct formal realities, represent a single formal reality in God (the divine essence)? Scotus' solution invokes his formal distinction, which allegedly does not involve any real distinction or multiplication, whence it is compatible both with divine simplicity and with the multitude of distinct creaturely forms that owe their real distinction precisely to the formal distinction of divine perfections.

But Ockham cannot accept Scotus' formal distinction in this case either, especially because he does not need it in his own account. Since on his nominalist conception a universal concept is universal *not* on account of its being the result of the intellectual grasp of some common nature existing individualized in its instances, but on account of its mere indifference of representation (not being a representation of *this* individual of a certain sort rather than *that* one), such a universal concept is capable of representing creaturely perfections and divine perfection indifferently. Of course, this representation can 'reach up' to divine perfection precisely on account of its indifference, its own imperfection in not giving a distinct, proper and adequate idea of the divine perfection itself. Still, it is a (however imperfect, indistinct and confused) representation of the divine essence itself, despite the fact that such a concept derives from the indifferent representation of some creaturely accident, such as wisdom or power. Thus, the multitude of attributes for Ockham simply boils down to the multitude of our imperfect, abstractive concepts of perfections as we know them in creatures; this, however, is certainly compatible with the unity and simplicity of the source of all perfections, which the aforementioned concepts indifferently and confusedly represent.

Divine ideas

But similar considerations drive Ockham's account of God's cognition of his creatures, that is, Ockham's theory of divine ideas. For Augustine, divine ideas are the universal exemplars of all creation in God's mind. They are basically Platonic Forms, except that they are not the ontologically independent exemplars a Platonic demiurge would have to look up to in shaping the world; rather, they are God's universal conceptions whereby he eternally preconceives the essences of all creatures actually realized in the singular creatures instantiating these essences.

However, the plurality of these ideas, matching the multitude of creaturely essences, is obviously in conflict with divine simplicity. For divine ideas cannot be creatures, as they are the creative exemplars of all creation; therefore, since everything is either a creature or the Creator, they must be identical with God. But how can several distinct ideas be one and the same absolutely simple divine essence? On Aquinas' solution, God preconceives his creatures indirectly, in and through cognizing the worthiest object of cognition, namely, divine essence. However, since this cognition is perfect, God cognizes divinity not only as it is in itself, but also in all possible ways in which it can even imperfectly be imitated or participated in. It is the diversity and multiplicity of these possible ways that accounts for the multiplicity of divine ideas, without, however, compromising divine simplicity; for of course the multiplicity of the ways in which a single object can be conceived does not entail the multiplicity of the object itself.

Ockham rejects this solution (as well as those of Henry of Ghent and Scotus), and simply identifies divine ideas with the creatures themselves. He can do so because he no longer takes divine ideas to be the universal archetypes of creation. According to his definition, an idea is "something cognized by an effective intellectual principle, looking to which something active can produce something in real existence" (1979: Ord. I, d. 35, q. 5: 486). In using this definition, Ockham exploits an existing ambiguity in the medieval usage of 'idea', which was taken to stand either for that *by which* something is cognized or for *that which* is cognized. Taking 'idea' in the latter way, Ockham can say that there is no conflict between the multiplicity of divine ideas and the simplicity of God, since the multiplicity of ideas is just the multiplicity of creatures, cognized by God in a single intuitive act of cognition from all eternity. As a consequence, according to Ockham, God does not even have universal ideas; the only universals in God's mind are the universal concepts of human beings existing in God's mind as its objects, just as any other created singular. Given that for Ockham abstraction is not the grasp of a common essence enabling one to have essential cognition of all singulars of a certain kind, but merely the indifferent cognition of any singular, for him the abstractive, universal cognition of any class of singulars is inferior to knowing each fully, intuitively. (Clearly, a teacher knowing each of his students personally by name knows them better than another knowing them merely as 'a student of mine'.) Thus, this conception, in tune with Ockham's nominalist epistemology, not only solves 'the simplicity problem' of divine ideas, but even provides a neat foundation for the claim of the perfection of the divine cognition of creatures.

The Trinity

But the absolutely perfect cognition, perfect not only in its mode but also in its object, is God's self-cognition, which, coupled with self-love, was traditionally construed as constituting the Trinity of divine persons. According to the Augustine/Boethius-inspired medieval doctrine, the three divine persons, each identical with the same divine essence yet distinct from one another, are distinct on account of the relative opposition there is between them, which, however, is not there between them and the non-relational divine essence. The divine persons are the subsistent relations constituted by divine knowledge and divine love, which provides their distinction on account of the relative opposition between the knower and the known and the lover and the beloved. This is so because the knower as such, in so far as it is the knower, is not the same as the known, in so far as it is known, even if it is the same God who is both the knower and the known. That is to say, the relations of knowing and being known and loving and being loved themselves, if they are subsistent entities (which in the case of God they have to be, since their being, on account of divine simplicity, has to be the same, indivisible existence of God), have to be distinct on account of their relative opposition, even if they have to be identical with the same non-relational absolute entity, namely, the divine essence, that is, God himself.

This doctrine as it stands, and especially with its further medieval refinements, runs directly counter to Ockham's philosophically motivated programme of 'ontological reduction'. For the doctrine essentially demands precisely the types of entities Ockham's programme was designed to eliminate (among others), namely, relational entities (in this case, even subsistent, and not merely inherent ones). Ockham's solution is simply to make an exception in the divine case: although there are no created relations signified by relative terms on top of substance and quality, there *are* such uncreated relations, namely, the divine persons, really distinct from one another, and (making *another* exception to his philosophical views) merely formally distinct from the divine essence. To be sure, Ockham may justifiably claim that supernatural relations are 'extraordinary'. However, this strategy soon becomes suspicious when this sort of solution becomes the rule rather than the exception, and indeed when the rule simply consists in making exceptions to otherwise universal rules.

The hypostatic union

This sort of strategy is clearest in the case of Ockham's interpretation of the hypostatic union, that is, the doctrine of the union of divine and human natures in the person of Christ. The traditional understanding of the doctrine would claim that just as in any other human being the individual human person, that is, the *suppositum* or *hypostasis* of human nature, instantiates this nature, so does the divine person of the Son in the case of Jesus Christ. Thus, Christ, the eternal Son of God, became truly a human being in the same species with us, having the same nature as we do, only in his case the hypostasis or suppositum instantiating human nature is one of the divine persons, the person of the Son, the divine Word, who, being identical with divine nature, is God himself. Thus, Christ is man and God on account of his two natures, but he, the uncreated divine suppositum of human nature, certainly cannot be identical with his created human nature, referred to by the abstract term 'humanity'.

On Ockham's logical doctrine of the relationship between concrete and abstract absolute terms, however, these terms are synonymous in their proper sense, and hence interchangeable and mutually predicable of each other, unless the abstract term is used as an abbreviation of a complex phrase (say, taking 'humanity' to mean 'man as such' or 'man in so far as man', which would falsify all accidental predications about 'humanity').[10] Thus, the concrete term 'man' and its abstract correlate 'humanity' are interchangeable, whence 'A man is a humanity' is just as true as 'A man is a man' is. This, however, does not mean that 'Every man is a humanity' is true, precisely because of the theological doctrine of the hypostatic union. On Ockham's proposal, even if for Aristotle this sentence would have to be true, for theologians it cannot be, for on their understanding the nominal definition of the term 'man' would have to be "A man is a nature composed of a body and an intellective soul, not sustained by any suppositum, or is some suppositum sustaining such a nature composed of a body and an intellective soul" (*SL* I, 7: 25), where the first member of this disjunction is true of any human being other than Christ, and the second is true only of Christ.

In Ockham's discussion it is not clear whether this nominal definition would be an indication that theologians would actually have to have a different concept of human beings than Aristotle did, although according to a strong interpretation of his doctrine of nominal definitions, he would be committed to this implication. In any case, his great follower, the Parisian philosopher John Buridan, would explicitly draw a similar conclusion in connection with the theological doctrine of the Eucharist: according to Buridan, Aristotle must have had a different concept of accidents from that of Christian theologians.

---

10. *SL* I, 8: 30. Thus, even if 'man' and 'humanity' stand for the same things in 'A man runs' and 'A humanity runs', taking 'humanity' to mean the same as 'man as such', the second predication is false even if the first is true.

The Eucharist

On the common medieval doctrine of the Eucharist, after consecration the substance of the bread and the substance of the wine are converted into the body and blood of Christ, which of course cannot be informed by the visible accidents (dimensions, shape, colour, taste and so on) of bread and wine; therefore, those accidents have to exist there miraculously, sustained by divine power without actually inhering in any substance. The metaphysical problem this account generated for medieval Aristotelian theologians was the very possibility of the miracle understood in these terms. For on Aristotle's description in the *Categories*, an accident is a being in a subject. But the miracle would require that accidents exist miraculously not in any subject. However, if for an accident to be is for it to be in a subject, then for it *not* to be in a subject is for it *not* to be at all. Thus, the miracle, requiring the existence of accidents not in a subject, apparently requires the verification of explicit contradictories, which was generally regarded as absolutely impossible, something that cannot be done even by divine power.

Still, Ockham would not find any difficulty in accounting for the separate existence of accidents. After all, the only accidents he acknowledges are absolute qualities, which are really distinct entities from substances. The rest of the Aristotelian categories having been reduced to these two, he only needs to account for the possibility of their supernatural separability. But since any two really distinct entities can be kept in existence by God alone, separately from each other, even if one is naturally dependent on the other, the separate existence of the accidents of bread and wine in the miracle of the Eucharist does not pose a separate problem for Ockham. Of course, he does have to account for the apparent quantity that is obviously there after the conversion of the substance of the bread into the body of Christ, but since he identified quantity with *either substance or quality*, even if the quantity identical with substance is gone, the quantity identical with quality may still remain (Ockham 1986: 84–5).

CONCLUSION: THE SEPARATION OF
RELIGIOUS AND SECULAR DISCOURSE

However, as Buridan makes it clear in his own discussion alluded to above (Buridan 1964: lb. 4, q. 6; Bakker 2001), this solution requires that theologians have a concept of accidents radically different from that of Aristotle. For on the Ockhamist theory of concepts, endorsed and further developed by Buridan himself, any categorematic concept is either absolute or connotative. But on his analysis, Aristotle's concept of an accident, even as conceived by means of a concept expressed by an abstract term, such as 'whiteness', must be connotative, for on Aristotle's conception any whiteness must be the whiteness *of something*. However, on the theologians' conception 'whiteness' is an absolute term, expressing an absolute concept. Thus

Ockham and the rest of Christian theologians on Buridan's Ockhamist analysis do not have the same conception of accidents in general that Aristotle himself did. Therefore, given the foundational character of the distinction between substance and accident in Aristotelian metaphysics, Aristotle and the theologians cannot be regarded as having the same conceptual idiom.

In view of this result, one may safely conclude that even if Ockham is *not* the religious heretic, philosophical sceptic or general destroyer of the scholastic synthesis that later (mostly Catholic) critics of his nominalism tend to depict him as, there is something in Ockham's nominalism that, viewed from the perspective of later developments, definitely points in the direction of these developments. In particular, Ockham's nominalism points in the direction of the modern separation of religious (theological) and secular (philosophical and scientific) discourse, the synthesis of which was one of the most important achievements of the great metaphysical theological systems of the thirteenth century, especially of the system of Thomas Aquinas.

FURTHER READING

Adams, M. 1987. *William Ockham*, vols I–II. Notre Dame, IN: University of Notre Dame Press.

Klima, G. 1993. "The Changing Role of *Entia Rationis* in Medieval Philosophy: A Comparative Study with a Reconstruction". *Synthese* **96**: 25–59.

Oberman, H. 1977. *Werden und Wertung der Reformation: Vom Wegestreit zum Glaubenskampf.* Tuebingen: Mohr.

Ockham, W. 1991. *Quodlibetal Questions*, vols I–II, A. Freddoso & F. Kelly (trans.). New Haven, CT: Yale University Press.

Panaccio, C. 2004. *Ockham on Concepts*. Aldershot: Ashgate.

Spade, P. 1999. *The Cambridge Companion to Ockham*. Cambridge: Cambridge University Press.

On THE EUCHARIST see also Vol. 3, Ch. 3. On THE TRINITY see also Chs 2, 8; Vol. 1, Chs 14, 17, 20; Vol. 3, Chs 3, 9, 17; Vol. 4, Ch. 4; Vol. 5, Chs 12, 23.

16

GERSONIDES

Tamar Rudavsky

Levi ben Gershom, also called Gersonides (1288–1344), has emerged in recent years as one of the most significant and comprehensive medieval Jewish philosophers. He has been constantly quoted (even if only to be criticized), and, through the works of Hasdai Crecas and others, Gersonides' ideas have influenced such thinkers as Gottfried Wilhelm Leibniz (*see* Vol. 3, Ch. 13) and Baruch Spinoza (*see* Vol. 3, Ch. 11). Emphasizing Gersonides' "religious rationalism in Judaism", Seymour Feldman describes Gersonides as one who "has taken seriously the fact that he has reason, who believes that this faculty is God-given, and who attempts to understand God with this instrument" (Gersonides 1984: 52). Attempting to show that philosophy and Torah or reason and revelation are co-extensive, Gersonides is a philosophical optimist who believes that reason is fully competent to attain all the important and essential truths in religion. And yet, at the same time, perhaps no other medieval Jewish philosopher has been so maligned over the centuries as Gersonides. Indeed, his major philosophical work *Milhamot Ha-Shem* (Wars of the Lord; hereafter *Wars*) was called 'Wars against the Lord' by one of his opponents, and was depicted as a radical rejection of traditional Jewish tenets.

Gersonides left few letters and does not talk about himself in his writings, nor is his life discussed at great length by his contemporaries. Hence, what is known of his biography is sketchy at best. Gersonides was born in Provence and may have lived for a time in Bagno sur-Ceze. Gersonides spoke Provencal; his works, however, are all written in Hebrew, and all of his quotations from Averroes (Ibn Rushd), Aristotle and Moses Maimonides are in Hebrew as well. One of the most prolific medieval Jewish philosophers, his output covers a variety of fields, including mathematics, astronomy, philosophy, logic, biblical commentaries, and philosophical commentaries on Averroes. His *Sefer Ma'aseh Hoshev* (The work of a counter; 1321) is concerned with arithmetical operations and uses of a symbolic notation for numerical variables. Gersonides' major scientific contributions in astronomy are contained primarily in book 5, part 1 of *Wars*, in which he reviewed and criticized astronomical theories of the day, compiled astronomical tables and described one of his astronomical inventions. This instrument, which he named *Megalle 'amuqqot* (Revealer of profundities) and which was called *Bacullus Jacob* (Jacob's staff) by his Christian contemporaries, was used to measure the height of stars above the horizon. Although there exists no explicit evidence that Gersonides read Latin, he may have learned of the views of Ockham, Nicholas Oresme and other scholastic thinkers in oral conversations with his Christian contemporaries (Sirat *et al.* 2003). There is some evidence that Gersonides had connections with high-ranking Christians during his lifetime. In 1342 Gersonides dedicated to Pope Clement VI the Latin version of a trigonometric treatise drawn from his astronomy. The astronomical parts of *Wars* were translated into Latin during Gersonides' lifetime, possibly at the request of the Papal court (Freudenthal 1996: 741). Also in 1342, Philippe de Vitry (future Bishop of Meaux) asked his advice about a mathematical theorem in connection with his own *ars nova* in musical theory (Chemla & Pahaut 1992). One of the craters of the moon, Rabbi Levi, is named after him. Gersonides also wrote philosophical commentaries on Averroes' commentaries on Aristotle. His innovative work in logic, *Sefer Ha-heqesh Ha-yashar* (Book of the correct syllogism; 1319), examines the problems associated with Aristotle's modal logic as developed in the *Prior Analytics*, and was translated into Latin at an early date, although Gersonides' name was not attached to it. Finally, Gersonides contributed to the corpus of philosophical biblical commentaries, including commentaries on the Book of Job (1325), Song of Songs (1326), Ecclesiastes (1328), Esther (1329), Ruth (1329), Genesis (1329), Exodus (1330), most of Leviticus (1332) and finally the remaining books of the Torah (completed in 1338).

GERSONIDES' PHILOSOPHICAL THEOLOGY

Faith and reason

In 1317 Gersonides began an essay on the problem of creation. This problem, which has vexed Jewish philosophers since Philo of Alexandria (*see* Vol. 1, Ch. 9), had recently received elaborate treatment by Maimonides. But Gersonides was dissatisfied with Maimonides' discussion and proposed to reopen the issue. This project was soon laid aside, however, for Gersonides felt that it could not be adequately discussed without proper grounding in the issues of time, motion and the infinite. By 1325 his manuscript had developed to include discussion not only of creation but also of immortality, divination and prophecy. By 1328 it included a chapter on providence as well. Books 5 and 6 were completed, by Gersonides' own dating, by 1329, and the final work was *Wars*. In this work, Gersonides' aim is to integrate the teachings of Aristotle, as mediated through Averroes and Maimonides, with those of Judaism. Gersonides specifies six questions to be examined in rigorous, scholastic fashion. Is the rational soul immortal? What is the nature of prophecy? Does God know particulars? Does divine providence extend to individuals? What is the nature of astronomical bodies? Is the universe eternal or created? With each issue, Gersonides attempts to reconcile traditional Jewish beliefs with what he feels are the strongest points in Aristotle's philosophy. Although a synthesis of these systems is his ultimate goal, it turns out that philosophy often wins out at the expense of theology.

Adhering to the ability of human beings to attain to an overarching truth comprising all of reality, Gersonides presents a unified cosmology rooted in a thoroughgoing epistemological realism based on reason. Gersonides laid down the general rule that "the Law cannot prevent us from considering to be true that which our reason urges us to believe" (Gersonides 1984: 98). His adherence to this principle is reflected throughout his work. In his introductory remarks to *Wars*, Gersonides upholds the primacy of reason, attributing to Maimonides the position that "we must believe what reason has determined to be true. If the literal sense of the Torah differs from reason, it is necessary to interpret those passages in accordance with the demands of reason" (*ibid.*). Gersonides believes that reason and Torah cannot be in opposition: "if reason causes to affirm doctrines that are incompatible with the literal sense of Scripture, we are not prohibited by the Torah to pronounce the truth on these matters, for reason is not incompatible with the true understanding of the Torah" (*ibid.*). Thus reason is upheld as a criterion for achieving truth. In contradistinction to Maimonides, who introduced allegory, metaphor and imprecise language into his work to convey the ambiguity of the subject matter, Gersonides saw it as his function to elucidate philosophical issues as clearly as possible. He contrasts his method with that of Maimonides, whose *Guide of the Perplexed* (hereafter *Guide*) he saw as unnecessarily obscure and esoteric (*ibid.*: 101).

Furthermore, Gersonides contends that "no argument can nullify the reality that is perceived by the senses, for true opinion must follow reality but reality need not conform to opinion" (Goldstein 1985: 24). That Gersonides clearly considered his own observations to be the ultimate test of his system is explicit from his attitude towards Ptolemy. The importance of empirical observation cannot be underestimated, he claims, and he values his own observations over those of others. "We did not find among our predecessors from Ptolemy to the present day observations that are helpful for this investigation except our own" (*ibid.*: 27), he says in describing his method of collecting astronomical data. Often his observations do not agree with those of Ptolemy, and in those cases he tells us explicitly that he prefers his own. Gersonides lists the many inaccuracies he has found when trying to follow Ptolemy's calculations (*ibid.*: 93ff.). Having investigated the positions of the planets, for example, Gersonides encountered "confusion and disorder", which led him to deny several of Ptolemy's planetary principles (Goldstein 1988: 386). He does warn his colleagues, however, to dissent from Ptolemy only after great diligence and scrutiny.

DIVINE PREDICATION: ON WHAT WE CAN SAY ABOUT GOD

Turning first to a brief discussion of Gersonides' analysis of divine predication, it is important to note that his comments occur as a response to Maimonides' theory of negative predication. In *Guide* 1.51–60, Maimonides developed an elaborate theory of divine predication, the purpose of which is to claim that human language is inadequate to predicate anything of God. In these chapters Maimonides argued that terms predicated of God must be understood in one of three ways. The first construes such terms as action predicates, descriptive of the "ways and the characteristics" of the deity (Maimonides 1963: 125). From these action predicates we infer corresponding mental states analogous to those states that human beings experience when exhibiting those actions. This leads to his second theoretical point, namely that the four essential attributes of God – life, power, wisdom and will – are of one simple essence; all other attributes are to be conceived either as descriptive of divine action, or as negative attributes. However, even these four attributes, when predicated of God, are used in a homonymous or equivocal sense. The difference between human and divine predicates is qualitative: since the terms are applied by way of perfect homonymity, they admit of no comparison between God and his creatures. In light of the linguistic implications of the doctrine of homonymous predication, Maimonides develops in *Guide* 1.58–60 his celebrated theory of negative predication, arguing that ultimately negative predication alone brings the human mind closer to an understanding of God: "Know that the description of God, may he be cherished and exalted, by means of negations is the correct description" (Maimonides 1963: 134). This third piece of Maimonides' theory of divine predication represents the logical culmination of his theory of language. By ascribing to God terms that do not begin to capture his transcendent nature, human beings are both insulting and denigrating God's true essence. Ultimately silence is the only appropriate linguistic response to divine predication: "silence with regard to You is praise" (*ibid.*: 139).

In response to Maimonides, Gersonides attempts to salvage the ability of human beings to talk meaningfully about God. Gersonides disagrees with Maimonides' doctrine, claiming that divine predicates are to be understood as *pros hen* equivocals rather than absolute equivocals (as Maimonides had argued). What this means is that according to Gersonides, predicates applied to God represent the prime instance or meaning of the term, whereas human predicates are derivative or inferior instances. So, for example, knowledge when applied to God is perfect knowledge and constitutes the standard for human knowledge, which is less perfect than divine knowledge: "the term 'knowledge' is predicated of God (may he be blessed) *primarily* and of others *secondarily*" (Gersonides 1987: 107). Gersonides denies that terms have completely different meanings when predicated of God and of human beings; it is only because of an underlying commonality of meaning that we can use language meaningfully at all.

DIVINE OMNISCIENCE, DETERMINISM AND ASTROLOGY

Turning to the relation between God and the world, Gersonides is able to analyse the details of this relation without violating the linguistic constraints he has established. The general problem is whether God's knowledge is limited to necessary states of affairs or extends to the domain of contingency as well. If the former, then God could not be said to have knowledge of human beings, and so divine providence would not be efficacious. But if God does know contingents, in particular, future contingent events, then it would appear that human freedom is curtailed by God's prior knowledge of human actions. This problem of the apparent conflict between divine omniscience and human freedom was discussed by many medieval philosophers. Gersonides does not follow the majority opinion on this issue: rather than claim that God does know particulars and that this knowledge somehow does not affect human freedom, Gersonides argues that God knows particulars only in a certain sense. In an apparent attempt to mediate between the view of Aristotle, who said that God does not know particulars, and that of Maimonides, who said that God does have such knowledge, Gersonides holds that God knows particulars only in so far as they are ordered. That is, God knows that certain states of affairs are particular, but he does not know in what their particularity consists. God knows individual persons, for example, only through knowing the species humanity.

Whereas Maimonides claimed that God's knowledge does not render the objects of his knowledge necessary, Gersonides maintains that divine knowledge precludes contingency. To retain the domain of contingency, he adopts the one option open to him, namely, that God does not have prior knowledge of future contingents. According to Gersonides, God knows that certain states of affairs may or may not be actualized. But in so far as they are contingent states, he does not know which of the alternatives will be the case. For if God did know future contingents prior to their actualization, there could be no contingency in the world. In an attempt to explain how prophecies are possible in a system that denies the possibility of knowledge of future contingents, Gersonides claims (in book 2) that the prophet does not receive knowledge of particular future events; rather, his knowledge is of a general form, and he must instantiate this knowledge with particular facts. What distinguishes prophets from ordinary persons is that the former are more attuned to receive these universal messages and are in a position to apply them to particular circumstances.

For Gersonides, the issues of divine omniscience, prophecy and contingency must be understood against the backdrop of astrological determinism. Most medieval philosophers accepted the distinction between astronomy as the study of the movements of the celestial bodies and the laws that govern these movements, and astrology as the study of the influence of the celestial bodies on the fates of peoples and individuals. Medieval Jewish philosophers, however, evinced a certain ambivalence toward astrology. Maimonides' trenchant rejection of astrology occurs against a culture that, at least *prima facie*, did not eliminate either natural or judicial astrology from theoretical considerations. In his *Letter on Astrology*, addressed to the rabbis of southern France, several sorts of considerations are adduced in opposition to astrology.[1] The very fact that Maimonides was called on to legislate on this issue is evidence of the popularity of astrology among Provencal Jews.

Perhaps one of the most outspoken Jewish proponents of astrology is Gersonides, whose astral determinism is explicitly developed in two contexts: in book II of *Wars* he interweaves astrological motifs into his discussion of divine providence and prophecy, while in book V astrology occupies a central role in the context of his cosmological speculations. Y. Tzvi Langermann emphasizes the teleological nature of astrology for Gersonides, its chief merit being its ability to provide "teleological explanations for the wide variety of stellar motions that are observed to take place" (Langermann 1999: 506). Gersonides disagrees with Maimonides over the ultimate purpose of the celestial bodies. For Maimonides it was not possible that a greater entity, the heavens, would exist for the sake of the sublunar universe. Gersonides disagrees, maintaining that it is not inappropriate that the more noble exist for the less noble. The stars, he argues, exist for the sake of things in the sublunar world (Gersonides 1999: 194). More explicitly, the heavenly bodies are designed for the benefit of sublunar existence, and they guarantee the perpetuation of life on earth.

This teleological cosmology is spelled out in *Wars* book 2, in which Gersonides is concerned to explain how divine knowledge operates, and to what extent divine foreknowledge of future contingents affects human choice. His major thesis is that divine knowledge is predicated to a great extent on knowledge of the heavenly bodies, which bodies are in turn "systematically directed toward his [man's] preservation and guidance so that all his activities and thoughts are ordered by them" (1987: 33). In support of this teleology, Gersonides argues that the celestial bodies have a purpose. This teleology is reflected by a "law, order and rightness" in the universe, implying the existence of an intellect that orders the nature of things: "you see that the domain of the spheres provides, in the best way possible, for the sub-lunar world" (Gersonides 1999: 137).

However, Gersonides must be able to account for individual variety in the sublunar realm. In as much as stellar radiation is the means by which stellar influences are conveyed, the wide variety of mixtures of stellar radiation guarantees a sufficient variety of 'influences' on terrestrial processes. The movers emanate from God who is construed as the "First Separate Intellect" (*ibid.*: 272). They are ordered in a rational system that governs the sublunar domain. If there were no one first intellect, Gersonides argues, the rational order we see in the heavens would be the result of chance, which is unacceptable. The agent intellect

---

1. For details of these arguments, see Rudavsky (2000).

thus functions as the link between these celestial bodies and human affairs. The kinds of information it transmits are of an astronomical type, as evidenced in the following example: "it [the agent intellect] knows how many revolutions of the sun, or of the diurnal sphere, or of any other sphere [have transpired] from the time at which someone, who falls under a particular pattern, had a particular level of good or ill fortune" (1987: 53). Gersonides goes on to explain that the information transmitted is of a general nature and does not pertain to the individual *qua* particular. The agent intellect serves as the repository for information communicated by the heavenly bodies. The patterns revealed in this communication between agent intellect and diviner (astrologer, prophet) are from the heavenly bodies, which themselves are endowed with intellects and so "apprehend the pattern that derives from them" (1987: 64). Each mover apprehends the order deriving from the heavenly body it moves, and not patterns that emanate from other heavenly bodies. As a result, the imaginative faculty receives the "pattern inherent in the intellects of the heavenly bodies from the influence deriving from them" (*ibid.*). This influence derives from the position of the heavenly bodies "by the ascendant degree or the dominant planet [in a particular zodiacal position]" (*ibid.*). However, in as much as the heavenly bodies do not jointly cooperate with one another (*lo yishtatfu*) in this process, it is possible for the communication to be misconstrued.

Of course, as we all know, astrologers often err in their predictions. One of the most compelling causes lies in human free will: our intellect and choice "have the power to move us contrary to that which is determined by the heavenly bodies" (*ibid.*: 34). Although Gersonides admits that on occasion human choice is able to contravene the celestial bodies, nevertheless this intervention is rare, and true contingency is a rare state of affairs indeed in Gersonides' ontology (see Rudavsky 2000). Gersonides presents an argument to show that human choice guided by reason can subvert the celestial bodies despite their general ordering of our lives. The heavenly bodies can order human affairs either by virtue of their difference of position in the heavens, or from the difference of the bodies among themselves. Astral bodies, however, will affect different individuals in different ways; they can also affect an individual differently at different times; and finally, two or more bodies can affect a single individual, resulting in multiple influences that can have contrary effects. Gersonides notes that human beings can contravene these effects: God has provided human beings with "the intellectual capacity (*sekhel ba'al yekholet*) that enables us both to act contrary to what has been ordered by the heavenly bodies and to correct, as far as possible, the [astrally ordained] misfortunes that befall us" (1987: 35). Nevertheless, he assures us that whatever happens by chance is "determined and ordered according to this type of determinateness and order" (*ibid.*: 34). Outdoing even Plato's hierarchical structuring in *Republic* book 4, Gersonides argues that the ultimate perfection and ordering of society is due to astrological influence (*ibid.*: 36).

INDIVIDUAL PROVIDENCE, EVIL, AND IMMORTALITY OF THE SOUL

A further dilemma surrounds the doctrine of divine providence. If God does not have knowledge of future contingents, how can he be said to bestow providence on his creatures; but if God does have knowledge of the future, how do we account for the presence of evil and suffering? This problem is discussed by Gersonides both in book 4 of *Wars* and in his commentary on Job. More specifically, Gersonides is concerned with two issues: the extent of God's providential activity and an explanation of the suffering of the righteous. Maimonides had dealt with both issues in *Guide* 3.17, arguing that individual divine providence extends only to those human beings who have achieved intellectual and moral perfection; providence for other species is only general. Gersonides, however, has already maintained that God cannot know particulars *qua* particular, and so Maimonides' solution is unacceptable to him. Gersonides must therefore revisit the theory of providence within the context of his theory of divine cognition.

In *Wars* 4.1 Gersonides summarizes three general views on providence: the philosophical view of Aristotle according to which there is no individual providence; the traditional Torah view, according to which divine providence extends over each member of the species as human beings; and the view of Maimonides, namely that divine providence extends to some but not all individual human beings. Most of book 4 is addressed to the second view. Gersonides makes use of the Book of Job to elucidate the various positions adduced, as well as to develop a theodicy that explains the existence of suffering and evil. Gersonides takes great pains to explain that his theory of divine cognition does not preclude providence. Gersonides argues that providence is general in nature: it primarily appertains to species and only incidentally to particulars of the species. God, for example, does not know the particular individual Levi ben Gerson and does not bestow particular providence on him. Rather, in as much as Levi ben Gerson is a member of the species humanity and the species philosopher, he is in a position to receive the providential care accorded to those groups. In his Commentary on Job, which complements book 4 of *Wars*, Gersonides claims that each of the characters in the Book of Job represents a different theory of divine providence. Gersonides' own position is a restatement of Elihu's theory that providence is not directed to particulars but rather to groups of individuals, or universals. Summarizing Maimonides' theory, Gersonides sees Maimonides as maintaining that "on Maimonides' theory of providence divine knowledge does not extend to particulars as particulars" (Gersonides 1987: 208).

Gersonides then turns to the more serious issue of theodicy. That instances of evil exist is a fact borne out by sense-experience, which shows "many righteous people suffering great evils most of their lives and receiving very few benefits ... moreover we observe that some righteous men suffer many evils despite their attempt to avert evils from coming to them, but they are not protected from these evils" (*ibid.*: 171). How, then, can we account for the suffering of the righteous? In order to account for the existence of human suffering, Gersonides distinguishes between 'general providence' that is embedded in nature itself, and 'special providence' that pertains to an individual's spiritual perfection: special providence is enjoyed in direct relation to the level of spiritual perfection attained by an individual. Only few individuals achieve the "kind of unity and conjunction with God" that provides individual providence (*ibid.*: 175). As noted above, those who are more strongly identified with the active intellect receive this communication in a more perfect manner.

But could it not be argued, in contradistinction to Gersonides' position, that God must be either evil or impotent: "[E]ither God (may He be blessed) can arrange it so that a man receives his due reward but He does not attempt to do so, and this would indeed be evil with respect to God (God forbid), or He cannot so arrange this, which also would be an imperfection in God" (*ibid.*: 182). Gersonides' response is twofold. First, he avers that this is the best of all possible worlds, and that this world exhibits "the best possible providential ordering and beneficence for sub-lunar things" (*ibid.*: 183). Secondly, he argues that the benefits of special providence, delegated to only certain individuals, are for the most part deferred to the world to come. What we call 'material evils' are the result ultimately of the material constitution of nature itself. In other words, evil is ultimately the result of matter, over which God has no control. Gersonides states that "evil derives from God only by chance and because of the necessity of matter" (*ibid.*: 167). Examples are adduced to show that evils are caused by chance, or by matter. The evils that befall human beings from the patterns determined by the arrangements of the heavenly bodies are not "essentially [evil] or primarily intended to be [evil]", but rather are chance occurrences not due to God (*ibid.*: 169). "That God cannot prevent or eliminate them [evil] is not a reflection of His impotence; the fact that they occur is a necessary consequence of the world's being what it is, i.e. material" (*ibid.*: 151).

The topic of the immortality of the soul is examined in detail by Gersonides in book 1 of the *Wars* in the context of a general theory of knowledge. This discussion must be understood against the backdrop of a notoriously difficult passage in Aristotle's *On the Soul* III.5. In this passage Aristotle seems to postulate the existence of an active intellect that is separable from the passive intellect and that is primarily responsible for the intellectual activities of the human mind. But what is the relation between the active and passive intellects, and which, if either, is immortal? Gersonides summarizes and criticizes four representative positions on this question. His own view is a version of that of Alexander of Aphrodisias, according to whom the active intellect is associated with the eternal 'agent intellect', that is, God, and is to some extent immortal. Gersonides agrees with Alexander that immortality of the soul consists in the perfection of the human intellect, but he disagrees with Alexander over the precise nature of this intellectual attainment. Unlike Alexander, who emphasized the process of conjunction between the human intellect and the agent intellect, Gersonides argues that the content rather than the process of knowledge is what matters. When the content of the human intellect mirrors that of the agent intellect, immortality is achieved. This knowledge, according to Gersonides, is of the complete ordering of particulars in the sublunary universe.

GERSONIDES ON CREATION

In book 6 of *Wars*, Gersonides turns finally to the question that had originally inspired him to write his work, namely the creation of the universe. Gersonides' discussion of creation reflects his attitude towards previous astronomers, coupled with his faith in human reason. In the *Guide* 2.13–26, Maimonides had gone to great lengths to maintain that the topic of creation was beyond rational demonstration. Gersonides, on the other hand, devotes many chapters in *Wars* book 6 to proving that the Platonic theory of creation out of an eternal formless matter is in fact rationally demonstrable. Further, the two disagree over the relation between the superlunar and sublunar spheres. Maimonides had claimed that no valid inference can be drawn from the nature of the sublunar sphere to that of the superlunar sphere. Gersonides, however, rejects any metaphysical bite to the distinction and argues that in as much as both spheres contain material elements, what we know about creation is based on astronomy, and astronomy is fundamentally no different a human science than physics (Samuelson 1991: 213). Astronomy can only be pursued as a science by "one who is both a mathematician and a natural philosopher, for he can be aided by both of these sciences and take from them whatever is needed to perfect his work" (Goldstein 1985: 23). Gersonides sees the ultimate function of astronomy as understanding God. Astronomy, he tells us, is instructive not only by virtue of its exalted subject matter, but also because of its utility to the other sciences. By studying the orbs and stars, we are led ineluctably to a fuller knowledge and appreciation of God (*ibid.*: 24).

In *Wars* 6.1.2, Gersonides lists three views of his predecessors who discussed the creation of the world. The first, that the world comes into existence and passes away an infinite number of times, has been associated with the rabbis as well as with certain ancient philosophers, such as Heraclitus and Empedocles (as attributed by Aristotle in *On the Heavens* I.10). The second view, that the world was generated only one time, is associated with two sets of proponents: first is the version of Plato that the world was created one time out of some thing, and second is the view attributed to the Islamic *kalām* theologians and to Maimonides, that the world was created out of absolute nothing (Gersonides 1999: 294). The third view is the eternity thesis of Aristotle: that the world is eternal and hence has not been created.

Gersonides' critical refutation of Aristotle's eternity thesis introduces the motif of time and its relation to motion. In contradistinction to Aristotle, who postulated the eternity of time and motion, Gersonides insists that both time and motion are finite. Gersonides hopes to refute Aristotle's eternity of the world by showing that the infinity of time and motion fail as exceptions to Aristotle's own finitistic universe (Feldman 1967). According to Gersonides, Aristotle offered at least nine arguments in support of the eternity thesis: of these, three have to do with temporality. Aristotle's first argument has to do with the nature of time in general, the second is based on the nature of the 'instant' and the third is based on the nature of temporal language. Gersonides concludes his summary of Aristotle's arguments with two general comments that link the metaphysical considerations to those of a more theological nature. Gersonides offers the suggestion that ultimately what may have motivated Aristotle to support the eternity thesis were theological considerations based on the nature of the deity. First, he argues that it would be inappropriate to suggest that the deity causes at one time rather than at another. Furthermore, it is not appropriate that the deity exist independently of the world that functions as the object of God's self-conception. And finally, Gersonides reminds us, as did Maimonides in the *Guide*, that Aristotle himself did not regard his arguments in favour of eternity as demonstrations but rather as containing fewer doubts than other arguments (Gersonides 1999: 302).

In order to reject Aristotle's eternity thesis, Gersonides must demonstrate the finitude of time. To this end he first makes a number of observations pertaining to the general characteristics of time that will affect his argument. Time, Gersonides argues, falls in the category of continuous quantity. We speak, for example, of the parts of time as being equal or unequal; time itself is measured by convention as opposed to by nature; and its limit is the 'instant' which itself is indivisible (*ibid*.: 329ff.). Further, Gersonides claims that time can be construed both as separate from its substratum and as residing in it. That time resides in its substratum is demonstrated from the fact that it has distinguishable parts: that is, present time is distinguished from both past and future time. Were these parts not distinguishable, argues Gersonides, then any part of time would equal the whole of time. Hence, time must reside in that which it measures. At the same time, it is separable from any substratum; for if it were in its substratum, there would be as many times as there are substrata. But we know that there is only one time and not a multiplicity of times. Hence time must not reside in its substratum (*ibid*.: 329–30). According to Gersonides, time is partly potential and partly actual. Gersonides now demonstrates that time must have been generated. We have seen that time is contained in the category of quantity. Gersonides will argue that just as quantity is finite, so too is time.

But Gersonides' rejection of Aristotle's eternity thesis, and his support of creation, do not commit Gersonides to a theory of creation *ex nihilo*. Arguing that creation out of nothing is incompatible with the facts of physical reality, Gersonides adopts a version of the second view, adopting a Platonic model of matter drawn ultimately from the *Timaeus*. Gersonides interprets the opening of Genesis to refer to two types of matter. *Geshem* is the primordial matter out of which the universe was created; not capable of motion or rest, it was characterized by negation and was inert and chaotic. This matter is identified with the primeval waters described in Genesis. *Homer* is prime matter, in the Aristotelian sense of a substratum always aligned with form. It contains within itself the potentiality to receive forms but is not an ontologically independent entity. Gersonides compares this matter to darkness: just as darkness is the absence of light, this matter represents the absence of form or shape. On this basis Gersonides argues that the world was created out of an eternally pre-existent matter (*ibid.*: 372). Gersonides' theory of creation, with its emphasis on the ontology of matter, thus reinforces his theodicy.

CONCLUSION

Gersonides' philosophical ideas went against the grain of traditional Jewish thought. Whereas his commentaries occupied a central place in Jewish theology, his philosophical work was rejected, or roundly criticized. Jewish philosophers such as Hasdai Crescas and Isaac Abrabanel, for example, felt obliged to subject his works to lengthy criticism. Only in recent years has Gersonides received his rightful place in the history of philosophy. As scholars have rediscovered his thought and have made his corpus available to a modern audience, Gersonides has finally been appreciated as an insightful, ruthlessly consistent philosopher, committed to logical argument even when it forces a reconceptualization of Jewish belief.

FURTHER READING

Feldman, S. 1978. "Gersonides on the Possibility of Conjunction with the Agent Intellect". *American Jewish Society Review* **3**: 99–120.

Feldman, S. 1997. "Levi ben Gershom (Gersonides)". In *History of Jewish Philosophy*, D. Frank & O. Leaman (eds), 379–98. London: Routledge.

Freudenthal, G. (ed.) 1992. *Studies on Gersonides: A Fourteenth-Century Jewish Philosopher-Scientist*. Leiden: Brill.

Goldstein, B. & D. Pingree 1990. *Levi ben Gerson's Prognostication for the Conjunction of 1345*. *Transactions of the American Philosophical Society* **80**(6). Philadelphia, PA: APS.

Kellner, M. 1979. "R. Levi Ben Gerson: A Bibliographical Essay". *Studies in Bibliography and Booklore* **12**: 13–23.

Manekin, C. 2003. "Conservative Tendencies in Gersonides' Religious Philosophy". In *The Cambridge Companion to Medieval Jewish Philosophy*, D. Frank & O. Leaman (eds), 304–44. Cambridge: Cambridge University Press.

Marx, A. 1926. "The Correspondence Between the Rabbis of Southern France and Maimonides about Astrology". *Hebrew Union College Annual* **3**: 311–58.

Nadler, S. 2001. "Gersonides on Providence: A Jewish Chapter in the History of the General Will". *Journal of the History of Ideas* **62**: 37–57.

Rudavsky, T. 1988. "Creation, Time and Infinity in Gersonides". *Journal of the History of Philosophy* **26**: 25–44.

Shatzmiller, J. 1972. "Gersonides and the Community of Orange in the Middle Ages". *Studies in the History of the Jewish People and the Land of Israel* **2**: 111–26 [Hebrew].

Touati, C. 1973. *La Pensée philosophique et théologique de Gersonide*. Paris: Les Editions de Minuit.

On COSMOLOGY see also Chs 4, 10; Vol. 1, Chs 6, 8, 14, 17. On EVIL/PROBLEM OF EVIL see also Vol. 1, Chs 18, 19; Vol. 3, Chs 13, 18, 19; Vol. 4, Chs 12, 18; Vol. 5, Chs 19, 22, 23. On FAITH see also Chs 6, 12, 18; Vol. 1, Ch. 13; Vol. 3, Ch. 8; Vol. 4, Chs 8, 10, 13; Vol. 5, Chs 7, 18. On IMMORTALITY OF THE SOUL see also Ch. 12; Vol. 1, Chs 2, 4; Vol. 3, Chs 10, 19. On PREDICATION see also Chs 11, 13; Vol. 5, Ch. 18. On PROVIDENCE see also Vol. 3, Ch. 15. On REASON see also Chs 10, 11, 12, 18; Vol. 3, Chs 8, 12, 16, 21; Vol. 4, Chs 4, 8.

17

JOHN WYCLIF

Stephen E. Lahey

Few medieval thinkers have evoked the reactions that Wyclif has. His admirers, from late medieval Oxford and Prague to post-Reformation historians and Protestant apologists, wax enthusiastic about the 'Evangelical Doctor' or the 'Morning Star of the Reformation'. On the other hand, his detractors, from his day into the present, revile him as heresiarch and apostate. Turning to his many extant works, one would expect dramatic prose, still smouldering with the whiff of the bonfire, from such a polarizing figure. After all, two distinct, widespread reform movements claim Wyclif's teachings as their inspiration. Lollardy beleaguered the English establishment into the fifteenth century, and the Hussite movement ended in full-scale war in Czech-speaking lands. Instead, the reader finds dense argument and scholastic terminology, dizzying repetition and endless reference to Scripture. Wyclif's appeal, and his danger, lie not in his popular availability, but in his solid foundation in the scholastic tradition. He envisaged himself as continuing the tradition of Augustine, Anselm and Robert Grosseteste, and even championing the synthesis of Aqunias, in the face of Ockhamism's threat to theology's pre-eminence among the sciences. Wyclif was less an innovator or a reformer than a radical reactionary, a zealot hungry to cleanse the Church and its theology of the intellectual and political poisons that had built up by the fourteenth century. But his call for a royal divestment of ecclesiastical and especially papal power, the widespread availability of vernacular Scripture and his rejection of transubstantiation seem more consonant with Reformation theology than with scholasticism. While earlier scholars concluded that Wyclif's thought presaged Protestantism, our understanding of later scholasticism, particularly of Oxford in the early fourteenth century, allows us to understand his ideas as products of his age.

Wyclif was born some time in the late 1320s or early 1330s, matriculated at Oxford in 1349 or 1350, and was associated with Merton College before becoming Master of Balliol College in 1360. He was ordained a priest in 1351, and income from benefices supported him throughout his early years in Oxford. He began studies in theology in 1363, and received his doctoral degree in 1372. At this point he was also engaged in service to John of Gaunt, the Duke of Lancaster and custodian of royal power during the dotage of Edward III and the childhood of Richard II. His conflicts with ecclesiastical authority began shortly thereafter, and despite papal condemnation and formal confrontation at Lambeth Palace, the Duke's authority afforded Wyclif assurance of continued protection. On being censured by a committee of theologians at Oxford for his Eucharistic teaching, Wyclif was forced to retire to Lutterworth in Leicestershire in 1381. There he lived out his final years as priest and instigator of dissent until his death on 31 December 1384. Following the condemnation of his ideas at the Council of Constance in 1415, where Hus was wrongly burned for having espoused heretical Wycliffism, his remains were exhumed and burned in 1428. Despite his conflict with ecclesiastical authorities and his heterodox theology, he was never excommunicated, probably because of his continued assertions of willingness to be corrected.

Wyclif's writings are defined by two primary collections of treatises. The *Summa de Ente* (Treatises on being; 1365–72), containing thirteen treatises, ranging over topics normally associated with a *Sentences* commentary, including the divine nature, being as such and its relation to humanity, and universals. The *Summa theologiae* (1375–81) contains ten treatises devoted to the practical application of his theology, including political and ecclesiological applications, and works on scriptural hermeneutics and exegesis. In addition, Wyclif produced a host of separate treatises, sermons, polemical tracts and short pieces, as well as a *postilla*, or expository summary, of the entirety of Scripture. Finally, he composed a substantial piece designed to introduce the laity to his theological vision, structured according to Peter Lombard's *Sentences*, as a three-way dialogue entitled *Trialogus*. The Middle English Bible and sermons associated with his hand by earlier scholars are probably not his work; probably none of the Wyclif Bible is the result of his translation, and we have no evidence that any of the extant Wycliffite writings are his, although some are translations of his Latin works. Over a century ago, scholars began producing editions of Wyclif's Latin works, which work continues; the past several years have even seen translations of his writings into English.

In the first half of the fourteenth century Oxford enjoyed a reputation as a centre for theological, logical and philosophical innovation. William Ockham's influence was significant; his thought was championed by Adam Wodeham (*d.* 1358), an important Franciscan advocate of Ockham's austere ontology, and its implications were explored by the Dominican Robert Holcot (*d.* 1349), whose thought dramatically questioned the cohesiveness of the great synthesis of Aquinas. While Holcot himself may not warrant the label of sceptic, his approach and those of Nicholas Aston (fl. 1361), and of an anonymous Benedictine known as the Black Monk (fl. 1341), among others, suggested the sceptical tendencies for which Nicholas of Autrecourt had been condemned in 1346. Both Ockham's ontology and the spectre of scepticism figure in Wyclif's thought as the teachings of 'doctors of signs' that threaten the health of the Church. But Oxford was not simply a hotbed of Ockhamism; a group of secular scholars at Merton College known as the Calculators introduced a mathematizing approach to philosophy beginning with the semantic analysis of propositions and proceeding to theorizing about fundamental aspects of what we now understand to be classical physics. A given ambiguous proposition such as 'Socrates is whiter than Plato begins to be white' can be parsed so that our assumptions about the degree of a quality like whiteness and its ratio to a lesser degree of whiteness can lead to more fundamental questions involving quantity and quality, and their relation to mathematical and physical speculation. This approach led to appreciation for the tremendous complexity involved in the mathematical analysis of physical reality, and in the theoretical understanding of force, resistance and velocity.

Two figures among the Calculators are very important for understanding Wyclif's thought. Walter Burley (c.1275–1344) was innovative in the analysis of problems of natural philosophy using the Mertonian approach, advocating a particularly robust philosophical realism, in which universals figure as central to our scientific understanding of physical phenomena. While Burley's realism seems not to have warranted much interest in Oxford during the 1320s, by the 1360s it was a rallying point for realist opponents of Wodeham and Ockhamism, including Wyclif. Thomas Bradwardine (c.1290–49) established a reputation for the mathematical analysis of physics in the 1320s, proclaiming that "Mathematics is the revelatrix of truth, has brought to life every hidden secret, and carries the key to all subtle letters" (quoted in Weisheipl 1959: 73). As his interest shifted to theology, Bradwardine began to explore the thorny problem of God's foreknowledge and future contingents. Ockham had famously argued that God's knowledge that 'x will occur at time t' is contingent, so that God's knowledge of future events has a different truth structure to his knowledge of events of the past and present. Bradwardine's reaction was to lead the theological reaction against what he (and others) decried as Pelagian heresy, and his massive *De causa Dei* (On God's causation) contains every conceivable argument against Ockhamist voluntarism. Bradwardine believed that the fundamental truth of theology is God's absolute causal power over creation, to the extent that God is co-agent in all human actions, and all good willing; it is only in willing evil that human beings act apart from God. To avoid problems such as double predestination and the fatalism attendant on later, Reformation versions of this position, Bradwardine carefully lays out a modal logic of necessity and possibility designed to preserve human agency while leaving clear God's necessary knowledge of all created events. Earlier readers have assumed that Bradwardine turned from his Mertonian mathematizing and adopted a radical 'Augustinianism' in *De causa Dei*, but the mind of a careful analyst of propositions and terms is clearly evident in the book's labyrinth of argument.

Wyclif's understanding of the relation of propositions to things lies at the base of his philosophical theology. His position, recently described as 'pan-propositionalism', is that whatever is, is a proposition. "A proposition, broadly speaking, is a 'being signifying in a complex way'; and so, because everything that is signifies in a complex way that it exists, everything that is can well enough be said to be a proposition" (Wyclif 1893: ch. 5, 14.1–4). Roughly, the individual reality of a creature, such as a human being or a stone, is a 'real proposition'. In it, there is subject and predicate; with Socrates, there is this person, an individuated particular of the human species, functioning as subject, and there is a human nature, which is essentially present in him as a predicate. Uniting the two is his essence, which functions as the actualization of the two, making the real proposition: Socrates [subject] is [essential actualization] a man [predicate]. A 'true proposition' is a truth signifying apart from the thing. The truth, 'to be a man', is a complex truth, reflecting the truth of a number of real propositions, or individual people. The existence of all the subjects having human being as a predicate essentially actualized in them must be a reality formulable into a more general proposition, 'to be a man'. So there are real propositions existing as individuals in creation, and true propositions existing as describing, and organizing, the individuals. The result is an isomorphism between the language we use to interpret the world and the ontological structure of the world. This position is directly opposed to the austere position of Ockham and his followers, in which things in the world are either of the genus substance or are qualities reliant on substances. The effect of Wyclif's approach is to hypostasize, to relate logical and epistemological issues directly to ontological criteria, which must provide the grounds for any sort of semantic distinction or variation that logic can recognize.

Understanding him as having argued for a propositional realism, a logically and semantically dictated ontology, provides an escape from the tendency to begin with Wyclif's realism in an account of his philosophy. Extended arguments arising from Wyclif's realism, which we will see are possible particularly with his thought on dominion, can easily lead to forgetting that ontology is grounded in propositional structure. Rather than explore his realism, it will be better to address the theological implications of Wyclif's 'pan-propositionalism'. What follows from this isomorphism between language and reality for a Christian philosopher? The answer depends on one's epistemology. If we can understand truth using natural reason, without Grace, we might develop a philosophical picture of reality that, while accurate as far as it goes, does not necessarily lead to the salvation made possible by the Incarnation. By Wyclif's time, philosophers were quite willing to recognize that human beings can understand scientific truths and the moral life by natural reasoning. As a result, many, like Ockham and Holcot, went so far as to describe theology as different in kind from science. But if we find truth only through divine illumination, as traditional Augustinian epistemology teaches, then Grace is a necessary prerequisite for any scientific, moral or theological understanding. The illumination theory of understanding, which Aquinas and Scotus had abandoned, was still a real philosophical option in the fourteenth century, largely because of Bonaventure and Henry of Ghent.

Wyclif's epistemology is based in recognition that all that we know, aside from self-evident first principles, involves an element of faithful assent, which is made possible through divine illumination. This allows him to argue that theology and the other sciences are not different in kind, and that we must include theological reasoning in any description of how we can know the truth. If we recognize type–token relations among things in the world, the logic of propositional realism compels us to recognize the reality of a type apart from its token. For example, when we perceive individuals and recognize them as human beings, we are led directly to the type Humanity, of which all these individuals are instances. This Humanity must have reality in some way not dependent on the being of the individual human beings, Wyclif reasons, because the universal does not change despite the transient nature of its particulars. The basis for the universal's being may be in the individual, as the semantic structure of 'Socrates is a Man' dictates. But propositions like 'Man is a rational animal' are about universals first and their particulars second; are universals as far as we can go? Wyclif argues that while we know a singular before we know its species, we have an innate tendency to proceed to the higher level of perfection, in which the species has its being. As Augustine teaches, universals have their basis in the contents of the divine understanding; they are the created actualization of God's ideas.

Wyclif is certain that our reason must lead us to recognize the necessity of God's being, and while he never does more than refer to arguments like those of Anselm and Aquinas, his conviction is that theology is central to the sciences. Any philosophy, then, that would allow one to conclude that the world is uncreated, or that God is not a Trinity, or that there are no uncreated, eternal truths at the base of created being, must inevitably be unfounded:

> Now a philosopher is described as a lover of prudence (*sapientia*), though it is evident that nobody is a philosopher insofar as he lapses into error. For then he is no different from a fool who hates prudence or wisdom (*sophia*), the very opposites of falsehood. Therefore, the greatest philosopher is none other than Christ, Wisdom itself, our God. Consequently, it is by following him that we too become philosophers, while in learning falsehoods we are straying from philosophy insofar as we drift away from the authentic understanding of the saints, who are the true philosophers.
>
> (*De veritate Sacrae Scripturae* I, ch. 2, trans. in Wyclif 2001: 60)

Wyclif's conception of Christ's nature lies at the heart of his philosophy of religion. Of all his scholastic forerunners, Wyclif held Grosseteste in the highest esteem, and Grosseteste's christology is paradigmatic for Wyclif's understanding of the Incarnation. Writing in 1235, Grosseteste argued that, far from being a divine response to human sin, the Incarnation completes the enfolding of creation, binding the universe in mystic union with its creator. Aside from arguing that the Incarnation would have occurred even had we not fallen, Grosseteste argues that Christ fulfils all law as the perfect moral agent. Given that Christ is also the great

Law-giver, mediating not only between God and human beings, but between all people in whatever attempt they make for truth and justice, Wyclif reasons that all created justice must rest on the law Christ ordained for all people, as given in the Gospels. This ideal serves as the opening motto for his massive *De civili dominio* (On civil lordship): "The divine law is presupposed by civil laws; natural dominion is presupposed by civil dominion".

Christ contains far more than normative law, though; the second person of the Trinity contains the divine ideas, the eternally known truths according to which created being is structured. As Augustine had taught in his homilies on the Gospel of John, God made use of eternal paradigms in creating the world. These divine ideas figure importantly in Wyclif's thought, as they define the very being of the Word, by whom all things are made. "We should understand how Christ ... is the essential foundation, which is with everything as internal vital being, according to John 1:3–4, 'What has come into being in him was life'" (Wyclif 1890: 39; see also 62–3; 1869: I, chs 8–9). Thus, Christ is the greatest philosopher simply because he defines truth; his eternal being is identical with uncreated truth, and all who would seek the truth must turn necessarily to him.

Wyclif proceeds outward from the being of Christ into creation by means of the truth Christ defines. In *De veritate Sacrae Scripturae* (On the truth of Holy Scripture; 1377–8) he presents five gradations, or equivocations, by which we can understand the identity of Christ with Scripture (in 1382 he would reduce the number to three). First is the Book of Life, described in Revelations 20:12, which represents the divine mind revealed in its true glory at the apocalypse as divine legislator and judge. Second are the truths contained within the Book of Life. These are not essentially distinct from the being of Christ, but formally distinct in that we can consider individual divine ideas apart from the being of the Word in which they have eternal being. Third are the truths considered as brought into effect in creation, each defining genus and species by which created being is organized. These are the universals that figure so importantly in Wyclif's ontology, directly corresponding to the divine ideas as created instantiations of the unchanging eternal truths. Fourth are the truths we comprehend when we encounter the world and gain understanding; these are the subject of epistemology, the concepts that reflect created beings that we use to recognize the universals. At this level are the concepts we glean from experience, as when we encounter people and formulate the concept 'Humanity'. This concept gives evidence of the universal Humanity, which itself is the created manifestation of God's idea of Humanity. Finally, at the lowest level of Christ's truth is Scripture, the written signs, manuscripts and so forth that tell us of the reality of Christ at the centre of the universe.

It is one thing to claim that Scripture is an iteration of Christ, but quite another to equate the two. It is not hard to reason that in so far as the Word is identical to the Eternal Law, and the divine law of Scripture is an iteration of the Eternal Law given to us to effect human salvation, one can say that the divine law of Scripture is an iteration of Christ. But it is something else again to say that Christ and Scripture are interchangeable. If Christ contains all created truth, the truths of mathematics, science and all the history of the universe, then so too must Scripture; how is this possible? Dismissing the possibility of discounting empirical truths such as 'Lincoln was shot in Ford's Theatre' or 'The atomic number of gold is 79' as somehow less true, we are left with a very strange, Bible-based philosophical approach.

Wyclif does not mean for us to look for truths of science, history and so on in the Bible; we are, instead, to look for corroboration of their truth in scriptural exegesis. In *Trialogus*, and two years later, towards the end of what was probably the last of his works, *De Antichristo* (Of the Antichrist), he lists five things that every seeker of truth must bear in mind when studying Scripture according to what he calls the 'logic of Christ'.

First, that they be instructed in right reasoning about universals. They consider the few by collecting their perceptions to what is universal, and with their words they enter into combat against those who would speak smoothly. Secondly, that they understand the teachings of Christ according to right metaphysics, the truth about the quiddity of time and of other accidents, which do not exist unless as dispositions formally inherent in their subjects. Thirdly, that they know that everything that was or will be between God and humanity is, in the great time, present to God. Fourthly, that they know that creatures have ideal eternal being in God, eternally antecedent existence in their kinds. And fifthly, that they know material essence to be perpetual, and material form to be of its dispositions, although they are the quiddities of species and genera (Wyclif 1869: III, ch. 31; Wyclif 1895: vol. 2, book IV, ch. 12, 325.17–326.30).

Anselm, Hugh of Saint-Victor, Bernard of Clairvaux and Grosseteste would agree in this, Wyclif believed; Scripture is the source of every valid system of logic, the eternal source of truth in creation, and to understand it one must recognize that it has its own, all-encompassing logic, and devote oneself to learning it. This was the point of studying philosophy. One does not enter into a college simply for entertaining word games, or to play with doubts about the veracity of revealed truth. For him, education is not an end in itself, but the means by which one gains access to the eternal truths embedded within Scripture. This is why Wyclif emphasizes preaching and study as foremost among a priest's responsibilities; because the vast majority of Christians lack the wherewithal to engage in this demanding intellectual labour, the clergy must make the logic of Christ clear to their charges in both their preaching and in the example of their lives. As we shall see, a priest ought to rely wholly on the alms of the people for his welfare, unencumbered by private property as were the apostles. Indeed, Wyclif's emphasis on the duty of the priest to live an exemplary life can teeter on the brink of Donatism, as when he suggests that clerics negligent through avarice or lechery may justifiably be deprived of the alms on which they rely, both by scriptural (2 John 10) and ecclesial (*Decretum I* d.32, c.5) authority. His clerical opponents perceived him as having plunged headlong into this heresy, condemning him for it both at Blackfriars in 1382 and at Constance in 1415.

Wyclif held that not only the familiar genera and species, which he termed 'universals by commonality' have reality distinct from their particulars, but universal relations and causal universals have this as well. These he understood to be the ongoing metaphysical ground for instances of relations, causal and otherwise, between created beings. An important instance is the dominion relation. Dominion, the subject of several of the first treatises of the *Summa theologiae*, is generally understood to be the classic relation holding between lord and subject, based in the lord's ownership of land, or of his subject liegeman, or both. Wyclif envisaged God's dominion to be the primary relation uniting God and creation, based in the divine act of creation *ex nihilo*. The hallmark of this relation, Wyclif explains, is God's love, which is realized in the divine creation, sustenance and nurturing of every created being. The Book of Genesis tells us that human beings were given dominion over the earth, in which ownership and property were unknown, and before the Fall human beings exercised their dominion relation over creation as created instances of the divine prototype relation.

The Fall robbed us of the possibility of this 'natural dominion', and with the advent of original sin came the idea of private property ownership. Prelapsarian human dominion was no longer possible, and 'civil dominion' came into being. This perversion of the universal dominion relation lacks the love characterizing God's dominion, and entails the subjection of one human being to another. The Incarnation allowed the return of 'natural dominion' by Grace; as Christ and his disciples lived in apostolic poverty, so too can his body on earth continue in this pure state of communal harmony. That the Church has relapsed into sin is clear by virtue of its extraordinary wealth, Wyclif argues, and he tirelessly declaims the need for radical divestment of ecclesiastical wealth and property. Thus far, Wyclif's arguments are strongly evocative of the poverty controversy that split the Franciscan Order earlier in the fourteenth century, although radical Franciscans did not frame their arguments for *usus pauper* in terms of a universal–particular relation holding between divine and just human dominion. Wyclif's innovation is to argue that God favours civil lords with Grace to protect the Church's 'evangelical dominion' by divesting it of its property and acting as its stewards on earth. This Grace-favoured civil dominion relation, he argues, is also an instantiation of the divine dominion relation, provided that the civil lord act with the love and nurturing care that characterizes divine dominion. Tyrannical civil lords or kings are certainly a possibility, but one must be very alert about the source of the accusation of tyranny; many a bishop's mind has been poisoned by the cloying venom of property ownership, prompting them to accuse just civil lords as tyrants, to employ the weapons of excommunication and interdict in defence of their own ill-held goods.

Ideally, Wyclif sees Christian life as free of property ownership, communally enjoying the goods of creation under the protection of a Grace-inspired civil lord, who serves as divine steward. The office of priest is still needed, although under the right circumstances all Christians are evangelical lords through Christ's

restoration of natural dominion; there is still a need for articulation and explanation of the Bible for those unable to find this for themselves, and so preachers
will always be necessary in the Christian life. While Wyclif described this ideal
in terms of universal divine dominion and particular created dominion relations, his detractors from his own day to the present have taken him to be moved
more by allegiance to John of Gaunt than to metaphysical realism in his political thought. The duke was frequently at loggerheads with the Church, and probably admired his liegeman's arguments, but his patronage was not the reason for
Wyclif's programme of ecclesiastical reform, which was inspired not by *realpolitik*
but by metaphysical realism.

Another issue with which Wyclif is frequently associated is his rejection of transubstantiation. By the later medieval period, Eucharistic theology had become the
quantum mechanics of the age; a forbidding thicket of philosophical complexity
had come to define the disputes about how the elements become Christ's body and
blood on the altar. Foremost among the theories is that of transubstantiation, in
which the substance of the element is replaced with the substance of Christ, while
the accidents (i.e. perceptible qualities) remain constant. To the eye, no change
occurs; the wafer remains white, circular and hard, but it ceases to be bread and
is Christ. In 1215, the Fourth Lateral Council's codification of transubstantiation
led to three distinct means by which the miracle occurs; each attracted their own
admirers, and each was judged a valid explanation. First, the substance of the
bread might remain along with the substance of Christ's body, which is consubstantiation. Where once there was one thing, bread, now there are two, for the
body of Christ begins to be in the same place. Secondly, the substance of the bread
might be annihilated and replaced by the substance of Christ's body. Thirdly, the
substance of the bread itself changes, becoming the substance of Christ's body,
without passing out of existence. Here, the substance itself converts from 'being
bread' to 'being body' without a change in the underlying subject.

Thomas Aquinas had rejected consubstantiation as allowing for the adora-
tion of something in addition to Christ, given the legitimacy of the veneration
of the consecrated host, and advocated the substantial change of the elements
into Christ, a conversion from one substance to the other. Scotus agreed that the
change took place by conversion from one substance to the other, though differing
with Aquinas as to how the change occurred. He was not as opposed to consubstantiation as Aquinas. God could, by absolute power, allow Christ to be present in
the substance of the bread, two things being in one place, but the teaching office of
the Church has shown that this is not what occurs. Both Scotus and Aquinas had
not chosen the annihilation of the substance of the elements as a possibility, but
Ockham did. Ockham's approach was to argue that the substance of the bread is
not reduced to absolute nothingness, but to the being it had as potential substance
in God's mind before creation. Once this occurs, the whole Christ is present in
the consecrated host under the species of the bread, transubstantiated into definitive place. Like Scotus, Ockham thought that, all things equal, consubstantiation

probably made more sense, but given that the Church had come to prefer transubstantiation, he was willing to submit to its authority. Ockham was called to account for his annihilation theory, the sacramental ramifications of which seemed excessive; he was made to answer charges at Avignon in 1325, where his Eucharistic theology was deemed within the bounds of orthodoxy, if only just.

Wyclif appears to have been very reluctant to turn the whole of his intellectual ability to the issue. Early on, he found annihilation to be repellent. Assuming that something that God created can be made not to exist is to assume that it is possible for an instance of a form to cease to be. Material form may change, it may become corrupted over time, but for it simply to wink out of existence would require a change within the universal it instantiates. If it were simply the elimination of one, isolated substantial composite of matter and form, it would be analogous to replacing one number in a series of numbers with a zero. This, it seems, is what Wyclif imagines his opponents to conceive. But because the substantial form of any given thing enjoys an identity relation with the universals it instantiates, dire consequences await the universals as well as the particular substance. For example, the substance of a plant instantiates the universal 'Rose' so that its form has identity with its universal. But the universal 'Rose' is a species of a larger genus, 'Plant', which is itself a species of 'Animal' (by Aristotelian biology), and so on up to 'Substance' itself. If the rose were annihilated, because of this identity, so would be 'Rose', 'Plant' and 'Substance' itself. On our mathematical analogy, annihilation would be multiplying the sum of a complex equation by zero; not only do you turn the sum into zero, you also render to nullity the complexity on the other side of the equal sign.

Given the eventual vigour with which he rejected the conversion theory of transubstantiation, it is natural to read Wyclif as having tacitly approved of consubstantiation. While he insisted that Christ was really present in the consecrated host, he could not bring himself to accept the arguments for Christ's substantial presence in the host. The approaches of neither Aquinas nor Scotus hold up under his criticism; as his thought progressed, he systematically rejected first Scotus' position, then Aquinas' as philosophically untenable. In part this was because his understanding of change over time was notably different from most of his scholastic predecessors'. The standard Aristotelian understanding of any continua was that they are infinitely divisible, allowing any given unit of time or space to admit the kind of conversion of substance from Eucharistic element to Christ that Aquinas and Scotus envisioned. A minority of Oxford philosophers believed that space and time are composed of indivisible atoms; in the generation before Wyclif, Walter Chatton and William Crathorn argued for this, prompting withering scorn from Adam Wodeham, among others. Wyclif's earliest writings argue for spatiotemporal atomism, in part arising from his belief in the isomorphism of language and reality. If we think of a body moving through space and time, while most philosophers of the day would have envisaged the media through which it moves to be infinitely divisible, Wyclif conceives of the two media as composed of points corresponding to propositions. There is a one-to-one correspondence of body to instant in time and in space, and the movement occurs through the succession of time. What Wyclif has in mind is a picture of time structured the way we watch films. Each frame of the film is in itself unified, a moment frozen in time. From one frame to the next, the subject portrayed seems to move, but in fact there is no movement distinct from the time in which it occurs, or the succession of frames.

Applying this model to the Thomistic conversion theory of transubstantiation, in which the change from bread and wine to body and blood is instantaneous, is disastrous. For an instantaneous change to occur to a substance, there must be a point at which the substance ceases being one thing and begins to be another. If we imagine a change in accident or property of a substance, this is not a problem, because the being of the underlying substance remains constant. We can say 'At time 1, the cat was still, and at time 2, the cat was moving'. But if we imagine a change in substances, as is necessary in transubstantiation, there is nothing to which the statement 'At time 1, this was bread, and at time 2, this is Christ' refers. To claim that 'this' refers to the bundle of accidents considered apart from their underlying substance, as Aquinas had argued, is simply nonsense. We are asked to believe that God would suspend the fundamental laws of creation to effect the conversion of the elements on the altar, Wyclif fumes, which is as good as saying that God causes our senses – and our reason – to lie to us in order to provide us with the salvific grace of the sacrament.

In his writings on both dominion and the Eucharist, Wyclif leads his reader back to the active complicity of negligence within the Church as the primary cause for error. Time and again, he argues, clergy have allowed themselves to be charmed by the enticements of the physical world. The Church was healthy until the terrible Donation of Constantine, when the papacy moved to declare itself sovereign in worldly power. Eucharistic theology was untrammelled by real error until Innocent III's contumacious demand that transubstantiation be the sole means by which the miracle could be explained. These errors, and many like them, arose when the Church drifted away from secure mooring in the logic of Christ. This hypnotic fascination with temporal goods seems to be accompanied by a rejection of universals and a biblical amnesia. Just as the Mosaic priesthood and the temple religion of the Jews had strayed from the fundamental truths of the Old Law in the time of Christ, so too has the ecclesiastical hierarchy and the panoply of earthly Christianity strayed from the truths of the New Law. Wyclif's later writings glow with an apocalyptic aura similar to the works of Joachim of Fiore in the twelfth century and the spiritual Franciscans a century earlier. From our vantage point, it is easy to associate that glow with the fires that would burn two centuries later, but dangerously anachronistic. Wyclif's importance in the history of philosophical theology lies in his articulation of so many of the strands of medieval theology; scholastic logic and metaphysics, scriptural hermeneutics, the ideology of clerical and ecclesiastical reform and sacramental theology all figure significantly in his thought and, in each case, his stance is a reactionary conservatism in the face of the evolution of the modern.

FURTHER READING

Benrath, G. 1966. *Wyclif's Bibelkommentar*. Berlin: De Gruyter.

Cesalli, L. 2005. "Le 'pan-propositionalisme' de Jean Wyclif". *Vivarium* **43**: 124–55.

Conti, A. 1993. "Logica intensionale et metafisica dell'essenza in John Wyclif". *Bullettino dell'Instituto Storico Italiano per il Medio Evo e Archivio Muratoriano* **99**: 159–219.

Courtenay, W. 1987. *Schools and Scholars in Fourteenth-Century England*. Princeton, NJ: Princeton University Press.

Fumigalli, M. & S. Simonietta (eds) 2003. *John Wyclif: Logica, Politica, Teologia*. Florence: SISMEL.

Herold, V. 1985. "Wyclif's Philosophy and Platonic Ideas". *Filozoficky Casopis* **33**: 47–96.

Hudson, A. & M. Wilks (eds) 1987. *From Ockham to Wyclif*, Studies in Church History, Subsidia 5. Oxford: Blackwell.

Hudson, A. 1988. *The Premature Reformation: Wycliffite Texts and Lollard History*. Oxford: Clarendon Press.

Kenny, A. (ed.) 1986. *Wyclif in His Times*. Oxford: Clarendon Press.

Lahey, S. 2008. *John Wyclif*. Oxford: Oxford University Press.

Levy, I. (ed.) 2006. *A Companion to John Wyclif, Late Medieval Theologian*. Leiden: Brill.

Oberman, H. 1958. *Archbishop Thomas Bradwardine, A Fourteenth-Century Augustinian: A Study of His Theology in Its Historical Context*. Utrecht: Kemink & Zoon.

Smalley, B. 1953. "John Wyclif's *Postilla super totam Bibliam*". *Bodleian Library Record* **5**: 186–205.

Wilks, M. 2000. *Wyclif: Political Ideas and Practice*. Oxford: Oxbow.

On LOGIC see also Chs 2, 4; Vol. 3, Ch. 3; Vol. 4, Ch. 19. On MATHEMATICS see also Vol. 3, Ch. 8. On TRUTH see also Vol. 1, Ch. 13; Vol. 3, Chs 3, 8, 13; Vol. 4, Chs 8, 18; Vol. 5, Ch. 4.

18

NICHOLAS OF CUSA

Jasper Hopkins

The German prelate Nicholas of Cusa (1401–64) belonged to a period of history that was rife with transitional cross-currents. Some scholars, such as C. Warren Hollister, call this period the Late Middle Ages; others, such as Paul O. Kristeller, refer to it simply as the Renaissance.[1] Furthermore, some intellectual historians who take soundings in the fourteenth and the fifteenth centuries claim to descry ripples of modern scientific enquiry as these issue forth from Theodoric of Freiburg's experiment of 1304, when, using glass balls, he ascertained that a rainbow results from light's passing through a medium whereby it is both reflected and refracted. And these same historians point to William Ockham's philosophical nominalism and to his doubts about the validity of natural theology. By contrast, other intellectual historians choose to emphasize the continuity of the fourteenth and fifteenth centuries with the past, as instanced by the unceasing ecclesiastical disputes and by the ongoing vigorous reactions to the incursions of Islam into the West. Nicholas himself is caught up in these historical cross-currents: in the flow towards modernity and towards new ways of conceptualizing, as well as in the ebb towards the past and towards traditional patterns of thought. While functioning in the Church as papal legate to Germany and as Bishop of Brixen in South Tyrol and as cardinal of St Peter in Chains in Rome, Nicholas nonetheless: (i) incorporated into his academic formation a time of study with the Italian Humanists in Padua (under whom he increased his knowledge of mathematics, astronomy and literature); (ii) journeyed to Constantinople with a Conciliar delegation (where he observed Islam at first-hand); (iii) wrote the dialogue *De staticis experimentis* (On experiments done with weight-scales); and (iv) espoused certain themes that

---

1. Primarily for heuristic reasons Hollister (1982) uses the following dates: 500–1050, Early Middle Ages; 1050–1300, High Middle Ages; 1300–1500, Late Middle Ages. Kristeller (1972: 110–55, esp. 111, 113) periodizes as follows: 500–1300/1350, Middle Ages; 1300/1350–1600, Renaissance.

are proleptic of later, more systematic philosophical frameworks (so that Ernst Cassirer labels him "the First Modern Thinker" [1927: 10]).

NO COMPARISON

One of the tenets that have been supposed to contribute to identifying Nicholas as a modern thinker is his strict adherence to the slogan '*Nulla proportio finiti ad infinitum est*' (There is no comparative relation of the finite to the infinite). By accentuating this theme – by making it a keystone of his philosophy of religion – Nicholas insists that the human mind has no knowledge, other than metaphorical, of *what* God is. For the infinite God is not like anything that a finite mind can either perceive or imagine or conceive. So although a theist rightly confesses that God *exists* and is *one* and is *good*, still it is no less true that God is neither existent nor unitary nor good in any way that resembles either our knowledge or our conceptualization of these properties. Thus, to say that God is good (Matthew 19:17) has the same cognitive status as to say that God is a consuming fire (Hebrews 12:29; Deuteronomy 4:24): that is, each of these statements is symbolical, or figurative. For we cannot know what God is, or is like, in and of himself. But we can and should, continues Nicholas, symbolize him in accordance with what we know to be perfections and in accordance with the teaching of Jesus, who spoke of God the Father as good, as perfect, as loving (Matthew 19:16, 5:48; John 14:21). So, as infinite, God is incomprehensible and beyond all description and attribution: even when we state that he is the creator of the world or the cause of the world, he is not creator or cause in any sense in which we either do understand, or can understand, the meaning of these words. Here Nicholas, by endorsing the *via negativa*, aligns himself with a tradition that runs through such diverse thinkers as Pseudo-Dionysius (*see* Vol. 1, Ch. 20) and Moses Maimonides, both of whom Nicholas mentions. In accordance with this tradition, we can rightly conceive only of what God is *not*: God is not *cause*, not *creator*, not *good*, not *existent*, not *being*, etc. But at this point Nicholas cautions us. For although God is not being, he is also not not-being; and although he is not good, he is also not not-good. He is beyond the entire distinction between being and not-being, between good and not-good and so on (*De Deo abscondito* [On the hidden God] 9, *De possest* [On actualized-possibility] 25).[2]

---

2. All references to Cusa's texts (except for his sermons) are in terms of my translations and divisions in Nicholas of Cusa (2001). By permission of Arthur J. Banning Press these translations also now appear online at www.cla.umn.edu/jhopkins/ (accessed May 2009). References to the sermons are to vols XVII–XIX of the Latin texts in Nicholas of Cusa (1983–2007). Besides being influenced by the negative theology of Pseudo-Dionysius, Nicholas is influenced by that of Eriugena. But whereas Eriugena (*De divisione naturae* [On the division of nature] II; *Patrologia Latina* [hereafter *PL*] 122:589B–C) states that God

Thus, Nicholas rejects Aquinas' claim that we have some imperfect, *analogical* knowledge of God: Aquinas' claim that there is some real resemblance between God and his creation, that there is some real (i.e. non-metaphorical) resemblance between, say, the human mind and the divine mind. Indeed, on Nicholas' view even a human person's rational-moral nature, in terms of which humanity is made in the image of God, does not constitute a real likeness. In this respect, then, Nicholas repudiates Aquinas' distinction between *proportio* (proportion, comparative relation) and *proportionalitas* (proportionality), a distinction that allows Aquinas to accept the slogan *'nulla proportio ...'* but without his altogether excluding analogical predication. As an example of a proportionality (which, as Aquinas says, is a similarity between proportions) he gives the following: the numbers six and eight are *proportionate* to each other in so far as each is a double. For just as six is the double of three, so eight is the double of four (Aquinas, *Quaestio disputata de veritate* [A controversial issue concerning truth], q. 2, a. 3, r. 4). Thus, six is to three as eight is to four. Another example – one that we may borrow from Nietzsche (*see* Vol. 4, Ch. 18) – also illustrates a proportionality: as today's man is to the ape, so the superman (*Übermensch*), when he comes, will be to today's man. If we extend this proportionality, and place it, as extended, into a theistic context, we might say along Thomistic lines: as the superman's intelligence would be to man's, so is God's intelligence to the superman's. In any event, Nicholas, unlike Aquinas, denies that any kind of proportionality will yield an acceptable analogy between humanity and God. For as God infinitely exceeds all proportion, so he also infinitely exceeds all proportionality: exceeds, that is, all similarity between proportions. And, thus, as concerns *what* God is, Nicholas is content to embrace agnosticism.

LEARNED IGNORANCE

The foregoing agnosticism is accompanied by our knowledge that we are, and must be, ignorant of God's nature. This awareness of a knowledge that we do not have, and cannot have, is called by Nicholas 'learned ignorance' (*docta ignorantia*), where the word 'learned' indicates, primarily, that we have come to be instructed – by individuals such as Cusanus, Maimonides and Pseudo-Dionysius – that God

---

is unknown even to himself, Nicholas (*De docta ignorantia* [On learned ignorance] I, 26 (88)) maintains that God is known only to himself. More specifically: whereas Eriugena states (*PL* 122:590D) that God knows himself but does not know or understand *what* he is (because he is beyond *essence* and is not *something*), Nicholas emphasizes that God *understands* himself (*De principio* [On the beginning] 9, *Cribratio Alkorani* [A scrutiny of the Qu'ran] II, 6 (102)), is the Essence of essences (*De docta ignorantia* I, 17) – indeed, *is* his own quiddity, which is his knowledge (Sermon CCLVIII (14)) – and is the "definition" of himself *qua* Not-other (*De li non aliud* [On not-other] 18). See Beierwaltes (1987).

is unknowable, because he is infinite. Yet, in a secondary sense, the meaning of the word 'learned' is also to be construed in accordance with the meaning that is associated with the pronunciation 'learn-ed', where this pronunciation conveys the idea of erudition. Still, *docta ignorantia* is not an inflated erudition but is the kind of humble erudition characteristic of Socrates, who deemed himself to be wiser than others simply because he *knew that he was ignorant*, whereas others were pompously unaware of their own state of unknowing. Like Socrates, but in a theological context, Nicholas wants to say that someone who knows that he is ignorant of what God is is wiser, more learn-ed, than are others who do not have this knowledge.[3]

One of Nicholas' favourite metaphors for God is that of 'Light': God is inaccessible light, as the Scriptures say (1 Timothy 6:16). Nicholas compares that divine light to the light of the sun:

> When our eye seeks to see the sun's light, which is the sun's face, it first looks at it in a veiled manner in the stars and in colors and in all participants in the sun's light. But when our eye strives to view the sun's light in an unveiled manner, it passes beyond all visible light, because all such light is less than the light it seeks. But since it seeks to see a light which it cannot see, it knows that as long as it sees something, this is not the thing it is seeking. Therefore, it must pass beyond all visible light. So if one has to pass beyond all light, the place into which he enters will have to be devoid of visible light; and so, for the eye, it will be darkness. Now, while he is amid that darkness, which is an obscuring mist: if he knows that he is within an obscuring mist, he knows that he has approached unto the face of the sun. For that obscuring mist arises in his eye as a result of the excellence of the light of the sun. Therefore, the more dense he knows the obscuring mist to be, the more truly he attains, within that mist, unto the invisible light.
>
> I see, O Lord, that in this way and in no other the inaccessible light and beauty and splendor of Your Face can be approached unveiledly.
> (*De visione Dei* [On the vision of God] 6 (22))

In propounding the doctrine of learned ignorance, then, Nicholas is endorsing a form of agnosticism that informs us of our necessary ignorance of God's nature as it is in and of itself. Even in the next life the redeemed shall have no such conceptual knowledge, he teaches. Nor do angels ever have it. For God is knowable only to himself. Yet, Nicholas' agnosticism concerns only God's nature, not God's existence. For one can know with reasonable certainty, thinks Nicholas,

---

3. With regard to Nicholas' use of '*docta*' in the sense of 'learn-ed', see *De possest* 41 and *Compendium* 1 (4) and 6 (18).

that God, who is the infinite source and sustainer of all things, exists. Nicholas offers no proofs, in the rigorous sense of 'proof'. Instead, he advances various sets of informal considerations that he regards as weighty enough to make it more reasonable to conclude that God exists than to judge otherwise (*De principio* 29). One such set of considerations, borrowed from Proclus, proceeds along the following lines:

> If there were many beginnings, assuredly they would be alike in this one respect, viz., that they would be *beginnings*. Therefore, they would partake of the One. But, surely, that which is partaken of is prior to its participants. Therefore, there are not many beginnings but there is a single Beginning, prior to multitude. But if you were to say that the beginnings are plural apart from their partaking of the One, that statement would self-destruct. For, surely, these plural beginnings would be both *alike*, by virtue of their not partaking of the One, and *not alike*, by virtue of their not partaking of the One.   (*De principio* 6)

In the foregoing reasoning Nicholas relies on a Neoplatonic framework, with its accompanying notion of participation. A cognate set of considerations is found in his dialogue *De genesi* (On the genesis [of all things]):

> *Nicholas*: When we say that what is different is different, we affirm that what is different is the same as itself. For what is different can be different only through the Absolute Same, through which all that is is both the same as itself and other than another. But whatever is the same as itself and other than another is not the Absolute Same, which is neither the same as another nor different from another. For how could it befit the Absolute Same to be the same as another? Nor is [the Absolute Same] different. For how could difference befit the Absolute Same, which precedes all difference and otherness?
> *Conrad*: I understand you to mean (1) that of all beings there is not one that is not the same as itself and other than another and (2) that, hence, the Absolute Same is no such being, although the Absolute Same is not *different* from anything that is both the same as itself and different from another.
> *Nicholas*: You are conceiving correctly. For it is not the case that the Absolute Same, which we also call God, is numerable with anything else ...   (*De genesi* I (146–7))

Here, again, Nicholas' reasoning occurs within a Neoplatonic metaphysical framework and is largely *a priori*. Instances of such *a priori* inferences of God's existence are to be found throughout his works: from the fact that there are *possible* occurrences, he infers that there is absolute possibility (*De apice theoriae*

[Concerning the loftiest level of contemplative reflection] 12–13), which he identifies with God; from the fact that there are truths, he infers that there is truth (Sermon CCIV (3)), which he identifies with God; from the fact that all that is seen is such as not to be the cause of itself, he infers that there must be something self-existent, which he identifies with God (*De possest* 3); and so on. But perhaps the best example of his *a priori* Neoplatonic reasoning about the existence of God (and about the symbolisms relevant to God's nature) has to do with his presupposition about *presupposition*! That is, he presupposes that "every question about God presupposes what is being asked about" (*De sapientia* [On wisdom] II (29)).

> So when you are asked whether God exists, reply by stating what is presupposed, viz., that He exists, for *being* is presupposed by the question. Likewise, if someone asks what God is, then since this question presupposes that there is quiddity, you will reply that God is Absolute Quiddity. A similar point holds true in all cases. And there is no doubt about this point. For God is the Absolute Presupposition of all things that are in any way presupposed – even as in the case of every effect a cause is presupposed. (*De sapientia* II (30))[4]

But even when Nicholas elsewhere seeks to make *empirical*, rather than *a priori*, inferences to God's existence, he does so informally. It is obvious, for example, that he considers the world to show evidence of orderliness and teleology: traces that he regards as warranting the inference of a divine craftsman (*Apologia doctae ignorantiae* [A defence of learned ignorance; hereafter *Apologia*] 19). However, in spite of his alluding to this line of thinking, he nowhere develops it systematically.

Still, there is a difference between Nicholas' reasoning about God's existence and his reasoning about God's nature. With respect to the former, he uses expressions such as "there is no doubt that …". But with respect to the latter he indicates that he is *surmising*. Indeed, much of his tractate *De coniecturis* (On surmises) deals with his surmises about God's nature: surmises that make use of symbolical illustrations, some of which are mathematical. In these surmisings Nicholas seeks "to comprehend the Incomprehensible" (*De sapientia* I (11)). In other words, he seeks to discern more readily the fact of God's incomprehensibility and to rejoice in this fact. For just as one who finds a treasure so vast as to be uncountable rejoices more than does one who finds a countable treasure, so Nicholas rejoices over the fact that the God whom he has found is something that is greater than can be conceived. And he takes comfort in paradox: "The better we grasp the Inaccessible's greater distance from us, the closer we come to [this] Inaccessibility" (*Apologia* 13).

---

4. See also Nicholas of Cusa (2000: 52–60).

COINCIDENCE OF OPPOSITES

All of the foregoing points about learned ignorance are re-expressed by Nicholas when he enfolds them into the meaning of the phrase '*coincidentia oppositorum*'; for God is, as he says, the coincidence of opposites. In places, he refers to God as *beyond* the coincidence of opposites. But this latter wording is intended to signify no more than does the former wording: namely, that God incomprehensibly transcends every distinction between *this* and *that*, every differentiation into *this* or *that*. For God is altogether undifferentiated into one thing or another. He is not *a* being; we may symbolize him as Being itself, as the power that creates all beings and that sustains them in existence for as long as they exist. Learned ignorance has shown us that God escapes all properties, all determination. He is not *other* than any finite thing, since he does not enter into the domain of comparison with finite things. Hence, we may symbolically name him 'Not-Other'.

To illustrate the Plotinian point about God's (the One's) being beyond being (and beyond not-being), Nicholas describes a scenario that could not actually occur but that nonetheless can to some extent be envisaged. We are familiar, he supposes, with the fact that a top that spins very fast *appears to be* at rest. If the top were spinning at infinite speed, he tells us, it would *actually be* at rest. For at infinite speed any given point on it would come full circle instantaneously, that is, with no intervening interval of time. So the top would be both in motion and at rest. In applying the illustration, he tells us that contradictory predicates can figuratively be ascribed to God. For example, we may say that "the eyes of the Lord run to and fro throughout the whole earth" (2 Chronicles 16:9); and we may equally well say "Jesus Christ the same yesterday and today and forever" (Hebrews 13:8). Or we may say that God is light in whom there is no darkness (1 John 1:5); but we may also say that he has "made darkness His secret place" (Psalms 18:11).

The doctrine of *coincidentia oppositorum* teaches that in God all things are God; but it also teaches that in all things God is all things (without being any of these things). Nicholas once again resorts to illustrations in order to elucidate these tenets. God is in all things as an original is in the mirror-images of itself; yet, God is not any of these things, even as the original is not a mirror-image. All things are in God as an effect is in its cause; yet, in God these things *are* God, even as in its cause an effect *is* the cause. What Nicholas never asserts, unqualifiedly, is that God is all things. For to say that *in all things God is all things* is not the same as saying, simply, *God is all things*. Because many interpreters have not noticed that Nicholas distinguishes these two statements, they have sometimes wrongly identified him as a pantheist or, at least, as someone displaying pantheistic tendencies. However, no interpretation could be farther from the truth, for Nicholas makes it abundantly clear that (on his view) God alone is uncontracted (i.e. unrestricted, undelimited, undifferentiated, absolute), whereas all else is contracted (*De docta ignorantia* II, 9 (148 & 150)); indeed, the universe "falls short of eternity, as what is contracted falls short of what is absolute – the two being infinitely different"

(*De docta ignorantia* II, 8 (140)). So when Nicholas writes that God's being "is the complete being of all the things which either are or in any way can be" (*De possest* 67), and reiterates that the creator is all the things "which are possible to be" (*De possest* 73; cf. *De docta ignorantia* I, 5 (14)), he means that in God all things are God and that, similarly, in all things God is present as Sustainer,[5] so that if God did not exist, finite beings would not exist (*De docta ignorantia* II, 3 (110)).

DESIRE FOR GOD[6]

Human beings, claims Nicholas, have an innate tendency towards seeking God. This tendency is encrypted into the rational image of God in humanity. Thus, a human being's desire for the good is, ultimately, a desire for God, who is the Good. "Although [each being] cannot comprehend That-which-it-desires-so-ardently, nevertheless it is not totally ignorant of it but knows most certainly that That-which-it-desires exists" (*De principio* 29). As Nicholas elsewhere writes: "You are Infinity itself, which alone I desire in every desire" (*De visione Dei* 16 (73)). The human heart, Nicholas instructs us, is restless, its hunger unsatisfied, until it finds repose and fullness in God (although, in its fullness, its desire for God does not cease but, rather, is intensified) (4 (13)). This Augustinian theme accords with Nicholas' further claim that no one can know himself unless he knows his cause, so that human self-knowledge depends on obtaining, through faith and commitment, a relationship of acquaintance with God. Not only does the human mind have an inborn tendency to seek God: it also has an innate *vis iudiciaria* – an innate power of rational judgement – that allows it to recognize the necessity of necessary truths and to discern the soundness of such moral maxims as the precept expressed by the Golden Rule. Each human being, by virtue of his or her rationality, has a concreated, inchoate sense of fairness that becomes more and more refined in the course of experience. At birth the mind has no concepts, not even the concept of God. But as human rationality develops and unfolds, through experience and growth, the innate power of judgement is stimulated to form *a priori* concepts such as the concept of number, the concept of fairness, the concepts of God, of good, of equality (*Compendium* 6 (17), 10 (34)).[7] Hence, Nicholas does not hesitate to use the expression 'logica connata' (concreated power

---

5. In the sun God is not the sun, and in the moon God is not the moon; rather, in them "He is that which is sun and moon without plurality and difference" (*De docta ignorantia* II, 4 (115)).
6. For this expression, see *De mente* (On mind) 15 (159).
7. Cf.: "The divine commandments are very terse and very well known to everyone and are common to all nations. Indeed, the light that shows us these commandments is created together with the rational soul." (*De pace fidei* 16 (59)).

of logic), thereby designating the tool by which philosophers (and others) pursue wisdom (*De venatione sapientiae* [On the pursuit of wisdom] 1 (5)).

ONE RELIGION

Partly on the basis of the presumed fact that each individual has a concreated tendency to seek God, so that *homo* is likewise *homo religiosus* (Sermon IV (6)), Nicholas pursues the question of whether there might be a set of religious beliefs to which individuals from different nations and traditions could be persuaded to subscribe, so that religious wars, hatreds and crusades would cease. In short, could there be *religio una in rituum varietate*: one religion amid a variety of rites? In *De pace fidei* (On peaceful unity of faith) he sets out to show how it is that Christianity is just such a religion; and he proceeds to furnish a series of rationales that he supposes will serve to persuade peoples from other nations that Christianity is compatible with – even inferable from – the basic beliefs that they already hold.

Let us take a single example of Nicholas' rationales: the example of how, presumably, it would be possible to persuade Jews and Muslims of the truth of God's triunity. At first glance, Nicholas' task seems to be not only formidable but also impossible. For no doctrine seems to be more at odds with these two religious traditions than is the Christian teaching that God is triune. Yet, Nicholas' account of learned ignorance and of the coincidence of opposites in God provides the needed opening. For as infinite, he says, God is "neither triune nor one nor any of those things that can be spoken of" (*De pace fidei* 7 (21)). Or, as he restates his point elsewhere: "Infinite goodness is not goodness but is Infinity. Infinite quantity is not quantity but is Infinity. And so on" (*De visione Dei* 13 (58)). So since Jews and Muslims do not disagree that God is infinite and is Infinity, they confess with Christians that God is not of a plural *nature*. And from this profession, thinks Nicholas, they can be led to see that in God threeness and oneness coincide, so that God is beyond any such *numerical* distinction. Nicholas next proceeds to the step of maintaining that God is *non-numerically* three and *non-numerically* one (*De visione Dei* 17 (77–8); *De pace fidei* 8 (23)), so that the ordinary concept of God's Oneness is infinitely distant from the true name of God (*De docta ignorantia* I, 24 (77)), who is ineffable. For in God plurality coincides with singularity, as could not happen if the plurality were numerical. Even Augustine, observes Nicholas, recognized that when you begin to number the Trinity, you depart from the truth (I, 19 (57)).[8] And Nicholas is certainly aware of the fact that Plato distinguished Ideal numbers from arithmetical numbers, the former not being numerical (see Aristotle, *Metaphysics* M.6, M.8).

---

8. Augustine makes this point generally throughout his *De Trinitate* (On the Trinity).

So although in and of himself – as Infinity – God is not Father or Son or Holy Spirit, we may legitimately symbolize him as Father, Son and Holy Spirit (*De docta ignorantia* I, 26 (87)). And this symbolism – once rightly understood to be a symbolism – will not scandalize either Jews or Muslims. Indeed, the Old Testament prophet Isaiah conveys to us God's words: "Shall not I that make others to bring forth children, myself bring forth?" (Isaiah 66:9, Douay translation). So divine begottenness and sonship are not notions inherently foreign to Judaism. Similarly, Muslims speak of God's having a word and a soul. But, notes Nicholas, whatever God *has* he *is*. So Muslims, too, speak of God in plural ways and do not deny non-numerical fecundity to be present in God. Thus, the one God's trinity may be spoken of in various ways. God is Father, Son and Holy Spirit. He is Oneness, Equality-of-Oneness and the Union of Oneness and Equality-of-Oneness. He is Loving Love, Lovable Love and the Union of Loving Love and Lovable Love. He is the Absolute Possibility-of-being-made, the Absolute Power-to-make and the Absolute Union of both. And so on. (See Hopkins 2003.)

UNION WITH GOD

Even if God cannot be cognized, he can be encountered: encountered mystically. The force of the word 'mystical' usually serves to indicate that the divine–human encounter takes place beyond the senses, the imagination, the intellect, so that the one who encounters God is at that moment no longer conscious of himself as a self, is no longer even forming a concept of God. But unlike Pseudo-Dionysius and Hugh of Balma before him (see Hopkins 2002), Nicholas does not allow that the mystical approach to God is one that occurs blindly, so to speak, and beyond all conceptualization, be it only a conceptual befigurement. Nicholas himself sought to have a mystical encounter with God; but it was not granted to him, he confides (*De visione dei* 17 (80)). Still, as he theorizes about such an encounter, he supposes that during its occurrence one will experience rapture, together with a sense of being enveloped by love, and that one will be aware that he is encountering God. Nicholas steers clear both of Meister Eckhart's assertion that in the mystical union the believer is "transubstantiated into God" and of Balma's assertion that the mystic is "transformed into God". For these notions are incompatible with Nicholas' claim that *in unione mystica* the believer can and does cognitively distinguish himself from God.

Different from mystical union is the phenomenon that Nicholas refers to as deification (*deificatio, theosis*) or as sonship (*filiatio*). This notion derives from John 1:12: "But as many as received Him [i.e. Christ], to them gave He the power to become sons of God, even to them that believe on His name". The idea here is that each believer in God becomes a son of God, even as Christ is *the* Son of God. Sonship begins in this lifetime with one's conversion; but it becomes perfected only in the next lifetime. Nicholas' use of the term 'deification' can be misleading, as can his use of the term 'absorbed' in *De docta ignorantia*: "Be aware that as someone's flesh is progressively and gradually mortified by faith, he progressively ascends to oneness with Christ, so that he is *absorbed into Christ* by a deep union – to the extent that this is possible on [this pilgrim's] pathway" (III, 11 (252); emphasis added). Now, the absorption and deification here being spoken of are absorption and transformation not into *Christ* but into Christ's *image* (III, 11 (253)). Such transformation is progressive, and it constitutes a *perfecting* of human nature rather than a *replacing* of human nature by the divine nature. Whereas if one experiences mystical union, he experiences it in this present lifetime, the perfection of sonship is found only in the future life. This perfection is an intellectual perfection in which God, although not attained as he is, nevertheless will be

> seen, in the pureness of our intellectual spirit, without any bedarkening sensory image. And this vision is clear to the intellect and is 'Face-to-face'. Since this mode of the manifestation of Absolute Truth is the ultimate, vital happiness of an intellect that is thus enjoying Truth, it is God, without whom the intellect cannot be happy.
>
> (*De filiatione Dei* [On being a son of God] III (62))

So in himself God is not knowable by us; rather, we know only a participated mode of God, who himself is above all mode. In the perfection of sonship a believer's intellect knows – both about God and about all things – as much as *it* can know, given that not all human intellects have the same range of knowledge. In sonship's future state of perfection the intellect (says Nicholas) *is* in a certain sense God; for it will then have become transformed perfectly into God's image.

FAITH AND REASON

Strong Cusan statements that de-emphasize the role of reason

Nicholas sometimes so accentuates the notion of faith that his doing so tends to downplay the role of reason. A prime example of this fact is found in his Sermon CCLXVIII (18), where he speaks of faith as vanquishing reason and where he goes as far as to assert: "it is necessary that reason die". For when a believer believes that after death he will one day be resurrected and live forever afterwards, he believes a proposition that has no basis either in experience or in rational demonstration. Thus, when Abraham believed that if he sacrificed Isaac he would receive him again from the dead (according to Hebrews 11), he believed what (from a purely human point of view) amounts to an impossibility. Yet, judges Nicholas, with God all things are possible (Matthew 19:26), so that all things are also possible for one who believes in God (Mark 9:23), since faith makes the impossible possible (Sermon CLXXXVI (21)). Two further Cusan statements seem also to minimize reason's role in religion: (i) God "is apprehended only where persuasive considerations cease and faith appears" (*De docta ignorantia* III, 11 (245)), and (ii) "where reason founders … faith bridges the gap" (Sermon IV (9)). Furthermore, "the Catholic faith teaches that God is believed in without proof and without evidentness" (Sermon IV (9)). Accordingly, true faith is *strong* faith: faith that dispels all doubt, faith that does not demand guarantees, faith that exalts the teachings of the Scriptures and of Christ above the teachings of the philosophers (Sermons CLXXXVI (9), CLXXXVII (16)).

Strong Cusan statements that emphasize the role of reason

On the other hand, Nicholas sometimes so accentuates the role of reason that reason seems indispensable to founding and buttressing faith. "The basis of faith", he writes, "is the fact that God exists" (Sermon IV (22)). And he gives *a priori* arguments to evidence God's existence, arguments such as those already examined and such as the following additional one:

> Since whatever things the perceptible world contains are finite, they cannot exist of themselves. For the finite can exist in a way different from the way it does exist; and so, its *being* is not eternity, which cannot exist in a way other than it does. Nor is [the world's *being*] infinity or absolute necessity. And so, if that which is not eternity itself were to exist from itself, it would exist before it existed – [something impossible]. Thus, then, we come, necessarily, to a Beginning of all finite things – [a Beginning] which is infinite …, etc.
>
> (Sermon CLXXXVII (2))

Elsewhere, Nicholas reminds us that that which is altogether unknown cannot be loved (Sermon CCLXXXVI (8)),[9] a reminder that implies some present 'knowledge by acquaintance', or, at least, a knowledge *that* God exists. Moreover, Nicholas speaks of faith as correlated with the faculty of intellect or of reason (Sermon IV (1)),[10] so that where there is no intellect (as in infants and animals) there is no faith (Sermon CLXXXVI (11)), because there is no understanding. Indeed, "to believe is to think with assent" (Sermon CLXXXIX (19)),[11] a statement that implies the intelligibility of faith.

---

9. This point is borrowed from Augustine's *De Trinitate* 8.4.6 (*PL* 42:951).

10. This point is borrowed from Hugo of Strassburg's *Compendium theologicae veritatis* (A compendium of theological truth), book V, ch. 18. See *S. Bonaventurae opera omnia*, A. C. Peltier (ed.) (Paris: Vivès, 1866), vol. 8. (Peltier wrongly ascribes Hugo's work to Bonaventure.)

11. This point is taken from Augustine's *De praedestinatione sanctorum* (On the predestination of the saints) 2.5 (*PL* 44:963).

Strong Cusan statements that balance the roles of faith and reason

In spite of Nicholas' strong assertions that seem sometimes to emphasize the priority of faith over reason and at other times to emphasize the priority of reason over faith, his overall viewpoint balances the relationship between these two approaches to God. And his viewpoint implicitly distinguishes three different senses of 'faith': faith as the act-of-believing (we may call it *saving* faith); faith as the content of belief (we may call it *propositional* faith); and faith as a body of belief, as the extended content of belief (we may call it *systematic* faith). Saving faith involves trust (*fiducia*): the believer trusts God, entrusts his life to God, believes *in* God (rather than merely believing that God exists). Propositional faith has to do with assent to the truth of a religious doctrine on the basis of an authority, as when on the authority of the book of Genesis or of Moses or of Christ one believes that the world was *created* and is not eternal. Systematic faith is illustrated by the meaning of expressions such as 'the Jewish faith', 'the Catholic faith', 'the Muslim faith'. With regard to propositional and systematic faith, Nicholas uses the expression "to know by faith", or "the knowledge of faith" (Sermon CLXXXVI (4)). Thereby he suggests that doctrinal belief on the basis of an authority puts one into contact with truth, given that the authority is reliable. But knowledge by faith is different from knowledge in the ordinary sense, even as Job's exclamation "I know that my Redeemer liveth" (Job 19:25) differs from the empirical knowledge that (according to the account) was the product of Thomas' having been summoned to place his hand in the risen Christ's side and to place his finger into the imprint of the nails in Christ's hands (John 21:24–9).

The crux of Nicholas' doctrine of the relationship between faith and reason is the same as it was for Augustine and for Anselm. For Nicholas' doctrine is triangulated coordinately with the twofold motto "Unless you believe, you will not understand" (Isaiah 7:9, in the Old Latin Version)[12] and, tacitly, "Unless to some extent you understand, you cannot believe" (because to believe is to think with assent, and because one cannot assent to that which makes no sense to one at all). This balancing of faith and reason is in tune with the Apostle Peter's instruction to the believer to "be ready always to give an answer to every man that asketh you a reason of the hope that is in you" (1 Peter 3:15). And it is in contrast to Søren Kierkegaard's later notions that "faith begins precisely there where thinking leaves off" (Kierkegaard 1941: 78) and that the deepest faith is characterized as "belief by virtue of the absurd" (*ibid.: passim*) (*see* Vol. 4, Ch. 13, "Søren Kierkegaard").

---

12. We must keep in mind that Augustine prescribed not only 'Believe in order to understand' but also 'Understand in order to believe'. See Sermon 43 (7.9) (*PL* 38:258).

CONCLUSION

The historical challenge of Nicholas' philosophy of religion lies in our being careful neither to overemphasize nor to underemphasize its modernity. *One under-emphasizes the modernity* if one rests content with starkly contrasting it with such modern thinkers as Kierkegaard, in the way that we have just done. For one must also note the proleptic parallels with a thinker such as Gottfried Wilhelm Leibniz (*see* Vol. 3, Ch. 13), adumbrations of whom we discern in a bevy of Cusan doctrines: for example the Cusan doctrine of (i) the identity of indiscernibles (*De ludo globi* [The bowling game] I (6)); (ii) the concreated power of rational judgement; (iii) the maximal perfection of the universe (which is as perfect as *it* can be); (iv) the infinite divisibility (in principle) of matter; (v) the surmising character of empirical judgements; (vi) the endorsement of the principle of sufficient reason (*De sapientia* II (35); *De beryllo* [On (intellectual) eyeglasses] 51); (vii) the use of mathematics to elucidate theological doctrines; (viii) the recognition that in the domain of objects that admit of being greater and lesser, we never arrive at a maximum or a minimum; (ix) the view that at infinity maximum and minimum coincide; (x) the claim that there is nothing in the intellect that was not first in the senses – nothing except the intellect itself. On the other hand, *one overemphasizes the modernity* of Cusa's philosophy (and of his philosophy of religion, in particular) if one neglects to mention that the theme of *nulla proportio* is not new with him but is drawn from Hugo of Strassburg (*Compendium theologicae veritatis*, book I, chapter 16), even as the theme of learned ignorance is appropriated from Pseudo-Dionysius.

What is new with Nicholas is not so much the themes themselves as the systematization of the themes, together with an extended application of them. A modern-day comparison might be helpful. Sigmund Freud neither discovered the unconscious nor was the first to introduce the concept of the unconscious. Nicolai Hartmann formulated this concept decades before Freud. Yet, that which Freud accomplished – that which links his name forever to the concept of the unconscious – consists in his having expanded the concept into a theory and then having placed that theory into an even more general theory, namely, a theory of human personality. In a remarkably similar way, the reason that Nicholas of Cusa's name will be forever associated with the concepts of *docta ignorantia, nulla proportio* and *coincidentia oppositorum* is that this fifteenth-century philosopher-theologian coherently worked an expanded version of these notions into a more general scheme that situated his philosophy of religion at the threshold of modernity. He was poised to step across that threshold when he intoned: "How will You, [O God], give Yourself to me unless You also *give me to myself*?" (*De visione Dei* 7 (26)). And he peered farther into the already looming modernity when he spoke of God's Paradise as surrounded by a *wall of absurdity* (12 (50)) – that is, by the wall of the coincidence of creating with being created – and when he spoke, in Hegelian fashion, of God as the Being of being and the *Not-being of not-being*

(Proposition V of the propositions appended to *De li non aliud*). Surely, then, if Cusa's God is "beyond the coincidence of contradictories", he is also, in the words of Paul Tillich, 'the God beyond the God of theism'.

FURTHER READING

Bellitto, C., T. Izbicki & G. Christianson (eds) 2004. *Introducing Nicholas of Cusa: A Guide to a Renaissance Man*. New York: Paulist Press.

Casarella, P. 2006. *Cusanus: The Legacy of Learned Ignorance*. Washington, DC: Catholic University of America Press.

Hopkins, J. (trans.) 2008. *Nicholas of Cusa's Didactic Sermons: A Selection*. Loveland, CO: Arthur J. Banning Press.

Kremer, K. 1999. *Nikolaus von Kues (1401–1464): Einer der größten Deutschen des 15. Jahrhunderts*. Trier: Paulinus. Published in English as *Nicholas of Cusa (1401–1464): One of the Greatest Germans of the Fifteenth Century*, F. Kann & H.-J. Kann (trans.) (Trier: Paulinus-Verlag, 2002).

Kremer, K. 2004. *Praegustatio naturalis sapientiae: Gott suchen mit Nikolaus von Kues*. Münster: Aschendorff.

Miller, C. 2003. *Reading Cusanus: Metaphor and Dialectic in a Conjectural Universe*. Washington, DC: Catholic University of America Press.

Santinello, G. 1987. *Introduzione a Niccolò Cusano*, 2nd edn. Bari: Editori Laterza.

Vansteenberghe, E. 1920. *Le Cardinal Nicolas de Cues (1401–1464): L'action – la pensée*. Paris. Reprinted (Frankfurt: Minerva, 1963).

On FAITH see also Chs 6, 12, 16; Vol. 1, Ch. 13; Vol. 3, Ch. 8; Vol. 4, Ch. 8, 10, 13; Vol. 5, Chs 7, 18. On KNOWLEDGE see also Ch. 11; Vol. 1, Ch. 6. On REASON see also Chs 10, 11, 12, 16; Vol. 3, Chs 8, 12, 16, 21; Vol. 4, Chs 4, 8.

19

ERASMUS OF ROTTERDAM

James McConica

The subject of this chapter, Erasmus of Rotterdam (*c.*1467–1536), was an anomaly in his own time, and remains so even today in the history of European thought. Most of Erasmus' important legacy is unacknowledged, as it was absorbed into classical and biblical scholarship, merged into the common literary heritage of the West, or was simply opaque to adherents of the theological and philosophical schools that developed in the immediate aftermath of the Reformation. Nevertheless, the growth of ecumenical dialogue, like the widespread interest in rhetorical expressions of religious conviction and sentiment, has led inevitably in our time to a reappraisal of the place of Erasmus in our culture. This chapter will deal briefly with his origins and the evidence for his early intellectual formation, then consider his humanism, the stated agenda of his life work, and the personal blend of religious and philosophical influences that found expression in a highly idiosyncratic if enduring understanding of the legacy of the Gospels.

ORIGINS AND EARLY FORMATION

Erasmus was born in Rotterdam in the late 1460s (Augustijn 1991: 21–4; Tracy 1996: 17–24). Little is known of him with certainty before his ordination to the priesthood in 1492. He was illegitimate, born probably into an extended family of some means, and while the exact date of his birth remains a subject of debate, *c.*1467 is widely accepted.

He and his brother Pieter (possibly a half-brother) were schooled in Gouda and later, about 1475, in Deventer at the school of the chapter of Saint-Lebuin, a place of high reputation. Later the brothers, orphaned by now, lived in a poor students' hostel run at 's-Hertogenbosch by the Brethren of the Common Life, whose pietism may be assumed to have influenced Erasmus to at least some degree, although he was later capable of excoriating criticism of the Brethren themselves. At any rate, first his older brother, Pieter, and in 1487 Erasmus himself, joined the Canons Regular of Saint Augustine, Pieter at Sion, near Delft, and Erasmus at Steyn, near Gouda.

It is from this period that we have the first direct evidence of his personal life, fragmentary as it is: some thirty personal letters, youthful poems in the classical mode and one finished work provide information sometimes supplemented by later references from his pen. It is clear that he had consciously rejected the dominant intellectual preoccupations of the century into which he was born, at least in so far as they were propagated in the universities and theological schools. While his own accounts are rarely to be taken at face value as he was frequently given to reshaping his own experiences to suit some temporary necessity, Erasmus' exchanges with his early correspondents make it clear that within the Augustinian cloister he was not alone in the rejection of late medieval scholasticism in favour of devotion to the pursuit of classical letters according to the tenets of the Italian humanist masters.

His was not a metaphysical mind. In his writings at least he paid scant attention to the numinous and, unlike some humanists of his generation, he opposed entirely the lure of the cabbala and indeed any form of esoteric learning. For him 'religion' meant the scriptural teachings of western Christianity. Judaism he regarded as a religion now supplanted by the Christian revelation. As for Islam, his views are notable for his insistence that the desirable conversion of the Muslim world must be achieved not by crusades and aggression, but only by the persuasive evidence of a reformed Christendom, peaceful, just and harmonious. His focus was on the need to achieve exactly that state of affairs in place of the contentious, often violent society of his day. His famous summary, *Pax et unanimitas summa nostrae religionis est* (The sum and substance of our religion is peace and concord)[1] was voiced as a fervent and, at times, bitter criticism of the Christian accomplishment as he saw it. Indeed, Erasmus' affinity with the humanistic priorities of his day is nowhere more evident than in his shunning of the speculative sciences and insistence on the practice of Christian living and the ethical demands of the Gospel (Erasmus 1989: letter 1334, l. 232; O'Malley 1979: 228).

The most informative single document from this early period is his educational manifesto, *Antibarbari* (Against the barbarians; Erasmus 1978). This text reveals a surprising familiarity with the tenets and resources of the movement that began in Italy in the fourteenth century, now generally known as Renaissance humanism. As a piece of sophisticated polemic, it situates him readily in relation to the philosophical movements of the late Middle Ages – the dominant culture of his youthful years – and the aspirations that dominated the rest of his life.

The *Antibarbari* was published in 1520 by the Froben Press in Basle, but by his own account its origins go back to the time when he first entered the monastery (Tracy 1996: 24ff.). While the published text was revised by Erasmus to supplant unofficial

---

1. This is from the preface to his 1523 edition of the writings of Hilary of Poitiers.

versions in circulation, we may reasonably understand it as an accurate representation of at least his first settled convictions about Christian humanism. It is a vigorous defence of the classical heritage – 'pagan learning' – against the attacks of religious fundamentalists. The work also reveals what proved to be his ruling conviction: that while the Christian revelation came into being in a pagan world with which it was in many ways in conflict, it also derived from that same world the instruments of culture, language and learning through which the Christian message was expressed, organized and proclaimed to others. Why, then, should not the wholesome elements in that legacy be adopted – 'baptized' so to speak – for the benefit of all?

ERASMUS' HUMANISM

The intellectual culture that gained the name 'Renaissance humanism' was never absent from the Christian West, but during the heyday of medieval scholasticism the philosophical mainstream, especially in the universities, rejected it. 'Humanists' revered the magisterial authors of classical Greece and Rome, and sought to read the foundational texts of the Christian era as well in light of that learning, while applying to them the same philological disciplines that were needed to comprehend the texts of the classics. As those texts revealed the ethos and morality of the classical *polis*, so those city-states of classical antiquity might inspire, as they fancied, a refashioned and revitalized Christian Europe.

Humanism was not a philosophy as such, nor did it oppose the Christian revelation to the fruits of pagan learning. It must, however, be said that the humanist community of Erasmus' day was in full reaction against the speculative sciences of the medieval university, rooted as they were in dialectic derived from the reception of Aristotelian logic. Erasmus saw that dominant university culture as one of the leading causes of Christian disunity and, what was worse, a perversion of the true aim of Christian philosophy, namely, to call men and women to a Christian life and to the active betterment of civil society. It follows from this that no systematic exposition of his philosophy of religion is to be expected from his own pen, but much can be inferred from a close reading of his works.

It is possible to discern even from Erasmus' earliest writings a distinctive commitment to the prospect of replacing the clerically dominated religious culture of the past with a lay oriented, scripturally informed Christian polity, one in which the informed citizen would be as much concerned with furthering the common good in this life as with securing eternal salvation in the next.

Thus we find in *Antibarbari* a tenet of his humanism more radical than anything mentioned to date. Erasmus' spokesman in the piece, a youthful friend named Jacob Batt, claims that the achievements of the pagans were more than admirable in themselves, or even as the foundation of European science and culture. Properly understood, they were nothing less than integral to the divine plan for the redemption of all humanity.

In law, in philosophy, how the ancients labored! Why did all this happen? So that we on our arrival could hold them in contempt? Was it not rather that the best religion should be adorned and supported by the finest studies? ... Many of the philosophers wore out their lives and their brains in seeking the highest good, but the real highest good, the perfect gift, was reserved by Christ for his own time. However, he did not intend all the rest to be useless and done to no purpose.

(Erasmus 1978: 60)

ERASMUS' REFORMING AGENDA

In all of this Erasmus was invoking the views of such early masters as Jerome and Augustine (*see* Vol. 1, Ch. 18), advocates in various ways of cleansing the legacy of antiquity to turn its learning to the service of Christendom. It was, however, to Augustine's *De doctrina Christiana* (On Christian doctrine) that Erasmus most clearly referred, linking the two worlds of the *doctus orator* of Quintilian and Cicero with that of the early Christian thinkers. Augustine's purpose was to build a bridge between the Ciceronian ideals of civil virtue and those of Christianity, and it was from that precedent that Erasmus developed his own agenda.

That agenda was to return to the theological culture of the world into which the Christian revelation was born, the 'ancient theology' or *vetus theologia*, formed by the Fathers of the Church within the grammatical and rhetorical legacy of Quintilian and Cicero. His early educational treatises[2] announce a mission to reawaken knowledge not only of the great texts of classical antiquity but those also of Scripture and the masters of the patristic era: the fabric of a true Christian culture. He blamed the scholastic enterprise on the one hand for evacuating the Christian message of its interior call to holiness in favour of mere intellectual speculation, and on the other for leaving the laity with arid, legalistic pieties where they might have been inspired with devotion to the person of Christ as found in Scripture.

Erasmus' hope was to revitalize the Christian world through a return to the methods of the 'ancient theology'. Where formerly, as he saw it, the reception of Aristotle in the West had engendered the scholastic debates and chronic argumentativeness that stifled knowledge of Scripture and true devotion, the 'ancient theology' would return to theological reflection in the manner of the Fathers, devout reflection grounded on respect for the integrity of the sacred text, while the high mysteries of the faith would be sought in allegory and poetry. Unlike the technical refinements of the scholastics, such a theology would cultivate clarity

---

2. These treatises were *Adagiorum collectanea* (Gathering of adages) of 1500; *De ratione studii* (On the method of study) and *De copia verborum ac rerum* (Foundations of the abundant style), both of 1512.

and refinement of style, be accessible to the non-specialist and be able to reach the far-flung and influential educated laity. A new evangelism should result: to Erasmus, it was essential that the Christian orator – priest, statesman or any devout baptized Christian – should be enabled to move his listeners to action, to conviction, in the following of Christ (McConica 1991: 20–23; Tracy 1996: 25–6).

In his rejection of the influence of Aristotle, as he described it, there was also a degree of receptiveness to the traditions of Platonism. These were derived less from Platonic texts directly than from the Fathers of the Church, notably from Origen (*see* Vol. 1, Ch. 14). In his *Enchiridion militis Christiani* (Handbook of the Christian soldier) dating from 1501 and published in 1503, Origen's influence is pervasive, notably in the work's moral optimism and doctrine of human nature. This 'Handbook', an amalgam – by no means mature or consistent – of Christian and pagan influences, provides nonetheless a revealing testimonial to the ethical bent and laicism of its author (Erasmus 1988). The same strain appears in his most famous work, the *Moriae encomium* (Praise of folly) of 1511, which Erasmus himself declared to be, like the *Enchiridion*, about the pattern of the Christian life, and in which the praise of Christian ecstasy is the final theme (Screech 1980: ch. 5; McConica 1991: ch. 6).

For Erasmus, then, the Christian revelation was definitive as the basis of religion. The further question, 'How is this God known?' leads us to his hermeneutic, where his educational formation at once enters the picture.

THE ANIMATING, ENLIGHTENING *LOGOS*

God is known through sacred Scripture, to improving the texts of which Erasmus devoted a great part of his life. Scripture in turn is known best through the optic of the culture of antiquity into which it was revealed, since the same eternal Spirit to which we owe our sacred writings fosters and informs the best of pagan learning and literature. God is known, then, from the revelation of God in Christ through the informed study of sacred Scripture, through the tutelage of the Holy Spirit and finally, from tradition.

The year 1515 may be said to mark the watershed between Erasmus' formative years in educational and literary studies, and the enterprise for which those studies were effectively a propaedeutic: the revision of the received text of the New Testament, the Vulgate. That enterprise led him to the work of Jerome and the development of the Greek text, all of which finally bore fruit in the *Novum instrumentum* (New testament) published by Froben in 1516. For the remainder of his life he worked at the revision of that text, including his all-important annotations on the Vulgate New Testament and his new Latin version. He had also to respond to the multitude of controversies that ensued, further complicated by the appearance of Martin Luther. For present purposes we shall focus on Erasmus' understanding of the New Testament and what we can learn from it about his way of proceeding in theology.[3]

Key to any understanding of Erasmus' conception of the Bible is a prefatory piece, *Paraclesis*,[4] a Greek term meaning a summons or exhortation. Like *Antibarbari*, it too was a manifesto, a striking assertion of the importance of sacred Scripture as a guide to life, and to the acquisition of the *philosophia Christi*. This latter term was of patristic origin, and indicates a love of the wisdom (*sophia*) that is incarnate in Christ. Such love alone has the power to transform our lives, and it is as accessible to the simple as to the educated. His conviction about the power of Scripture to make Christ present is at times almost mystical:

> And He [Christ Himself], since He promised to be with us all days, even unto the consummation of the world, stands forth especially in this literature, in which He lives for us even at this time, breathes and speaks. I should say almost more effectively than when He dwelt among men. (Olin 1987: 105)

Again, speaking of the reverence due to the Bible as compared with that given to popular religious images, he comments:

> The latter represents only the form of the body – if indeed it represents anything of Him – but these writings bring you the living image of His holy mind and the speaking, healing, dying, rising, Christ Himself, and thus they render Him so fully present that you would see less if you gazed upon Him with your very eyes. (*Ibid.*: 108)

Helpful insight into Erasmus' distinctive understanding of the role of Scripture comes from his controversial revision of the opening of the Gospel of John in the Vulgate text: "In the beginning was the Word". Erasmus' Latin rendering of the Greek text at John 1:1 replaced '*In principio erat verbum*' with '*In principio erat sermo*', where the Latin word for discourse bore an entirely different connotation from that of *verbum*, 'word'. He was here translating the Greek noun, *logos*, a term that he argued evoked an active, creative reality that is the second, eternal person of the Trinitarian Godhead, rather than the static concept contained in *verbum*. The reality, *logos*, is that which is incarnate in the person of Jesus of Nazareth, who as a living individual could be seen as the discourse of God. It is a daring and dynamic way of envisaging the ongoing revelation of God in Christ, a revelation that continues in the risen Christ after the crucifixion and resurrection.

---

3. For a summary account of Erasmus' approach to the New Testament, see McConica (1991: 34ff.).
4. See the text in Olin (1987).

Again, Erasmus' conflict with Luther is instructive. In their debate he reveals much about his conception of the part played by the Christian Scriptures in the ongoing revelation of God, and we can discover as well an implicit ontological foundation for his hermeneutic (McConica 1969).

The early contacts between the two men, who were separated by a generation, were positive if somewhat tentative on both sides, given that they had much in common in their concern about the state of Christendom. Both rejected scholasticism, both turned to the New Testament as the foundational text of any reform programme, both urged an interior devotion to the Jesus of the Gospels and condemned religious formalism, both turned to the princes to take the needed reform in hand. Their approaches, however, were quite different, as events proved.

The collision came through a variety of circumstances[5] and the chosen battleground was over freedom of the will, an issue of critical importance to Erasmus' programme for reform. We have seen that Erasmus' intellectual formation was humanistic. That of Luther was scholastic. Erasmus initiated the debate in a reply to Luther's response to the bull of Leo X, *Exsurge domine* (Arise O Lord; 15 June 1520), rejecting Luther's views. Article 36 of the bull proclaimed the freedom of the human will, and Luther in turn in his *Assertio omnium articulorum Martini Lutheri per bullam Leonis X novissimam damnatorum*[6] emphatically reasserted all of the views that had been condemned in the bull, including those in Article 36. He thus repudiated the received Catholic teaching that human beings, by their own freely willed deeds, performed in a proper relationship to divine grace, might contribute to their own salvation.

Erasmus now rose to defend the teaching of the bull with his treatise, *De libero arbitrio* (A discussion of free will) of 1524. Given the approach Erasmus took to all religious matters, a systematic doctrinal exposition was scarcely to be expected, although it was second nature to Luther. Luther's reply, *De servo arbitrio* (On the enslaved will) of 1525 repudiated Erasmus' argumentative approach with point-by-point rebuttal. Persuaded by the violence of his reply that Luther was determined to disrupt Christendom and that attempts at reasoned discussion were useless, Erasmus then composed a lengthy response, the *Hyperaspistes distribae adversus ... Martini Lutheri*,[7] which appeared in stages over the following year.

Without entering into the details of the debate, it provides us with a valuable opportunity to study the way in which Erasmus went about theological enquiry and exposition. From his earliest misgivings about Luther, Erasmus exhibited little interest in doctrinal issues. In that arena, his typical attitude is that controversial points should be referred to the wise and learned, and that nothing should

---

5. See, for example, the account in Augustijn (1991: chs 10, 11).
6. 'Assertion of all the articles of Martin Luther that were quite recently condemned by a bull of Leo X', September 1520. See Erasmus (1999).
7. 'A warrior shielding a discussion of free will against the enslaved will by Martin Luther'; see Erasmus (1999, 2000).

be done in haste. Likewise, writing to princes and other authorities touched by the growing dispute, Erasmus typically urged caution, consultation and negotiation rather than confrontation. What concerned him from the start was Luther's aggressive assertion of his views and evident indifference to causing dissension in the Christian commonweal.

Was this the posture of an irresolute or dissembling actor in the drama? Many thought so, among them Luther himself. Yet the principle of accommodation and debate was deeply rooted in Erasmus' conception of the way in which the Christian community is instructed by divine providence.

It should be recalled that long before Luther appeared on the scene, Erasmus included among his objections to the scholastics their adoption of dialectic and disputation as the necessary procedures in theological enquiry. His attitude is clear in a notable letter to Martin Dorp in May 1515, in which he defends his satires in the *Moriae encomium*, particularly with respect to resentments among the theologians of the university.

> What can Christ have in common with Aristotle? What have these quibbling sophistries to do with the mysteries of eternal wisdom? What is the purpose of these labyrinthine *quaestiones*, of which so many are pointless, so many really harmful, if for no other reason, as a source of strife and contention? (Erasmus 1976: letter 337, ll. 435–9)

So also with Luther: he is a source of dissension. At all costs peace and concord – *pax et concordia* – must be maintained among Christians so that truth will eventually emerge. Concord is a distinguishing trait of the Christian community, formed by the action of Christ through the Holy Spirit. As is implied in the quotation above from his preface to the edition of Hilary, peace and unanimity are inseparable.[8] By 1526, when Erasmus abandoned any hope of fruitful discussion with Luther, his final objections are not to any of Luther's teachings as such, but to his 'arrogant, impudent, seditious temperament' productive only of ruinous discord, an attitude that must call into question his claim to be a true reformer (McConica 1969: 80).

In contrast to Luther, Erasmus held that Christians do not share in the headship of Christ as individuals; rather, as sharers in common of baptism and the other sacraments they are made one among themselves by the Holy Spirit. While the teaching authority of the Church is associated with the bishops in particular, so bishops must also be acquainted with the mind of the faithful, as their first responsibilities are pastoral. This is true equally of the successors of Peter. Whenever Erasmus turns to questions of faith, the term that repeatedly recurs is 'consensus'. That term is the key to understanding his entire outlook on the history and fate of Christendom.

---

8. See note 1.

In the many educational works of Erasmus, intimately associated with his desire to revive the culture of antiquity, there is a Stoic belief in a universal order of nature that is informed and created by the *logos*. As such, it is intrinsically intelligible and spontaneous (McConica 1969: 89ff.). It is also intrinsically in harmony with the Christian intellect, since in baptism and the sacraments the individual receives the gift of the *logos* in Christ. The deeper importance of Erasmus' insistence on *sermo* rather than *verbum* in the introduction to the Gospel of John is now apparent.

In explaining his decision, he drew on Augustine's view that the Father generated the Word by interior deliberation: *Sermo* is the Word in eternal dialogue (McConica 1969: 90). The importance of this view for exposition of the text of Scripture is apparent: within the letter is the spiritual essence of the *logos*, the inner meaning emanating from the Incarnate Word. In Scripture we learn about the highest mystery of all, the secret plan of God for all creation, and the voice of Scripture is the voice of Christ himself. Thus, for a 'true' (i.e. old) theology there is no organizing principle. The only organizing principle is the sacred text itself. Dialectical refinements of doctrine and the constructions of a systematic theology are mistaken responses to the tuition of the Spirit. What is needed is the penetration of divine mystery contained in Scripture by theological allegory, and the proclamation of the Word in a fashion that will move the hearts and mould the convictions of men and women everywhere.

In matters of doubt, Erasmus invokes the rule of the Fathers themselves. Given that the minds of individuals are instructed by the Spirit in common with those of other Christians, dialogue with those who have the necessary learning (biblical languages and a grasp of the original texts is fundamental) should lead to a 'consensus of all' (*consensus omnium*; McConica 1969: 93–6). Peace too, is essential to preserve the community of discourse within which the Holy Spirit works. As a reflection of the harmony of the Holy Trinity, peace is a sign of truth in and of itself.

Erasmus' methodology came from the traditions of patristic exegesis, from the disciplines of the classical grammarians and from Stoic notions of the intelligible harmony of all creation. While this anchored his views strongly in tradition (to him, as to others, the scholastics were the 'modernists'), his view of the Church was dynamic. As a community of belief nourished by the sacraments and animated by the Holy Spirit, it develops through time. Peace, however, is essential if the Church so considered is to avoid rupture through dissension; without peace, the Spirit cannot function and the problems of faith must remain unsolved. In this world, the consent and affirmation of all – *consensus omnium* – is the very principle of intelligibility (McConica 1969: 89–99).

ERASMUS' INFLUENCE

This highly idiosyncratic view won few adherents in Erasmus' lifetime, and never became a significant element in the reformation debate.[9] Doctrinal issues and the overriding question of ecclesiastical authority swamped the accommodating, consensual approaches of the Dutch humanist on both sides of the debate. Where he did leave his mark, however, was in the resolute use of the humanistic method with respect both to the texts of classical antiquity and those of the Bible and early Church, including the writings of the Fathers. His success in placing texts emanating from the origins of Christianity into their historical context displaced the traditional approaches to the Bible embodied in the *Glossa ordinaria* and in like medieval commentaries, and effectively initiated a wholly new era of biblical scholarship.

The appearance of the New Testament with Erasmus' annotations and accompanied by a Greek text in itself forever changed the nature of biblical scholarship. Of itself it would have ensured that followers of Erasmus were to be found on all sides of the reformation debate, and the fact that Luther used it ensured its celebrity, despite his differing exegetical strategies. In point of fact, as the base text for Robert Estienne's Greek Testament (Paris, 1550) it influenced strongly that of Théodore de Bèze and underlay both the King James Version and the Elzevir Greek Testament of 1633, which proclaimed it the 'received text'. As the foundation of Protestant biblical scholarship for three centuries it undoubtedly provides the most persuasive testimony to the enduring influence of Erasmus' enterprise.

For a full account it would be necessary to explore as well the history of educational philosophies, of classical scholarship and of international politics in his lifetime. In subsequent centuries, the perception of Europe as a Christian commonweal, the promotion of international peace and concord and of religious irenicism have reflected in every age Erasmus' dedication to his seemingly ill-fated enterprise.

FURTHER READING

Adams, R. 1962. *The Better Part of Valor: More, Erasmus, Colet, and Vives on Humanism, War, and Peace.* Seattle, WA: University of Washington Press.
Boyle, M. 1983. *Rhetoric and Reform: Erasmus' Civil Dispute with Luther.* Cambridge, MA: Harvard University Press.
Chomarat, J. 1981. *Grammaire et rhétorique chez Érasme*, 2 vols. Paris: Belles Lettres.
IJsewijn, J. 1969. "Erasmus *ex Poeta theologus*". In *Scrinium Erasmianum*, J. Coppens (ed.), vol. 1, 378–89. Leiden: Brill.

---

9. There is a comprehensive and well-considered account of Erasmus' influence in the early sixteenth century and subsequently in Augustijn (1991: ch. 15).

Payne, J. 1969. "Toward the Hermeneutics of Erasmus". In *Scrinium Erasmianum*, J. Coppens (ed.), vol. 1, 13–49. Leiden: Brill.

Rummel, E. 1989. *Erasmus and His Catholic Critics*, 2 vols. Nieuwkoop: De Graaf.

Schoeck, R. 1990. *Erasmus of Europe: The Making of a Humanist, 1467–1500*. Edinburgh: Edinburgh University Press.

Schoeck, R. 1993. *Erasmus of Europe: The Prince of Humanists, 1501–1536*. Edinburgh: Edinburgh University Press.

Tracy, J. 1972. *Erasmus, The Growth of a Mind*. Geneva: Droz.

Woodward, W. 1904. *Desiderius Erasmus, Concerning the Aim and Method of Education*. Cambridge: Cambridge University Press.

On FREE WILL see also Chs 2, 7, 9; Vol. 1, Ch. 18; Vol. 3, Chs 9, 15; Vol. 5, Ch. 22. On HUMANISM see also Ch. 19; Vol. 3, Chs 5, 16; Vol. 5, Ch. 6. On LOGOS see also Ch. 19; Vol. 1, Chs 9, 11, 13. On SCRIPTURE see also Vol. 1, Chs 9, 13, 17; Vol. 3, Chs 3, 4, 15; Vol. 4, Ch. 3; Vol. 5, Ch. 12.

CHRONOLOGY

511   Death of Clovis, founder of the Merovingian kingdom in Gaul, widely regarded as the 'father' of France

*c.*525   Death of **Boethius**, executed by King Theodoric on charges of treason.

526   Death of Theodoric the Great, king of the Ostrogoths who conquered Italy.

529   Emperor Justinian closes the Platonic Academy in Athens.

541   Plague of Justinian, the first recorded outbreak of bubonic plague in Europe.

*c.*547   Death of Benedict of Nursia, founder of the Benedictine order and of Western monasticism.

552   Buddhism is introduced into Japan from Korea.

553   Fifth Ecumenical Council, convened in Constantinople with the aim of putting an end to the Nestorian and Monophysite controversies.

*c.*560   Death of Dionysius Exiguus, theologian, mathematician and astronomer who introduced the use of 'Anno Domini' in dating historical events.

565   Death of Justinian I, Byzantine emperor who recovered many of the territories of the western Roman empire, and is noted for his codification of laws known as the Codex Justinianus and the rebuilding of 'Hagia Sophia', the Church of the Holy Wisdom in Constantinople.

570   Death of Gildas, regarded as the earliest British historian for his account of the Roman invasion and Anglo-Saxon conquest of England.

581   Commencement of the Sui dynasty in China, which unified the country after four centuries of fragmentation.

597   Death of Columba, missionary who played a leading role in the conversion of Scotland to Christianity.

604   Death of Pope Gregory I (Gregory the Great), church reformer and founder of the medieval papacy, which exercised both secular and spiritual power.

605   Death of Alexander of Tralles, regarded as the 'most modern' of Byzantine physicians, and author of a twelve-book medical encyclopedia.

632   Death of Muhammad, regarded by Muslims as the last messenger and prophet of God who received various revelations that are recorded in the Qur'an. Following Muhammad's death, Abu Bakr becomes the first caliph, or successor.

636 Death of Isidore of Seville, archbishop who is best known for his encyclopedic work the *Etymologies*, which became one of the most studied works in the Middle Ages.

637 Arab Muslims conquer Jerusalem.

644 Death of Umar, companion of Muhammad and second caliph, under whose reign the Islamic empire became a major power.

649 Death of Emperor T'ai-tsung, dynamic ruler of the Tang dynasty of China.

664 Death of Xuanzang, Buddhist monk and Chinese pilgrim to India, who is best known for his voluminous translations of Buddhist scriptures into Chinese.

673 Death of Yan Liben, leading painter of the early Tang dynasty in China.

680 Sixth Ecumenical Council, held in Constantinople, condemns Monothelitism, according to which there is a single will in Christ.

711–13 Muslims from North Africa invade and conquer the Visigothic kingdom of Spain.

735 Death of Bede the Venerable, Benedictine monk and author of an influential history of the rise of Christianity and the growth of Anglo-Saxon culture in England.

741 Death of Charles Martel ('the Hammer'), Frankish ruler and grandfather of Charlemagne, who stemmed the Muslim expansion into Europe and established a power base for the Carolingian empire.

767 Death of Ibn Ishaq, Arab Muslim historian who wrote the first biography of the prophet Muhammad.

787 Seventh Ecumenical Council, held in Nicaea, declares icons worthy of veneration.

793 First Viking raid in England, on the abbey on the island of Lindisfarne.

800 Celtic monks on the island of Iona begin working on the Book of Kells.

c.800 Birth of **Johannes Scottus Eriugena**, Irish philosopher whose major works were deemed heretical and condemned.

814 Death of Charlemagne, ruler of the Franks, who briefly established a large European empire (excluding England and Scandinavia).

820 Death of Shankara, Hindu ascetic, philosopher and theologian in the Advaita Vedanta School.

833 Death of Al-Mamun, great Islamic patron of philosophy and science who established a library and academy in Baghdad.

839 Death of Egbert, King of Wessex, key agent in the political unification of England.

850 Norse settlers arrive in Iceland.

867 Accession of Basil I inaugurates the Macedonian dynasty of the Byzantine Empire.

869 Death of Cyril, who together with his brother, Methodius, received the title 'apostles to the Slavs' for their mission to the Slavic peoples, which included the invention of a Slavic alphabet based on Greek characters.

870 Death of Al-Bukhari, compiler of a canonical collection reporting the sayings of Muhammad.

c.870 Birth of **al-Farabi**, Islamic philosopher who valued human reason above revelation.

877 Death of **Eriugena**.

879 Death of Rurik, Norman founder of the first Russian state of Novgorod.

891 Death of Photius, patriarch of Constantinople, leading figure in ninth-century Byzantine Renaissance and (regarded by some as) chiefly responsible for the schism between the Eastern and Western Christian churches ('the Photian schism').

899   Death of Alfred, King of Wessex, renowned as a lawmaker and translator of ancient writings.

907–60   Division of China on the fall of the Tang dynasty, inaugurating the period known as the Five Dynasties and Ten Kingdoms.

923   Death of al-Tabari, Islamic scholar who laid the foundations for Koranic studies.

935   Death of al-Ashari, Islamic theologian who founded Islamic scholastic philosophy.

950   Death of **al-Farabi**.

960–79   Sung Taizu, founder of the Sung dynasty, reunites China.

973   Death of Otto the Great, German king who in 962 had become ruler of the Holy Roman Empire.

980   Birth of **Avicenna** (Ibn Sina), pre-eminent Islamic philosopher and scientist, who made important contributions to most of the arts and sciences, including medicine and music.

1001   Leif Eriksson establishes Viking settlement in Vinland.

1033   Birth of **Anselm**, Archbishop of Canterbury, who had one of the greatest minds of the Middle Ages.

1035   Death of Canute, Viking ruler of England, Denmark and Norway.

1037   Death of **Avicenna**.

1039   Death of al-Hassan, major Arab scientist who made contributions to optics, astronomy, physics and the understanding of the atmosphere of the earth.

1040   Macbeth becomes King of Scotland, succeeding Duncan I who was slain in battle.

1048   Death of al-Biruni, Arab scholar who worked in astronomy, physics and geography.

1054   The 'Great Schism' rends the Roman Catholic and Eastern Orthodox churches.

1058   Birth of **al-Ghazali**, Muslim jurist, theologian and mystic.

1066   Norman conquest of England in the Battle of Hastings.

1071   Seljuk Turks defeat Byzantine army at the Battle of Manzikert, signalling the decline of the Byzantine Empire.

1076   Ghana Empire crumbles with the sacking of its capital, Kumbi.
Death of Pi-Cheng, Chinese commoner who invented printing with moveable type.

1079   Birth of **Peter Abelard**, French philosopher and theologian, whose colourful life and love affair with Heloise is recorded in his *Historia calamitatum* (History of my troubles).

1085   Founding of the cathedral school in Lund, Sweden, the oldest school in Scandinavia.

1086   Completion of *Domesday Book*, William the Conqueror's great English census.

1088   The first university in Europe is established at Bologna, Italy.

1090   Birth of **Bernard of Clairvaux**, Cistercian abbot who became one of the most influential figures in Western Christendom of his time.

1099   First Crusade captures Jerusalem.
Death of El Cid, Spanish warrior who led the liberation of Toledo from the Muslims.

1102   King Coloman unites Hungary and Croatia under the Hungarian crown.

1105   Death of Ramanuja, influential Indian theologian.

1109   Death of **Anselm**.

1111   Death of **al-Ghazali**.

1119   Foundation of the Knights Templar.

1123   Death of Omar Khayyám, Persian poet, philosopher, mathematician and astronomer, who developed geometrical techniques for solving algebraic equations, and who devised the most accurate calendar then in existence.

1126   Birth of **Averroes** (Ibn Rushd), Islamic philosopher best known for his commentaries on Aristotle and his defence of the philosophical study of religion.

1135   England slides into civil war and unstable government under King Stephen.

1138   Birth of **Moses Maimonides**, Jewish philosopher, juror and physician, and author of *The Guide of the Perpelexed*.

1142   Death of **Abelard**.

1145   Launch of the Second Crusade in response to the fall of the County of Edessa.

1148   Death of Ari, Icelandic historian and 'father of Icelandic literature'.

1153   Death of **Bernard of Clairvaux**.

1170   Assassination of Thomas Becket, Archbishop of Canterbury, defender of the special privileges of the clergy.

1179   Death of Hildegard of Bingen, author, composer and religious visionary.

1189   Launch of the Third Crusade.

1193   Death of Saladin, Egyptian ruler who captured Jerusalem during the Third Crusade.

c.1193   Birth of Albertus Magnus, German philosopher, bishop and teacher of **Thomas Aquinas**.

1197   Destruction of Nalanda, the great Indian Buddhist educational centre.

1198   Death of **Averroes** (Ibn Rushd).

1200   Annihilation of the Toltec empire by Chichimec warriors.

1204   Fourth Crusade sacks Constantinople and creates the Latin Empire.
Death of **Maimonides**.

1212   Battle of Las Navas de Tolosa begins Christian reconquest of the southern half of the Iberian Peninsula.

c.1214   Birth of **Roger Bacon**, English philosopher widely regarded as the founder of modern experimental science.

1215   King John of England is forced to sign the Magna Carta, a foundational text for constitutional monarchy.

1217   Death of Peter Waldes, founder of the Waldenses religious movement.

1221   Death of Dominic, Spanish churchman who founded the Dominican order, which emphasized scholarship and a universal mission of preaching.

1224/5   Birth of **Thomas Aquinas**, leading figure of medieval scholasticism, who was to become the most influential philosopher of the Roman Catholic Church.

1226   Death of Francis of Assisi, founder of the Franciscan order and one of the most venerated saints in church history.

1227   Death of Genghis Khan, fearsome Mongol ruler who established an empire that stretched from Northern China to the Black Sea.

1238   Establishment of Kingdom of Sukhothia in Thailand, with Theravada Buddhism as the state religion.

1240   Death of Ibn al-Arabi, prolific Islamic mystic, author of *The Meccan Revelations*.

1241	Death of Snorri Sturluson, Icelandic poet and historian, who wrote sagas on Norwegian kings and retold old Norse myths.
1266	Norway cedes the Isle of Man to Scotland under the Treaty of Perth.
*c.*1266	Birth of **John Duns Scotus**, eminent Scottish philosopher and theologian.
1274	Death of **Aquinas**.
1279	With the death of the last Sung emperor, the Mongols take control of all China.
1280	Death of Nicola Pisano, Italian sculptor who introduced a classical style into Italian medieval art. Death of Albertus Magnus.
*c.*1287	Birth of **William Ockham**, English scholastic philosopher and theologian best known for advocating a form of nominalism.
1288	Birth of **Gersonides**, prolific Jewish philosopher.
1291	Formation of the Swiss confederation. Death of Shaikh Muslih-al Din Sadi, great ethical and worldly wise Persian poet.
1292	Death of **Bacon**.
1294	Death of Kublai Khan, Mongol emperor who became the first foreigner to rule China, and who established a fabled court in Beijing.
1308	Death of **Scotus**.
1315	Commencement of Great Famine, which kills millions in Europe.
1321	Death of Dante Alighieri, Italian poet and author of the *Divine Comedy*, the first masterpiece written in a modern European language.
1324	Death of Marco Polo, Italian traveller who became governor of Yangzhou.
1325	Foundation of the Aztec city of Tenochtitlan.
1327	Death of Meister Eckhart, German theologian and speculative mystic.
*c.*1330	Birth of **John Wyclif**, whose work was condemned by synod in London and by Pope Gregory XI.
1336	Harihara I founds Vijayanagara Empire in Southern India.
1337	Edward II lays claim to the French throne, initiating the Hundred Years War. Death of Giotto di Bondone, founder of the Florentine school of painting.
1344	Death of **Gersonides**.
1347	Death of **Ockham**.
1348–50	Black Death, resulting in the loss of one-third of the European population from the bubonic plague.
1350	Beginning of the Renaissance in Italy, spreading thereafter to the rest of Europe.
1368	Beginning of the Ming dynasty in China.
1374	Death of Francisco Petrarca, Italian poet and scholar of classical antiquity, widely regarded as the founder of humanism.
1375	Death of Giovanni Boccaccio, Florentine poet and scholar who helped to lay the foundations for the Renaissance.
1378	Great Schism of the West, which leads to three simultaneous popes.
1381	Death of Wat Tyler, leader of a peasant uprising against serfdom and oppressive labour laws.
1384	Death of **Wycliff**.

1385	Union of Krewo between Lithuania and Poland.
1389	Death of Shams ud-Din Mohammed, Persian poet and theologian.
1400	Death of Geoffrey Chaucer, English poet whose works mark the beginning of a distinctively English literature.
1401	Birth of **Nicholas of Cusa**.
1402	Beginning of the Spanish Empire with the conquest of the Canary Islands.
1415	Battle of Agincourt. Death of Jan Huss, Czech preacher and religious reformer who anticipated the Lutheran Reformation and who was burned at the stake for heresy
1430	Death of Andrey Rublev, Russian monk and artist renowned for his iconography. Death of Christine de Pizan, French author, critic and rhetorician.
1431	Death of Joan of Arc, leader of the French army to victory over the English at Orleans, burned at the stake on charges of heresy.
1433	Death of Cheng-Ho, commander of several famous naval expeditions during the early Ming dynasty.
1438	Pachacuti founds the Incan Empire.
1441	Death of Jan van Eyck, Flemish painter who perfected the newly developed technique of oil painting.
1446	Death of Filippo Brunelleschi, Florentine sculptor, architect and engineer who pioneered early Renaissance architecture.
1453	Battle of Castillon, the final engagement in the Hundred Years War. The fall of Constantinople marks the end of the Byzantine Empire.
1455	Commencement of the dynastic civil war known as the War of the Roses (between supporters of the rival houses of Lancaster and York, for the throne in England). The first printed book, the Gutenberg Bible, is published in Germany.
1462	Ivan the Great becomes the first Tsar of Russia.
1464	Death of **Nicholas of Cusa**.
1466	Death of Donatello, master Italian sculptor.
c.1467	Birth of **Erasmus**, Dutch humanist known for his critical and satirical writings and his disputes wth **Martin Luther** (*see* Vol. 3, Ch. 3).
1468	Death of Johannes Gutenberg, the inventor of moveable-type mechanical printing in Europe.
1472	Death of Leon Battista Alberti, Italian architect, painter, poet, composer and inventor.
1481	Commencement of the Spanish Inquisition.
1492	Christopher Columbus founds the first New World colony on Hispaniola. Expulsion of Jews from Spain. Death of Lorenzo di Medici, Italian statesman and patron of literature and art.
1494	The Treaty of Tordesillas partitions the non-European world between Spain and Portugal.
1497	Vasco de Gama's first voyage to India.
1498	Death of Girolamo Savonarola, Dominican priest, leader of Florence, and religious reformer who was excommunicated and later burned at the stake.

BIBLIOGRAPHY

Abelard, P. 1885. *Opera omnia*, J.-P. Migne (ed.), Patrologia Latina 178. Paris: Garnier.

Abelard, P. 1969a. *Commentaria in epistolam Pauli ad Romanos*. In *Opera theologica I*, E.-M. Buytaert (ed.), Corpus Christianorum continuatio mediaevalis 11. Turnhout: Brepols.

Abelard, P. 1969b. *Theologia Christiana*. In *Opera theologica II*, E.-M. Buytaert (ed.), Corpus Christianorum continuatio mediaevalis 12, 72–372. Turnhout: Brepols.

Abelard, P. 1971, *Ethics*, D. Luscombe (ed. & trans.). Oxford: Clarendon Press.

Abelard, P. 1974. *The Letters of Abelard and Heloise*, B. Radice (trans.). Harmondsworth: Penguin.

Abelard, P. 1976–7. *Sic et non: A Critical Edition*, B. Boyer & R. McKeon (eds). Chicago, IL: University of Chicago Press.

Abelard, P. 1978. *Historia calamitatum*, J. Monfrin (ed.). Paris: Vrin.

Abelard, P. 1984. "Peter Abelard, 'Soliloquium': A Critical Edition", C. Burnett (ed.). *Studi Medievali*, 3rd series, **25**: 857–94.

Abelard, P. 1986. "Peter Abelard, *Confessio fidei 'universis'*: A Critical Edition of Abelard's Reply to Accusations of Heresy", C. Burnett (ed.). *Mediaeval Studies* **48**: 111–38.

Abelard, P. 1987a. *Theologia 'scholarium'*. In *Opera theologica III*, E.-M. Buytaert & C. J. Mews (eds), Corpus Christianorum continuatio mediaevalis 13, 313–549. Turnhout: Brepols.

Abelard, P. 1987b. *Theologia 'summi boni'*. In *Opera theologica III*, E.-M. Buytaert & C. J. Mews (eds), Corpus Christianorum continuatio mediaevalis 13, 85–201. Turnhout: Brepols.

Abelard, P. 2001. *Collationes*, J. Marenbon & G. Orlandi (eds & trans.). Oxford: Oxford University Press.

Adams, M. 1987. *William Ockham*. Notre Dame, IN: University of Notre Dame Press.

Aelred of Rievaulx 1971. *Opera omnia I*, A. Hoste & C. Talbot (eds), Corpus Christianorum continuatio mediaevalis 1. Turnhout: Brepols.

Aertsen, J. 1996. *Medieval Philosophy and the Transcendentals: The Case of Thomas Aquinas*. Leiden: Brill.

Alan of Lille 1855. *Opera*, J.-P. Migne (ed.), Patrologia Latina 210. Paris: J.-P. Migne.

Alaoui, J.-E. 1986. *Le Corpus Averroicum* [in Arabic]. Casablanca: Toubkal.

Al-Fārābī 1895. *Mabādi' Arā' Ahl al-Madīnat al-Fāḍila*, F. Dieterici (ed.). Leiden: Brill.

Al-Ghazali 1957. *Iḥyā' 'Ūlūm al-Dīn* [The revival of the sciences of religion], 4 vols. Cairo.

Al-Ghazali 1962. *Al-Iqtiṣād fī al-I'tiqād* [Moderation in belief], I. Cubcku & H. Atay (eds). Ankara.

Al-Ghazali 1998. *The Niche of Lights*, D. Buchman (trans.). Provo, UT: Brigham Young University Press.

Al-Ghazali 2000. *The Incoherence of the Philosophers*, 2nd edn, M. Marmura (trans.). Provo, UT: Brigham Young University Press.

Anselm of Canterbury 1940. *Opera omnia II*, F. Schmitt (ed.). Edinburgh: Thomas Nelson.

Anselm of Canterbury 1968. *Sancti Anselmi Cantuariensis Archiepisopi opera omnia*, F. Schmitt (ed.). Stuttgart-Bad Cannstatt: Friedrich Frommann.

Anselm of Canterbury 2007. *Anselm: Basic Writings*, T. Williams (trans.). Indianapolis, IN: Hackett.

Aquinas, T. 1882-. *Sancti Thomae de Aquino opera omnia*, Leonine edn. Rome. [*Summa theologiae*, vols 4–12; *Summa contra Gentiles*, vols 13–15; *Quaestiones disputatae de veritate*, vol. 22.1; *Compendium theologiae, etc.*, vol. 42; *De principiis naturae ... De ente et essentia, etc.*, vol. 43; *Super Boetium de Trinitate*, vol. 50.]

Aquinas, T. 1929. *Scriptum super libros sententiarum*, vols 1–2, P. Mandonnet, (ed.). Paris: Lethielleux.

Aquinas, T. 1950. *In duodecim libros Metaphysicorum Aristotelis expositio*. Turin: Marietti.

Aquinas, T. 1953. *Quaestiones disputatae*, vol. 2. Turin: Marietti.

Aquinas, T. 1962. *Summa theologiae*. Rome: Editiones Paulinae.

Augustijn, C. 1991. *Erasmus: His Life, Works, and Influence*. Toronto: University of Toronto Press.

Averroes 1924. *Die Epitome der Metaphysik des Averroes*, S. van der Bergh (trans.). Leiden: Brill.

Averroes 1932, 1942, 1948. *Great Commentary on the Metaphysics*, 3 vols, M. Bouyges (ed.). Beirut.

Averroes 1953. *Averrois cordubensis commentarium magnum in Aristotelis De anima libros*, F. Crawford (ed.). Cambridge, MA: Medieval Academy of America.

Averroes 1954. *Tahafut al Tahafut: The Incoherence of the Incoherence*, S. van den Burgh (annot., intro. and trans.). London: Luzak.

Averroes 1967. *Averroes: On the Harmony of Religion and Philosophy*, G. Hourani (trans.). London: Luzac.

Averroes 1974. *Commentary on Plato's Republic*, R. Lerner (trans.). Ithaca, NY: Cornell University Press.

Averroes 1977. *Averroës' Three Short Commentaries on Aristotle's "Topics", "Rhetoric", and "Poetics"*, C. Butterworth (ed. & trans.). Albany, NY: SUNY Press

Averroes 1984. *Ibn Rushd's Metaphysics*, C. Genequand (trans.). Leiden: Brill.

Averroes 1986. *Averroes' De substantia orbis*, A. Hyman (comm. & trans.). Cambridge, MA: Medieval Academy of America.

Avicenna 1952. *Madkal*, M. al-Khudayri, F. al-Ahwani & G. Anawati (eds). Cairo: Organisation Générale des Imprimeries Gouvernamentales.

Avicenna 1959. *Avicenna's "De anima" (Arabic text), Being the Psychological part of Kitab al-Shifa'*, F. Rahman (ed.). Oxford: Oxford University Press.

Avicenna 1983. *al-Samaœ al-tabiœi*, S. Zayed, (ed.). Cairo: General Egyptian Book Organization.

Avicenna 1985. *al-Najat*, M. Danishpazhuh (ed.). Tehran: Danishgah-yi Tihran.

Avicenna 2005. *The Metaphysics of "The Healing"*, M. Marmura (ed. & trans.). Provo, UT: Brigham Young University Press.

Bacon, R. 1859. *Opera quaedam hactenus inedita (= Opus tertium, Opus minus, Conpendium studii philosophiae, Epistola de secretis operibus artis et naturae, et de nullitate magiae)*, J. Brewer (ed.), Rolls Series: Rerum Britanicarum Medii Aevi Scriptores. London: Longman, Green, Longman and Roberts. Reprinted (Nendeln, Lichstenstein: Kraus, 1965).

Bacon, R. [1897] 1900. *Opus maius*, 3 vols, J. Bridges (ed.). Oxford: Clarendon Press. [Corrected vol. 3 (London: Williams & Norgate, 1900); reprinted (Frankfurt Am Main: Minerva Press, 1964).] Full Latin text available at www.archive.org/stream/opusmajusofroger02bacouoft/opusmajusofroger02bacouoft_djvu.txt (accessed June 2009).

Bacon, R. 1953. *Moralis philosophia (= Opus maius, part seven)*, E. Massa (ed.). Zurich: Thesaurus Mundi.

270

Bacon, R. 1978. "*De signis*. An Unedited Part of Bacon's *Opus maius: de signis*", K. Fredborg, L. Nielsen & J. Pinborg (eds). *Traditio* **34**: 75–136.

Bakker, P. 2001. "Aristotelian Metaphysics and Eucharistic Theology: John Buridan and Marsilius of Inghen on the Ontological Status of Accidental Being". In *The Metaphysics and Natural Philosophy of John Buridan*, J. Thijssen & J. Zupko (eds), 247–64. Leiden: Brill.

Beierwaltes, W. 1987. "Eriugena und Cusanus". In his *Eriugena Redivivus. Zur Wirkungsgeschichte seines Denkens im Mittelalter und im Übergang zur Neuzeit*, Abhandlung der Heidelberger Akademie der Wissenschaften: Philosophisch-historische Klasse, Abhandlung 1, 311–43. Heidelberg: C. Winter.

Bernard of Clairvaux 1953–80. *Omnia opera*, 8 vols, Rome: Editiones Cistercienses,

Bernard of Clairvaux 1957–77. *Sancti Bernardi opera*, vols 1–8, H. Rochais & J. Leclercq (eds). Rome: Editiones Cistercienses.

Bernard of Clairvaux 1970. *On Precept and Dispensation*, C. Greenia (trans.). In *The Works of Bernard of Clairvaux*, vol. 1. Spencer, MA: Cistercian Publications.

Bernard of Clairvaux 1976. *On the Song of Songs*, vol. II, K. Walsh (trans.). Kalamazoo, MI: Cistercian Publications.

Bernard of Clairvaux 1977a. *On Grace and Free Choice*, D. O'Donovan (trans.). Kalamazoo, MI: Cistercian Publications.

Bernard of Clairvaux 1977b. *On the Song of Songs*, vol. I, K. Walsh (trans.). Kalamazoo, MI: Cistercian Publications.

Bernard of Clairvaux 1979. *On the Song of Songs*, vol. III, K. Walsh & I. Edmonds (trans.). Kalamazoo, MI: Cistercian Publications

Bernard of Clairvaux 1980. *On the Song of Songs*, vol. IV, I. Edmonds (trans.). Kalamazoo, MI: Cistercian Publications.

Bernard of Utrecht 1970. *Accessus ad auctores*, with Conrad of Hirsau, *Dialogus super auctores*, R. B. C. Huygens (ed.). Leiden: Brill.

Black, D. 1990. *Logic and Aristotle's Rhetoric and Poetics in Medieval Arabic Philosophy*. Leiden: Brill.

Black, D. 1996. "Al-Fārābī". In *History of Islamic Philosophy*, S. Nasr & O. Leaman (eds), 178–97. London: Routledge.

Black, D. 1999. "Fārābī: ii. Logic". In *Encyclopaedia Iranica*, vol. 9, E. Yarshater (ed.), 213–16. New York: Bibliotheca Persica Press.

Black, D. 2006. "Knowledge (*'Ilm*) and Certitude (*Yaqîn*) in Al-Farabi's Epistemology". *Arabic Sciences and Philosophy* **16**: 11–45.

Blund, J. 1970. *Tractatus de anima*, D. Callus & R. Hunt (eds). Oxford: Oxford University Press.

Boethius 1973. *De Trinitate* Opuscula Theologica, S. Tester & E. Rand (eds), Loeb Classical Library. Cambridge, MA: Harvard University Press.

Boethius 1983. *The Theological Tractates* and *The Consolation of Philosophy*, H. F. Stewart, E. K. Rand & S. J. Tester (eds & trans.). Cambridge, MA: Harvard University Press.

Boethius 2000. *Boethius: De consolatione philosophiae, and Opuscula sacra*, C. Moreschini (ed.). Munich: K. G. Saur.

Brower, J. 2005. "Medieval Theories of Relations". *Stanford Encyclopedia of Philosophy*, E. Zalta (ed.) (Fall 2005 edition), http://plato.stanford.edu/archives/fall2005/entries/relations-medieval/ (accessed May 2009).

Buridan, J. [1518] 1964. *Quaestiones in Aristotelis Metaphysicam: Kommentar zur Aristotelischen Metaphysik*. Frankfurt: Minerva.

(Pseudo-)Campsall, R. 1982. *Logica Campsale Anglicj, valde utilis et realis contra Ocham*. In *The Works of Richard Campsall*, vol. 2, E. A. Synan (ed.), 79–420. Toronto: Pontifical Institute of Mediaeval Studies.

Casey, M. 1988. *A Thirst for God*. Kalamazoo, MI: Cistercian Publications.

Cassiodorus 1937. *Institutiones*, R. Mynors (ed.). Oxford: Oxford University Press.

Cassirer, E. 1927. *Individuum und Kosmos in der Philosophie der Renaissance*. Leipzig: Teubner.

Chemla, K. & S. Pahaut 1992. "Remarques sur les ouvrages mathematiques de Gersonides". In *Studies on Gersonides: A Fourteenth-Century Jewish Philosopher-Scientist*, G. Freudenthal (ed.), 149–98. Leiden: Brill.

Clanchy, M. 1999. *Abelard: A Medieval Life*. Oxford: Blackwell.

Clarembald of Arras 1965. *Tractaculus super librum Genesis*. In *Life and Works of Clarembald of Arras: A Twelfth-Century Master of the School of Chartres*, N. Häring (ed.), 226–49. Toronto: Pontifical Institute of Medieval Studies.

Colet, J. 1869. *Two Treatises on the Hierarchies of Dionysius*, J. Lupton (ed. & trans.). London: Bell & Daldy.

Contreni, J. & P. Ó. Néill (eds) 1997. *Glossae divinae historiae: The Biblical Glosses of John Scottus Eriugena*. Florence: Sismel, Edizioni del Galluzo.

Crispin, G. 1986. *The Works of Gilbert Crispin*, A. Abulafia & G. Evans (eds). London: British Academy.

Cross, R. 2005. *Duns Scotus on God*. Aldershot: Ashgate.

Dahan, G (ed.) 1991. *Gersonide en son temps*. Louvain-Paris: Peteers.

Daley, B. 1984. "Boethius's Theological Tracts and Early Byzantine Scholasticism". *Mediaeval Studies* **46**: 158–91.

Davidson, H. 1972. "Alfarabi and Avicenna on the Active Intellect. *Viator* **3**: 109–78.

Davidson, H. 2004. *Maimonides: The Man and His Works*. Oxford: Oxford University Press.

Davies, B. 2001. "Aquinas's Third Way". *New Blackfriars* **83**: 450–66.

Davies, B. & B. Leftow (eds) 2004. *The Cambridge Companion to Anselm*. Cambridge: Cambridge University Press.

Druart, T.-A. 1999. "Fārābī: iii. Metaphysics". In *Encyclopaedia Iranica*, vol. 9, E. Yarshater (ed.), 216–19. New York: Bibliotheca Persica Press.

Elm, K. (ed.) 1994. *Bernhard von Clairvaux. Rezeption und Wirkung im Mittelalter und in der Neuzeit*. Wiesbaden: Harrassowitz.

Endress, G. 1995. "Averroes' *De caelo*: Ibn Rushd's Cosmology in His Commentaries on Aristotle's *On the Heavens*". *Arabic Sciences and Philosophy* **6**: 9–49.

Endress, G. 1999a. "Le projet d'Averroès: constitution, réception et édition du corpus des œuvres d'Ibn Rušd". In *Averroes and the Aristotelian Tradition*, G. Endress *et al.* (eds), 3–31. Leiden: Brill.

Endress, G. 1999b. "Averrois Opera". In *Averroes and the Aristotelian Tradition*, G. Endress *et al.* (eds), 339–81. Leiden: Brill.

Erasmus, D. 1976. *The Correspondence of Erasmus: Letters 298 to 445*, R. Mynors & D. Thomson (trans.), Collected Works of Erasmus 3. Toronto: University of Toronto Press.

Erasmus, D. 1978. *Antibarbari/The Antibarbarians*. In *Literary and Educational Writings, 1 and 2: Volume 1: Antibarbari/Parabolae*, C. R. Thompson (ed.), Collected Works of Erasmus 23, 16–122. Toronto: University of Toronto Press.

Erasmus, D. 1988. *Enchiridion/Handbook of the Christian Soldier*. In *Spiritualia: Enchiridon/De contemptu mundi/De vidua Christiana*, C. Fantazzi (trans.), Collected Works of Erasmus 66, 8–124. Toronto: University of Toronto Press.

Erasmus, D. 1989. *The Correspondence of Erasmus: Letters 1252–1355*, R. Mynors (trans.), Collected Works of Erasmus 9. Toronto: University of Toronto Press

Erasmus, D. 1999. *Controversies: De libero arbitrio, Hyperaspistes 1*, C. Trinkaus (ed.), P. Macardle & C. Miller (trans.), Collected Works of Erasmus 76. Toronto: University of Toronto Press.

Erasmus, D. 2000. *Controversies: Hyperaspistes 2*, C. Trinkaus (ed.), C. Miller (trans.), Collected Works of Erasmus 77. Toronto: University of Toronto Press.

Eriugena, Johannes Scottus 1853. *Johannis Scoti opera quae supersunt omnia*, H.-J. Floss (ed.), Patrologia Latina 122. Paris: J.-P. Migne.

Eriugena, Johannes Scottus 1968/1972/1981. *Iohannis Scotti Eriugenae Periphyseon*, vols I–III, I. Sheldon-Williams (ed.), Scriptores Latini Hiberniae. Dublin: Institute for Advanced Studies.

Eriugena, Johannes Scottus 1975. *Iohannis Scoti Eriugenae expositiones in ierarchiam coelestem*, J. Barbet (ed.), Corpus Christianorum continuatio mediaevalis 21. Turnhout: Brepols.

Eriugena, Johannes Scottus 1976. *Periphyseon (On the Division of Nature)*, M. Uhlfelder (trans.). Indianapolis, IN: Bobbs-Merrill.

Eriugena, Johannes Scottus 1987. *Eriugena: Periphyseon (The Division of Nature)*, I. Sheldon-Williams (trans.), J. O'Meara (rev.). Montreal: Bellarmin.

Eriugena, Johannes Scottus 1988. "Homily on the Prologue of John", J. O'Meara (trans.). In J. O'Meara, *Eriugena*, 158–76. Oxford: Clarendon Press.

Eriugena, Johannes Scottus 1998. *John Scottus Eriugena: Treatise on Divine Predestination*, M. Brennan (trans.). Notre Dame, IN: University of Notre Dame Press.

Eskenasy, P. 1988. "Al-Fārābī's Classification of the Parts of Speech". *Jerusalem Studies in Arabic and Islam* **11**: 55–82.

Feiss, H. 1992. "*Bernardus scholasticus*: The Correspondence of Bernard of Clairvaux and Hugh of Saint Victor on Baptism". In *Bernardus Magister*, J. Sommerfeldt (ed.), 349–78. Spencer, MA: Cistercian Publications.

Feldman, S. 1967. "Gersonides' Proofs for the Creation of the Universe". *Proceedings of the American Academy for Jewish Research* **35**: 113–37.

Freddoso, A. 1999. "Ockham on Faith and Reason". In *The Cambridge Companion to Ockham*, P. Spade (ed.), 326–49. Cambridge: Cambridge University Press.

Frede, M. 1987. "The Unity of General and Special Metaphysics". In his *Essays in Ancient Philosophy*, 81–95. Minneapolis, MN: University of Minnesota Press.

Freudenthal, G. 1996. "Levi ben Gershom (Gersonides), 1288–1344". In *The Routledge History of Islamic Philosophy*, S. Nasr & O. Leaman (eds), 739–54. London: Routledge.

Geoffroy, M. 1999. "L'almohadisme théologique d'Averroès (Ibn Rušd)'". *Archives d'histoire doctrinale et littéraire du moyen âge* **66**: 9–47.

Geoffroy, M. 2005. "À propos de l'almohadisme d'Averroès: l'anthropomorphisme (tağsīm) dans la seconde version du Kitāb al-Kašf ʿan manāhiğ al-adilla". In *Los almohades: problemas y perspectivas*, M. Fierro & L. Molina (eds), 853–94. Madrid: Consejo Superior de Investigaciones Científicas.

Gerson, J. 1998. *Early Works*, B. P. McGuire (trans.). Mahwah: Paulist Press.

Gersonides 1984/1987/1999. *The Wars of the Lord*, 3 vols, S. Feldman (trans.). Philadelphia, PA: Jewish Publication Society of America.

Gilson, E. 1955. *History of Christian Philosophy in the Middle Ages*. London: Sheed & Ward.

Goldstein, B. 1975. *The Astronomical Tables of Rabbi Levi ben Gersom*. Hamden: Shoestring Press.

Goldstein, B. 1985. *The Astronomy of Levi ben Gershom (1288–1344)*. New York: Springer.

Goldstein, B. 1988. "A New Set of Fourteenth Century Planetary Observations". *Proceedings of the American Philosophical Society* **132**: 371–99.

Gracia, J. 1994. "Cutting the Gordian Knot of Ontology: Thomas's Solution to the Problem of Universals". In *Thomas Aquinas and His Legacy*, D. Gallagher (ed.), 16–36. Washington, DC: Catholic University of America Press.

Grane, L. 1970. *Peter Abelard: Philosophy and Christianity in the Middle Ages*. London: Allen & Unwin.

Gutas, D. 1988. *Avicenna and the Aristotelian Tradition*. Leiden: Brill.

Gutas, D. 1999a. "Fārābī: i. Biography". In *Encyclopaedia Iranica*, vol. 9, E. Yarshater (ed.), 208–13. New York: Bibliotheca Persica Press.

Gutas, D. 1999b. "Fārābī: iv. Fārābī and Greek Philosophy". In *Encyclopaedia Iranica*, vol. 9, E. Yarshater (ed.), 219–23. New York: Bibliotheca Persica Press.

Gutas, D. 1999c. "The 'Alexandria to Baghdad' Complex of Narratives: A Contribution to the Study of Philosophical Medical Historiography among the Arabs". *Documenti e studi sulla tradizione filosofica medieval* **10**: 155–93.

Hackett, J. 1995. *Roger Bacon: An Annotated Bibliography*. London: Taylor & Francis.

Hackett, J. 2000. "Aristotle, Astrology and Controversy at the University of Paris, 1266–1274". In *Learning Institutionalized: Teaching in the Medieval University*, J. Van Engen (ed.), 69–110. Notre Dame, IN: University of Notre Dame Press.

Hackett, J. 2002. "Roger Bacon and Maimonides: Did Roger Bacon Read Maimonides?". In *Medieval Philosophy and the Classical Tradition in Islam, Judaism and Christianity*, J. Inglis (ed.), 279–309. London: Curzon Press.

Hackett, J. 2005. "Roger Bacon and the Reception of Aristotle in the Thirteenth Century: An Introduction to His Criticism of Averroes". In *The Reception of Aristotle in the Thirteenth Century*, L. Honnefelder, M.-A. Aris, M. Dreyer & R. Wood (eds), 219–47. Münster: Aschendorff Verlag.

Hartshorne, C. 1965. *Anselm's Discovery: A Re-examination of the Ontological Argument for the Existence of God*. LaSalle, IL: Open Court.

Henninger, M. 1989. *Relations: Medieval Theories 1250–1325*. Oxford: Clarendon Press.

Hollister, C. 1982. *Medieval Europe: A Short History*, 5th edn. New York: Wiley.

Hopkins, J. 1972. *A Companion to the Study of St Anselm*. Minneapolis, MN: University of Minnesota Press.

Hopkins, J. 2002. *Hugh of Balma on Mystical Theology: A Translation and an Overview of His "De theologia mystica"*. Minneapolis, MN: Arthur J. Banning Press.

Hopkins, J. 2003. "Verständnis und Bedeutung des dreieinen Gottes bei Nikolaus von Kues". *Mitteilungen und Forschungsbeiträge der Cusanus-Gesellschaft* **28**: 135–64.

Hugh of St Victor 1939. *Didascalicon*, C. Buttimer (ed.). Washington, DC: Catholic University of America.

Hugh of St Victor 1951. *De sacramentis ecclesiae*, R. Ferrari (ed.). Cambridge, MA: Medieval Academy of America.

Hugh of St Victor 1966. *Epitome Dindimi in philosophiam, opera propaedeutica*, R. Baron (ed.). Notre Dame, IN: University of Notre Dame Press.

Hyman, A. 1973. "The Letter Concerning The Intellect". In *Philosophy in the Middles Ages*, A. Hyman & J. Walsh (eds), 215–21. Indianapolis, IN: Hackett.

Ibn Bājja 1968. *Opera metaphysica*, M. Fakhry (ed.). Beirut: Beirut, Dār al-Nahār li-l-Nashr.

Ibn Kahallikān 1842–71. *Biographical Dictionary*, 4 vols, B. de Slane (trans.). Paris: Oriental Translation Fund for Great Britain and Ireland.

Ibn Khaldūn 1958. *The Muqaddima*, F. Rosenthal (trans.). New York: Pantheon.

Inglis, J. (ed.) 2002. *Medieval Philosophy and the Classical Tradition*. London: Routledge.

Isidore 1909. *Etymologiae*, W. Lindsay (ed.). Oxford: Oxford University Press.

Ivry, A. 1972. "Towards a Unified View of Averroes' Philosophy". *Philosophical Forum* **4**: 87–113.

Jeauneau, É. (ed.) 1969. *Jean Scot: L'Homélie sur le Prologue de Jean*, Sources Chrétiennes 151. Paris: Editions du Cerf.

Jeauneau, É. (ed.) 1972. *Jean Scot: Commentaire sur l'Evangile de Jean*, Sources Chrétiennes 180. Paris: Editions du Cerf.

Jeauneau, É. (ed.) 1988. *Maximi confessoris ambigua ad Iohannem iuxta Iohannis Scotti Eriugenae latinam interpretationem*. Turnout: Brepols.

Jeauneau, É., with M. Zier (eds) 1995. *Iohannis Scotti Eriugenae Periphyseon (De divisione naturae) Liber Quartus*, J O'Meara & I. Sheldon-Williams (trans.), Scriptores Latini Hiberniae 13. Dublin: Dublin Institute for Advanced Studies.

Kasher, H. 1998. "Biblical Miracles and the Universality of Natural Laws: Maimonides' Three Methods of Harmonization". *Journal of Jewish Thought and Philosophy* **8**: 25–52.

Kenny, A. 1980. *The Five Ways: St. Thomas Aquinas' Proofs of God's Existence*. Notre Dame, IN: University of Notre Dame Press.

Kierkegaard, S. 1941. *Fear and Trembling*, W. Lowrie (trans.). Princeton, NJ: Princeton University Press.

Klima, G. 1999. "Ockham's Semantics and Ontology of the Categories". In *The Cambridge Companion to Ockham*, P. Spade (ed.), 118–42. Cambridge: Cambridge University Press.

Klima, G. 2000. "The Medieval Problem of Universals". In *Stanford Encyclopedia of Philosophy* (Fall 2000 edition), E. Zalta (ed.) http://plato.stanford.edu/entries/universals-medieval/ (accessed May 2009).

Klima, G. 2005. "The Essentialist Nominalism of John Buridan". *Review of Metaphysics* **58**: 301–15.

Klima, G. 2006. "Nominalism". In *Elsevier's Encyclopedia of Language and Linguistics*, vol. 8, 2nd edn, K. Brown (ed.), 648–52. Oxford: Elsevier.

Knuuttila, S. 1993. *Modalities in Medieval Philosophy*. London: Routledge.

Knuuttila, S. 2004. "Anselm on Modality". In *The Cambridge Companion to Anselm*, B. Davies & B. Leftow (eds), 111–31. Cambridge: Cambridge University Press.

Kretzmann, N. 1983. "Goodness, Knowledge, and Indeterminacy in the Philosophy of Thomas Aquinas". *Journal of Philosophy: Supplement* **80**: 631–41.

Kretzmann, N. 1997. *The Metaphysics of Theism: Aquinas's Natural Theology in Summa Contra Gentiles I*. Oxford: Clarendon Press.

Kretzmann, N. 1999. *The Metaphysics of Creation: Aquinas's Natural Theology in Summa Contra Gentiles II*. Oxford: Clarendon Press.

Kristeller, P. 1972. "Renaissance Philosophy and the Medieval Tradition". In his *Renaissance Concepts of Man and Other Essays*, 110–55. New York: Harper & Row.

Kukkonen, T. 2002. "Averroes and the Teleological Argument". *Religious Studies* **38**: 405–28.

Langermann, Y. 1999. "Appendix". In Gersonides, *The Wars of the Lord*, vol. 3, S. Feldman (trans.), 506–19. Philadelphia, PA: Jewish Publication Society of America.

Langermann, Y. 2004. "Maimonides and Miracles: The Growth of a (Dis)belief". *Jewish History* **18**: 147–72.

Leclercq, J. 1982. *The Love of Learning and the Desire for God*. New York: Fordham University Press.

Lee Jr, R. 2001. "Being Skeptical about Skepticism: Methodological Themes concerning Ockham's Alleged Skepticism". *Vivarium* **39**: 1–19.

Leftow, B. 1991. *Time and Eternity*. Ithaca, NY: Cornell University Press.

Lekai, L. 1977. *The Cistercians: Ideals and Reality*. Kent, OH: Kent State University Press.

Lettinck, P. 1999. "Ibn Sina on Atomism". *al-Shajarah* **4**: 1–51.

Lindberg, D. 2003. "The Medieval Church Encounters the Classical Tradition: Saint Augustine, Roger Bacon, and the Handmaiden Metaphor". In *When Science and Christianity Meet*, D. Lindberg & R. Numbers (eds), 7–32. Chicago, IL: University of Chicago Press.

Lovejoy, A. 1965. *The Great Chain of Being: A Study of the History of an Idea*. New York: Harper & Row.

Lutz, C. (ed.) 1939. *Iohannis Scotti annotationes in Marcianum*. Cambridge, MA: Medieval Academy of America.

MacDonald, S. 1984. "The *Esse/Essentia* Argument in Aquinas's *De ente et essentia*". *Journal of the History of Philosophy* **22**: 157–72.

MacDonald, S. 1991. "Aquinas's Parasitic Cosmological Argument". *Medieval Philosophy and Theology* **1**: 119–55.

Macy, J. 1986. "Prophecy in al-Fārābī and Maimonides: The Imaginative and Rational Faculties". In *Maimonides and Philosophy*, S. Pines & Y. Yovel (eds), 185–201. Dordrecht: Nijhoff.

Madec, G. (ed.) 1978. *Iohannis Scotti de divina praedestinatione*, Corpus Christianorum continuatio mediaevalis, Series Latina L. Turnhout: Brepols.

Mahdi, M. (trans.) 1962. *Alfarabi's Philosophy of Plato and Aristotle*. New York: Free Press of Glencoe.

Mahdi, M. 1970. "Language and Logic in Classical Islam". In *Logic in Classical Islamic Culture*, G. von Grunebaum (ed.), 51–83. Wiesbaden: O. Harrassowitz.

Mahdi, M. 1971. "Al-Fārābī". In *Dictionary of Scientific Biography*, C. Gillispie (ed.), 523–6. New York: Scribner.

Mahdi, M. 1999. "Fārābī: vi. Political Philosophy". In *Encyclopaedia Iranica*, vol. 9, E. Yarshater (ed.), 225–9. New York: Bibliotheca Persica Press.

Maimonides, M. 1938. *Maimonides' Treatise on Logic (Makalah fi-sina'at al-mantik): The Original Arabic and Three Hebrew Translations*, I. Efros (ed.). New York: American Academy for Jewish Research.

Maimonides, M. 1963. *The Guide of the Perplexed*, S. Pines (trans.). Chicago, IL: University of Chicago Press.

Maimonides, M. 1964. *Mishnah 'im perush rabenu moshe ben maimon*, Y. Kafih (ed.). Jerusalem: Mossad Harav Kook.

Maloney, T. 1995. "Is the *De doctrina Christiana* the Source for Bacon's Semiotics?". In *Reading and Wisdom: The De doctrina Christiana of Augustine in the Middle Ages*, E. English (ed.), 126–42. Notre Dame, IN: University of Notre Dame Press.

Manekin, C. 2000. "The Conservative Reaction in Christian Spain". In *The Jewish Philosophy Reader*, D. Frank, O. Leaman & C. Manekin (eds), 263–81. London: Routledge.

Mann, W. 2004. "Anselm on the Trinity". In *The Cambridge Companion to Anselm*, B. Davies & B. Leftow (eds), 257–78. Cambridge: Cambridge University Press.

Marenbon J. 2003. *Boethius*. New York: Oxford University Press.

Marenbon, J. 2005. *Le temps, l'éternité et la prescience de Boèce à Thomas d'Aquin*. Paris: Vrin.

Martin, C. 1991. "The Logic of Negation in Boethius". *Phronesis* **36**: 277–304.

McConica, J. 1969. "Erasmus and the Grammar of Consent". In *Scrinium Erasmianum*, vol. 2, J. Coppens (ed.), 77–99. Leiden: Brill.

McConica, J. 1991. *Erasmus*. Oxford: Oxford University Press.

McGuire, B. P. 1988. *Friendship and Community: The Monastic Experience 350–1250*, Kalamazoo, MI: Cistercian Publications.

McGuire, B. P. 2005. *Jean Gerson and the Last Medieval Reformation*. University Park, PA: Pennsylvania State University Press.

Mews, C. J. 1999. *The Lost Love Letters of Heloise and Abelard: Perceptions of Dialogue in Twelfth-Century France*. New York: St Martin's Press.

Mews, C. J. 2002. "The Council of Sens (1141): Bernard, Abelard and the Fear of Social Upheaval". *Speculum* **77**: 342–82.

Mews, C. J. 2008. "William of Champeaux, Abelard, and Hugh of Saint-Victor: Platonism, Theology, and Scripture in Early Twelfth-Century France". In *Bibel und Exegese in Sankt Viktor zu Paris: Formen und Funktionen eines Grundtextes in europäischem Rahmen*, R. Berndt (ed.), Corpus Victorinum. Instrumenta 3, 118–52. Münster: Aschendorff.

Najjar, F. 1963. "Alfarabi: The Poltical Regime". In *Medieval Political Philosophy: A Sourcebook*, R. Lerner & M. Mahdi (eds), 31–57. New York: Free Press of Glencoe.

Nederman, C. 2000. *Worlds of Difference: European Discourses of Tolerance (1100–1550)*. University Park, PA: Pennsylvania State University Press.

Newhauser, R. 2001. "Inter scientiam et populum: Roger Bacon, Pierre de Limoges and the *Tractatus moralis de oculo*". In *Nach der Verurteilung Von 1277: Philosophie und Theologie an der Universität Paris im letzten Viertel des 13. Jahrhunderts: Studien und Texte*, J. Aertsen, K. Emery Jr. & A. Speer (eds), *Miscellanea Medievallia* **28**: 682–703. Berlin: De Gruyter.

Nicholas of Cusa 1983–2007. *Nicolai de Cusa opera omnia*. Hamburg: Meiner.

Nicholas of Cusa 2000. *Metaphysical Speculations: Volume Two*, J. Hopkins (trans.). Minneapolis, MN: Arthur J. Banning Press.

Nicholas of Cusa 2001. *Complete Philosophical and Theological Treatises of Nicholas of Cusa*, J. Hopkins (ed. & trans.). Minneapolis, MN: Arthur J. Banning Press.

Ockham, W. 1974. *Summa logicae*. In *Opera philosophica*, vol. I, P. Boehner *et al.* (eds). St Bonaventure, NY: The Franciscan Institute.

Ockham, W. 1979. *Ordinatio*: Guillelmi de Ockham *Scriptum in librum primum sententiarum ordinatio: Distinctiones XIX–XLVIII*. In *Opera theologica*, vol. IV, G. Etzkorn & F. Kelley (eds). St Bonaventure, NY: The Franciscan Institute.

Ockham, W. 1980. *Quodlibeta septem, opera theologica*, vol. IX. St Bonaventure, NY: The Franciscan Institute.

Ockham, W. 1984. *Summula philosophiae naturalis*. In *Opera philosophica*, vol. VI, S. Brown (ed.). St Bonaventure, NY: The Franciscan Institute.

Ockham, W. 1986. *Tractatus de quantitate*. In *Opera theologica*, vol. X, C. Grassi (ed.). St Bonaventure, NY: The Franciscan Institute.

Oderberg, D. 2003. "Review of John Buridan: *Summulae de dialectica*". *Times Literary Supplement* (6 June): 9.

Olin, J. (ed.) 1987. *Christian Humanism and the Reformation: Selected Writings of Erasmus*. New York: Fordham University Press.

O'Malley, J. 1979. *Praise and Blame in Renaissance Rome: Rhetoric, Doctrine, and Reform in the Sacred Orators of the Papal Court, c.1450–1521*. Durham, NC: Duke University Press.

Owens, J. 1965. "Quiddity and Real Distinction in St Thomas Aquinas". *Mediaeval Studies* **27**: 1–22.

Owens, J. 1981. "Stages and Distinction in *De ente*: A Rejoinder". *The Thomist* **45**: 99–123.

Owens, J. 1986. "Aquinas's Distinction at *De ente et essentia* 4:119–123". *Mediaeval Studies* **48**: 264–87.

Pelzer, A. 1922. "Les 51 articles de Guillaume d'Occam censurés, en Avignon, en 1326". *Revue d'Histoire Ecclésiastique* **18**: 240–70.

Poirel, D. 2002. *Livre de la nature et débat trinitaire au XIIe siècle: le De tribus diebus de Hugues de Saint-Victor*. Turnhout: Brepols.

Proclus 2001. *On the Eternity of the World*, Greek text with intro., trans. & comm., H. Lang & A. Macro (eds). Berkeley, CA: University of California Press

Rashed, M. 2008. "Al-Fārābī's Lost Treatise on Changing Beings and the Possibility of a Demonstration of the Eternity of the World". *Arabic Science and Philosophy* **18**: 19–58.

Reisman, D. 2005. "Al-Fārābī and the Philosophical Curriculum". In *The Cambridge Companion to Arabic Philosophy*, P. Adamson & R. Taylor (eds), 52–71. Cambridge: Cambridge University Press.

Relihan, J. 2006. *The Prisoner's Philosophy: Life and Death in Boethius's Consolation*. Notre Dame, IN: University of Notre Dame Press.

Rescher, N. 1962. *Al-Fārābī: An Annotated Bibliography*. Pittsburgh, PA: University of Pittsburgh Press.

Rescher, N. 1963. *Al-Fārābī's Short Commentary on Aristotle's "Prior Analytics"*. Pittsburgh, PA: University of Pittsburgh Press.

Rogers, K. 2000. "A Defense of Anselm's *Cur Deus Homo* Argument". *Proceedings of the American Catholic Philosophical Association* **74**: 187–200.

Rosier-Catach, I. 1998. "Roger Bacon, al-Farabi et Augustin: Rhètorique, logique et philosophie morale". In *La Rhétorique d'Aristote: Traditions et commentaires de l'antiquité au XVIIe siècle*, G. Dahan & I. Rosier-Catach (eds), 87–110. Paris: Vrin.

Rudavsky, T. 2000. *Time Matters: Time, Creation, and Cosmology in Medieval Jewish Philosophy*. Albany: SUNY Press.

Russell, B. 1946. *History of Western Philosophy*. London: Allen & Unwin.

Saadia Gaon 1948. *Saadia Gaon: The Book of Beliefs and Opinions*, S. Rosenblatt (trans.). New Haven, CT: Yale University Press.

Samuelson, N. 1991. "Elements and Matter in Gersonides' Cosmogony". In *Gérsonide en son temps*, G. Dahan (ed.), 199–233. Louvain-Paris: E. Peeters.

Scotus, J. Duns 1639. *Opera omnia*, L. Wadding *et al.* (eds). Lyons.

Scotus, J. Duns 1950–. *Opera omnia*, C. Balić *et al.* (eds). Vatican City: Vatican Polyglot Press.

Scotus, J. Duns 1982. *A Treatise on God as First Principle*, 2nd edn, A Wolter (ed. & trans.). Chicago, IL: Franciscan Herald Press.

Screech, M. 1980. *Ecstasy and the Praise of Folly*. London: Duckworth.

Sharples, R. (ed.) 1991. *Cicero: "On Fate" and Boethius: "The Consolation of Philosophy" IV.5–7,V (Philosophiae Consolationis)*. Warminster: Aris & Phillips.

Shogimen, T. 2007. *Ockham and Political Discourse in the Late Middle Ages*. Cambridge: Cambridge University Press.

Sirat, C., S. Klein-Braslavy & O. Weigers (eds) 2003. *Les méthods de travail de Gersonide et le maniement du savior chez les scolastiques*. Paris: Vrin.

Söder, J. 1999. *Kontingenz und Wissen: Die Lehre von den futura contingentia bei Johannes Duns Scotus*. Münster: Aschendorff.

Sorabji, R. 1983. *Time, Creation and the Continuum*. London: Duckworth.

Southern, R. 1962. *Western Views of Islam in the Middle Ages*. Cambridge, MA: Harvard University Press.

Southern, R. 1966. *Saint Anselm and his Biographer*. Cambridge: Cambridge University Press.

Spade, P. 1994. *Five Texts on the Mediaeval Problem of Universals*. Indianapolis, IN: Hackett.

Spade, P. (ed.) 1999. *The Cambridge Companion to Ockham*. Cambridge: Cambridge University Press.

Stern, J. 2000. "Maimonides on Language and the Science of Language". In *Maimonides and the Sciences*, R. Cohen & H. Levine (eds), 173–226. Dordrecht: Kluwer.

Stump, E. & N. Kretzmann 1981. "Eternity". *Journal of Philosophy* 78: 429–58.

Taylor, R. 2007. "Intelligibles in Act in Averroes". In *Averroès et les averroïsmes juif et latin: Actes du colloque tenu à Paris, 16–18 juin 2005*, J.-B. Brenet (ed.), 111–40. Turnhout: Brepols.

Thierry of Chartres 1971. *Commentaries on Boethius by Thierry of Chartres and His School*, N. Häring (ed.). Toronto: Pontifical Institute for Mediaeval Studies.

Thomas of Chobham 1993. *De arte praedicandi*, F. Morenzoni (ed.), Corpus Christianorum continuatio medievalis 82. Turnhout: Brepols.

Torrell, J.-P. 2005. *Saint Thomas Aquinas, vol. 1: The Person and His Work*, R. Royal (trans.). Washington, DC: Catholic University of America Press.

Tracy, J. 1996. *Erasmus of the Low Countries*. Berkeley, CA: University of California Press.

Urvoy, D. 1978. *Le Monde des Ulémas andalous du V/XIe au VII/XIIIe siècle*. Geneva: Droz.

Urvoy, D. 1991. *Ibn Rushd (Averroes)*. London: Routledge.

Van Steenberghen, F. 1980. *Le Problème de l'existence de Dieu dans les écrits de S. Thomas d'Aquin*. Louvain-la-Neuve: Éditions de l'Institut Supérieur de Philosophie.

Velde, R. te 1999. "The Concept of the Good according to Thomas Aquinas". In *Die Metaphysik und das Güte: Aufsätze zu ihrem Verhältnis in Antike und Mittelalter*, W. Goris (ed.), 79–104. Leuven: Peeters.

Velde, R. te 2006. *Aquinas on God: The 'Divine Science' of the Summa theologiae*. Aldershot: Ashgate.

Visser, S. & T. Williams 2008. *Anselm*. Oxford: Oxford University Press.

Walzer, R. (ed. & trans.) 1985. *Al-Farabi on the Perfect State: Abū Naṣr al-Fārābī's Mabādi' Arā' Ahl al-Madīnat al-Fāḍila*. Oxford: Oxford University Press.

Weisheipl, J. 1959. *The Development of Physical Theory in the Middle Ages*. London: Sheed & Ward.

Weisheipl, J. 1985. *Nature and Motion in the Middle Ages*, W. Carroll (ed.). Washington, DC: Catholic University of America Press.

William of Saint-Thierry 1845. *Sancti Bernardi vita prima*, J.-P. Migne (ed.), Patrologia Latina 185. Paris: J.-P. Migne.

Wippel, J. 1984. *Metaphysical Themes in Thomas Aquinas*. Washington, DC: Catholic University of American Press.

Wippel, J. 2000. *The Metaphysical Thought of Thomas Aquinas: From Finite Being to Uncreated Being*. Washington, DC: Catholic University of America Press.

Wippel, J. 2007. *Metaphysical Themes in Thomas Aquinas II*. Washington, DC: Catholic University of America Press.

Wisnovsky, R. 2003. *Avicenna's Metaphysics in Context*. Ithaca, NY: Cornell University Press.

Wyclif, J. 1869. *Trialogus, cum supplemento trialogi*, G. Lechler (ed.). Oxford: Oxford University Press.

Wyclif, J. 1890. *De dominio divino libri tres*, R. Poole (ed.). London: Wyclif Society.

Wyclif, J. 1893. *Tractatus de logica*, M. Dziewicki (ed.). London: Wyclif Society.

Wyclif, J. 1895. *Opus evangelicum*, 2 vols, J. Loserth (ed.). London: Wyclif Society.

Wyclif, J. 2001. *On the Truth of Holy Scripture*, I. Levy (trans.). Kalamazoo, MI: Medieval Institute Publications.

Zagzebski, L. 1991. *The Dilemma of Freedom and Foreknowledge*. Oxford: Oxford University Press.

Zimmermann, A. 1998. *Ontologie oder Metaphysik? Die Diskussion über den Gegenstand der Metaphysik im 13. und 14. Jahrhundert*, 2nd edn. Leuven: Peeters.

Zimmermann, F. 1981. *Alfarabi's Commentary and Short Treatise on Aristotle's De Interpretatione*. Oxford: Oxford University Press.

INDEX